Arnie
& Jack

Ian O'Connor is a Pulitzer-nominated
journalist. He has worked for the *New
York Times* and *USA Today*, among many
others. He is the author of one previous
book, *The Jump*, about college basketball.

ALSO BY IAN O'CONNOR

THE JUMP: SEBASTIAN TELFAIR AND THE
HIGH-STAKES BUSINESS OF HIGH SCHOOL BALL

Arnie & Jack

PALMER,
NICKLAUS,
AND
GOLF'S
GREATEST
RIVALRY

Ian O'Connor

Yellow Jersey Press · LONDON

First published in the United States by Houghton Mifflin Company 2008

Published by Yellow Jersey Press 2009

10 9 8 7 6 5 4 3 2

Copyright © Ian O'Connor 2007

First published in Great Britain in 2008 by
Yellow Jersey Press
Random House, 20 Vauxhall Bridge Road,
London SW1V 2SA

www.rbooks.co.uk

Addresses for companies within The Random House Group Limited
can be found at: www.randomhouse.co.uk/offices.htm

The Random House Group Limited Reg. No. 954009

A CIP catalogue record for this book is available from the British Library

ISBN 9780224082518

The Random House Group Limited supports The Forest Stewardship
Council (FSC®), the leading international forest certification organisation.
Our books carrying the FSC label are printed on FSC® certified paper.
FSC is the only forest certification scheme endorsed by the leading
environmental organisations, including Greenpeace. Our
paper procurement policy can be found at
www.randomhouse.co.uk/environment

MIX
Paper from
responsible sources
FSC® C016897

Printed and bound in Great Britain by Clays Ltd, St Ives PLC

To Mom,
the rock of our childhoods.
Until we meet again.

To Kyle,
my best friend and all-time favorite golf partner.
You're living proof that angels walk the earth.

To Tracey,
my forever love and inspiration.
You're the heroine who makes every word worth
writing and every breath worth taking.

Contents

Part III

Introduction

TIGER WOODS, billionaire-to-be, had just run the tip of a three-dollar pen across his seventy-dollar slacks. He was the only player in the locker room at the Doral resort in Miami, and he was inspecting his ink stain the way he would an eight-foot putt.

"Shit," he said. "These pants are done."

I extended my hand and explained the purpose of my intrusion, and Woods kindly agreed to hear me out. I was wondering if Tiger felt cheated by the players who were pursuing him. I was wondering if he wished he had what Jack Nicklaus had in Arnold Palmer, and what Arnie had in Jack.

His omnipresent Nike cap tucked low over his brow, Woods measured the thought for a moment and loosed that killer smile of his. "No," he said.

He went on to talk about the greater depth of talent on today's PGA Tour and about the players he considered worthy major championship challengers—the Phil Mickelsons and Vijay Singhs. Woods made it clear he was far more interested in winning than in the substance and style of the opponents he vanquished in the process.

No, Tiger didn't need any defining rival. He needed only a fair-and-square chance to break Nicklaus's record of eighteen major titles, the target he'd famously posted on his childhood walls.

Woods stands at thirteen at the start of the 2008 season, and none of his contemporaries expected to compete in the Masters has won more than three. Mickelson is the closest thing to a true Tiger rival, and the heat that radiates between them is marketable and real.

But Woods-Mickelson didn't unfold when television was a burgeoning phenomenon in search of live passion-play programming; Palmer-Nicklaus did. Arnie and Jack represented the perfect conflict in personality, background, and style at the perfect time — just as TV was starting to plant larger-than-life figures in America's living rooms and dens.

By the time Tiger and Phil came along, golf fans were well aware of what an intense rivalry meant to a sport. Arnie and Jack had taught them well.

They made for simple good guy–versus–bad guy stuff, the kind that attracted drama-starved viewers and the network executives and advertisers forever trying to reach them. Palmer was the protagonist and Nicklaus the antagonist, and they needed each other on a golf course the way any sheriff and outlaw needed each other for a gunfight.

Arnie was the first man to prove a golfer could be an athlete, a TV star, and a sex symbol rolled into one. Jack was the first man to prove Ben Hogan would not go down as the greatest player of all time.

Palmer and Nicklaus battled each other across five decades and never staged the kind of near-brawl experience Mickelson and Singh shared inside Augusta National's champions locker room in 2005, when Phil and Vijay went nose to nose over the spike marks Mickelson allegedly left on the twelfth green. Arnie and Jack were too smart for that.

But without ever throwing a punch, without ever spilling a single drop of each other's blood, Palmer and Nicklaus went after each other with the same snot-busting fury that defined the clashes between Muhammad Ali and Joe Frazier.

Only there was something about Palmer that Nicklaus could never lay a glove on. "Arnold had something well below his skin that attracted people to him," said Frank Chirkinian, the longtime producer of Masters telecasts on CBS. "He looked like the type of fellow you could walk up to and say, 'Let's have a beer,' and he would."

Arnie had the fans and wanted the trophies; Jack had the trophies and wanted the fans. In the struggle permanent scars were left on each side.

Six years ago one of Arnie's granddaughters would hear from a kindergarten classmate that "Jack Nicklaus is more of a legend than Arnold Palmer." But to this day Jack hears and feels a vastly different sentiment from vocal galleries.

"I still get hurt [by Palmer's fans], you know," Nicklaus said, "and I know how to live with it because I expect it. We can play the Skins Game in Hawaii and I still get it. I just accept it. It's not me. You learn that it's not you. It's Arnold. Nobody's going to replace Arnold from that standpoint with the public."

When told that Nicklaus admitted he could still get hurt by Arnie's Army, Palmer said of the man who defeated him on the golf course more often than not: "You can only be so many things in your life."

In other words, Arnie's brother Jerry said, "there can only be one Arnold Palmer."

To recapture the flaming spirit of golf's greatest rivalry, I conducted extensive interviews with Nicklaus and Palmer, the most fascinating one taking place at forty-seven thousand feet, somewhere between Calgary and Palm Beach on Nicklaus's spacious Gulfstream V. Jack talked right through the four-course meal served by his wife, Barbara. He talked for five hours and could've gone for five more.

So much ground to cover; so many lessons to share. Nicklaus and Palmer have lived incredibly rich and profound lives. They stand as American icons chiseled into golf's Mount Rushmore, giants who aren't even six feet tall.

Johnny Miller, the golfer and broadcaster, would say that playing with Palmer in the early seventies "was definitely tougher than playing with Tiger today." He said a two-round pairing with Arnie and his rambunctious gallery "was like a four-shot penalty."

Gary Player, third member of the Big Three, would say that a thirty-year-old Nicklaus would've beaten a thirty-year-old Woods if both had equal access to golf's nuclear-powered technology.

"If you gave Jack that equipment," Player said, "I think Jack would've been better."

In the end Woods will have more trophies than Jack and more fans than Arnie. But long before golf produced a prospective billionaire named Tiger, two lions fought like hell for control of an evolving and exploding sport.

In the course of researching and writing this book, I was often asked some variation of this question: Who do you think won the battle, Arnold Palmer or Jack Nicklaus?

My answer was always the same: It depends on how you keep score.

Howard Baker Saunders, Jack Nicklaus, Amold Palmer, and Dow Finsterwald at the 1958 Athens, Ohio, exhibition where Amie and Jack met for the first time.

• Athens

THE ELDERS AT the Athens Country Club had cobbled together a big day to honor one of their own, Dow Finsterwald, and needed to fill the last slot on their VIP list. They wanted a man and settled for a boy instead.

Fred Swearingen, club president, had been struck by a sudden thought. He would call up this hot-shot kid in Columbus and ask him if he would care to play eighteen holes of golf with Finsterwald, the brand-new winner of the PGA Championship, and Dow's good friend Arnold Palmer, brand-new winner of the Masters.

Swearingen found a listing for Charlie Nicklaus's drugstore. Charlie answered the phone.

"Is your boy interested in playing with the PGA champ and the Masters champ?" Swearingen asked.

"I'm sure he is," Charlie said. "He's right here. I'll put him on."

Without blinking, Jack Nicklaus told Swearingen he'd be happy to bring his game to the southeast corner of the state. "I'll get my dad to take me," Jack said.

He was eighteen years old in September of 1958, and his father would drive him to his first face-to-face encounter with Palmer, who was just days removed from his twenty-ninth birthday and just months removed from his first victory at Augusta National, the one that hinted at the dawn of a new era in professional golf.

1

This wouldn't be the first time young Nicklaus had seen Palmer in the flesh. At the 1954 Ohio amateur championship outside Toledo, Jackie was a fourteen-year-old qualifier who stumbled upon a dark, solitary figure on the Sylvania Country Club driving range, raging at ball after ball in a biblical rain.

Nicklaus didn't know the man's identity; he was mesmerized all the same. Under cover, from about forty yards away, Nicklaus stared at the stranger in the rain suit for forty-five minutes.

Palmer was western Pennsylvania born and bred, made eligible for the Ohio event by his time in Cleveland as a member of the coast guard and, of all things, the fraternity of frustrated paint salesmen. He was pounding his nine-irons, making them turn right to left, commanding them with a musculature that belonged to a middleweight fighter. In his mind's eye Nicklaus saw a relentless series of angry line drives that never rose more than six feet off the ground.

This was two days before the start of the state championship, and Nicklaus was the only other competitor on the course. The storms hadn't let up. Jackie was soaked, but he couldn't tear himself away from a scene that could've been cut right out of a Tiger Woods credit-card ad nearly half a century later.

There are no rainy days.

Palmer didn't even know young Nicklaus was there. Arnold was unwittingly giving the heir to his future throne a lesson in hard-earned royalty. Nicklaus loved the raw commitment, the brute strength. He had never seen anyone attack a golf ball quite like this.

Finally, Jackie stepped inside the clubhouse. "Who is that guy out on the driving range?" he asked. "Man, is he strong."

A voice identified Palmer as the defending state champ.

Palmer would make it two in a row long after Nicklaus lost to someone named Dale Bittner on the nineteenth hole. Bittner was a fleeting thought, gone just like that. Nicklaus went home to tell friends and neighbors all about the golfer swinging in the rain, the carnival strongman who crushed opponents with his frighteningly large hands.

Four years later, when Charlie Nicklaus made the seventy-five-mile drive with his growing boy for the date with Palmer, Jack had left his awe back at home, left it there in a closet cluttered with everything else he'd outgrown.

"The guy had basically just started winning majors," Nicklaus said.

"Did I know Arnold Palmer was a good player? You're darn right. But was I ever in awe of what he did? Probably not."

No, the teenage Nicklaus wasn't short on confidence. He had built himself a remarkable youth record.

He'd won the Ohio State Open as a sixteen-year-old competing against pros. He'd already played in two U.S. Opens, making the cut at Southern Hills in Tulsa. He'd won a national Jaycees championship, and he'd contended in his first pro tour event, standing one shot off the lead after two rounds of the 1958 Rubber City Open before placing twelfth.

Jack wasn't about to make any fuss over Palmer, who had "only" one major professional championship to his name to go with the one U.S. Amateur title he captured in 1954. Nicklaus would let the people of Athens do the fussin' for him.

Palmer was quite a catch for a community in the Appalachian foothills, a college town of fifteen thousand residents, about half of them students at Ohio University. To the coal miners and farmers of the depressed pockets surrounding the sanctuary of higher education, Palmer's arrival, according to George Strode, sports editor of the *Athens Messenger,* "was like the second coming of Christ."

The son of an Athens attorney, Finsterwald was the one who booked the main attraction. His friendship with Palmer was born of the matches they played as college rivals, Dow a star at Ohio U., Arnold a star at Wake Forest.

Palmer shot 29 across the first nine holes they shared. In one Ohio-Wake match, with Arnold and Dow tied at the turn, Palmer declared, "I'll bet you a tub of beer I shoot 32 or better on the back side."

Palmer shot 31. The pecking order in their relationship established forevermore, Palmer and Finsterwald became what one pro described as "asshole buddies."

Dow told everyone to count Arnold in. "Give him a call," Swearingen said.

"Hell, give him a call yourself," Finsterwald responded. "Here's his number. He's there right now."

Sure enough, Arnold was home in Latrobe, Pennsylvania, and eager to participate in a day to honor Athens's favorite son. Swearingen told Palmer he'd send him a plane ticket, fly him into Columbus, and pick him up at the airport for the drive into town.

"You've got an airport in Athens, don't you?" Palmer asked.

"Well, we've got a landing strip at the university," Swearingen answered.

"I don't need a ticket then. I'll fly right in."

If Palmer hadn't chosen golf as his vocation, he likely would've become a commercial pilot. At first he was scared to death to fly. He was an amateur golfer en route to Chattanooga on a DC-3 once when he was startled by a ball of fire rolling up and down the aisle. "I immediately found out it was static electricity," Palmer said, "and that's when I decided I would learn to fly and learn to understand what was happening."

He overcame his fear of flying out of necessity—he wanted to spend as much time at home with his family as he could, and driving from tour stop to tour stop was no way to accomplish that.

So he earned his pilot's license. Over time the only thing Palmer loved as much as the sight of his ball soaring toward the green was the sight of a plane streaking through the sky.

He flew into Athens with his wife, Winnie, and Swearingen picked them up in his station wagon and tossed Palmer's Wilson bag into the back of the car. He drove Arnold and Winnie to the home of Jean Sprague, Finsterwald's cousin, where they would spend the night and then rise early on the morning of September 25, 1958, so Arnold could pay tribute to his best friend and play golf with Jack Nicklaus for the very first time.

Swearingen would plan the day around a parade and a match involving two-man teams. The fourth competitor was a local amateur, Howard Baker Saunders, a six-time Southeastern Ohio Golfing Association champ out of Gallipolis and a lead player on the Ohio State team fifteen years before Nicklaus filled the same role. Saunders would've turned pro if he hadn't suffered from osteomyelitis, an infection of the bone that left him with a bad limp. With one leg shorter than the other, Saunders wore one shoe with a five-inch heel to level his playing field.

He would ride along in the Finsterwald parade. Court Street was packed for the morning festivities, as Swearingen celebrated his own birthday with a gift to Dow: a July Fourth supply of marching bands. The route was less than a mile long and yet stamped by so many monuments to Americana—a family department store, a courthouse, an armory, a car dealership, a bookstore, Swearingen's sporting goods store, and the bars forever kept busy by hard-partying Ohio U. boys and girls.

This could've been a homecoming football parade. Finsterwald, Palmer, Nicklaus, and Saunders rode in their own convertibles, tops down, waving like returning war heroes at a delirious crowd of twelve hundred. The mayor presented Finsterwald with a key to the city. Speeches were given, autographs were signed, pictures were taken. Michael DiSalle, busy running a successful campaign for the governorship of Ohio, joked that he had picked the wrong day to be in Athens.

No politician could match the golfers' star power. And nobody cared that more people had come to see Arnold than to see Dow.

When the hourlong ceremony was complete, Swearingen had the golfers go fishing before it was time to head to the club. He grabbed some rods out of his store; gave them to Finsterwald, Palmer, and Nicklaus; and steered them to a pond full of catfish.

Finsterwald and Palmer knew their way around the hills and streams of Appalachia, "but Jack was a city boy," Swearingen said.

Jack cast his line over the hillside and got it caught in some rocks. He refused to go down and loosen it: he was afraid a snake or two might be waiting for him.

"No, Jack wasn't roaming any hills in Columbus," Swearingen said. "The only hills he ever roamed were at Scioto Country Club in that real nice suburb of his, Upper Arlington."

Over time Nicklaus would grow sensitive to any talk that he was a rich little daddy's boy, especially when the talk was inspired by Palmer's past. Arnold was the son of a greenskeeper, the sod-stained child on the other side of the country club glass. People adored his Horatio Alger tale and assumed Nicklaus never spent a day of his youth with any tool in his hands that didn't come out of a shiny new golf bag.

But as an eighteen-year-old prodigy driven by blind ambition, Nicklaus carried something of a pauper's chip on his shoulder. Remarkably enough, the kid refused to treat his first meeting with Palmer as a brush with uncommon skill and fame. He merely saw the reigning king of Augusta National as just another hurdle to clear, just another guy to beat.

"I don't think he was so excited to play [Palmer]," Swearingen said.

Nestled atop a sun-splashed hill, five miles from the parade route, Athens Country Club was a playground for the university professors and administrators, and for the doctors, dentists, and businessmen who had them as patients and clients. Theirs was a simple nine-hole Donald Ross course, with alternate tees used for scoring on the second nine. When the layout was doubled up, the test measured 6,382 yards and a par of 72.

The course was lined with pine trees and graced by the acoustic charm of chirping birds. With a single dirt road running into the club, barely wide enough for two cars passing in opposite directions, Athens hardly looked like the center of the golf universe.

But with the heart of the tour season already accounted for, this was the biggest game on the schedule. The skies were benign and the temperatures were in the upper sixties. Somehow, some way, a gallery of about fifteen hundred fans poured onto the scene. Fans parked along the seventh fairway. In fact, they parked in the yards of everyone who lived just off the golf course.

The sides were picked, and Palmer — considered the strongest player — was paired with Nicklaus — considered the weakest, if only because of his age. The four participants were warming up when the mischievous forces of fate intervened.

Nicklaus and Palmer would go head-to-head after all.

As Palmer and Finsterwald were swatting practice drives from the elevated tee on the 321-yard first hole, Nicklaus and Saunders were sent to the nearby ninth green to hit balls toward the ninth tee. Jack swung away with all his teenage might and immediately caused a stir.

A witness approached Kermit Blosser, the Ohio U. golf coach and de facto master of ceremonies. "Hey," the man told Blosser, "you ought to get that Nicklaus kid to hit against Arnold on number one. He's really moving it down there."

Blosser knew all about Jack; he'd tried and failed to sign him to play for Ohio U. Charlie Nicklaus had already locked in on a vision for his son's future. Jack was attending Ohio State, Charlie told Blosser, because he wanted his boy in OSU's pharmacology program.

Blosser figured he'd send Jack to the school of hard knocks instead. He summoned Nicklaus to the first tee, where Palmer was flexing his comic book arms. The golf coach had a microphone, and he was about to become a play-by-play man. A short, precise driver known for his cautious, anti-Arnold game, Finsterwald stepped to the side as Palmer accepted the good-natured challenge. This was a heavyweights-only fight, and Finsterwald didn't make the cut.

The fairways were dry and running hard, allowing the mad bombers to add an extra fifteen or twenty yards to their prodigious drives. Palmer and Nicklaus took a few warm-up swings. Jack's technically sound form appeared torn from the pages of a manual, with one exception: his right elbow flew away from his side, like that of a free-throw shooter gone awry, and Palmer couldn't help but notice the flaw.

Arnold wasn't in any position to mock another player's mechanics. His swing was punctuated by the least aesthetically pleasing follow-through in golf. In the immediate wake of impact, Palmer abruptly jerked his club above his head and appeared to begin wrestling with a rattlesnake, a gushing water hose, or both.

Nicklaus, meanwhile, enjoyed a full follow-through that featured none of Palmer's gyrations. Their games were as different as their backgrounds and body types. Nicklaus came from German stock, Palmer from Scotch, Irish, and English. Nicklaus had thighs that looked like redwood trunks; Palmer had hands that could crush a watermelon.

On this day in Athens, Palmer showed up tan and fit. As always, he was distracting the ladies with his rugged, man-of-the-earth looks.

Palmer carried himself with a John Wayne swagger and an Errol Flynn flair. He didn't walk to his tee shots; he marched. After surveying his target and flicking his cigarette to the grass, Palmer approached his ball as if he were a cowboy loading up at the O.K. Corral.

He'd hitch up his pants, puff out his chest, and defy the smooth and effortless strokes of the greats before him. Palmer wasn't interested in the sweet science of Sam Snead's swing, nor was he hoping to match Ben Hogan's relentless quest for technical perfection.

He was just trying to land his ball on the moon.

Nicklaus? He looked like an extra on Palmer's movie set. "A little plump kid with real short hair," Swearingen said. The blond Nicklaus walked around with a God-awful buzz cut, and his pale skin could blotch up in the summertime; it would never accommodate Palmer's even tan.

Arnold and Jack both stood about five feet ten, so they looked each other squarely in the eye when they shook hands on a tee box for the first time. For all of Palmer's smoky, leading-man looks, Nicklaus might've had an advantage here: even as a kid his piercing blue eyes had already cut through many a foe on the first tee.

Blosser had arranged for four of his Ohio U. players to serve as caddies, and he had Dow Reichley, Bill Santor, Larry Snyder, and Charlie Vandlik make their way down to the first green to shag the driving-contest balls. "I know they had a bet," Reichley said of Palmer and Nicklaus. "I don't know how much it was for."

Something more important than a few bucks was on the line here. Palmer was a pro, Nicklaus an amateur. Palmer was a man, Nicklaus a boy.

Hundreds of fans closed in around the first tee box, giving it the feel of a boxing ring. The golfers and fans looked out from their elevated perch at a hole that turned slightly left to right. On the right side of the fairway, rows of pine trees stretched out toward the green. Two bunkers were lurking to the left of the putting surface, one about thirty yards short of the fringe.

The third green sat thirty-five downhill yards behind the first green. Nobody in his right mind believed either competitor could drive his ball there, not with the equipment in play — persimmon clubs and balata balls.

Nicklaus took the honors, and his first drive was a monster. "He hit it so high," Santor said, "you could barely see it up in the sky."

The ball cleared the first green and stopped rolling only after it had traveled 356 yards. Santor picked up Nicklaus's ball on the third green.

The caddie knew a thing or two about Jack's tape-measure power. As an entering high school senior in 1955, Santor had played in the same field with Nicklaus, an underclassman, in the state Jaycees tournament.

Santor placed second. Nicklaus only beat him by twelve strokes.

Palmer had no such intimate knowledge of Nicklaus and his game. He'd heard a few vague tales of the boy wonder from the Columbus area, sweeping through the amateur ranks, but Palmer had enough to worry about with his own generation to lose any sleep over the next one.

Only in Athens the future was suddenly now. Palmer teed up his ball, knowing he had almost no chance of matching the kid's first drive. He lashed at it with vile intentions, hoping against hope to power his ball down to the third green.

It stayed low, like most Palmer drives. Much lower than Nicklaus's ball.

"Arnold hit a big hook," Swearingen said. "It hit short of the first green and bounced downhill to the left."

Nicklaus ripped off his second drive. As he stood near the first green, Santor squinted to track the ball's high, majestic flight. Again, Nicklaus had placed his drive on the third green, some 356 yards away.

Again, Palmer failed to match it, unleashing another low, screaming hook shot into oblivion.

"Jack was out-hitting Arnold by thirty-five, forty yards," Santor said. "I could hear the crowd yelling around the first tee."

His face three different shades of red, Palmer shot an incredulous look at Nicklaus. "My God," he said. "No man hits it that far. It's men like you who make problems for us."

Blosser was dumbfounded. He had never seen a player of any age put a drive from the first tee onto the third green, never mind two drives. The de facto master of ceremonies decided to make a show of it.

"Mr. Palmer," Blosser barked loudly enough for the masses to hear, "can you tell me why you're hooking that ball so violently?"

"Because I'm trying to hit it too goddamn hard just to keep up with this kid," Palmer responded.

It was a lost cause. Palmer would later claim he won this long-ball contest, but witnesses reported the players hit about fifteen drives each, and with the aid of some friendly bounces Arnold kept up with Jack maybe three or four times.

Palmer was embarrassed, and a little pissed that Blosser called extra attention to that embarrassment. But he still had the regulation best-ball match coming up, and even if Nicklaus would be his teammate, he could still outplay him. Still show the boy what was what.

Blosser's players drew straws to see who would caddie for whom. Snyder got Palmer, Vandlik got Nicklaus, Santor got Finsterwald, and Reichley got Saunders.

Finsterwald and Saunders represented the favorites, as most assumed that young Nicklaus would amount to a handicap for Palmer. Dow knew every blade of grass and grain of sand on the Ross design; he owned the course record of 63. Palmer had never seen the place, but he caught a major break in the form of his caddie, Snyder, the Athens member who had just won his fifth consecutive club championship. Snyder was in command of whatever local knowledge Palmer might need.

All but emasculated by Nicklaus in the game before the game, Palmer opened the team match with a fury, hitting his first approach shot to within a foot of the hole, tapping in for the easy three while the others made par. Palmer then added birdies on two of the next three holes.

He chipped his third shot to within two feet for birdie at the par-five second, then birdied the par-four fourth after driving his ball 290 yards into the fairway and then landing his approach three feet from the hole.

If Palmer couldn't beat Nicklaus in the driving contest, he would make damn sure everyone saw him carry Nicklaus during this match.

Snyder held the nine-hole record of 29 at Athens, and he was certain that would go down in flames. Palmer would solicit his advice on strategy. Sometimes he listened to Snyder; sometimes he didn't. "He'd say, 'Larry, what would you hit here?'" Snyder said. "I'd tell him it was 175 yards and I'd probably hit the five-iron. And he'd hit the four-iron and almost knock it in the hole for a gimme birdie.

"On the sixth hole, par five, he hooked his tee shot over into the rough. He says, 'How far away?' I say, 'Probably two hundred yards. I'd hit the four-wood.' And he hit the three-iron or four-iron and knocked it on the green."

Palmer dropped a twenty-five-foot putt on the 476-yard hole to get his eagle three. He was already playing a game the kid on his bag could hardly believe.

Snyder had been caddying for ten years. He used to shag balls for Finsterwald for eight hours a day, fifty cents an hour, and he would try to mimic Dow's beautiful swing.

"But Dow didn't have the personality that Arnold had," Snyder said. "Not very many people did."

Palmer nearly aced the par-three eighth with a four-iron after Snyder advised him to clear the pond with a five-iron. Another birdie. On the next hole Palmer had a twelve-foot putt to tie Snyder's record of 29; he missed it, much to his caddie's relief.

Palmer settled for a six-under 30 on the front side; his teammate, Nicklaus, made the turn at 35. Saunders kept his team in the match with a 33, while Finsterwald struggled to a 36. At the break Palmer-Nicklaus held a three-hole lead.

Not that the team competition was the be-all, end-all. The crowd was buzzing over the possibility that Palmer could shoot 59, or that he could at least break Finsterwald's course record. Among the caddies Nicklaus was also a prime subject of conversation.

Like Santor, Snyder had seen Jack up close in tournament play. In 1952 a fourteen-year-old Snyder went up against a twelve-year-old Nicklaus in the district juniors, and the older player prevailed on the nineteenth hole. "And I bet he outweighed me by forty pounds," Snyder recalled. "By the time Jack was eighteen, his power was phenomenal."

That power moved the earth in Athens, and the older Ohio U. players serving as caddies couldn't fathom the noise made when Nicklaus's club face made contact with the ball. "The crack, the boom," Reichley said. "It was a supersonic sound."

Nicklaus drove the 330-yard tenth hole, landing his tee shot pin-high and six feet from the cup. He missed the eagle putt and settled for a three. Palmer also birdied the hole, turning the gallery on its ear.

"Watching Jack and Arnie," Reichley said, "we were awestruck."

Finsterwald went on a birdie binge to make up for his lackluster front nine, but Saunders faded to negate the effect. Palmer and Nicklaus were in the clear. Both were out-muscling the course, though Palmer was the one making more putts.

The caddies were watching Palmer's every purposeful step. He was the leading money winner on the tour at that point, having banked more than forty-four grand for the season, and yet he didn't walk with an air of superiority.

"So down-to-earth," Snyder said. "He never said an unkind word to me, never frowned, never acted like I should've known better to do this or that."

The Ohio U. boys also watched the body language between Palmer and Nicklaus. No one could imagine then that these two figures — separated by more than ten years of age — would someday make for the greatest rivalry the game has ever known. But there was no extra effort on either player's part that day to bridge their generation gap.

"Arnold and Jack were cordial," Reichley said, "but Nicklaus wasn't much of a talker . . . He kind of stuck to the business of the day."

That business was drumming every available player on the course. Nicklaus wasn't nearly as interested in winning the team competition as he was in posting the lowest score.

He didn't want to defeat Finsterwald and Saunders. He wanted to defeat Finsterwald and Saunders and Palmer.

Nicklaus would win only low amateur honors, his 68 beating Saunders's 71. Finsterwald saved face in his own backyard, edging Nicklaus by a single shot. Palmer sank a fifty-footer at the sixteenth and managed an easy two-putt par on the eighteenth for a 62, celebrating Finsterwald's day by breaking his Athens record by one.

Palmer said a few kind words about Nicklaus afterward but wasn't effusive in his praise. Over the decades, whenever asked about this day, Palmer would inevitably talk about that flying Nicklaus elbow, the one conspicuous flaw.

"I thought he was potentially good," Palmer said. "I noticed he had his right elbow, it was unattached. Let's say it swung out ... Until he got that elbow under control or kept that elbow closer, he might have had some problems with his game.

"He had some problems [with accuracy] at the time. He drove it long and he was good; I mean, it was obvious he was very good. But the consistency was something at the time I thought might have been of some concern."

The exhibition wasn't about Nicklaus anyway. "I think the whole thing was just the fact that I was there to appease a good friend," Palmer said, "and that was Dow Finsterwald. It had nothing to do with Jack Nicklaus, other than the fact that I was happy to see him and make his acquaintance, and to understand he was an upcoming player to be reckoned with at some point. And that was it."

After the exhibition Palmer gave a dozen Wilson balls to Snyder and three apiece to the other caddies. The Ohio U. boys were paid ten dollars for their priceless experience, and the golfers were off to a dinner held in Dow's honor.

Palmer and Finsterwald helped themselves to a few cocktails while Charlie Nicklaus kept close watch over his boy. "I don't think either Arnold or I realized how great Jack was going to be," Finsterwald would say. "We didn't appreciate ... the significance of what was taking place."

Finsterwald did make a speech at the dinner, and in it he predicted Nicklaus would have a "wonderful future" in golf. The other players spoke as well, and Nicklaus handled himself with surprising ease at the podium.

Palmer told the audience he liked Jack's putting stroke. At the close of the evening, the man and the boy shared their final handshake and went their separate ways, Arnold back to the tour, Jack back to Ohio State.

Swearingen, the event organizer, would go on to become an NFL referee, the one who would make the most controversial call in league history: the "Immaculate Reception" call that decided the Oakland Raiders–Pittsburgh Steelers playoff game in 1972.

But first he officiated golf's Immaculate Conception, the birth of a rivalry that would fuel the surging popularity of the sport in the 1960s.

A driving contest in Appalachia. A meaningless exhibition on a middling nine-hole course.

"That was the start of the whole Palmer and Nicklaus thing," Swearingen said.

That was the start of a lifelong clash of titans that would play out in fairways and boardrooms across the globe.

Part I

CHAPTER 1

• Poor Boy

ARNOLD DANIEL PALMER was not like the other school-boys who worked the grounds of Latrobe Country Club. In fact, as much as Palmer thought the members' children were living a charmed existence in the Allegheny foot-hills, the caddies figured Arnold was the one who had it made in the apple trees' shade.

Palmer's father, Deacon, was Latrobe's greenskeeper and head pro — the latter title granted when Depression-era reality forced the club to assign two jobs to one man. Deacon never let his son forget that he wasn't a member's kid, that he had no business on the greener side of the club's economic divide.

But the caddies were sons of men even lower on the western Pennsylvania food chain than Deacon Palmer. They wore tattered sneakers, not polished golf shoes, when allowed to play the course on Monday mornings, and Monday mornings only.

Arnold had superior footwear and equipment. He carried bags here and there, even served as caddie master for a bit. But Arnold was more often a part of the grounds crew and an aide in the pro shop. As Deacon's son, he rode the tractor and got to play the course in the evenings, when he'd cover as many holes as daylight allowed once the members were through with their rounds.

Truth was, Deacon found his boy to be a lousy employee, worse than any who had left to fight in the war. "The worst person he ever hired, his own son," said Joe Tito, Arnold's friend. "Deacon told everyone that."

It didn't make a difference. Arnold's only concern was finishing his tasks quickly enough, or closing the pro shop surreptitiously enough, so he could go to work on his game.

The way the caddies saw it, Arnold had everything going for him. The caddies were envious of his job and the opportunities they thought he had in front of him. "Arnold made the most of what little edge he had over the rest of us," said Ed Matko, his friend.

The club members came out of the white-collar corners of Latrobe, and its employees came out of the ethnic strongholds of neighboring Youngstown and Baggaley, home to the region's steelworkers and coal miners and a place where residents didn't think twice about calling one another hunkies and Polacks and dagos — with a laugh, of course.

Mingling between the social classes wasn't encouraged at the club. While the caddies waited for their loops, they played penny ante and talked about the boy who rode the tractor, mowed the grass, and hit a golf ball harder than anyone his age had a right to hit it.

Arnold would play with Matko and two other caddies on Monday mornings. Deacon's son didn't impress only with his power and his aggressive approaches to the green, but with his blind faith in himself.

The caddies didn't have that confidence. They marveled at Arnold's brashness, his cockiness. They couldn't believe someone so young could be so sure of his ability to play an impossibly difficult game.

Arnold's cockiness would show up in the fantasy matchups the caddies created during their rounds. Like millions of American boys who imagined themselves as Joe DiMaggio or Joe Louis in their backyard dreams, Arnold and the others in his foursome would step onto the final Monday morning tee and borrow the identities of the game's enduring winners.

Matko would say he was Sam Snead. Another caddie would say he was Byron Nelson. Another would say he was Bobby Jones. The three caddies rotated their allegiances almost on a weekly basis, working in the likes of Sarazen, Hagen, and Hogan.

Only the greenskeeper's son would never deviate from his personal script.

"I'm Arnold Palmer," he'd say every single time.

Arnold always said it slowly and with the self-assuredness of a seasoned sage. "Like he knew he would end up alongside those legendary names," Matko said. "It was written all over Arnold that he was destined for greatness."

Doris and Milfred Jerome "Deacon" Palmer paid fifteen dollars a month in rent for their two-story frame house off the sixth tee of the Latrobe Country Club, where they made do without the luxury of a toilet. Their outhouse was back by the maintenance shed, and in the dead of winter it wasn't an enjoyable walk.

The Palmers raised chickens and pigs to help make ends meet. They grew and canned their own vegetables and jellies and fermented their own wine.

Arnold and his kid sister, Lois Jean, shared one upstairs bedroom, Deacon and Doris the other. The Palmers didn't have a furnace, but they did have fireplaces in every room that would accommodate one. The family didn't have a bathroom and a shower until a teenage Arnold helped his father install them in the early forties.

Born less than seven weeks before the stock market crashed and burned in October 1929, Arnold was raised on the value of a buck. He was already hustling for money as a barefoot five-year-old with a cowboy pistol hanging from his hip, standing by the sixth tee and offering to hit the ladies' balls over a drainage ditch 120 yards out for a nickel a pop.

Arnold's father was a high school dropout who suffered from polio as a child, though his limp never discouraged him from putting in an honest day's work. Deacon compensated for his weak legs by hardening his upper body through endless reps of one-arm chin-ups and by serving as a teenage member of the construction crew that built the nine-hole course owned by Latrobe Steel, the course that would serve Latrobe Country Club.

He would dig ditches, plant trees, run a poolroom, and work in a steel mill. He would cater to all the country clubbers' whims from 6:00 a.m. until whenever the last range lesson was complete.

Deacon earned his nickname while working a painting job with his grandfather in Connellsville. Some kids were mocking a black minister or deacon on the street, and young Palmer interceded on the man's behalf. The kids started calling him Deacon after that, and the name stuck to him like a nail hammered down to its head.

Deacon was a man of modest size who relied on his large and powerful hands, the most obvious physical trait he passed down to his oldest child. Arnold called his old man "Pap." He followed his father around the golf course, helping him maintain it, but mostly he was interested in wrapping his own monstrous mitts around the grip of a club.

"Watch me, Pap!" he'd yell over and over to Deacon while practicing, enough to move the old man to say, "You'd get so sick of him you'd feel like hitting him a lick." Arnold painted the white golf balls red so he could drive them into the winter snow, retrieve them, and drive them again.

Anything to keep playing. Arnold was the first of four Palmer children—Lois Jean was born twenty-one months later, and Jerry and Sandy arrived a full fifteen and nineteen years after Arnold's birth—and the one most intent on making the game an integral part of his life. Lois Jean was a more diligent worker than her older brother. Everyone called her "Cheech"—as an infant Jerry kept spitting out "Chi-Chi" instead of Lois Jean, and Deacon later shortened it to Cheech. She was the only lifeguard at the country club pool, working six days a week. She was on duty from the time the first member jumped into the water until the time the last member climbed out of it, and she made fifty dollars a month for the privilege.

Sometimes she hated watching those rich kids swim and splash about. "But Daddy was a good man who kept his place," Cheech said. "It was his idea that we were not members; we were children of the staff." The Palmer children were allowed in the pool only when it was otherwise empty.

The lifeguard secured her own form of payback. Cheech and Arnold were among those who would swim in the creek water that was pumped into the pool, so the members' kids were, in effect, wading in their backwash and swimming in their piss. Sometimes the membership water was so dirty, Cheech said, "you could write your name in the bottom of the pool."

Things would change by the time Jerry and Sandy grew up; they were the beneficiaries of their father's rise up the Latrobe staff ladder and of Arnold's widening reputation as a golf phenom.

Despite Deacon's protests, Jerry and Sandy would dive into the pool and roam the club grounds as quasi members. That didn't stop Deacon from drawing fresh lines in the country club sand, for himself and his kids. He ate his meals in the club kitchen. He wouldn't enter the locker room and dining room and clubhouse unless invited by a member.

Most of these were lines the Palmer children wouldn't cross. At home and at work, Deacon's word was law. The children held their knives and forks the proper way. If one of them was moved to sneeze at mealtime, he or she was expected to leave the room. There would be no sneezing at Deacon Palmer's dinner table.

Nobody wanted to defy Deacon's law. And nobody felt the full force of that law quite like the firstborn.

"He was relentless," Arnold said of his father. "He never let up."

Physically they were alike — all shoulders and forearms, with high hairlines and hips too narrow to hold up their britches. Their life in the sun left their skin dirt brown. In fact, Deacon and Arnold were practically the mirror images of each other, and close enough to be called good friends. "But I was very aware of him," Arnold said, "and certainly lived in the shadow of knowing that if I did something wrong, I got my ass kicked."

Deacon could hand out an ass-kicking with the best of 'em, too. He rose before dawn every morning and busied himself reading newspapers and Zane Grey westerns. But between sunrise and the inevitable moment he fell asleep on the couch watching the evening news, his volcanic temper could blow in a flash, his rage often fueled by alcohol.

Drunk on Arnold's sixteenth birthday, enraged by his son's nerve in confronting him over the way he was talking to Doris, Deacon picked up Arnold by the shirt and threw him against a galvanized stove pipe, crushing the pipe against the wall.

Most in the family saw Deacon as a kind and generous man, an old-school patriarch and disciplinarian whose drinking didn't significantly detract from his value as a loving parent.

At least one family member would come to see him as a functioning alcoholic.

Either way, Deacon assigned his wife to handle the girls' discipline, and Doris also assumed the role of good cop with the boys after her husband left them in dire need of a hug. The children craved her soft touch. "The peacemaker," Arnold called her.

Arnold was a boy's boy, and if he got into mischief at school he would pay a heavy price at home. Doris would console her son and tell Deacon that he should let up, that he was being too hard on their child. Deacon dismissed her suggestions as signs of weakness.

He was his own man, Deacon Palmer was. Stubborn as the day was long. He would tell Sandy he would be extremely disappointed in her if she ever smoked as Arnold and Cheech and Jerry had, as her entire generation had, as even Deacon had. The second a woman put a cigarette to her lips, Deacon would say, was the second she surrendered her sex appeal.

Sandy never once smoked a cigarette. She didn't care as much about losing her sex appeal as she did about losing her father's respect.

Deacon never conceded an argument. And no, he never challenged anyone's right to Deacon's opinion.

"You could've been the Lord standing right in front of him," Arnold said, "and he was going to tell you what he thought."

Deacon's stubbornness ultimately drove his son to the top of the golf world. Whenever he stepped onto a tee box, in high school, college, and the pros, Arnold was a golfer on a singular mission: to prove he could be the man his father wasn't sure he'd be.

That motivated Arnold more than his second-class citizenship at the club. After taking all of those ass-kickings without launching any retaliatory strikes, Arnold was going to show Deacon how much fight he'd kept locked inside.

He would be a product of his upbringing; he'd succeed or fail as a Palmer, because of the Palmers. No outside influences needed. No third-party instruction desired.

Deacon wanted it that way. He embraced a cardinal rule in the molding of his son: nobody would advise him on what Arnold should or shouldn't do.

Club members would tell the father, "Deke, you're handling that kid wrong. He's never going to amount to anything." A lot of those members treated Arnie as a dead-end cause. "One man in particular," Cheech said, "a man that was Daddy's boss for a while, he just thought Arnie wasn't worth anything. He said, 'All he'll ever do is dig ditches.'"

Deacon would bark at the critics—"He's my kid. I'll raise him. Mind your own business"—and these were the only occasions he'd step out of his soiled employee's clothes and confront the members.

Deacon might've been quick to remind his children that they weren't Latrobe royalty; he just didn't want the royals to do any of the reminding for him.

All in all, the Palmers successfully bridged the gap between their roots and the higher social standing of the WASPs-only Latrobe membership. Doris and Deacon never segregated their guests when they hosted parties at their home. Family and friends from Youngstown were welcome to mix with those Latrobe doctors grounded enough to accept an invitation from a hired country club hand.

But like a Bowery Boy pressing his face against a Saks Fifth Avenue window on Christmas Eve, coveting a forbidden world on the other side, Arnold never forgot that he was on the outside looking in. "He definitely felt that glass wall," said his classmate and friend Mary Moran, "because he often brought it up . . . I think he felt that very strongly. He felt it more strongly than it actually was."

The teenage Arnold wasn't so insecure about himself away from the club. He was never shy around the high school girls and he preferred to keep the company of older students. Matko, two years his senior, worked with Arnold at Jimmy Peretto's nightclub, the Mission Inn, a popular hangout that featured dancing under the stars. Palmer and Matko cleaned tables and parked cars and ate the leftover spaghetti and ham barbecues in the small hours of night, after the partygoers cleared out; Peretto's mother made the best pasta Arnold had ever tasted.

Palmer and Matko talked about girls, of course, about how Arnold always seemed to do better with them than his older friend. "I couldn't keep up with him," Matko said. Arnold was mature, even charismatic at such an early age. The girls noticed, and so did the boys. Arnold was envied as much as he was adored.

"You'll never be a golfer like Palmer," the Latrobe High golf coach, Bill Yates, would tell Matko, "because you don't have his big hands."

Arnold could've been an even bigger man on the Latrobe High campus. He was fast enough and athletic enough to have made for a hell of a high school halfback, but Deacon didn't want his boy getting hurt playing football. So that was that.

Arnold, Matko, and their friends instead played a game called rough and tumble, hard-tackle football without the pads. When Deacon wasn't around, they played it on country club grounds.

Deacon put a stop to rough-and-tumble the moment he caught

wind of it. He wanted his boy to stay healthy for the non-contact drills of golf.

As always, Arnold had one instructor for those drills. And that instructor had one instruction.

Deacon advised his son to hit the ball hard, find it, then hit it harder.

The boy was a good listener. Arnold paid no attention, in his words, "to all this stuff about hitting high shots and different types of shots." Arnold would identify a target, aim, and fire. Then he would do it all over again.

Arnold first started driving with a sawed-off, hickory-shaft brassie given to him by his father. Deacon had taught him the Vardon grip, the overlapping grip, when his son was barely out of diapers.

Soon enough Arnold was overpowering the par-34 Latrobe course, this before the club upgraded to a par-36 and then to a full eighteen-hole layout. Arnold collected junior tournament and high school tournament trophies as easily as one collected pennies or stamps: he would rip off five Western Pennsylvania Amateur championships.

His strength and athleticism, which could've made him a football hero in a football-mad place (Latrobe was once considered the Cooperstown of the sport, at least until the Pro Football Hall of Fame recognized Pittsburgh as an earlier nineteenth-century birthplace),instead made him a young star in a game most mill-town boys dismissed as a soft exercise for the frail and rich.

Arnold occasionally flashed a temper on the course, once hurling his putter over some poplar trees in his father's presence. During the car ride home, Deacon wasn't interested in congratulating his son for a victory earned on the final hole. He told Arnold the next time he threw a club in his presence, while living under his roof, would be the last time he ever played the game of golf.

Deacon didn't care how other players exploded over a missed putt and embarrassed themselves in public; his boy wasn't allowed to do the same. "One of the rules of Deacon Palmer's house," Arnold said, "was get angry if you want to, but don't show yourself. Don't show how stupid you are, and he meant it. There was nothing to gain ... Making an ass of yourself is not something that he permitted."

Deacon didn't allow any conspicuous show of on-course parenting, either, not from his end. If Doris was up front and center, letting everyone know that the boy with the big arms and bigger lead was hers, Deacon would retreat into the shadows of the pines and oaks, watching his flesh and blood from a safe distance.

Arnold learned to play to the gallery while watching Babe Didrikson dazzle the fans during an exhibition in Latrobe. He first sensed a connection with the golfing public while competing in the 1947 Western Pennsylvania Amateur, where the crowd helped carry him to victory in a quarterfinal match, its cheers growing louder with each successful stroke. The feeling that came over him, Arnold said, "reached all the way down to my toes." The louder the cheers, the better the shots.

Palmer played his first pro tour event that year, as a high school student, when he entered the Dapper Dan Open in Pittsburgh. "I wrecked my father's car going to the tournament," Arnold said, "and I didn't make the cut. But I got cut when I got home."

He secured a scholarship to Wake Forest, though not an academic one; Arnold was an average student at Latrobe High, nothing more. He had made the acquaintance of Buddy Worsham, a long-hitting amateur bound for Wake and the younger brother of Lew Worsham, the pro at the revered Oakmont Country Club and a playoff winner over Sam Snead at the 1947 U.S. Open. Buddy helped land Arnold a free-ride spot on a Wake team with a losing tradition.

They became good friends, and soon enough Arnold was Wake's number-one player and an emerging presence on the national landscape. He beat North Carolina's Harvie Ward, regarded as the finest college player in America, to win the Southern Conference championship after predicting he would do just that.

"The Wake Forest College muscleman," the Associated Press called Arnold.

Palmer built up his arms by pushing his father's mowers around Latrobe and by doing bricklaying work in the mills while on vacation from Wake. He wasn't a stylist in the mold of Bobby Jones, Byron Nelson, and Sam Snead. With a club in his hand, Palmer was as refined as a raging bull.

He could smack a one-iron shot like nobody else. Palmer was a player who went for the pin from any corner of the course, doglegs be damned. He was just as aggressive with a three-wood in his hands as he was with a putter, which he used to sink thirty-five-footers that would've traveled fifty-five feet if the back side of the cups hadn't reached up and sucked them down.

Everyone suspected Palmer was blazing a path to greatness. Don

January, lead player on the powerful North Texas State team, was completely outclassed by Palmer when the two went head-to-head. "Arnold had a peculiar style," January said, "but he got it all done."

Deacon ordered Arnold never to alter that peculiar style. Across his time at Wake, Palmer heeded his father's counsel and refused to let anyone mess with his unorthodox swing. He made one exception: Buddy Worsham.

Arnold would struggle at times with a severe hook. Worsham fiddled with his grip, and the duck hooks soon disappeared.

Arnold was regularly beating the big names at the big schools. If he wasn't much for going to class, he did enough to get by, barely.

Buddy was his running mate, his wingman. Buddy was his teammate, confidant, and unofficial swing coach. He would visit Arnold in Latrobe, where he grew close to Deacon and Doris. Palmer and Worsham were brothers in every figurative way; Buddy even briefly dated Arnold's sister.

"A neat kid," Cheech called him, "but he was as wild as he could be."

With Arnold at Wake, Cheech was going to school and working in Washington, DC, training to become a computer programmer for the federal government. Deacon and Doris couldn't afford to send their daughter to a private or state college, so Cheech found a way to get ahead on Uncle Sam's dime.

She made arrangements to meet with Arnold and Buddy at a Wake Forest football game in Winston-Salem. Cheech would bring the man she would marry, Ron Tilley, and two of her roommates to pair up with Arnold and Buddy for blind dates. "We were all going to have a big weekend," Cheech said.

The night before their meeting, Buddy asked Arnold to go with him to a dance in Durham. Arnold was planning on taking in a movie with their teammate Jim Flick and asked Buddy to stay behind and join them.

Buddy stuck to his original plan. He went to Durham with Flick's roommate, Gene Scheer, and never came back.

Arnold was asked to identify the battered bodies resting side by side on a funeral home table. He would find Buddy's Buick nearly ripped in half at a junkyard; the car had flipped over and crushed its occupants.

"I was mentally and physically and every other way shaken by the fact Buddy was killed," Palmer said, "and I realized life can have a destiny and you sometimes can't control that."

Palmer controlled his destiny at Wake Forest, and the haunting thoughts of Buddy and what might have been had Arnold accepted his invitation compelled him to leave school. He didn't lose his appetite for competitive golf, but Palmer craved a fundamental change in his life, if only for a temporary escape. He decided on military service, and the coast guard demanded the shortest commitment and offered the best opportunity to continue playing the game.

The only action Palmer saw during the Korean War presented itself on domestic golf courses. Arnold was transferred from Cape May, New Jersey, to Cleveland; his military duty didn't stop him from competing in — and winning — amateur tournaments before his discharge. Three years after leaving school because he couldn't cope with Buddy Worsham's death, Arnold returned to Wake Forest and reestablished himself as a dominant collegiate force, becoming the first man to win a title in the new Atlantic Coast Conference.

Palmer left Wake without a degree but with a singular purpose: he wanted to win the U. S. Amateur championship, one of the few titles of consequence that had eluded him.

Palmer didn't want his father's life, the life of a club pro. A man spent too much time being demeaned in that life, being treated like a towel boy by hundreds of country club snobs. Arnold saw the U.S. Amateur championship as a vehicle to greater things. If he could win it, perhaps he could win and win big on the professional tour, too.

He entered the U.S. Amateur at the Country Club of Detroit as a paint salesman. The job was a joke, as Palmer's employer more or less hired him to play golf with clients. Just as he wasn't much of a pro shop aide, Arnold wasn't much of a salesman. But it was a way to make a few dollars and pass the time until golf took him wherever he was meant to go.

In his fifth crack at the Amateur title, Palmer was fixing to go the distance. He burned to make a full-time occupation out of golf, and he needed a major national championship to convince himself he wouldn't have to make a career out of peddling paint.

If Palmer privately doubted that he could close the deal, he betrayed no such concern on the course. Some of his friends and competitors called him "Crow" because Palmer "was always yakking and making noise," said Steve Pipoly, who had lost to Arnold at the Ohio State Amateur.

No, Palmer wasn't shy or hesitant with a ball at his feet. That's why Matko and a couple of his buddies spilled into his 1952 Studebaker and made the 330-mile drive to suburban Detroit in late August 1954. "We specifically went there to watch Arnie win the Amateur," Matko said.

A series of tense, exhausting matches landed Palmer in the final four. In the fifth round he'd defeated the heir to the Champion Spark Plug fortune, Frank Stranahan, a two-time British Amateur winner, body-building fiend, and good friend who previously had Arnold's number. In the quarterfinals Palmer came from behind to beat Don Cherry, a singer and Canadian Amateur champ.

Next up was Ed Meister, thirty-seven-year-old former captain at Yale. Deacon and Doris drove all night to get there for a match that would go down as the longest semifinal in Amateur history.

Arnold took a one-up lead after the morning round but unraveled on the first nine of the second eighteen, landing in bunker after bunker and shooting a 39 on the par-70 course. Palmer's putter suddenly came to life over the final nine, and on the thirty-sixth hole, with the match all square, Arnold made a near-miraculous recovery shot from behind the green — maybe the damnedest golf shot he'd ever hit — and stood forever over a five-foot sidehill putt that would either eliminate him or force a playoff.

"I waited until I was sure I would make it," Palmer said.

He beat Meister on the thirty-ninth hole.

On August 28, 1954, Palmer rose to his hour of reckoning. The Amateur final would pit the greenskeeper's son against a man who was everything the twenty-four-year-old Palmer was not. Robert Sweeny, forty-three-year-old investment banker and socialite out of Sands Point, New York, was Oxford educated and a dues-paying member at places that would make Latrobe Country Club seem as prestigious as a waffle house.

Sweeny helped his brother Charles assemble the Eagle Squadrons of volunteer American fighter pilots who served the Royal Air Force during World War II. He won a Distinguished Flying Cross after leading a successful mission against enemy submarines in 1943 and was rumored to have inspired the James Bond character that Ian Fleming would turn into a cottage industry.

Sweeny was a member of Seminole in Jupiter, Florida, and Sunningdale in London, ultra-exclusive enclaves for the ultra-rich and ultra-connected. He had won the British Amateur in 1937 and was making his sixth attempt to win the American title.

The greenskeeper's son? He was looking for direction, for a reason to turn pro.

More than anything, he was looking for the approval of Milfred Jerome "Deacon" Palmer.

If the United States Golf Association used a ring announcer at the first tee, the introductions would've been simple: "In this corner, blue collar. In that corner, blue blood."

On cue the dashing Sweeny came dressed for a polo match. He wore a white visor, a light knit shirt sporting the Lacoste status symbol — the crocodile logo — and white linen slacks that appeared to be buckled around his armpits. All legs and thin as a flagstick, Sweeny was the living, breathing picture of privilege, the ultimate symbol of golf's elitist present and past. He was a Palmer foil out of Central Casting.

Just as Sweeny was sure to represent his people, Palmer was sure to represent his. Arnold arrived at the flat 6,875-yard course looking ready either to carry Sweeny's bag or to paint Sweeny's home on the French Riviera. He wore dark pants and the kind of open-collared, short-sleeved shirt that had "laborer" written all over it, the sleeves high enough to show off Palmer's considerable biceps. Arnold's shirt wasn't properly tucked; it spilled over his black belt buckle. He was missing only a pack of Liggett & Myers rolled up in his sleeve and a number-two pencil tucked behind his ear.

High society was colliding with its wait staff in this thirty-six-hole final, a battle of the classes witnessed by some thirty-five hundred fans. Palmer was the exception at a time when accomplished amateurs were old money men of the highest social standing, golfers who could support their globe-trotting expeditions without dipping into a single trust fund.

So the underdog at the Country Club of Detroit was easy to identify and easier to pull for.

"The crowd was definitely rooting for Arnie," Matko said.

He gave them nothing to cheer about over the first four holes: Sweeny birdied numbers two, three, and four with putts of thirty-five, eighteen, and twenty feet to take a three-up lead. Palmer didn't know what hit him. He was dazed, dismayed, and a bit ashamed that his parents had come all the way from Latrobe to see this.

He had survived half a dozen brutal matches in four days to earn this crack at Sweeny. Palmer was starting to wonder if he'd even make it to the twentieth hole.

And then Sweeny made a crucial mistake out of the goodness of his heart. Upon leaving the fifth tee, he wrapped an arm around his bloodied opponent and said, "This can't last forever."

Palmer won that hole on a Sweeny three-putt. He won the eighth, ninth, and tenth holes to square the match, to give himself hope, to give Sweeny a reason to doubt his own ability to hold off a younger, stronger, longer man.

Sweeny finished the morning eighteen with a two-up lead, but the dynamic of the match had changed from those first four holes. Palmer realized he had a chance. He'd absorbed Sweeny's best punch and stayed on his feet.

Sometimes Palmer dropped to his knees by choice, to get a better read on a putt. Arnold would plant his knees and elbows on the green while cupping his eyes and studying his line. This was not a pose Sweeny would've ever struck.

Palmer erased his deficit on the front nine of the afternoon round, squaring the match on the twenty-seventh hole, where Sweeny drove into the right rough and missed the green on his approach. After Sweeny won the twenty-eighth hole to recapture the lead, Palmer took the thirtieth on a six-foot putt to forge another tie. He would never trail again.

Palmer two-putted from twenty-five feet — after Sweeny missed the green — to win the thirty-second hole and claim his very first lead of a long, taxing day, retrieving the ball with his right hand, lifting it ear-high, and pumping it for punctuation. Palmer then sank a ten-foot birdie at the thirty-third to go two up with three to play. Sweeny showed some resilience on the thirty-fifth, getting out of the sand and dropping an eight-footer to cut Palmer's lead to one.

All Palmer had to do to win the U. S. Amateur was halve the final hole. Sweeny drove into the rough, again, and missed the green on his approach, again. Palmer was safely on in two, and after Sweeny left his third shot seven feet from the hole, Arnold ran his forty-five-foot putt three inches short of pay dirt.

The man who encouraged an overwhelmed Palmer at the fifth hole conceded the match to him on the thirty-sixth. Sweeny calmly approached Palmer and offered his hand in congratulations. The greenskeeper's son and paint salesman was the undisputed king of American amateur golf.

Palmer embraced his mother, who was crying. Deacon was predictably late to the scene of the celebration, but he cut through a circle of reporters and photographers and stepped around the brass band that was surrounding Arnold and preparing to play "Hail to the Chief."

Deacon grabbed Arnold's hand and offered the trace of a smile. "You did pretty good, boy," he said.

It was the nicest compliment Deacon had ever paid his son.

The Palmers posed for a picture. Arnold wrapped his right arm around his mother, who was wearing a white hat and patterned summer dress, with a clubhouse pass and three-dollar event ticket dangling from her waist. Doris planted a kiss on the champion's right cheek while the man to Arnold's left, dressed in a golf shirt and sweater vest, looked on and smiled.

Arnold had his left arm wrapped around Deacon's shoulders, but the old man held firm, resisting the urge to get pulled in too tightly.

The Amateur title would change Arnold's life forever. Newspapermen filled their pages with breathless tales of a swashbuckling poor boy who could beat the elitists at their own game.

Was his go-for-broke style too reckless to work on the tour? "A lot of guys won the National Amateur," Don January said, "and couldn't stick their fingers in their butts in the pros."

Didn't matter to Palmer. At the Country Club of Detroit, he knew he was good enough to become a professional golfer.

He didn't know this championship would dramatically alter his personal life—it earned him an invitation to a tournament at Shawnee on Delaware, where he would meet and propose to the woman he'd marry, Winifred "Winnie" Walzer.

Palmer had new responsibilities and more reasons to turn pro. But beyond a husband's financial obligations, Palmer's flame was stoked by a familiar motivational spark: the man he called Pap. Arnold wanted to show Deacon he could beat the big boys.

Before his son headed out on tour, Deacon's final marching orders went like this: "Just play your own game. Don't listen to all the guys who'll criticize you and tell you what to do and how to play.

"If you start listening to other people, anyone, you can always come back and cut fairways for me."

Arnold didn't need to reserve his old seat in Deacon's tractor. His instincts were confirmed while competing against the pros at the Azalea Open in Wilmington, North Carolina, where he was paired with Ted Kroll and Bob Toski.

Kroll and Toski were taken by Palmer's all-American, Jack Armstrong looks. They were also struck by how nervous the Amateur champ appeared.

At the first tee, on Kroll's suggestion, Toski told Palmer some dirty jokes to relax him. "You're playing with two Polacks today," Toski finally said, "so relax and have some fun."

Palmer shot 65.

"Jesus Christ, you didn't have to loosen him up that good," Kroll told Toski. "Did you see the size of those divots he was taking? They were a half foot long and flying out there thirty yards. If he learns to take a thin divot he's going to be a hell of a player."

"No," Toski said, "he's going to be a hell of a player with a thick divot."

"Do you think he's going to turn pro?" Kroll asked.

"Yes."

"Well, there goes another money place."

"Money place? This guy's not going to play for money; he's going to play to win. Arnold Palmer is going to be a star. A big star."

CHAPTER 2

• Stardom

ON EASTER SUNDAY, 1958, Arnold Palmer was standing over his drive at the thirteenth hole of the Masters when he confronted the first seminal moment of his professional major career. He could lay up short of the creek with an iron, or go for broke with a wood.

Palmer was no longer the penniless and clueless kid who first pulled up to Augusta National in 1955 hauling a trailer behind his two-door Ford. Arnold and Winnie would park in a trailer camp next to a drive-in movie theater back then and hope for the best.

By the spring of 1958, Palmer had won eight pro events in a little more than three seasons on tour. Weeks before arriving in Augusta, the 1956 champ, Jack Burke Jr., told him, "I just dreamed you won the Masters."

But as he stood in position to realize another man's dream, Palmer was a nervous wreck. He'd just walked away from a stare-down with a rules official at the par-three twelfth that he feared could cost him the tournament. With the course soaked by earlier rains, Palmer had plugged his tee shot in the muddy bank between a rear bunker and the green.

Palmer believed he was entitled to a free drop under the foul-weather provisions the Masters had adopted for the day—embedded balls could be cleaned and dropped without penalty. The official, Arthur Lacey, maintained he had to play his ball without a lift because it was only half embedded. Palmer flubbed his chip and made a double-bogey five before playing a second ball inches from the original landing spot, leaving the matter in the hands of the rules committee.

Palmer made par on his second ball, and his playing partner was furious. Ken Venturi was a protégé of Byron Nelson and Ben Hogan, and once a Yankees prospect who shagged fly balls for Joe DiMaggio. He nearly won the 1956 Masters as an amateur but shot a wind-blown 80 in the final round when paired with Sam Snead, who was alleged to have given Venturi the silent treatment.

The leader was traditionally paired with the neighborly Nelson, but Clifford Roberts, the New York investment banker and Augusta National cofounder, forever made up the rules as he went along, and he decreed that Venturi's relationship with Nelson was cause to start a new trend.

It was Venturi's bum luck. But that was then; this was now. Some thought Venturi would be the next megastar on tour in 1958; some thought Palmer. The ruling at twelve would begin to settle the debate.

As Palmer and Lacey argued, Venturi told Palmer to ignore the official. "Arnold," he said, "you can't be half pregnant. Take a drop."

Palmer didn't take his advice, not immediately anyway. The discussion continued as Venturi putted out for par. Only after making his five did Palmer state his intention of taking a drop, according to Venturi, who saw this as a clear violation of the rules.

"You can't do that," Venturi told Palmer. "What if you holed out your first ball [on the chip]? Would you still be playing a second [ball]?"

As Palmer readied to hit his second ball, Venturi turned to his caddie and said, "I think we're going to win the tournament."

Palmer would later claim he had informed Lacey of his intentions before flubbing his first-ball chip. And even if Palmer hadn't, the rules of golf at the time stated that a competitor failing to announce his second-ball intentions before striking his first ball would still be credited with whatever score his second ball produced.

But Palmer walked to his drive on the 475-yard, par-five thirteenth still unsure if he was one shot ahead of Venturi or one shot behind him. "They're going to give me a five," Palmer said.

"You bet your ass they're going to give you a five," Venturi responded.

Venturi played his second shot short of the creek fronting the green, hoping for a pitch-and-putt birdie. Palmer pondered his next course of action. His sense of dread over the pending verdict was at odds with the rage he felt over several slights.

Upon arriving in Augusta, sleep-deprived after the drive from North Carolina and a Monday playoff loss to Howie Johnson (who benefited, ironically enough, from a one-stroke penalty Palmer called against himself), Arnold played dreadfully in a practice round with his friend Dow Finsterwald and their opponents, Burke and Ben Hogan. In the locker room after that round, with Palmer nearby, Hogan asked Burke, "How in the hell did he get in the Masters?"

Burke answered that Palmer was in fact among the hottest players on tour.

Hogan shook his head. "He played like he couldn't even find his ball most of the time."

Palmer didn't confront Hogan, but he was ripshit all the same. He was already steamed that Hogan, winner of nine majors and a player the Scots called the "Wee Ice Mon," never referred to him by his first name, always calling him "fella" instead. Truth was, Hogan, the perfectionist, had no use for Arnold's Wild West game.

"Pissed me off," Palmer said. "*P-i-s-s-e-d.*"

By the morning of the final round, with Hogan seven shots back, Palmer had directed his attention toward a clear and present danger. Sitting in his hotel with Ron Green of the *Charlotte News,* eating a breakfast of corn flakes, Palmer pulled his head out of a newspaper long enough to say, "I don't see how they can make a fella like Ken Venturi such a heavy favorite in the tournament."

Hours later, in the thirteenth fairway, Palmer argued with himself over the proper method to beat the heavy favorite. It was no contest. Palmer had left burn marks on the tee boxes all tournament, his slashing style stamped by his own mark of Zorro.

He had riled up the soldiers on leave from Fort Gordon, the men working the scoreboards and wielding their pro-Palmer signs and starting what would become the "Arnie's Army" craze. Arnie had thrilled the Sunday crowd, estimated at more than thirty thousand, a Masters record, and he wasn't about to disappoint the soldiers or fans by playing it safe down the stretch.

If Palmer needed any additional motivation, it arrived in the form of Bobby Jones, the Grand Slam champion of 1930, cofounder of Augusta

National, and the only man to have received two ticker-tape parades in New York. Jones showed up in a green cart with his partner, Clifford Roberts; the fifty-six-year-old Jones could no longer walk the course, as he was suffering from syringomyelia, a spinal cord disorder that would paralyze him. The cart was marked "Official." It was the jury box for the trial of Palmer over his alleged crime at number twelve.

Arnold was inspired by the sight of the legendary figure, even though Jones was a shell of the man he used to be. He grabbed a three-wood out of his bag, took dead aim at the pin, and swung as hard as he could. The ball stopped eighteen feet from the hole. Jones would say it was the best golf swing he'd seen since he watched Gene Sarazen make his famous double-eagle shot on the fifteenth hole at the 1935 Masters.

When Palmer sank his eagle putt, he dropped his putter and raised his arms in touchdown form. On the fifteenth hole Palmer was summoned to Jones's cart and told that his second-ball score of three at the twelfth would stand.

A rattled Venturi proceeded to three-putt his way out of contention. Palmer bogeyed two of his final three holes to finish at four-under 284, then barely sat still as he watched a TV monitor showing Doug Ford and Fred Hawkins miss putts at eighteen in failed bids to force a playoff.

Palmer was the twenty-eight-year-old champion of the Masters, and a hug and kiss from his pregnant wife, Winnie, would have to do. Deacon and Doris had stayed back in Latrobe to watch their younger son, Jerry, join the family's Lutheran church in Youngstown, St. James Evangelical.

But another stern figure had filled the void left by Arnold's Pap. Hogan's ridicule had driven Palmer to this breakthrough victory.

"Hogan was another one of the goddamn guys on tour as far as I was concerned," Palmer said. "He was no big guy. He was no big deal, and I didn't care what he said. All I wanted to do was beat him, and I did."

Along the way Palmer had breathed life into a fresh piece of Augusta National lore. Herbert Warren Wind of *Sports Illustrated* was so moved by Arnold's Sunday drama that he coined the phrase "Amen Corner" for the eleventh, twelfth, and thirteenth holes.

Once it was clear he had won, Palmer was escorted into Roberts's clubhouse suite, where an informal ceremony would be broadcast on

CBS. Jim McKay, the lead network announcer, was wearing large headphones over his cap, and binoculars and a microphone around his neck, when he wrapped CBS's coverage of the closing holes and threw it to his colleague, John Derr. As Derr handed Roberts a mike, the co-founder looked at it as if it were a pipe bomb.

Roberts quickly passed it to Jones as the wire dangled straight across the investment banker's lap. Jones told Palmer how his swing at thirteen reminded him of Sarazen's at fifteen, and later, off air, Palmer heard the great Grand Slammer pay him a compliment he would never forget.

"Arnie," Jones said, "if I had to have a putt for my life, you can putt it for me."

Arnold Palmer was one shot down at the 1960 Masters with two holes to go. He was peering through his own cirrus clouds of cigarette smoke and thinking that the course owed him one.

The year before, Palmer had blown the Masters on seventeen and eighteen. A CBS camera would find him in the immediate wake of his 1959 defeat, shaking his head. "You're looking on the clubhouse porch at one of the most disconsolate young men in the world," the announcer, Jim McKay, told millions. "That's Arnold Palmer, the defending Masters champion. He's been dethroned."

And now one year later, on the seventeenth hole of the 1960 Masters, Palmer wanted his crown back. He was the pre-tournament favorite to win — Art Wall Jr., the defending champ, was out with a kidney ailment and bum knee — as he'd taken four tournaments leading into Augusta, including one stretch of three in a row.

Ken Venturi was already in the clubhouse at five under, which looked like the winning score. Palmer had sent a long putt through the shadows that bounced off the flagstick at sixteen, a development suggesting this wouldn't be his day. He shook his head in disgust; maybe he should've taken out the stick before he putted.

Venturi and Arnold's asshole buddy, Dow Finsterwald, had gone out almost a full hour ahead of Palmer, in the 12:33 p.m. pairing. Venturi and Finsterwald started the day the same way Ben Hogan, Julius Boros, and Billy Casper had — one stroke off Palmer's lead.

But after some thirty thousand fans poured through the Sunday gates, and after a couple of early Palmer bogeys, Venturi and Finsterwald pulled ahead of the pack and engaged in a classic match-play struggle. Poor Dow, best known for his bridesmaid ways. He would've been in sole possession of the lead down the back-nine stretch if not for the two-shot penalty he earned by taking an illegal practice putt in the middle of his first round.

Venturi outplayed Finsterwald by a stroke. He headed to the clubhouse believing he had finally won himself a green jacket.

All Venturi had to do was sit back and watch. Sit back and wait for Arnold Palmer to play seventeen and eighteen as he had in losing to Wall the year before.

Palmer needed to cover the final two par-four holes in one under to force a playoff, and he was looking at a downwind 400-yard seventeenth with a pin placement toward the back of the green. After landing his drive in the fairway, Palmer hit an eight-iron shot that on contact felt like a flawless stroke.

But the ball checked up below the hole much more quickly than Palmer thought it would, leaving him with an uphill thirty-footer he positively had to have. As he approached the green and realized his ball wasn't closer to the cup, Palmer yanked a smoldering L&M from his lips and spiked it into the ground.

The other half of his pairing, Billy Casper, missed a long putt, and then Palmer stalked his own ball like a panther measuring its prey. Arnold moved into putting position, then backed away. He stared into the crowd, commanding silence and stillness without saying a word. When he stepped back to his ball, not a single witness doubted this cold, hard fact:

Arnold Palmer wouldn't leave this putt short. He never, ever left a putt short.

It was either going in the hole, or it was going at least ten feet past on the attempt. Never up, never in. This was Arnie's article of Augusta National faith.

He crouched low to study his line, his late-afternoon shadow tracking his every move. Palmer gave himself one practice stroke and then pulled the trigger. Two-thirds of the way to the hole, his ball bounced an inch off the putting surface, as if tripping over a spike mark, the sure sign of a miss.

Not this time. The putt almost didn't make it to its destination, a rare Palmer development, but his ball didn't hang on the front lip for long. "It's up and up and up and up ... *and in!*" cried the CBS announcer, Jim McArthur.

Palmer threw both arms into the air and did a strange little jig, punctuating it by swinging his right arm and fist through the air. The crowd let out a roar that thundered through the theater in the pines.

Back in the clubhouse a reporter informed Venturi that Palmer had just nailed a long one at seventeen. "Oops," Venturi said.

Palmer was five under, tied for the lead. He marched to the seventy-second tee with his rail-thin caddie, Nathaniel "Iron Man" Avery, who was wearing number thirteen on the left side of his white overalls. Lucky number thirteen.

Palmer never thought Avery was much of a caddie. "He was about to be fired any minute . . . from the first day he started," Arnold said.

Avery had been caddying for Palmer at the Masters since 1955, and Arnold kept him on the bag because he felt obliged. Somehow, their fragile marriage worked.

Arnie needed one more birdie for his second Masters title, and the waiting newsmen couldn't have been happier. Venturi was an intriguing figure, but Palmer made for better copy.

"Everyone looked at his swing," Venturi remarked, "and they said, 'I love that guy. He looks just like me.'"

As the Fort Gordon soldiers were inspiring the "Arnie's Army" headline in the *Augusta Chronicle* — written by a copyeditor named Johnny Sands — that put a name to a movement, fans and viewers were coming to see Palmer as the perfect American star. He was the Marlboro Man chain-smoking L&Ms. He was a clean-cut Elvis whose contortions were deemed appropriate for all viewing audiences. He was a most photogenic and charismatic sportsman in a day when 87 percent of U.S. households had TV.

More than anything, he was a swing-for-the-heavens slugger at a time when America was first fathoming the possibility of putting a man on the moon.

"The first time I ever watched Arnold Palmer hit golf balls," said Gary Player, the 1959 British Open champ, "I said, 'Wow, this guy's going to be a champion.' It's like when you see a beautiful woman; you don't have to look at her ten times to know it. I looked at this guy's swing and I saw the flair, and I saw the man."

On April 10, 1960, that was the package Palmer carried to the eighteenth tee. A golf addict, Dwight D. Eisenhower, was president, honing his putting stroke on the practice green he had installed at the White House. Coverage of the sport had come a long way since ABC broadcast the Tam O'Shanter World Championship from outside Chicago with one camera in 1953, when Buddy Worsham's brother, Lew, staged the perfect ending by sinking a 115-yard wedge shot from the fairway for an eagle and a first prize of $25,000.

A flamboyant promoter named George S. May was willing to pay ABC $32,000 to show his $100,000 Tam O'Shanter event. By 1960 this financial arrangement was turned upside down. The networks were now paying tens of thousands of dollars in broadcast fees, and Palmer was quickly becoming the lead actor in a running series of unscripted dramas.

The rich man admired his putting. The common man admired his high-handicapper swing, the one that almost always left Palmer tripping over his own feet.

The final hole at the Masters only secured Palmer's hold on the public's imagination. He hit his tee shot against the wind, landing it in the fairway some 260 yards from the point of impact. Palmer was dying for a piece of chewing gum; his frayed nerves had left his mouth as dry as a sand trap.

"I was afraid I was going to lose," Palmer said, "and that scared the shit out of me. That made me play even harder ... A lot of people are frightened by winning; I was frightened by losing."

Palmer had held the lead after the first three rounds, and now he was three good shots away from a playoff, two very good shots away from his second green jacket. With the crowd spilling into the fairway and trailing Palmer to his ball, CBS's McKay told his viewers, "And the mob closes in on the marshals. Still a well-behaved crowd down here at Augusta, though."

The word *mob* was no more welcome at Augusta National than a civil rights demonstration, but McKay survived the slip. Palmer chatted with Casper and then pulled out a six-iron. "He's a golfer who always plays to win," McKay told his viewers.

Casper had already hit a perfect — if irrelevant — approach to within three feet of the hole, and as Palmer prepared to match it, McKay reminded his CBS audience that the 1958 Masters champ had bogeyed away his chance to repeat the following year before McKay's broadcast partner, Wall, went on his winning birdie run.

Venturi was watching and listening on a clubhouse TV when Palmer struck his next shot as if he had heard McKay's every word. With the ball in the air, McKay loudly and breathlessly gushed, "Here it comes . . . with a five- or a six-iron . . . the ball on the green . . . and *within approximately three feet of the pin,* a magnificent shot by Arnold Palmer. He's got a chance to win the championship with this putt."

The distance separating Palmer from his second Masters triumph was more like five feet, this after the ball landed two feet to the right of the pin and skipped left and past the hole. The masses surrounding eighteen made the ground tremble. Palmer's dear friends from Latrobe, Ken and Susie Bowman, ran through the woods to get up to the green, burning off all those carbs from the spaghetti dinners they ate at the Palmers' rented home.

They felt the history in the air. Everyone with a pulse did.

Standing on the green, the fans still roaring their approval, Palmer scanned the leaderboard, that signature tuft of hair on his forehead flapping gently in the cool Georgia breeze. Though he was closer to the hole, Casper decided to putt first to get out of his playing partner's way.

Palmer walked across the green and sat down near the bunker on its right side, next to Iron Man. Casper missed and then tapped in. Palmer rose to his feet and considered his putt from every possible angle, this as the swelling crowd below the green, in the fairway, fidgeted behind the marshals' ropes.

He settled on his read and walked toward his ball. A kneeling marshal under a straw hat held up a sign demanding quiet, then lowered it as Palmer backed away from his putt and looked over his shoulder and into the crowd. "And now we're going to be very quiet," McKay said into his mike, "because Arnold was glancing this way. The wind blowing onto the green may carry our voice more than we realize."

Palmer returned to his putt. He'd already won more than $26,000 on tour for the season and had a shot here to add another $17,500 to that sum. But this five-footer had very little to do with the money he could earn for his wife, Winnie, and their two young girls, Peg and Amy. It had nothing to do with Palmer's growing celebrity, his simmering sex appeal, or his popular standing as a go-for-broke athlete in a country that was prospering and always reaching for more.

These five feet were all about Deke Palmer's son and his golfing legacy.

"Arnold Palmer has been thirty years on this earth," McKay said in a solemn tone. "He has never had a more important moment than this one."

Palmer had already developed a reputation for staring a ball into the hole, for willing it into the hole. He took two practice swipes with his putter as the low sun threw his shadow to the left of him, away from the cup. Casper stood to Palmer's right; Iron Man and the marshal were kneeling next to each other nearby, studying the scene.

Finally, from his pigeon-toed, knock-kneed stance, Palmer drew back his blade and then jabbed hard at the ball. The putt started left, quickly broke right, and dropped into the middle of the cup.

"*Arnold Palmer is the Masters champion of 1960!*" McKay shouted. Palmer grabbed his ball out of the hole and then threw his head back and started hopping up and down. Casper raced over to shake his hand and throw an arm around his shoulder.

"One of the greatest displays of courageous golf that anybody has ever seen any place," McKay cried.

Palmer walked toward the scorer's table as the marshal patted him on his back. He handed his putter to Iron Man and slapped both hands against his forehead in disbelief. Palmer plopped into a chair, looked over his scorecard, and then leaned back to exhale, blowing away all that bottled-up stress as if it were a cloud of L&M smoke. A man tapped the winner on the right shoulder to inform him that America was trying to catch his attention through the CBS camera to the rear.

Palmer turned his head over his right shoulder, then swiveled it back over his left. He smiled for the camera and waved. Soon enough Arnold grabbed his wife, Winnie, and lowered her into the kind of passionate kiss a sailor would give his woman after ten months at sea.

McKay threw it to the cabin and McArthur, who was standing behind the seated co-lords of Augusta National, Bobby Jones and Clifford Roberts, both wearing green jackets and giant microphones clipped to their chests. McArthur introduced Jones as president of the Augusta National "Country Club."

"*Golf* Club," Roberts barked into his mike. "Golf Club, not Country Club."

Stern and stiff and wearing thick glasses, Roberts took control of the proceedings and told viewers that players were still out on the course, that this ceremony would only honor "the apparent trophy winners . . . Someone still might beat them out, although it's highly unlikely."

Jones, looking infirm, turned to Palmer and Venturi, sitting to his left. As far back as 1954, at the funeral of the sportswriter and myth-maker Grantland Rice, Jones had trouble getting around. He was to serve as an honorary pallbearer and needed his friend John Derr of CBS to walk with him down the aisle to keep him from falling.

But six years later Jones was still strong enough and stubborn enough to preside over the crowning of the Masters winner. "What we've had today is the most dramatic finish that I can remember," Jones said in his southern drawl. "We saw a couple of heartbreaks and one li-onhearted finish."

Venturi looked like a boy who has just discovered his bicycle has been stolen. "I thought I had it won," he said, "but I never did think I was the champion, because with Arnold out there, you can never trust him."

Palmer apologized to Venturi for beating him. "I wanted to win more than anything, Ken," Palmer said. "But I'm truly sorry it had to be this way."

The next morning, April 11, 1960, President Eisenhower would play golf with the two-time champ. At the time the prime minister of South Africa, Hendrik Verwoerd, a champion of white supremacy, was fight-ing for his life after he was shot twice in the head by a white farmer, throwing the apartheid regime into chaos. The Soviets were rushing to send a man into space before NASA could do the same. Red China was blasting America's military policies. Castro's Cuba was detaining two U.S. pilots. The Senate was passing a civil rights bill to enforce "Ne-gro" voting rights, a measure attacked by members from the South.

And the president of the United States pulled up to Augusta Na-tional in a black limousine to go eighteen holes with Arnold Palmer.

They had a blast, too, becoming fast friends by the time they hit the third green. Ike was making his twenty-sixth trip to Augusta to play golf (the club built a cabin for him on the grounds), and Palmer was just then being likened to the iconic American sports champions of the past — the Ruths and Dempseys, the Tildens and Joneses. John F. Ken-nedy, the presidential candidate, had already named Palmer among his heroes.

Dwight D. Eisenhower, the president, was in the process of doing the same. Ike was a member at Cherry Hills outside Denver, and he told the Masters winner he thought the course would agree with him at the upcoming U.S. Open. But Palmer wasn't thinking about the Open just yet. Done golfing with the president, he was only thinking about the 610-mile drive back to his friends and neighbors in Latrobe, Pennsylvania.

Palmer loaded Winnie, the Bowmans, and his Wilson golf bag into his black Chrysler and headed north. Deke's boy was so eager to get home, so unwilling to take the time even to make bathroom stops, that Susie Bowman developed a bladder infection from the ride.

She forgave Palmer, who was starting to transcend the game he played. It wasn't just *Sports Illustrated* that gushed over him — "an authentic and unforgettable hero," *SI* called Arnie — but *Time* and *Life* magazines as well.

The words were different, but the angle was not. They all agreed Arnold Palmer had established himself as the one and only successor to Ben Hogan and Sam Snead.

CHAPTER 3

• Rich Kid

HIS FRIENDS LAUGHED at him. Stan Ziobrowski, six-teen, had traveled all the way from upstate New York to the United States Junior Amateur championship in Tulsa just to get matched against a thirteen-year-old kid.

Jackie Nicklaus. "A nobody," Ziobrowski said.

The buddies who made the trip with Stan in the summer of 1953 would not let up. His three fellow golfers from New York told Zio-browski his first-round pairing was as good as a first-round bye. Over and over they told him he'd walk through Jackie Nobody just like that.

Ziobrowski worked for the Edison Club outside Schenectady, where the head pro took up a collection to pay the boy's way to Tulsa. Stan went by train, connecting through Chicago, lugging his golf bag from one station to the next. He was bone-tired by the time he made it to his room at the University of Tulsa, and after his first practice round in the searing Oklahoma heat, he was in no mood to discover he was playing the youngest competitor in the field.

Their match was the first on the morning schedule at Southern Hills Country Club, and Nicklaus almost missed his tee time. He made it with thirty seconds to spare, and only after the starter, Colonel Lee S. Reed of Kentucky, had called his name for a third time.

As Reed and Joe Dey of the USGA lectured Nicklaus on his tardi-ness, warning him that he'd be one down heading to the second tee next time around, Ziobrowski was off in his own little world. Finally,

Stan heard from Reed. Through the eyes of a sixteen-year-old, Reed was a large older man with a handlebar mustache and a ten-gallon hat.

The Kentucky colonel told the Schenectady schoolboy to go ahead and hit.

"I'm waiting for the kid I'm supposed to play," Ziobrowski said.

"He's right here," Reed said, pointing to the boy with the red face, blue eyes, white eyebrows, and hair the color of straw.

Jackie was big for his age, and his opponent had mistaken him for a caddie. Ziobrowski gave Nicklaus the once-over and assumed the kid would be spraying the ball all over the lot. He told himself it would be a long day.

Ziobrowski had no idea it would be the longest day of his young golfing life.

He had no idea Jackie was already good enough to break 70 from the back tees at his home course in Columbus, Ohio — Scioto Country Club, where Bobby Jones won the 1926 U.S. Open. The kid shot 34 on the front side one afternoon, rushed home for dinner with his father, Charlie, then raced back to the course to beat the fading sun.

Jackie got to the eighteenth hole just in time that evening and needed to sink a thirty-five-foot eagle putt for his 69. The sprinklers around the green sprang to life as he surveyed his line. Charlie shut them off, then watched his son curl in the putt.

Charlie knew he had something in Jackie. Trailing Nicklaus and Ziobrowski throughout their match at Southern Hills was a man in a trench coat, scribbling notes onto a pad, making like a detective from Scotland Yard. Ziobrowski thought the stranger was a referee or a spotter, or some official making himself available in case the boys had a question or three. He couldn't believe the stranger's choice of attire on another dust-bowl day in Tulsa when a short-sleeved golf shirt felt like a winter jacket.

Stan was never introduced to the man but later found that he was "a person Jack's father hired and was being groomed as his mentor . . . I was flabbergasted, all for a thirteen-year-old."

The mystery man remained unidentified, but his presence did nothing to steady Stan's nerves. Jackie was showing remarkable composure for his age, hitting shots Ziobrowski hadn't seen even from high school seniors. The child could hit the ball from one side of Oklahoma to the other, his power rising up from his man-sized thighs.

The older boy was playing fairly well himself. Ziobrowski kept shooting par golf, which was nothing to apologize for at Southern Hills. But par golf wasn't going to be good enough with Jackie Nicklaus on the prowl.

Ziobrowski became unnerved when he couldn't stop the Nicklaus onslaught of birdies. Stan was cocky. He arrived in Tulsa thinking there wasn't a high school player in America who could beat him.

The thirteen-year-old beat him six and five, meaning Jackie was six holes up with five holes to play, the equivalent of a twenty-five-point rout in basketball. Ziobrowski felt as if his world had come to an end.

He wished Nicklaus well and quickly retreated to the locker room, hoping against hope he wouldn't run into his buddies from New York — Ronnie from Binghamton, Jerry from Syracuse, and Ross from Westchester.

Ziobrowski never heard the end of it. His three friends had him for lunch, dinner, and dessert.

Stan could only counter with a word of caution. He was less than two years away from accepting a golf scholarship to Florida State, so he knew his way around a course. But Ziobrowski's response to the teasing sounded less like prophecy and more like the desperate rationale of a humiliated boy.

"Let me tell you something," he said to his friends. "If this kid stays with the game, you're going to be hearing about him for a very long time."

Jack William Nicklaus was conceived in a second-floor room above his father's drugstore and delivered inside White Cross Hospital of Columbus, Ohio, at 3:10 a.m. on January 21, 1940. Charlie and Helen Nicklaus would tell people their boy was not born into any embarrassment of riches but into the traditional comforts of middle-class suburbia.

Charlie was an all-everything athlete in high school. He was a broad, ham-faced freshman end and lineman at Ohio State before playing semipro football under an assumed name for the Portsmouth Spartans, the team that evolved into the Detroit Lions. Charlie was a local tennis champ and a devoted Bobby Jones fan.

But if Charlie harbored one sporting dream for his Jackie, it was for his only son to play football for the almighty Buckeyes. They went to their first Ohio State game together when Jackie was six. Charlie could close his eyes and picture his son, the fullback, blasting holes through the Michigan line.

That vision was altered by a severe ankle injury Charlie suffered playing volleyball, one that required surgery. The doctors told him he could strengthen his ankle by playing golf. Charlie grabbed his clubs and headed to Scioto, and young Jackie tagged along.

Charlie would teach his boy the interlocking golf grip. But the swing? That would be assigned to Jack Grout, the new pro in town.

Out of Oklahoma, a tall and thin man with wavy black hair, Grout had been something of a failure on tour, his luck as bad as his sore feet. He turned instructor to make up for it. In his days as an assistant pro in Fort Worth, Grout had spent many rounds in the company of two local up-and-comers named Byron Nelson and Ben Hogan. What he didn't learn about the golf swing from Nelson and Hogan Grout discovered later from Henry Picard, his boss at the Hershey (Pennsylvania) Country Club and the 1938 Masters champ.

If Grout couldn't beat the best, maybe he could teach someone else to do it for him. Grout decided to start a juniors clinic at Scioto in the spring of 1950, every Friday morning, two hours a pop. Jackie Nicklaus was among the four dozen boys and girls who signed up.

Grout called Kaye Kessler at the *Citizen-Journal* and asked if the paper would be interested in taking a photo of the would-be Byrons and Bens. The *Citizen-Journal* dutifully took the shot. A couple of months later Kessler's phone rang again.

"Remember that picture you took of our kids?" Grout asked him.

"Yeah," Kessler said.

"One of those boys is a ten-year-old who just shot 51 for the first nine holes he ever played."

Kessler could hardly believe it. Scioto was a hell of a course and no place for a grade school novice trying to learn the difference between a nine-iron and a wedge. Kessler did a little write-up on Jackie. Three years later, with Nicklaus growing into a full-blown prodigy, mowing down the older boys in his path, Kessler did a cover story on him for the newspaper's Sunday magazine.

In the photo the featured subject was wearing a scaled-down version of Sam Snead's straw hat. "Move over Snead," the headline read. "Here Comes Jackie."

Suddenly, Grout had what every teacher would die for: a Mozart in his midst. He'd pull Jackie out of formation and have him demonstrate shots for the lesser lights in the class.

The Scioto golf shop manager, Dom Lepore, would go out in the dead of January and sweep away the snow from the first tee and the ninth green so Grout could watch Jackie hit balls while wearing a hooded jacket and gloves. Staffers put up a Quonset hut, complete with a space heater and mat, so Jackie could comfortably practice in the driving snow or rain.

It didn't matter that Jackie was a yes-sir, no-sir type of child, reared by Charlie and Helen to be respectful of his elders, even the staffers who were there to serve the Scioto elite. Jackie's fellow members didn't appreciate the hut's lack of aesthetic value. Fortunately for the Nicklaus boy, they didn't have the clout to get it taken down.

Jackie had a gift, and Grout would nurture him morning, noon, and night. He loved teaching Jackie. He loved it so much he would stop billing Charlie for the privilege. Truth was, Grout loved teaching any player who hinted at a bright golfing future to come.

But if a prospective student couldn't play a lick, Grout couldn't spare the time. One day he told a high-handicapped member that he simply couldn't help him anymore. "You should never tell a person that," Lepore said. "You should always encourage a player."

Grout encouraged Jackie, anyway. Many days the boy would pound three or four hundred range balls and play twenty-seven holes, forcing his mother to call Lepore and send him out on the course to get her son home for dinner. Jackie was a little bigger, a little stronger, and a lot longer than the other boys under Grout's watch. He was also more determined, more willing to listen and learn.

Jackie could be a little erratic on the practice tee, but he knew how to compete. "Once you said 'junior tournament,' Jack became special," said Jay Weitzel, Grout's assistant. "He had a great desire to win."

At age twelve Jackie could drive a ball 285 yards, or 25 yards past his father's ball. He was a powerful athlete, not just a precise golfer.

Charlie would teach Jack how to play tennis, showing him four or five different serves. He would teach him how to crouch behind the plate and receive a fastball. He would teach him how to throw, catch, and punt a football properly; in their backyard Jackie would boot field goals through two trees he imagined as goalposts. He became a reliable straight-on kicker but couldn't kick soccer-style if his life depended on it.

Jackie would develop into a good young quarterback, a switch-hitting catcher, an accurate shooting guard, and a sprinter fast enough to cover one hundred yards in eleven seconds flat.

As a thirteen-year-old Jackie weathered a polio scare and lost twenty-five pounds in two weeks. His younger sister, Marilyn, was stricken by a much more severe case shortly after her brother recovered. Marilyn was hospitalized and couldn't walk for three months, spending that time in bed or on the couch. Charlie and Helen lived in fear of losing their eleven-year-old girl. When a teary-eyed Charlie would carry Marilyn down the stairs, Jackie would ask, "Is she going to live?"

She lived long enough to realize her brother was blessed (or cursed) with an uncommonly blind focus. When Jackie was watching TV, it never mattered how loudly Marilyn screamed his name to get his attention. "I don't think he even hears me," she complained.

Theirs was the life in Upper Arlington, a leafy suburb to the northwest of Columbus. Jack's mother was the housewife who doted on her children. Jack's father was the gregarious breadwinner who took his son to see Joe DiMaggio play in Yankee Stadium and Jackie Robinson play in Ebbets Field, and who spent as many hours in the backyard playing sports as his boy desired.

Charlie grew up in Columbus delivering newspapers and working at a local pharmacy run by a kindly man he came to adore, Doc Mebs, who would later take a job under Charlie. Jackie's father was a worker's worker. "A great provider," Marilyn said.

The son of a railroad man, Charlie was bringing in $30,000 to $35,000 a year, enough to carry the Nicklauses across the line separating middle class from upper middle class and enough to afford his membership at Scioto. He was growing his business, from one family drugstore near the Ohio State campus to four scattered about, and Jackie would sometimes stand before a mirror and try on his father's smock.

As a towheaded child Jackie ran up and down the pharmacy aisles and stuffed candy in his pockets. Sometimes the Ohio State football players would come into the store and tease the little boy on the soda-pop stool. "But that kid was full of piss and vinegar," one of the players said. "He always came back at you. He didn't back off."

In later years Charlie had everything mapped out for his son. Jackie was an accomplished baseball catcher and basketball guard at Upper Arlington High, good enough to attract interest from a number of colleges. But Charlie wasn't interested. Jackie would go to Ohio State (without a scholarship) and enter its highly regarded pharmacology program — there was never any doubt about that.

"Jack was going to be a pharmacist," said his best friend, Robin Obetz, "and then things changed."

The winning changed everything. The winning of more golf trophies than the Nicklauses could polish. The more Jackie won, the more he threw himself into his lessons with Grout.

The instructor or one of his aides would grab the front of Jackie's hair, hold it nice and tight, and then tell him to lash at the ball without shifting his head. Sometimes Jackie was moved to tears, but the drills were working. Jackie was developing into a fundamental genius.

Grout wanted his prize student to hit the ball high the way Jones did, the way all the great Open players did, so his ball would stick on the greens. Grout wanted a left-to-right flight pattern, too, for he knew that right-to-left players often become the victims of duck hooks when the pressure makes their throats tighter than their grips.

The kid wasn't sure if Grout was the greatest teacher in the world, and he didn't care. Jackie cared only that Grout spent so much time with him, boosted his confidence, treated him the way a surrogate father would. "He cares about me," Jackie told his friends. That sentiment was far more important than the prodigy's swing thoughts.

"Jackie, young fella," Grout would tell him, "you're going to be unbeatable . . . You hear me? . . . Unbeatable."

By the time he was fifteen, Jackie was beginning to see golf as something more than another game to juggle in his sports-crazed youth. He would spend hours in his cellar striking balls off a mat and toward a bull's-eye painted on a padded wall. He would dust a field of older boys in the 1955 Ohio Jaycees tournament, hardening his reputation as the best young prospect in the state.

Between rounds of that thirty-six-hole event, organizers ran a cookout for the players. Jackie was sitting around with ten or twelve competitors, shooting the shit, when the conversation took an unexpected turn toward the future.

With a hamburger in one hand and a hot dog in the other, each boy was asked by the others what he wanted to be when he grew up. The question produced a flurry of predictable answers. The youngsters said they wanted to be doctors, teachers, lawyers, and police officers.

Finally, they asked the boy whose name was posted at the top of the leaderboard.

"What do you want to be?"

Jackie Nicklaus didn't hesitate as he looked up from his half-eaten lunch.

"The greatest golfer who ever lived."

In the middle of September 1959, Jack Nicklaus was standing on the first tee at the Broadmoor, sucking in the crisp Colorado Springs air. He was a nineteen-year-old college student at Ohio State, close enough to full-blown manhood to have lost the boyish *ie* that had been tethered to his given name.

Nicklaus was playing in the United States Amateur championship, and Bob Jones III, son of the one and only, was his opponent in the first round.

What an incredible coincidence. Bobby Jones was Jack's idol, the reason he was playing golf. Nicklaus had finally met him at the 1955 U.S. Amateur on the James River Course of the Country Club of Virginia, Jack's first appearance in the Amateur. Jones was sitting in a cart near the eighteenth green, basking in the glow of the twenty-fifth anniversary of his Grand Slam–punctuating victory at Merion.

At the end of a practice round, the fifteen-year-old Nicklaus landed his ball on the 460-yard hole in two. He was startled when the great Jones waved him in for a chat.

Nicklaus walked over with his father, who was more starstruck than Jackie. "Young man," Jones said, "I want to meet you. I've been sitting here quite a while, and you're only the second person to reach the green in two. I was very impressed by that. And I'm going to watch you come out and play some holes tomorrow."

Sure enough, Jackie was walking to the eleventh tee with a one-up lead over Bob Gardner the next day when he spotted Jones arriving in his cart. Spooked, Nicklaus immediately devolved into an unseemly mess, going bogey, bogey, double bogey, and sending Jones on his way.

Gardner won, and Jackie got over it. The following year Jackie and his MacGregor Mity Mite putter held their own in an exhibition with Sam Snead.

Grout and Charlie were pouring more time and energy into the boy's game than ever before. Young Nicklaus had started hanging out with a new Scioto range worker named Paul Bondeson, a big, blond, teenage bomber just like Jack and the one prospect Nicklaus saw as his equal.

Bondeson was raised poor, the son of a divorced waitress who had moved him from Michigan to St. Petersburg, Florida. A friend of his was working the bag room for Grout and recommended that the Scioto pro hire Bondeson for the summer.

The new kid on the block envied Nicklaus's focus. "He knows where he's going," Bondeson thought to himself, "and I don't have a clue." But Bondeson out-drove Nicklaus the first time they played together, getting Jack's attention. Bondeson hit his balls high and with a fade, just like Nicklaus. Tee to green it was a dead heat, though Nicklaus had the edge with the putter. They took turns beating each other with subpar rounds.

"If Paul wanted it," Nicklaus would say, "nobody would've ever heard of me."

But Grout had already put his money on the horse with the proper pedigree. While Nicklaus was playing with his shiny new MacGregor clubs, Grout took an ill-fitting demo set he received free of charge and sold it to Bondeson—who was making $100 a month—for $150.

Feeling isolated in his cabin room between the clubhouse and range, Bondeson began to drink. He was all alone, with no idea how to live. He kept a closet full of dirty socks because he didn't know how to do his laundry. Charlie was angry that Bondeson kept Jack out late one night, and when Bondeson returned to Scioto after a trip to New York, where his drinking led to drug use, Grout told him he was no longer an employee of the club.

"I can't have you back," the pro told him. "Charlie thinks you're a bad influence on Jack."

Drunk and high, Bondeson would end up sleeping in New York subway stations while the Nicklaus band played on. Jack won the Trans-Mississippi tournament as an eighteen-year-old, the same year he made the cut at the U.S. Open and contended at the Rubber City Open.

Nicklaus played with the likes of Charlie Sifford, Tommy Bolt, and Julius Boros in the Rubber City and didn't look overmatched, though the hot-tempered Bolt intimidated him the way Bolt intimidated golfers twice Jack's age.

Nicklaus had fully devoted himself to golf by then. When he wasn't practicing at Scioto, he could be found at the nearby muni course, Raymond Memorial, where he'd park the little Mercury convertible Charlie had bought for him, flip his hat into the passenger seat, and go practice some more.

Woody Hayes, the Ohio State football coach and Nicklaus family friend, had long told Charlie that his son should forget about football. Hayes had made a good living on his cherished blood sport, but he didn't want Charlie's kid to endanger his future on the fairways in a fourth-and-one cloud of Big Ten dust.

So Jack Nicklaus was going to be a golfer. And in September of 1959, Bobby Jones's own son was going to find that out for himself.

Entering the opening round of the 1959 U.S. Amateur, Nicklaus had established himself as a phenom committed to doing things his own way. He'd been invited to play in his first Masters that April, and when he found out that the amateurs staying in the upstairs clubhouse quarters known as the Crow's Nest were charged only a dollar for breakfast, a dollar for lunch, and two dollars for dinner, Nicklaus and another cocksure amateur, Phil Rodgers, seized the moment. They ordered steak and eggs in the morning, steak in the afternoon, and Chateaubriand in the evening until the attendants advised that they had to pay more than four bucks a day for the privilege.

Nicklaus missed the cut at the Masters and did the same at the U.S. Open at Winged Foot, where Doug Ford, the 1957 Masters champ known for playing fast, was angered by the kid's pace over the first and second rounds. "He's got to speed up," Ford told Charlie after the second round.

Charlie listened. His son didn't.

Jack could show up fashionably late at the Ohio Intercollegiate, as a brash Buckeye, and still dominate the competition. On a day when players had to carry their own bags over thirty-six holes and endure forty-degree temperatures and a raw drizzle, Nicklaus could show up ten minutes before his tee time, slap at two or three practice putts, and shoot 71.

Gary Player, the rising South African star, had already predicted that Nicklaus would become a great champion on the pro tour. In turn, Nicklaus took one look at Player's swing and told himself, "Don't have to worry about him. He'll never make it."

At the Broadmoor, 1959, this was the buzz saw into which thirty-two-year-old Bob Jones III was walking at the worst possible time. He'd just shaved his handicap down to a plus three, and he'd been excitedly talking up his prospects with his father, only the most decorated amateur of them all.

A player needed to reach the quarterfinals of the Amateur to qualify for the Masters, which Jones had personally elevated into a major championship of unparalleled prestige.

Jones feared the burden of carrying his surname would be too heavy to bear, so he harbored no desire for his family members to make a career out of golf. But he made an exception here. Nothing would have pleased the wheelchair-bound Grand Slam hero more than the sight of his son playing in the Masters.

So Jones and Bob III spent months mapping out their strategy, planning their assault on the Broadmoor. Bob III bloodied his hands hitting range balls. He felt good about his chances of playing his way into the Augusta National field, and so did his father, who counted on somehow feeling strong enough to fly from Atlanta to Colorado Springs to watch his boy play.

"I don't see how I can't get to the quarterfinals unless I draw Jack Nicklaus in the first round," Bob III told his father, "or something crazy like that."

As the Amateur approached, Bob III called his old man.

"Are you coming?" he asked.

"Have you seen the pairings?" his father answered.

"No, I haven't."

"You're playing Jack Nicklaus in the first round. Son, I don't think it's worth it for me to fly out to Colorado for twelve holes."

Father and child were equally stunned and deflated. Nicklaus had just helped the American team to a resounding Walker Cup triumph in Scotland. The U.S. Open winner at Scioto, Jones was developing a mentor-protégé bond with Nicklaus. He appreciated the young man's immense strength and skill, and he knew his son didn't stand a chance.

With his father staying put in Atlanta, Bob III showed up at the Broadmoor anyway and met Nicklaus at an elevation of 6,400 feet. The underdog felt good. The possibility of a huge match-play upset pumped life into his Rocky Mountain high.

Bob III had the honors on the first tee, and he leaned hard into a 265-yard drive with a slight fade, a perfect shot and a strong opening statement. Bob III had gotten off to a good start, a critical part of his master plan. He stood to the side, sized up Nicklaus, and waited to see how his nineteen-year-old foe would respond.

The elevation would add about 10 percent of distance to each player's shots, a frightening thought given Nicklaus's Ruthian length at sea level. Jack was some sight on that first tee. He was all ass and thighs, and his midsection spilled over his belt. His diet at Ohio State had caught up to him—his Phi Gamma Delta frat brothers were already calling him "Blob-o"—but the extra pounds did nothing to diminish his swing.

After staring down the enemy shot in the distant fairway, Nicklaus unleashed a mammoth blast. Bob III's heart sank as he eyed the soaring, shrinking ball. Nicklaus's drive was still rising when it passed his opponent's ball, and it came to rest well beyond 300 yards from the tee.

Bob III was overcome by a singular thought. "It's over," he told himself. No man can spot another player forty to fifty yards on every drive, spot him three or four irons on the approach shots, and still devise a way to beat him.

Bobby Jones never did show up at the Broadmoor, and the match ended exactly where he predicted it would: on the twelfth green. Jones would joke with his defeated son about that, even if some thought his stated prophecy was an awfully cruel thing for a man to share with his child.

Nicklaus felt fortunate that Bob III's old man didn't make an appearance: he admitted he could barely hit a competent shot with Bobby Jones looking on.

Jones won thirteen major titles before retiring on the brink of his prime, at age twenty-eight. Within months of the Broadmoor event, Jack would say, "Jones is the greatest golfer who ever lived and probably ever will live. That's my goal, Bobby Jones. It's the only goal."

Charlie Coe was no Bob Jones III. In fact, Coe was more like Bob III's father. He was the captain of the 1959 Walker Cup team and the defending U.S. Amateur champion, a two-time winner of the event.

"Beating Charlie Coe in the Amateur," said Ward Wettlaufer, another Walker Cup star, "would be like beating Arnold Palmer on tour."

In 1959 Coe was bidding to become the first player since Jones to win this event at least three times. An Oklahoma oilman who was sixteen years older than Nicklaus, Coe was a lifelong amateur, a golfer of independent means, and a man fully expected to defeat a boy in the U.S. Amateur final.

Only Nicklaus wanted this one badly: he'd lost a first-round heartbreaker to Harvie Ward at Olympic in San Francisco the year before. To beat Coe in the final, Nicklaus would need Bobby Jones's prescription for all on-course ills: an ability to solve problems on his own.

Jones believed he became a good golfer only when he realized he couldn't go scurrying back to his instructor after every wayward swing, and Nicklaus would come to embrace the same philosophy. With Jack Grout in the background, staying clear of the practice tees during tournaments and presenting himself only when his straight-A student walked off the fairways and over to his shade trees, Jackie became a one-boy wrecking crew who would win five consecutive Ohio State Junior championships.

In the finals of the 1959 Amateur, neither Jack Grout nor Charlie Nicklaus would beat Charlie Coe. Jack Nicklaus would have to do the job himself. So earlier in the tournament, over dinner, Jack cut off his father when Charlie tried to correct a mistake he'd seen his son make earlier in the day.

"Wait a minute, Dad," Jack told him, positioning his hands like a basketball coach signaling for a stoppage in play. "Time-out. You know you and I are best friends, but I've got to do this my way."

Charlie Nicklaus never again tried to offer a piece of golfing advice to his son.

On September 19, 1959, Jack Nicklaus would go it alone. His match with Coe was a thirty-six-hole, one-day struggle that came down to the last stroke.

An intense competitor and pure ball striker, Coe knew he'd have to play his best golf to win, as he'd seen Nicklaus's talent firsthand at the Walker Cup. He opened with three birdies (Nicklaus answered with two) and shot two-under 69 in the morning round, taking a two-hole lead at the midway point.

Nicklaus, who shot 71 in the morning, evened the match, fell behind again, and pulled even again with six holes to go. As it turned out, Nicklaus walked to the thirty-sixth tee with the contest all square. This finish at the 430-yard, dogleg-right hole sealed their match as one of the greatest in Amateur history.

Nicklaus had won his semifinal over Gene Andrews by sinking a par-saving, downhill-running twenty-five-footer on the Broadmoor's 613-yard seventeenth hole, stunning everyone who saw it—including Nicklaus. Jack wasn't going to shrink from the challenge in the championship round. He was going to make Coe beat him.

Wearing a red Oklahoma Sooners baseball cap, Coe hit a flawless three-wood shot into the fairway. Nicklaus followed with a similar tee shot, only five yards longer. Up first, Coe lofted an eight-iron right at the stick, an approach that appeared in midflight to be one that could win the oilman his third Amateur title.

That look was deceiving. Coe's ball landed hard on the green and rolled off the back and down into a patch of thick grass, convincing Nicklaus to hit a shorter club. His nine-iron approach found the front of the green and stopped crawling eight feet from the cup.

Coe was in deep grass and in deep trouble. He would have to get up and down and save par to have any chance of sending the match into overtime, but Coe knew Nicklaus better than that. He played his third shot as if he needed to sink it.

Showing all the touch and nerve that made him a feared champion, Coe took his sand wedge, plunged it into the grass, pitched his ball over the back crest of the green, and watched it make a dead run for the hole as the crowd grew louder with every slow and sure revolution. When the ball was halfway to the cup, Nicklaus knew it was going in. He knew he'd have to nail his eight-footer just to force a thirty-seventh hole.

And then the ball stopped, without warning, a half revolution from history.

"It should've gone in," said Wettlaufer, who was standing behind the hole. "It was right on the lip. It had to go in."

But it didn't. Nicklaus exhaled and tried to tame his breakaway heartbeat when Coe did the unthinkable: he picked up his ball before his opponent conceded the putt. Under the rules of golf, this not-so-venial sin could have cost Coe the match.

"Oops," Nicklaus said to him. "I want you to leave it there so I can use it as a backstop."

"OK," Coe said. "I picked it up. The match is over."

"I won't take it that way," Nicklaus answered. "I'll win it fair and square."

He circled around the putting surface separating his marker from the hole. Nicklaus crouched behind the ball for a final look, and then he hunched over the putt, Wettlaufer said, "for what felt like an eternity."

Nicklaus took his practice strokes, gently placed his putter behind his ball, and finally let it roll. This was not the stroke of a teenage amateur. "There was never a doubt," Wettlaufer said. "It was going in the hole."

Nicklaus had scaled this Rocky Mountain peak. He had beaten the great Coe and captured his first major championship. At nineteen years and eight months, he had become the youngest U.S. Amateur champion in fifty years.

He would accept Coe's congratulations, accept the trophy, and then join his father and Wettlaufer on the flight back to Columbus. But before he boarded the plane, Charlie Nicklaus had to spread the glorious news.

He called up his dear Helen, the woman who had been called "Sis" or "Sissy" as far back as childhood. Charlie gave his bride the results of the Nicklaus-Coe match, caught his breath, and then told her that their dreams for their only boy were about to come true.

"Sis," Charlie said, "I think our son's been born to greatness."

CHAPTER 4

• Cherry Hills

T HE WORLD WAS SPINNING at a dizzying pace for Arnold Palmer in the weeks after he won the 1960 Masters. Offers of print ads and TV exhibitions and appearances were flooding in, and his business manager, Mark McCormack, wasn't going to make any money by turning them down.

The day McCormack first laid eyes on Palmer in 1950, he was mesmerized much the way a fourteen-year-old Jack Nicklaus would be the first time he saw Palmer practicing four years later. McCormack was a freshman golfer at William and Mary, prepping for a match against Wake Forest, when he found a bronzed opponent with blacksmith arms blasting long irons as he thought only Sam Snead could.

Years later, as an ambitious young lawyer in Cleveland who was booking exhibitions for a handful of top pros, McCormack approached Palmer and asked if he and his partner at National Sports Management, a PR man named Dick Taylor, could represent him.

At first Palmer wanted no part of it. "My wife and I had a deal," Arnold said. "Winnie and I ran the books and the business, and I was very comfortable with that. The one thing I never wanted to do was get myself in a position where I had to depend on someone else to do things for me.

"When Mark came to me, I hardly knew him. When he started talking to me about how he would help me in my business . . . I said, 'Hell, no, I don't need you.' I didn't say that, but in my mind that was my thought."

McCormack persisted; he was a convincing salesman. He knew Winnie couldn't solicit lucrative offers for Palmer as he could. McCormack told Arnold he could get him upward of five hundred dollars an appearance to start and then build from there.

"What do I have to do to get exclusivity with you?" McCormack asked Palmer.

Arnold thought of the Augusta National partnership between Clifford Roberts and Bobby Jones. Palmer admired Roberts and figured it would be nice to have a money man manage his affairs the way Roberts managed Jones's.

"That was the thing that turned me around with McCormack," Palmer said. "I told him, 'You can run my business . . . but it has to be exclusively with me, no one else.'"

It wasn't an easy choice for McCormack, who had to surrender his partnership with Taylor and his ties to the accomplished likes of Dow Finsterwald, Billy Casper, Doug Ford, and Gene Littler.

"Mark thought Dow was going to be the next Ben Hogan," said McCormack's wife, Nancy.

But Palmer made this condition a deal breaker. McCormack could represent him, or he could represent everyone else. McCormack followed his gut.

Palmer and the agent agreed to the deal on a handshake.

Arnie was banking five figures—about sixty grand a year—when he brought in McCormack. But Augusta, 1960, altered the landscape. There were nearly 46 million TV households in America by then, up from 3.88 million in 1950, and Palmer's breathless triumph had turned him into a full-blown television sports star, his popularity rivaling that of Mickey Mantle, Willie Mays, and Johnny Unitas.

After his second Masters triumph, Arnold turned up on *The Perry Como Show* and in ads for L&M cigarettes, his smoke of choice. McCormack could suddenly secure $1,000 per exhibition match and $2,500 per TV appearance.

Palmer's income was soaring into six figures. Of course, he had the look that played perfectly on the small boxes that kept popping up in America's living rooms.

"He was just the all-American boy," said Nancy McCormack. "I never thought Arnold was drop-dead attractive, but a lot of people did."

Arnold was more accessible than most game-day heroes, as he didn't wear pads, a helmet, or even a hat in competition. Palmer wasn't separated from his fans by any stadium walls or guardrails.

He could be touched, literally, by the crowds that followed him, crowds that easily warmed up to his humble beginnings. Regular Joes and Janes saw Palmer as one of them. Arnold was their human bridge to what had largely been an aristocratic domain.

McCormack capitalized on this appeal at every turn. The attorney had already come a long way from the National Sports Management days when he and Taylor and their wives would send out letters to clubs all over the country to solicit their interest in hosting exhibition matches and in paying their clients to compete in them.

McCormack had learned a lesson or two from George S. May, the colorful carnival barker whose annual Tam O'Shanter tournament outside Chicago attracted the game's biggest stars with an unheard-of $50,000 first-place prize and an unheard-of option for the winner to play in fifty exhibitions around the country at $1,000 a pop.

A former Bible salesman, May was the Bill Veeck of golf. He was smart enough in 1953 to see the potential value of television to the sport, and innovative enough to believe that paying ABC to broadcast his event would start a business relationship between network TV and golf that would ultimately lead to the network boys doing the paying rather than the receiving.

May's $25,000 first prize in 1953 was greater than the total purse of any PGA event. Lew Worsham's hole-out from 115 yards was the first winning shot broadcast on national TV, and as May predicted, the networks kept coming back for more.

"The PGA didn't like George May stealing their spotlight, so he eventually canceled the tournament and Mark saw the vacuum there," Nancy McCormack said. "Mark knew a lot of little towns couldn't afford a tournament but could host an exhibition."

Suddenly Palmer was in demand for those exhibitions like no other player in golf. "A lot of it had to do with television happening at the same time," Nancy said. "It was just a wonderful serendipity of everything coming together at once."

Everything including the 1960 U.S. Open at Cherry Hills.

Past, present, and future were colliding at the manic intersection that was the 1960 Open, and Palmer, the present, was not ready to be sent careening out of his prime.

Only there he was for the final round at Cherry Hills, an innocent and irrelevant bystander left standing at the curb. Palmer was a country mile out of the lead, and he was all but ignored while the generations before and after his were represented by challengers closing fast on the Open crown.

Hogan was making his last stand, and Nicklaus was making his first. The forty-seven-year-old Hogan loomed largest among the contenders, at least in Arnold's eyes. Palmer had little use for him. He hated how this not-so-gentle Ben had refused to refer to him by name and had generally dismissed him as a homemade hacker.

Nicklaus, meanwhile, stirred almost no emotion in Palmer, even though the kid Arnold had met at Finsterwald's exhibition two years earlier was threatening to become the first amateur to win the Open since Johnny Goodman did it in 1933.

Palmer was curious about Nicklaus, but he was plenty more concerned about Hogan. As he weighed the far-out possibilities of a comeback in the Rockies that would dwarf the one he pulled off at Augusta, Arnold figured the old man would put up the nastiest fight.

Palmer believed he could still win the national championship, even if he was the only player on the course holding fast to that opinion. He hadn't reached golf's summit just so he could be immediately and decisively replaced as king of the hill.

But his newfound fame and fortune wouldn't be worth a single stroke at Cherry Hills, where Palmer found himself seven shots down with eighteen holes to play. Arnold decided he couldn't count on the field coming back to him, so he went out and hunted down the field.

On the first tee of the final round, Palmer's playing partner, Paul Harney, thought the man was positively mad. Arnold had pulled a driver out of his bag with the same urgency as a pirate ripping a sword from his sash.

Ironically enough, despite his feelings for the player the Scots called the Wee Ice Mon, Palmer was using a Hogan driver. He loved the club, if not the man whose name graced it.

Palmer had 346 yards to the green, and Harney thought the obvious play was a safe two-iron and a simple pitch. The first hole at Cherry

Hills was guarded by a creek on the right side, which had victimized Palmer on his very first shot of the Open.

All these wayward strokes later, Palmer figured it was time to victimize the creek.

"He's nuts," Harney thought to himself.

Enraged was more like it. Palmer had just stormed out of the locker room and away from a lunchtime conversation that would ultimately define the tournament.

He had finished his morning round on this marathon thirty-six-hole day, a round that left him out of earshot of Mike Souchak's lead. Palmer was pissed at his position, pissed at his clubs, pissed at himself. He was blowing his big chance to win back-to-back majors. He was dishonoring all that faith put in him by TV hosts, advertising executives, and the newspaper and magazine writers who had penned adoring profiles in the country's most prominent publications.

And then Palmer ran into his good friend Bob Drum of the *Pittsburgh Press* and Dan Jenkins of the *Fort Worth Press*. Between bites of a burger he was inhaling during his short break between rounds, Palmer announced he would do what he'd tried and failed to do all tournament: drive his ball onto the first green.

"Get outta here, boy," Drum told him. "Go make your usual eight birdies and eight bogeys."

"If I drive the first green and get a birdie," Palmer responded, "I might shoot a 65."

"So what?" Drum shot back. "You're four thousand shots behind."

"That would give me 280. Doesn't 280 always win the Open?"

"Yeah," Jenkins interjected. "When Hogan shoots it."

Jenkins heard Palmer laugh as he pushed through the locker room door, but this wasn't a man in any joking mood. Palmer was hoping Drum would console him, make him feel better about failing to post a single subpar round in his first three attempts on a 7,004-yard, par-71 course that many pros thought was too forgiving to be a worthy Open venue.

Palmer took out his anger on some range balls, heard his name called to the first tee, and then stalked his way toward a redemptive strike. He was thinking driver before his exchange with Drum and Jenkins; their ridicule sealed the deal.

Two days earlier, in the first round, Palmer went for the green and landed his tee shot in Little Dry Creek instead. The ball ran downstream. Joe Dey, executive director of the United States Golf Association and an official with a well-earned reputation for being all business, all the time, identified a drop area—a point near the ball's entry into the creek—that didn't sit well with Palmer.

"Let's just let it wash on down, Joe, until it gets to the green," Palmer told him. "Then I'll drop it out."

"Now, Arnold," Dey answered, "you know better than that. I have the spot marked right here."

Palmer hit a tree on his next shot and made a double-bogey six.

He played with Jack Fleck, the million-to-one upset winner over Hogan at the 1955 U.S. Open, for the first thirty-six holes and spent much of the time loudly ripping into his caddie, Bob Blair. "Arnold, what are you arguing with your caddie for?" Fleck asked. "The tournament just started. There's a long way to go."

In the second round, at the fourteenth hole, Palmer would hit his tee shot over a fence and out of bounds—a transgression that didn't cost him a stroke penalty under USGA rules at the time. It was the only break he got across the first half of the tournament.

This painful reality did nothing to temper his flame at the start of the final round. The 4-to-1 favorite to win the Open was done taking punches from a course that was supposed to pack a lightweight punch despite its small and hard elevated greens; Palmer was going for the knockout with a vicious right hook.

It was 1:42 p.m. on June 18, 1960, a warm and sunshiny day in the Rockies, when the tour's leading money winner approached his propped-up ball. Standing to the side, the other half of his twosome wanted to shake his head. Harney was a damn good pro out of Worcester, Massachusetts, a three-time winner on the tour. He watched with a two-iron in his hands, and he just knew Palmer was about to make a very big mistake.

Harney wasn't alone. Among the fans surrounding the tee box was Joe Curtis, a Masters regular and Palmer loyalist who had made the trip from Macon, Georgia. Curtis had first met Arnold in 1956, when the pro at Augusta National, Ed Dudley, introduced Palmer to the air force colonel by saying, "Joe, this kid is going to be one of the greatest golfers ever."

Colonel Joe had served in World War II and was a bomber pilot in the Korean War, and before he would complete an improbable and unholy trinity by seeing action in Vietnam, he would whisper a prayer at Cherry Hills' first tee, asking the Good Lord to let Arnie win.

Curtis had come to love the guy, but even he didn't believe this prayer would be answered. Though he was right there in April when his man came back to seize the Masters, Curtis figured there was almost no chance Palmer could hurdle fourteen players in eighteen holes to win his first Open title.

And then he saw what Harney saw: a driver in Palmer's hands.

"What the heck is he pulling that out for?" Curtis asked himself. "Just try to get on in two and make the birdie putt."

That wasn't the Arnold Palmer way. He'd been racking up tour victories and capturing America's imagination by firing for the stick and damning the consequences.

Wearing a visor, a white golf shirt, and light gray slacks, Palmer addressed his ball and took dead aim at the big names above him on the leaderboard.

Settling into his wide stance between two red cherry-shaped tee markers, Palmer looked out from his elevated stage at the snowcapped peaks in the distance. A row of marshals sat behind him; one official stood in doubled-over form, hands on knees, watching through dark shades.

The gallery wasn't what a Palmer gallery should be for the final round of a major. But Hogan and Nicklaus were playing two groups ahead, and the fans were fascinated by the matchup and the prospect of a historic Hogan sendoff. They assumed what Harney had assumed: Palmer had already shot himself out of the running.

Only Arnold hadn't surrendered to the dim prospects. He surveyed the downhill fairway, eyed the trees on the left and the stream on the right, and slowly pulled his club face away from the ball. At the top of his backswing, with tree branches swaying in the mountain winds behind him, Palmer tapped the brakes, then unleashed his rage on the ball.

He nearly bounced his head off his right shoulder to punctuate his follow-through. Palmer took three quick steps forward after making contact, walking his ball toward the target.

"He hit it a little right-to-left," Harney said. "A beauty."

A sight to behold. The ball bounced through the tangly rough that guarded the front of the green, hopped onto the putting surface, and stopped twenty-five feet from the hole.

The crowd noise around the green announced that Palmer would have a putt for eagle. Almost nine years after Bobby Thomson homered off Ralph Branca on the single most famous swing in baseball history, Arnold Palmer had just hit another shot heard round the world.

He race-walked for his ball, feeling an orgasmic rush of hope rising from his toes. Palmer knew he was on the cusp of a charge that would make this the wildest and craziest day in the history of the U.S. Open.

Arnie would chase the legend, Hogan, and the phenom, Nicklaus, in a tri-generational race across a mountain course that forced players to use portable oxygen tanks to avoid the headaches and shortness of breath that burdened some in practice rounds.

Palmer wasn't just going to vacate his throne. Someone with brass balls was going to have to knock him off his mile-high hill.

With six holes to play at Cherry Hills, Jack Nicklaus was not the least bit surprised that he was leading the U.S. Open. His father, Charlie, had told Jack before the tournament that he was listed as a 35-to-1 shot.

"Thirty-five to one?" Jack said incredulously. He was the reigning U.S. Amateur champion, conqueror of Charlie Coe. So, yes, Jack was insulted.

"Do you want some of that?" Charlie Nicklaus asked his son.

"Yeah."

"How about twenty bucks?"

Jack was preparing to marry his college sweetheart, Barbara Bash, and sure could've used an unexpected source of income. He bet twenty bucks on himself to win.

"Do you want anything for place or show?" his father asked.

"Are you kidding me?" Jack answered. "I want nothing but win."

The moment he arrived at Cherry Hills, Nicklaus thought he could and would win. It didn't matter that he missed the cut at Winged Foot in 1959: he entered every tournament feeling the same way, including the recent Masters, where he tied for thirteenth in only his second Augusta National appearance. Why should the U.S. Open be any different?

Nothing changed at Cherry Hills after Nicklaus shot a pair of 71s to stand seven strokes off the lead with one thirty-six-hole Saturday to go. Nothing changed after his father delivered the news bulletin that would've reduced most twenty-year-olds to a petrified puddle of goo.

"Guess who you're playing with tomorrow," Charlie said.

"Who am I playing with?" Jack responded.

"Ben Hogan."

"Fan-tastic."

Jack wasn't that fifteen-year-old kid rattled by Bobby Jones's presence anymore. Sure, he was nervous: the Scots named Hogan the Wee Ice Mon for a reason. His flat white cap pulled low over his brow, the five-foot-eight Hogan was a dark and silent force, as tough mentally and physically as any golfer who ever lived.

His father, a Texas blacksmith, shot himself to death while nine-year-old Ben watched. Hogan came from nothing. He was a newspaper boy and a Fort Worth caddie who sometimes slept in a sand trap at the Glen Garden club so he could be first in line for a sixty-five-cent loop the next morning. He grew up with his fellow caddie and future rival, Byron Nelson, and was a self-made golfer who tamed a wild hook to become an all-time great.

Hogan was a chain-smoking terminator who won three major championships in 1953, four years after nearly dying at the wheel in a head-on collision with a ten-ton Greyhound bus. He earned a ticker-tape parade in New York for his trouble, and in 1955 he was on the verge of becoming the first man to win five U.S. Opens when Jack Fleck, the muni course pro out of Iowa, closed strong at the end of regulation and then beat his idol, Hogan, in a playoff while using a set of Hogan's clubs.

Five years later, with just one tour victory since his heroic 1953 season, Hogan wasn't given much of a chance at Cherry Hills. There was one flicker of pre-Open greatness in 1960 that suggested Hogan shouldn't be completely counted out. He had just used the Memphis tour stop as a tune-up and summoned enough of the old magic to make it into a playoff that Tommy Bolt would win.

And now Hogan was locked in an improbable duel to the Open death with Jack Nicklaus of Ohio State, this while Arnold Palmer was charging like a colt from the rear.

Mike Souchak, the thirty-six-hole leader who had shattered the Open record with his seven-under 135, was busy fading into the scenic backdrop. Souchak was a beast of a man, a former football player at

Duke with no neck and arms the size of his competitors' legs. "Like an ape," said one pro.

Souchak had been a big winner on the circuit—he erased a huge Palmer lead to beat him in the Western Open the year before—and in 1955 his twenty-seven-under 257 at the Texas Open set a tour scoring record. But he hadn't won a single Grand Slam event, leaving many to believe that his three-shot lead over Doug Sanders, another star with no major victories, and five-shot cushion over Fleck, Dow Finsterwald, and Jerry Barber could be had.

Bob Rosburg, winner of the 1959 PGA Championship, was among the Cherry Hills competitors who gave voice to the doubts about Souchak's credibility.

"Jack, you're in great position to win another Open," Rosburg told Fleck at dinner on the eve of the thirty-six-hole final.

"What are you talking about, Bob?" Fleck responded. "Souchak's way out there."

"Jack, don't worry about [Souchak and Sanders]. Neither one of those guys can win the Open."

Rosburg then patted his left breast.

"They don't have it here," he said.

On the final hole of the third round, Souchak started to come undone. "Some idiot snapped a camera in my downswing," he said. He hit his ball out of bounds, made double bogey, then headed for the clubhouse.

Souchak was so upset he couldn't eat any lunch. He couldn't even get down half a milkshake. He still had the lead, but he'd just let the field back in play. His head told him to make it up over the final eighteen holes; his heart told him he'd just given away the U.S. Open.

Seven strokes back, with more than a dozen players to hurdle, Souchak's fellow Pennsylvanian had knocked his first tee shot of the last round onto the par-four green, defying the nearby creek and the doubting sportswriters, Dan Jenkins and Bob Drum.

Colonel Joe Curtis and the other fans gathered around the tee had little problem making it down to the green to watch Palmer putt for eagle; the crowd around Arnold had thinned out, and for good cause.

"Arnold Palmer was out of the tournament," said Deane Beman, the accomplished amateur who had missed the cut before choosing to walk thirty-six holes with Hogan and Nicklaus.

Palmer almost put himself out of the tournament for keeps on the first green. After missing his eagle bid, a dismayed Palmer carelessly slapped at his birdie tap-in. "And the damn thing almost didn't go in," said Paul Harney, his playing partner. "He didn't take any time with it, and it almost lipped out."

Almost. Palmer chipped into the cup from thirty feet at number two, and suddenly he was off on a blitz of four consecutive birdies and six birds over his first seven holes. As the cheers grew louder with each daring stroke, making the mountainside rumble, fans deserted other pairings and ran toward the commotion. Palmer was the Pied Piper of the Rockies. This was his Augusta National charge times ten.

Palmer made the turn in 30, and on the tenth tee he spotted two familiar figures pressing up against the ropes. "Fancy seeing you guys out here," Palmer said to Drum and Jenkins. He stole Jenkins's Coke and pack of Winstons and resumed his assault on the course.

Up ahead, Hogan and Nicklaus were winning their war with Cherry Hills, and Palmer was focused on only one of them. "I wasn't even aware of Jack," he said. The feeling was mutual.

"I never even thought of Arnold Palmer," Nicklaus said. "He wasn't even in the tournament."

The Ohio State Buckeye was mostly thinking about those seven hundred bucks he would win on his bet if he managed to protect his score of five under over the final six holes.

Nicklaus and Hogan had put on some show, each shooting 69 in the morning to stand three shots off the lead. On the back nine of the afternoon round, it appeared the winner would come from their group. A bizarre Saturday at the Open, with as many as ten players legitimately contending for the victory in its closing hours, centered around this twosome.

Hogan and Nicklaus. It looked like a father-son outing.

Even at his advanced age, Hogan could still strike a golf ball better than any other man alive. His putting was failing him, sometimes freezing him over his ball for what felt like an hour, but he was still the ultimate tee-to-green automaton.

Nicklaus would later tell friends he was embarrassed by how perfectly Hogan struck the ball. The Wee Ice Mon had been enthralling practice-range crowds at Cherry Hills with his marksmanship. He'd send out his caddie a couple of hundred yards — with a shag bag — and hit hooks, then fades, then two-irons, then three-irons, his caddie never moving more than two steps to his right or his left to retrieve the balls.

Hogan's aim and his aura had no ill effect on Nicklaus for their first thirty holes together, as the young amateur stepped onto the thirteenth green two ahead of Hogan and one ahead of Palmer, Fleck, and Julius Boros. Nicklaus's best friend, Robin Obetz, had flown into Denver that morning and made it to Cherry Hills nine holes into the third round for this very reason:

"Jack's going to win the Open as an amateur," Obetz had told his father.

Woody Hayes was also on the grounds and acting as Charlie Nicklaus's valet. It was a great day for Charlie, as he'd laid out about $35,000 to finance Jack's youth and amateur golf career. "Most wonderful money I ever spent," Charlie said. "I figure it's like living my life all over again. I always wanted to be a champ."

But Hayes was upset that no Columbus-area sportswriters were there to cover what was developing into one of the enduring major championship stories of all time, the story of Jack Nicklaus winning the Open. Hayes called Kaye Kessler, whose *Citizen-Journal* didn't have a Sunday paper, and then Paul Hornung, whose *Dispatch* did, and gave a running account of young Jack's remarkable play.

Nicklaus stood a dozen feet away from another birdie and a two-shot lead on the field at number thirteen when he ran his putt eighteen inches past the hole. "Oh, shit," said Beman, his friend in the gallery, after sizing up the delicate putt that remained.

Nicklaus had thoroughly enjoyed the seven hours he'd spent in Hogan's company, and not simply because he was routinely driving his ball between fifteen and forty yards past Hogan's. Jack had heard all the stories. He knew there would be precious little conversation, as Hogan was known to say only two words to his playing partners: "You're out."

But Nicklaus found that he loved playing with Hogan. Neither competitor suffered fools easily, and Hogan had a deeper respect for Nicklaus's swing than he did for Palmer's slashing and gashing.

"Hogan was staggered by the things he saw Jack doing," Beman said. "I'm not sure Hogan had ever played with anyone who could do all the things Jack could do."

They exchanged pleasantries at the appropriate time, Hogan and Nicklaus did, but suddenly the kid found himself melting under the gaze of the Wee Ice Mon. Jack spotted the uneven remains of a ball mark between his par putt and the thirteenth cup, and he was paralyzed by fear.

The fear of asking Hogan if he could repair the mark. The fear of Hogan belittling him for not knowing the rule.

Nicklaus was allowed to fix the indentation, but he'd never find out. "My God, if I ask him," Jack thought to himself, "he'll think I'm kind of stupid to ask a question like that."

So Nicklaus didn't ask the question. He hit the ball mark and missed the putt instead.

Nicklaus bogeyed the next hole, too, surrendering his share of the lead, losing his fighting spirit, and leaving Hogan and Palmer as the main principals in this raucous battle royal. Hogan finally made a putt — a twenty-footer for birdie at fifteen — to secure a share of the lead with Fleck, the ghost from his most devastating defeat, and with Palmer, who had settled into a conservative par-golf approach — for once in his life — after his blistering start.

Fleck's putter betrayed him, so he wouldn't haunt Hogan at Cherry Hills as he had five years earlier at Olympic. Hogan was tied for the lead as he stood in the seventeenth fairway, and he couldn't believe that Palmer — two groups back — was right there with him at four under.

The Wee Ice Mon was content all the same. His own putter was torturing him, reducing him to an almost pathetic figure as he agonized over the shortest tap-ins, and yet he had a record fifth Open title in reach with two holes to go.

As he prepared to strike his third shot on the 548-yard, par-five seventeenth, Hogan knew he'd pitched a perfect Saturday game: he'd hit thirty-four greens in regulation in thirty-four attempts. If time and stress and age hadn't stripped him of all his touch and nerve on the greens, Hogan would've been leading the Open by six or seven strokes.

At forty-seven, his legs battered by the accident, Hogan couldn't afford to take his chances with an eighteen-hole playoff. He needed a birdie. Even with the seventeenth green a virtual island surrounded by troubled waters, Hogan needed to go for the pin.

He needed to play it the Palmer way, not the Hogan way. He stood about fifty yards short of a moat that was some eighteen feet wide; the hole was cut twelve treacherous feet from the front of a rock-hard green that sloped toward the watery grave. Half cloaked by his own cigarette smoke, Hogan attached his hands to his hips; scanned the fairway, the hazard, and the green; and identified the spot where he wanted to land his ball.

Palmer was standing on the seventeenth tee as Hogan gripped his pitching wedge and measured his next move. When Hogan punched the ball, it was clear the shot was loaded with backspin.

He hit it some twenty inches short of perfection. Hogan's ball froze for a moment on the slope, then slowly but surely trickled into the water as a horrified crowd gasped.

"When that happened," Nicklaus said, "Hogan deflated like a balloon."

Hogan checked his ball in the moat, then sat on the bank to remove his right sock and shoe. He rolled up his pants, slipped as he planted his bare foot in the water, and slid his shoe back on while leaving his discarded sock on the front fringe. Hogan again lowered his right foot into the moat, blasted out his fourth shot, and then missed the twelve-foot putt for par.

Tied with Nicklaus, one shot behind Palmer, Hogan unraveled on the eighteenth, hooking his tee shot into the water and making a sad march up eighteen. Hogan was a beaten figure as he finished off his triple-bogey seven by missing—what else?—a short putt. He winced and stiffened his spine as if he'd received some unexpected jolt. Hogan tipped his flat cap with his right hand and then disappeared for good.

For some reason Nicklaus had also given up. His unbreakable concentration had been broken by Hogan's shocking meltdown; Nicklaus didn't realize he was only one shot off Palmer's lead as he stood over his chip shot off the edge of the eighteenth green. Joe Dey of the USGA was cleaning debris and cigarette butts near the ball as Nicklaus thought to himself, "What are you doing? I'm out of it."

In his white cap, white shirt, and dark pants—perfect for NBC's black-and-white broadcast—Nicklaus hit an indifferent chip to within six feet of the cup, missed the par putt, and retreated to the clubhouse to watch Palmer finish on TV. Fifteen minutes later, when Palmer and his score appeared on the screen, Nicklaus realized how badly he'd screwed up.

Palmer was to the left of the eighteenth green, under a tree and eighty feet from the hole. Had Nicklaus merely made his par putt, Palmer would've felt the pressure to get up and down to avoid a playoff.

Nicklaus started counting his blown back-nine opportunities. He bogeyed three of his final six holes and missed a short birdie putt at sixteen. "I should've won this golf tournament," he told himself.

Hogan agreed. The Wee Ice Mon would tell Jenkins of the *Fort Worth Press* that he'd played with a kid who would've won the Open by ten shots "if he knew what he was doing," though it was often reported that Hogan said Nicklaus would've won "if he had a brain in his head."

For a change, Palmer was leading with his brain rather than his heart. He played seventeen and eighteen the Hogan way, not the Arnie way. He hit a safe approach at the penultimate hole and then used a one-iron off the tee to avoid the water on eighteen. Palmer missed the final green with a four-iron, then slapped his third shot low and through the shadows, the ball stopping three feet from the hole.

He needed only to two-putt from there, but Palmer wanted to win in appropriate style. He knocked in his par putt to complete his round of 65-280 — the very numbers he'd told Jenkins and Drum that would claim the tournament — and to punctuate the most breathtaking comeback the Open had ever seen.

Palmer picked up his ball, took a jump step under the earsplitting din, and grabbed his visor with his right hand. This snapshot, this scene, would find its way onto the front pages of newspapers all across the land. Palmer threw his visor toward the back of the green like a boomerang; it spun high in the air and banked left. When the visor landed, a kid jumped out of the crowd to retrieve it.

NBC announced Palmer as the winner, though there were still twenty-nine players out on the course. Playing in a final group that was almost an hour and a half behind Palmer, part of the only threesome in the field, Bob Rosburg couldn't believe his ears. "Goddamn it," he told Howie Johnson and Bill Johnston. "They're giving the guy the trophy and I still have a chance."

Rosburg finished ten strokes back. Nobody was catching Palmer, whose wife, Winnie, was traveling with family members toward their winter place in Pennsylvania's Lehigh Valley when she caught a static-laced radio bulletin out of Denver over the prattle in her father's car.

"Daddy," Winnie said, "I think I just heard that Arnold won the Open. Can we hurry home?"

The phone was ringing when Winnie rushed through the door.

"Hiya, lover," said the excited voice on the line. "Guess what? We won!"

Palmer told Winnie to pack up and meet him at Idlewild Airport in New York the next day for the flight to Dublin for the Canada Cup matches, and then to St. Andrews for the British Open. Palmer could have floated across the Atlantic. His comebacks at the Masters and Open had people wondering if he was destined to shatter the records of all the golfing legends who preceded him.

Back in the Cherry Hills clubhouse, the pharmacology student out of Ohio State was beginning to sink into a depressed state. Jack Nicklaus's total of 282 was the best amateur score in U.S. Open history, better than any Bobby Jones round, but he wasn't throwing a party over his consolation prize. "I didn't win," he would say. "Nobody ever remembers who finished second at anything."

Nicklaus would be on his way to the NCAA Championship at the Broadmoor in Colorado Springs, where he'd won the U.S. Amateur, and soon enough he'd be on his way to marry Barbara Bash.

Before Jack left Cherry Hills, his best friend and best-man-to-be, Robin Obetz, cornered Joe Dey in the clubhouse. Dey wasn't a small talker or the type who liked to be bothered by strangers in the hour following the conclusion of the USGA's biggest event.

But at the end of this remarkable marathon day in the mountains, with the blue sky beginning its slow fade to black, Dey was going to hear from a young prophet forecasting the demise of Arnold Palmer's empire.

"Listen to me," Obetz told the USGA man.

"Jack Nicklaus is going to be the greatest player of all time."

CHAPTER 5

● Oakmont

J ACK NICKLAUS DID NOT arrive at the 1962 U.S. Open with the sole purpose of slaying Arnold Palmer before all of Arnie's family, neighbors, and friends.

To Jack, the Oakmont Country Club could have been in western Pennsylvania or the south of France.

"Arnold Palmer was never even a thought on my mind," Nicklaus said. "I didn't even know it was his backyard."

No, Jack was not talking tough after his second-place finish at the Thunderbird tournament in Clifton, New Jersey. He was just young and naive.

He simply didn't care that Palmer's Latrobe home was forty miles from Oakmont, or that Palmer was the reigning British Open champ who had just won his third Masters title, beating Dow Finsterwald and Gary Player in a playoff.

A thirty-two-year-old Arnie was just another guy a twenty-two-year-old Jack figured he could beat.

It was a hell of a way to look at it, given Palmer's stature in the game. Two months before the Open at Oakmont, Palmer sank a magical, mystery forty-five-foot downhill chip shot on the sixteenth hole of Augusta National right in front of the flabbergasted Player, who had won the Masters the year before when Palmer suffered an inexplicable meltdown on the final hole.

Palmer won the 1962 playoff after being down three shots to the five-foot-seven, 143-pound Player at the turn, but it was the chip shot in regulation from off the back edge of the green—with Palmer two shots behind—that hardened his standing as a fearless charger.

"We've got him now," Player, a fierce South African flyweight, told his caddie in the anxious moments preceding the chip. "He can't get down in two from there."

Palmer got down in one from there after absorbing a disturbing commentary from the TV tower above. Palmer heard the announcer and three-time Masters champ Jimmy Demaret tell his audience that Palmer had no shot.

"I'll show that son of a bitch," Arnie thought to himself.

As the ball raced toward the pin, fans rose from their foldup seats in anticipation. As the ball hit the stick and dropped, Palmer's caddie, Iron Man, fell backward from his kneeling position and threw his right arm out as if he'd been struck dead by a lightning bolt. Player leaned his putter against his hip and started clapping. "Nobody has ever holed a shot from there in the history of golf," the South African would say.

Two days later the lead Masters story by *Augusta Chronicle* sports editor Johnny Hendrix started like this: "Arnold Palmer, the greatest comeback player golf has ever seen, made up five shots in the last nine holes Monday to win the 26th Masters Tournament by three shots."

The greatest comeback player golf has ever seen. Palmer had been fueling all sorts of "greatest this" and "greatest that" talk for three seasons, starting with his come-from-behind victories at the 1960 Masters and U.S. Open. He was even changing the language of golf.

On his way to the 1960 British Open at St. Andrews, Palmer and his sportswriting pal Bob Drum were talking over drinks when Arnold said he'd like to win the British and then the PGA to collect a Grand Slam of pro majors.

Drum wrote it, the idea stuck, and the term *Grand Slam*—once defined as calendar-year victories in the U.S. and British Opens and U.S. and British Amateurs—took on a new shape, much to the dismay of Bobby Jones, 1930 winner of the old Grand Slam, who thought Palmer's remodeled version was silly.

It didn't matter so much that Palmer lost the 1960 British Open by a shot to Australian Kel Nagle, or that he felt he would've won if his momentum hadn't been stalled by an unprecedented St. Andrews rainout. Just by showing up, Palmer restored the British Open's prestige.

He captured the British title in 1961 at Royal Birkdale, and the top American players who once bypassed the tournament because of the expense, the travel, the relatively small purse, and the Open's demand that all competitors survive treacherous qualifying rounds were suddenly moved to make it a must-stop on their schedules.

Palmer didn't just change the language of the game. He changed the game itself.

So he was something of a living legend by June of 1962, when he pulled up at Oakmont, a course he'd played more than one hundred times since the age of twelve, including his appearance as a U.S. Open rookie in 1953. Palmer was a 5-to-1 favorite to take the 1962 Open, even if the oddsmakers were concerned about the injury he suffered at the Latrobe, Pennsylvania, airport while moving luggage from his plane to the trunk of his car.

Already burdened by a cold, fatigue, and a thirty-fifth-place finish at the Thunderbird, Palmer slashed the third finger on his right hand on a jack and required stitches to repair it.

He was terrified that doctors would rule him out of the Open; they didn't. Palmer was also concerned about the state of his game. He'd asked Thunderbird officials if he could quit their tournament after the third round to get in some much-needed pre-Open work at home, and they successfully begged him to stay.

None of this tempered the Oakmont buildup, which was ratcheted up by the USGA's decision to pair Arnie, the three-time Masters winner, with Jack, the two-time U.S. Amateur champ. In an attempt to ease the heavy hometown expectations, Palmer tried fitting his playing partner in the role of tournament shoo-in.

"It favors Nicklaus, undoubtedly," Palmer said of a course known for its 208 bunkers, furrowed greenside traps, and putting surfaces that ran faster than marble tile.

"Nicklaus drives the ball farther on the fly than I do and can hit over much of the trouble. He's stronger than I am."

This was not an easy confession for a man's man to make, but there was some gamesmanship involved. Palmer had carnal knowledge of Oakmont, and Nicklaus had played the course only a couple of times before Open week. Yet on the heels of Jack's showing at the Thunderbird, Palmer figured he could make Oakmont the perfect track for the highly touted rook. Make everyone believe Nicklaus should be the odds-on choice to win, and then see how the fat boy from Ohio handles that.

Only Nicklaus didn't seem bothered by much of anything at Oakmont, other than the zero in his professional victory column. With all of his amateur hardware, Nicklaus was most comfortable in this USGA setting.

He had a strong relationship with USGA officials, especially with Joe Dey, the executive director, and considered following Bobby Jones's lead and remaining a career amateur. But the golf world was no longer the same place that Jones had dominated. So in a letter to Dey dated November 7, 1961, Nicklaus wrote the following: "After much thought, I have concluded that due to the several sources of income available to me at the professional level, it would be unfair to my family not to accept this new responsibility."

Nicklaus's first pro payout came at his first tour stop, the Los Angeles Open. Bank of America check number 2679 was made out to Jack Nicklaus from the Los Angeles Junior Chamber of Commerce. Dated January 28, 1962, the check for Jack's dead-last finish was worth a grand total of $33.33.

His placements and prize money improved from there, thanks to the George Low Wizard 600 Sportsman putter he started using, the one with two notches in the club face — Jack carved in the second notch to line up the ball. By the time Nicklaus reached the first tee at Oakmont in the early afternoon of June 14, 1962, he had earned $28,000 and change on tour. Palmer occupied his familiar seat as the tour's leading money winner with more than $60,000 in earnings, and a victory at the Open would send him past his own earnings record of $75,263, set in 1960.

Oakmont was a worthy arena for their battle, the layout as rugged as Palmer's looks. The Pennsylvania Turnpike knifed right through the course; a narrow overhead bridge carried fans from one side to the other. For the first round of the 1962 Open, that bridge was far more congested than the turnpike.

Palmer was wearing a bright red sweater over a white shirt and a bandage over his injured finger. Nicklaus was dressed in a white shirt and cap and gray slacks. Arnold wore a white glove, Jack a black glove.

The 17,837 fans in attendance — a record opening-day crowd for this tournament — made the other 148 players in the field feel as invisible as Claude Rains.

Palmer had won five majors and thirty tournaments; Nicklaus had nearly won the 1960 Open at Cherry Hills and the 1961 Open at Oakland Hills and had shot an incredible eleven-under 269 for the United States at the 1960 World Amateur Team Championship at Merion, merely eighteen shots better than Ben Hogan's score at Merion in the 1950 Open.

Four months after John Glenn orbited the Earth, this main event was about stars from different galaxies, men with striking differences in appearance, personality, upbringing, and style. Palmer was the son of a country club employee; Nicklaus was the son of a country club member. Palmer was fit; Nicklaus was fleshy. Palmer ran a fast break; Nicklaus slowed the game to a crawl.

Palmer had a deep but friendly voice; Nicklaus sounded like someone who'd spent ten minutes sucking helium from a balloon. Palmer hit the ball right to left; Nicklaus hit it left to right. Palmer hit it low; Nicklaus hit it high. Palmer landed balls in ponds and hayfields; Nicklaus landed them on fairways and greens. Palmer had a hacker's cut only a mother could love; Nicklaus enjoyed a user's manual swing. Palmer was a stab-and-jab putter; Nicklaus stroked through the ball. Palmer made eye contact with everyone; Nicklaus made eye contact only with the pin. Palmer was prompt for his appointments; Nicklaus was often tardy.

These opposites attracted a huge following for Thursday's first round on a course soaked by heavy Wednesday rain. Nicklaus and Palmer greeted each other on the first tee. Jack was so unnerved by the Arnie-crazed masses, he went out and birdied the first three holes.

At number three he chipped into the hole after driving into Oakmont's famous "church pew" bunkers, the low mounds of thick grass separated by sand. Palmer was already wobbling against the ropes. He answered Nicklaus's 3-3-3 with a 4-6-4.

The double bogey at the 355-yard, par-four second made no sense, until one factored in Palmer's own angst. He was only seventy-five yards from the green in one when he walked up to the fringe to confirm what everyone knew: nobody wanted to be above the stick on this hole.

Palmer returned to his ball and promptly struck it too hard, sending it slightly over the green and into thick rough. "Ridiculous," said his caddie, John Garbo. "Absolutely ridiculous."

Garbo was hardly thrilled that Palmer assigned the blame to him.

"John," he said, "we should've talked that shot over."

"Well," the caddie answered, "you went up and looked at the pin. I thought you knew what you wanted to do."

Palmer chipped about twenty feet past the hole and three-putted from there.

"Geez," he said on the walk to the fourth tee. "Five strokes."

Five strokes behind Nicklaus, three holes into the tournament.

Jack cooled off and scored his own double bogey out of the sand and a ditch at the par-five ninth. Meanwhile, Arnold steadied his putter on the back nine and ripped off five consecutive threes, punctuated by a birdie at the 292-yard seventeenth, where his tee shot reached the green.

Palmer and Nicklaus each made par at eighteen and signed for scores that sat well with the pro-Palmer crowd. Jack shot a 72, Arnold a 71. They were both within easy striking distance of the leader and defending champ, Gene Littler, who came in with a two-under 69.

"The way he was playing out there," Palmer said of Nicklaus, "I figured he was using magic. When he knocked the ball in on the third hole, from off the green, I figured maybe I could sit around and watch all day. He was fantastic."

Palmer drove home to Latrobe and slept in his own bed. He was making the forty-five-minute drive back and forth each day, sometimes catching a ride with his friend Joe Tito.

Nicklaus, meanwhile, was stuck in a hotel with a crying baby, Jackie, a nine-month-old who wouldn't heed his mother's pleas for quiet so his father could sleep. This was a part of Palmer's home-court advantage, part of the reason he was everyone's pick to win.

Friday, round two, did nothing to disabuse anyone of that notion. Palmer and Nicklaus each birdied the first hole, but Arnie outscored Jack for a second straight day, his three-under 68 two shots lower than his playing partner's sum.

But the story wasn't Palmer's three-stroke advantage over Nicklaus after thirty-six holes, or Palmer's share of the lead with Bob Rosburg. It was the fans, and what those fans were and were not doing to Jack Nicklaus.

"They treated him like a dog," said Gary Player, who shared Nicklaus's score of 142.

More than anything, the crowd mocked Jack's weight. *Sports Illustrated* once did a cover piece on Nicklaus with the headline "One Whale of a Golfer," and Palmer's more boisterous fans took it from there.

When the Palmerites weren't calling him "Fat Guts" and "Fat Jack," they were calling him "Ohio Fats." The gallery was full of laborers — Palmer's kind of people — and it took on the personality of a beered-up Pittsburgh Steelers crowd.

"Miss it, Fat Guts!" the fans would shout.

As at Cherry Hills two years earlier, Woody Hayes was shepherding Charlie Nicklaus through the masses. Woody walked those first thirty-six Palmer-Nicklaus holes on Thursday and Friday in a jacket and tie, and he watched Charlie Nicklaus get hotter under the collar with every step.

Charlie was growing furious over the insults strangers were hurling at his son. His wife, Helen, always walked on the outer perimeter of the hustle and bustle, out of harm's way, which was a wise choice at Oakmont. Her husband was flirting with an all-out coronary as he barreled through enemy lines.

Charlie was a burly man with a burr cut, "and you could see his neck bulging and turning red," said Kaye Kessler, the Columbus sportswriter who was walking with him. Fans kept cheering for Nicklaus bogeys, and Charlie kept inching closer to an atomic blast. Finally, the old man blew.

He wheeled on a heckler and started going for him when Hayes, of all peacemakers, held him back.

"Charlie, you can't do that," Woody said. "Calm down. Calm down."

In another incident one of Jack Nicklaus's frat brothers from Ohio State shoved an older heckler in the chest, nearly knocking the man off his feet. Jack's wife, Barbara, was another gallery member who couldn't ignore the verbal venom as successfully as her husband did. "You can't not hear some of it," she said.

In the crowd of nearly twenty thousand, a record for the second day at the Open, Barbara Nicklaus was easy to spot. Howard Baker Saunders, who played in the 1958 Athens, Ohio, exhibition with Arnie and

Jack, was in that partisan Oakmont gallery with his wife, Alice, when "Miss it, Fat Guts" was about the nicest thing being barked.

Nobody was cheering for the rookie out of Ohio State. "Not one person," Alice Saunders said. Alice and Howard stumbled upon Barbara Nicklaus near one of the greens. "She was alone," Alice said. "All alone . . . She looked uncomfortable."

Twenty-seven marshals in helmets patrolled the mob. According to Jerry Izenberg of the *New York Herald Tribune,* one of the many prominent writers on the scene, the reporters tracking Nicklaus and the Palmer fans "felt like they were covering a lynching."

Through that same gallery walked a Milwaukee Braves catcher named Joe Torre, in town to play the Pirates at Forbes Field. Torre knew a hostile crowd when he heard one, and Oakmont's surely qualified.

"These people hate Jack," he told himself.

The fans weren't alone in that sentiment.

"All of us hated Jack Nicklaus," said Arnold Palmer's sister Cheech. "We thought he was another one of those spoiled little rich kids, and he was." Still, Cheech Palmer called the fans' treatment of Nicklaus "embarrassing."

Only Jack was most determined to marginalize the rough steel-town crowd. He'd begun developing his thick skin as a basketball star at Upper Arlington High, where he was a three-year starter good enough to draw box-and-one defenses.

Nicklaus would go head-to-head with Mount Vernon's Richie Hoyt, who would play with Jerry Lucas, John Havlicek, and a reserve named Bob Knight on the Ohio State team that won the 1960 NCAA title. Nicklaus would take all the lessons learned in Mount Vernon's raucous shoebox gym — "The opposing crowd noise never bothered me," he said — and apply them to the golf course.

The Oakmont crowd eased up on Saturday's thirty-six-hole final, if only because Nicklaus was paired with Billy Maxwell and Palmer with his co-leader, Rosburg. Arnold was feeling good and liberated. His damaged finger wasn't stopping him from hitting the ball, tee to green, as soundly as he could hit it. Palmer was ready to attack this most familiar course to the delight of his family, friends, and neighbors and to pull away from a field accustomed to choking on his last-day dust.

But his short game wouldn't cooperate. In his morning round

Palmer three-putted his way back to the pack. He was bothered by quick-fingered photographers, and then by an airplane that buzzed him on the eighteenth green, where Palmer somehow missed from two feet and closed with another bogey that quashed the joy he felt over his long eagle putt at seventeen.

Palmer flipped his putter in disgust as he trudged off the green. "Man," he said, "if I had a BB gun I'd have shot down that plane."

Palmer was madder than hell. He rushed off the green and marched into Lew Worsham's pro shop, where he planted his putter in a vise and started hammering away. Palmer removed the putter, looked it over, put it back in the vise, and started hammering some more.

Palmer's two-over 73 left him in a tie with Bobby Nichols. Nicklaus, who adored Oakmont's lightning-fast greens, shot a 72 to land two shots off the lead at 214. Over the first fifty-four holes Nicklaus didn't have a single three-putt; Palmer had seven. If Arnold had just put together an average round on the greens, the hometown boy would've been leading his hometown Open by three strokes.

The fourth and final round started under a hot afternoon sun, Nicklaus and Maxwell going out one group ahead of Palmer and Rosburg. Energized by a ham sandwich, a Coke, and a pint of chocolate milk, Palmer began seeing a cup that finally looked bigger than an ant hole.

He sank a six-footer for birdie at the 355-yard second, the hole he'd doubled in the first round, and then he sank a four-foot birdie putt at the fourth. The fans shouted his name and appealed for more. Some of them cheered when Nicklaus suffered his first three-putt on the first green of the last round.

With eleven holes to play, Nicklaus found himself five shots behind Palmer. Jack was out of the conversation, out of contention. And then he wasn't.

Palmer put him back in the tournament at the par-five ninth, right when Arnold had a chance to drive a near-fatal dagger into Jack's hopes. After hitting a three-wood into the rough to the right of the green, Palmer grabbed a wedge and planned for an up-and-down birdie. He was pin-high, three under for the Open, ready to widen his lead.

Palmer could sink the chip for an eagle. He could knock it close and tap in for a birdie. Or he could do exactly what he did: flub the shot.

Palmer advanced the ball a few inches, no more. He looked ready to blow snot out of his ears when he stepped back to his ball for a second chip, a shot that would be considered a success only when measured against the one that preceded it.

Just when he needed his trademark aggressiveness, Palmer backed off. He hit his do-over chip too delicately and left himself a ten-footer for par.

He missed it. For the first time all day, Palmer thought he might lose the tournament.

"Earthshaking," he would call that flubbed wedge.

Up ahead, Nicklaus was shaking the earth with something of a Palmer charge. After making birdie at number nine, Nicklaus shaved another shot off par by sinking a fourteen-footer at number eleven.

The game was back on. Sensing an epic upset that 99 percent of the Oakmont crowd didn't want, the steelworkers and ironworkers from Palmer country started back in on Fat Jack.

Nicklaus held firm. He put himself back on the enemy court at Mount Vernon High, blocked out the noise, and fixed his eye on the goal.

Nicklaus made par at number thirteen, and right behind him Palmer sent his six-iron shot at the par three into a trap. Arnold blasted out to fifteen feet, and then his putter failed him again.

Five holes to play, and Arnold Palmer and Jack Nicklaus shared the lead in the U. S. Open.

The tension was thicker than the humidity, as a sweat-stained crowd of 24,492 — another Open record — closed in on the only two groups that mattered. Including practice rounds, nearly eighty thousand fans had passed through Oakmont's gates, and almost every single one of them was clinging to the same endgame scenario, the same definition of the Open's happily-ever-after: Palmer, the beloved pauper turned king, beating Nicklaus, the rich kid, on a daring stroke of genius and grit.

At the fifteenth Palmer let loose a sixteen-foot birdie attempt that would've reclaimed the lead. With the ball halfway to its planned destination, a marshal in a green military outfit rose from his knees and waved his bony hands toward his hollow chest, begging the ball to find the cup.

It didn't. The marshal winced and doubled backward, then waved his right hand in disgust before clearing the sea of fans and their official U.S. Open cardboard periscopes so Palmer could walk to the next tee.

Still tied for the lead with Palmer, Nicklaus nearly gave everyone the perfect opening to their ideal ending by trying to drive the seventeenth green and landing his ball in a bunker instead. His playing partner, Maxwell, was standing off to the side of the trap as Nicklaus was digging his heels into the sand.

Over time Maxwell and Phil Rodgers and the other contenders had dropped off the pace, leaving Nicklaus and Palmer to settle it. Maxwell knew Nicklaus was hell-bent on winning; the only words Jack said to Maxwell all day were "You're out," which was always the extent of Ben Hogan's conversations with his playing partners.

From the green Maxwell would turn to the rear and watch Palmer's tee shots. "And Jack was always ten or twenty yards ahead of Arnold on every drive," Maxwell said. "I'd look back to see; Jack wasn't looking back to see Palmer. He was concentrating on golf."

But Maxwell just didn't believe Nicklaus was ready to defeat Palmer. Maxwell was even more convinced Nicklaus was going down when he watched the sand shot at seventeen come out soft and waver on the bunker's lip.

"It could've easily gone back into the trap," Maxwell said. "It was one in a million. The ball didn't have to go forward; it almost went backward. One inch shorter and it would've gone backward."

A relieved Nicklaus pitched his third shot four feet from the stick and then faced the biggest putt of his Open.

Bobby Jones was watching the NBC telecast from his home as Nicklaus sized up his line to the hole. Jones knew this putt could be the difference between winning and losing the national championship.

It was a double breaker that would travel at the speed of sound, and Nicklaus figured the best available option was a hard and straight putt that would bypass the breaks in the green. He knew if he missed, he'd have a treacherous bogey attempt coming back.

Nicklaus decided he had to take this calculated risk. Palmer's fans were raising hell behind him, and Nicklaus couldn't afford to hand their man a one-shot lead at this stage of the game.

He aimed and fired. The ball hit the back of the cup with blunt-trauma force and dropped straight down. Watching this putt fall on his TV, Jones nearly jumped out of his chair.

Still tied with Palmer, Nicklaus stormed to the eighteenth tee and unleashed a ferocious drive into the fairway. He followed with an approach shot that landed fifteen feet from the stick, where Jack would have a perfect uphill look at a birdie that could claim the Open.

Thousands of fans had moved ahead of the Nicklaus and Palmer groups to surround the eighteenth green and wait for their photo finish. The rookie out of Ohio State had weathered the pro-Palmer storm, and he had only fifteen feet to pay dirt. Fifteen feet to cover before silencing the abusive fans for good.

Jack hovered over his ball for a week, just as he always did. He finally pulled the trigger and watched as his putt drifted to the left of the hole by a nose hair. Nicklaus winced and buckled his knees ever so slightly. He tapped in for par, removed his cap, and extended his hand to Maxwell. Jack Nicklaus was in the U.S. Open house at 283, Hogan's winning Oakmont score in 1953.

Now all eyes were locked on Palmer, who needed a birdie on the seventy-second hole to claim his second Open championship and avoid an eighteen-hole playoff with Nicklaus. Arnie followed Jack's beautiful drive with one of his own, but it was already clear that the three-time Masters winner and reigning British Open champ couldn't match the rookie pound for pound, yard for yard.

Nicklaus had hit a six-iron into the eighteenth green; Palmer was going with a four-iron. This manhood concession didn't affect the shot. Arnold took a wicked cut at the ball, and his flying divot split into two considerable chunks, one crash-landing to the left, the other to the right. Palmer's ball occupied a low flight pattern, of course, and landed in front of the green. It took two big bounces, and then three tiny ones — like a stone skipping across a country pond — before stopping ten feet to the left of the flag, inspiring the crowd to explode with the sound of certain triumph.

Palmer had overcome the severely sloped greens, the bad finger, and the worse putting. He was one birdie away from a most exhilarating victory.

Winning the Open at home. Defending his throne. Beating the defiant prince the Palmer family loathed.

Arnold walked up to the green to his one-of-a-kind reception, and he waved his right hand to the crowd. Down in the fairway, fans who had broken through the ropes swarmed like honeybees behind a human chain of hand-holding marshals. If Palmer sank the putt, his $15,000 first prize would put him well on his way to the first $100,000 season in golf.

If he missed, an apocalyptic duel with Nicklaus would be the consolation prize.

Fans watched through their white periscopes; they were so frozen by the moment, one might've thought they were all looking through a U-boat lens at an approaching Allied warship. Palmer stalked his putt, then dropped down on his right knee for a better look. He got up, walked to his ball, dug himself into his own personal batter's box, and focused on getting halfway to a Grand Slam.

Nicklaus was standing to the right of Palmer's stage, taking in this incredible scene. Pigeon-toed and knock-kneed as always, Palmer took one last peek at the hole as the crowd turned quiet. Rosburg, Palmer's friend, putted out and then walked by Arnold and said, "If you were ever going to make a putt, make this one, will you?"

"I sure hope so," Palmer responded.

Arnold talked more that day than he usually did. Nerves, Rosburg figured. "Arnold really wanted this one," he said. "Badly."

Palmer decided this putt was a left-to-right proposition. In the thick, oxygen-deprived moments before Palmer struck his ball, Rosburg told himself he'd never heard such deafening silence in his life.

Arnold steadied himself, pulled back his blade, and then thrust it forward, jabbing at the ball in perfect Palmer form.

Three-quarters of the way there, it was clear Arnold had read too much break. His putt was a couple of inches too high, and as it grazed by the hole and traveled an extra two feet, the gallery gasped and groaned. Palmer stiffened up and stared at the ball with a look of sheer disdain.

His shoulders and hands sagged. Palmer looked at his caddie, John Garbo, and then finished off his par. Rosburg offered his right hand for congratulations and reserved his left hand for condolences, placing it on Palmer's back as he whispered in his ear. Rosburg patted his friend three times on the stomach and then disappeared as a dejected Palmer staggered off the green.

Arnold recovered quickly, put a smile on his face, and mugged with Jack for the cameras.

"Frankly," Palmer would say of his playoff opponent, "I wish it was someone else besides that big, strong dude."

J ack Nicklaus was not about to share any money with Arnold Palmer. They were warming up at Oakmont, preparing for a one-on-one, eighteen-hole playoff for the U.S. Open championship, when Palmer approached the rookie and whispered an offer he could refuse.

"Do you want to split the purse?" Palmer asked.

Purse-splitting wasn't an uncommon practice at the time, but Nicklaus was too new to the pro game to know it.

Jack paused for a brief review of his options.

"No, thanks," he told Palmer. "Why don't we just play for it?"

This was Sunday, June 17, and two proud young dads were hoping to ruin each other's Father's Day. Palmer was dressed in a light blue shirt with sleeves short enough to expose those biceps he started building in his greenskeeping youth forty miles to the east. Nicklaus was dressed in a looser white shirt that cloaked his less impressive arms. He was wearing a cream-colored cap on a hot Pennsylvania day when the crowd would let him know he was wearing a black hat whether he liked it or not.

Nicklaus was busy enjoying a cigarette when Palmer stunned him with the proposal. The Open carried a $15,000 first prize, with $8,000 going to the runner-up, and the go-for-broke gambler actually chose to play it safe. Palmer wanted to guarantee that each man received $11,500 regardless of the cards in his hands.

Nicklaus wanted only to protect the distinction between the winner and the loser.

This wasn't about money, either. The week before, at the $100,000 Thunderbird, Nicklaus received an oversized cardboard replica of his $10,000 runner-up check before John Derr of CBS and some print guys went into the locker room to question him about the tournament and the upcoming Open.

"You don't want to interview me," a dour Nicklaus told them. "I didn't win."

"Yeah," Derr said, "but you finished second, Jack."

"I didn't come out here to win checks; I came out here to win tournaments. Here, John, you can have this."

With that, Nicklaus heaved his cardboard check across the locker room and toward a stunned Derr. Nicklaus was frustrated and tired. He was six months into his professional career and he had yet to score his first tour victory.

And now here he was seven days later, right in the middle of Arnold Palmer country, telling the undisputed champion of professional golf that he would not agree to blur even slightly the line separating first place from second.

Jack did think it was a nice gesture on Palmer's part, and certainly not the first. Four months earlier Palmer and Nicklaus were paired together for the final round of the Phoenix Open when Palmer—who would win the Phoenix title by a twelve-shot margin—moved to comfort the frayed kid on the final hole.

"You can birdie this hole and finish second," he told Nicklaus. "Just play it smart and do it."

Nicklaus finished in a tie for second and never forgot those friendly big-brother words or other acts of Palmer kindness. Relative strangers at Cherry Hills just two years earlier, Palmer and Nicklaus quickly became acquaintances in Jack's short time as a pro.

Arnold let Nicklaus fly on his airplane. He advised Jack to putt from just off the green rather than chip because, Palmer told him, "your worst putt will be every bit as good as your best chip."

Above all, Palmer let Nicklaus sign with his business manager, Mark McCormack, with whom Palmer had negotiated an exclusive partnership.

Arnold had already allowed Gary Player into McCormack's fold, but this was still a huge concession. Palmer had told McCormack he needed to remain his only client, only to grant exceptions for his biggest foreign and domestic threats.

When it came down to it, Arnold was simply an agreeable man who had a hard time saying no. "I saw an opportunity to help [Nicklaus]," Palmer said, "and I thought it was the right thing to do." He came to see Jack, the prodigious talent with the flying elbow, as a "young good friend."

But on that fateful playoff Sunday at Oakmont, with the U.S. Open hanging in the balance, the field cut from 150 players to 2, things were different. This was the national championship, not the Phoenix Open, and Nicklaus had absorbed some serious verbal abuse from Palmer's hometown fans.

Arnie would apologize to Nicklaus for the behavior of his loyalists —"They don't understand," he'd tell Jack—and Nicklaus would say that he blocked out the jeers, that he never even heard them. Nonetheless, the hostile tone had been set.

As it was, Nicklaus didn't find the humor in a Palmer quote delivered before the start of the Open. "Everybody says there's only one favorite, and that's me," Palmer said. "But you'd better watch the fat boy."

Now they were even. He didn't say so publicly, but Palmer was not happy that Nicklaus refused his offer to split the U.S. Open purse. *No, thanks. Why don't we just play for it?*

Who the hell did this rookie think he was?

Nicklaus was 0 for 17 in pro tournaments, and here he was shutting down the winner of five majors and countless endorsement deals.

Maybe Jack didn't know that those who disrespected Palmer usually paid the price. Roger Maris, New York Yankees slugger, found out the hard way eighteen months earlier at the Hickok Belt banquet to honor the professional athlete of the year.

When Palmer walked through the door as a candidate for the award, Maris turned to him and said, "What the fuck are you doing here?" Palmer just stopped and stared at him. He figured the best way to prove to Maris that golfers are indeed athletes would be to beat out the Yankee for the award.

"That's what my father taught me," Palmer said. "He said, 'Don't say anything, just do it.' I didn't say a goddamn word to [Maris] . . . I didn't say a word until after it was all over, and then I didn't need to say anything."

On his way out the banquet door, Palmer made sure to walk past Maris with the alligator-skin, diamond-encrusted belt in his hands.

On the way out of Oakmont, Palmer wanted to walk past Nicklaus carrying the Open trophy.

Yes, he'd been helpful to young Jack: if the Palmer family "hated" Nicklaus as Cheech Palmer said, Arnold did a fairly good impression of someone who didn't share the in-house sentiment.

But at 1:45 p.m. on June 17, 1962, high noon at Oakmont, Palmer's first sporting act of the day — the offer of a fifty-fifty share of a pot Arnie was favored to win — was also scheduled to be his last. He wanted to teach a little lesson to the country clubber who turned pro and immediately declared his intention to be "the greatest golfer the world has seen."

"I want to win this one more than any tournament I've ever played," Palmer said.

On the big day Jack showed up in his favorite pair of twelve-dollar pants, the same God-awful olive-green iridescent pants he'd worn for Saturday's steamy thirty-six-hole final. Tommy Bolt once took a look at those pants and Jack's beer-barrel thighs stuffed inside them and said, "They ought to put that guy in the army pushing tanks."

Nicklaus wasn't about to compete in the playoff without them. "So I just sort of stood them up in the corner at night," he said.

It was some night, too. Frankie Avalon was performing in Nicklaus's hotel, and his voice was cutting through the paper-thin walls of Jack's room, separating the rookie from his much-desired sleep. Nicklaus ultimately descended into a deep, ten-hour slumber, during which his wife, Barbara, took their infant son, Jackie, to the downstairs coffee shop.

Little Jackie caused a scene while his father slept. He heaved a jar of baby food and yanked a tablecloth full of breakfast ware to the floor. Later, with Barbara's mother-in-law playing babysitter so Barbara could watch the playoff, Jackie spit up right in Avalon's presence. "Oh, my God!" the singer cried. "The kid puked."

The kid's dad didn't. Nicklaus wasn't the least bit jittery when he made his way to Oakmont with his MacGregor clubs. He felt he was on top of his game, and when he was on top of his game, he believed there wasn't a man alive who could beat him on a golf course, Arnold Palmer included.

"This is my tournament," Nicklaus told himself. He wasn't about to treat Palmer any differently than he had treated sixteen-year-old Stan Ziobrowski, the opponent he defeated as a thirteen-year-old in the United States Junior Amateur championship.

"Arnie's not that much better than anyone else," Jack said. "Everybody thinks Palmer will win, and he has come from behind often enough so that pretty soon the player facing him thinks so, too. Well, maybe it's a certain cockiness in me, but I can't really admit to myself that Palmer or any other player is a better golfer than I am."

Palmer was the more anxious of the two as he drove in from Latrobe. Nicklaus had only one three-putt green over seventy-two regulation holes; Palmer had four in the third round alone. Arnold knew he couldn't keep up with Jack off the tees, and now he wasn't sure if he could match him on the greens.

The pressure on Palmer was immense. "There was never any question in my mind that he was going to win," said Palmer's younger sister, Sandy. "And I think everyone felt the same way . . . Arnie felt it, too. He thought he was going to win. He wanted to win for himself and for all of western Pennsylvania, for all of his friends and family."

Losing to Jack Nicklaus simply was not an option. "We didn't like Jack," Sandy Palmer said. "I mean, we didn't want Jack to win."

Nicklaus and Palmer posed side by side for a photo, Arnie holding up his Hogan driver, Jack holding up his MacGregor. On the first tee Arnold slipped on his white glove, Jack his black glove. Arnold was introduced to wild cheers, Jack to a far less hysterical sound. They shook hands, and then Palmer stepped into the box. If he was still angry over the rookie's refusal to split the $23,000 combined purse for the first- and second-place finishers, the ball would feel every ounce of the man's wrath.

Palmer took a violent public-course cut on his drive, falling back from the swing on impact. It was a good, healthy knock, but the ball veered right. Palmer's drive landed in the rough.

Eager to seize upon the opening and make a statement, Nicklaus teed up his ball and — with a tighter, more disciplined swing — sent a booming drive into the fairway that traveled nearly three hundred yards.

And then they were off. Walking with them, in the gallery, was another golfing phenom from Ohio State, a nineteen-year-old named Tom Weiskopf, who couldn't believe the length of Nicklaus's ball. "I walked it off," he said. "Twenty-eight paces past Arnold on the fly, thirty-four yards with the roll.

"Arnold walked over the top of that first hill at Oakmont, and he saw that drive, and . . . surprise! His head went up. A double take, almost."

Nicklaus had landed the first blow, and the way Weiskopf saw it, "he was going to show everybody, 'Is that the best Arnold can do? Is that the best they can throw at me? Well, I'm going to destroy the best.'"

Palmer missed the green long on his approach and couldn't get down in two; Nicklaus made a routine two-putt par and took a one-shot lead to the second tee, much to the dismay of an ornery crowd.

"For Jack," said Jay Weitzel, the former aide at Nicklaus's home club and one of the precious few Nicklaus fans behind the Oakmont ropes, "it was like going into Yankee Stadium and sixty thousand people were for the Yankees."

Arnold was Ruth, DiMaggio, and Mantle, and Jack was just this spoiled, moon-faced man-child who dared to challenge the people's champ.

"If he gets tired of golf," wrote Jim Murray of the *Los Angeles Times,* "[Nicklaus] can make a living as a department store Santa . . . Arnold Palmer has a belly like a washboard and a back like a chimney. He flies his own plane. Jack Nicklaus has a front like a pile of old clothes and a back like an unmade bed. He gets any heavier, and he'll have to fly as freight."

Nicklaus dropped a birdie putt on the par-four fourth for a two-shot lead. The crowd was growing restless. At one point a fan, apparently enraged by the obstructed views provided by the procession of reporters on the players' side of the ropes, grabbed Don Weiss of the Associated Press and sent him tumbling into a sand trap.

Frustrated extremists were urging Palmer to resort to unsportsmanlike conduct. "Walk around while he's putting, Arnie," they pleaded.

"The hard hats were everywhere," Jerry Izenberg of the *Herald Tribune* said of the steelworkers. "These guys didn't understand anything. Every time Nicklaus was ready to line up a putt, they started to stamp their feet. The freaking ground was shaking, hundreds stamping their feet. It sounded like the fucking army coming over the hill."

Arnie's Army.

"The only golf course I've ever seen become a home court," Izenberg said.

But the visiting team wasn't rattled; the home team was the one that looked completely out of sorts. At the par-three sixth Palmer's putter foiled him yet again; he missed a par attempt after Nicklaus dropped a seven-footer for birdie. Jack was no longer threatening to beat Arnold; he was threatening to humiliate him.

On his way to the eighth tee, four shots off Nicklaus's pace, Palmer started whining to his caddie, John Garbo, over the size of the deficit.

"What the hell is four shots?" Garbo shot back. "You've made four shots up a lot of times. You don't have to worry about four shots."

Palmer was doing the slowest of burns, smoldering in his own L&M smoke. Nicklaus was playing at his usual glacial pace — he was practically smoking a pack of cigarettes while examining each and every putt — and it was driving Palmer mad.

"He was a rabbit," Nicklaus said, "and he wanted to go. Maybe I was the tortoise."

Palmer was already annoyed on the first hole, and not only because Nicklaus had rejected his split-purse offer. Jack had taken his sweet time joining Arnie on the tee, and Arnie suspected the kid was trying to rattle him, trying to stall for effect.

Nicklaus swatted away the suggestion the way he would an annoying horsefly. "I think I had to go take a crap," he said.

Jack swore he had never intentionally slowed his pace of play to unnerve an opponent, but he also maintained that no man would make him speed up either. "He couldn't fast-play me," Nicklaus said of Palmer. "I wouldn't move."

As they crossed the narrow bridge over the Pennsylvania Turnpike on the way to the ninth tee, Nicklaus and Palmer were escorted by four state troopers and the match referee, Fred Brand, an Oakmont member. Behind the group, above everyone's head, the mobile scoreboard told a most shocking tale.

PALMER   +3

NICKLAUS   −1

"Whatever Arnie did," said Palmer's younger brother, Jerry, "Jack just did a little better."

Heading to the clubhouse side of the turnpike, the side of holes one and nine through eighteen, Palmer wore a look of grim determination. Maybe it was his caddie's little pep talk. Maybe it was the memory of Cherry Hills and the 1960 Masters and all the other comeback victories that had earned him the reputation of the game's ultimate charger.

Either way, Palmer wore the expression of a man who believed his 9–3 playoff record was about to move to 10–3.

At the par-five ninth — the hole that cost him a victory in regulation — Palmer scored a little revenge by chipping out of the rough to four feet and putting up a four to Nicklaus's five. The lead was down to three, and it was the first time the gallery lathered up since Palmer's opening introduction.

In the midst of this Father's Day crowd walked two young mothers, acting as if they were on their way to a church social. Barbara Nicklaus and Winnie Palmer had met before, but they were mere acquaintances at the time their husbands squared off on the first playoff tee.

But now? Nine holes deep into a U.S. Open playoff that felt more like a tar-and-feathering?

This was love at first slight.

"Once I started talking to Winnie," Barbara said, "it was like we'd been best friends for a hundred years."

The women kept their heads while thousands of men around them lost theirs.

If most saw it as odd that the wives and closest confidantes of two fierce competitors could spend an eighteen-hole playoff acting like old sorority sisters catching up, Barbara and Winnie didn't care. Neither had ever met a stranger. Barbara and Winnie were disarmingly sweet and quick with a smile. They were attractive, intelligent, and well versed in all the issues facing young mothers with husbands entrenched in the nomadic existence of the golf pro.

"We connected," Barbara said. "I don't want to sound blasé, like, 'Oh, yeah, we were out there together in the playoff.' But we were just very comfortable with each other."

That comfort level would shrink along with the Nicklaus lead. When Arnold sank a five-footer for birdie at the 372-yard eleventh, and then a three-footer for birdie at the 598-yard twelfth, the gap between the Nicklauses and the Palmers was down to one stroke with half a dozen holes to play.

Jack wasn't afraid. He figured everyone expected him to lose anyway, so there was no point in fearing the consequences.

The crowd moved in for the kill around the par-three thirteenth, and Nicklaus didn't appear the least bit worried. He was a twenty-two-year-old pro with Palmer right in front of him, not the twenty-year-old amateur paired with Hogan at Cherry Hills while Palmer was making his move out of a different group.

Nicklaus never lost his nerve. On the tenth hole, when a USGA official had asked him to play faster, Nicklaus didn't budge. He was doing it his way, the officials and the opponent be damned.

"You play too slow," Palmer had told him once, to no avail.

Arnold loved to march, hit, hitch up his pants, and do it all over again. Nicklaus was breaking that rhythm, and the fans couldn't do a thing about it.

Palmer even believed the crowd was inadvertently helping Nicklaus, hardening his focus, driving him into a me-against-the-world cocoon. "I don't think there's any question about it," Arnie said.

Nicklaus was wearing blinders at Oakmont, but Arnold had his opening at the short thirteenth. A birdie would likely mean a tie and a whole new ball game. Nicklaus couldn't withstand an onslaught of birdies forever, could he?

Palmer turned to his caddie, Garbo.

"Is a five-iron enough?" he asked.

"Yeah, a five-iron's enough," Garbo answered.

Palmer pulled out the club, studied the target, then returned to the caddie and his bag. His gut was telling him he needed a four-iron, and Arnold Palmer was a golfer who lived and died on gut feelings.

It was a curious choice, as Palmer felt the adrenaline surging through his veins. A golfer on a hot streak would normally take less club to account for that adrenaline, and Palmer chose the opposite route. The man who never eased up decided to ease up on a four-iron. The results were disastrous.

The pin was on the left, and Palmer pushed his low, line-drive tee shot out to the right. He got a lucky bounce and the gallery reacted favorably, but Palmer was still a good sixty feet from the hole. Meanwhile, Nicklaus's high fly landed fourteen feet from the stick.

Palmer's first putt — an uphiller breaking to the left — stopped seven feet short. Nicklaus missed his birdie try and tapped in for par. Now Palmer needed a make to stay one shot behind. This was his moment of hometown truth.

Feeling every ounce of those local-boy burdens after a long week in the sun, Palmer lurched over his putt, let it rip, and missed to the left. He whipped his torso to the right and angrily pumped his left fist toward his belly button.

Palmer's extreme facial expressions always stood in stark contrast to Nicklaus's robo-stare and made him more human to his fans. This time his face was a teeth-baring brew of rage and despair. Palmer was two shots down with five holes to play.

"It wasn't the same after that hole," Garbo said. "It just wasn't the same."

Arnie and his army had run out of ammo.

So there they were on the eighteenth hole, Palmer looking deflated and defeated before nine million NBC viewers, wearing the body language of a bitter runner-up. Still up two shots, Nicklaus had sent his tee shot whistling into the left rough. As Jack was trying to find his drive, and then as Jack was trying to determine if a fan had stepped on his ball or if his ball had settled into an animal hole, Palmer grew agitated in the fairway.

Finally, with Nicklaus hemming and hawing in the rough, talking to an official who was on his hands and knees inspecting the ball, Palmer slashed away with a three-iron. "Worst shot he hit in the whole tournament," Garbo said.

Palmer hit it fat and to the right, short of a bunker. Nicklaus was taken aback. He couldn't believe Palmer would be so careless.

"It was like a give-up," Nicklaus said of Arnie's second shot.

The give-up made Jack's next choice a simple one. Nicklaus hit his wedge short of a fairway bunker rather than risk clearing it. He calmly knocked his third shot onto the green and left of the pin and then watched as Arnie made a desperate pitch for birdie.

From near the bunker Palmer threw an aggressive shot at the stick, hoping it would bank and fall. The ball took two hops and appeared ready to do exactly what Palmer wanted it to do. "Oh, God," Nicklaus told himself, "it's going in."

The ball just missed the stick and ran to the back fringe.

Palmer knew he couldn't win. As he crouched in the rough behind his putt, his knees almost in the grass, his back nearly brushing against the low ropes, the long-faced fans to his rear held their chins in their palms. To Arnold's left knelt a state trooper. To Arnold's right knelt his caddie, Garbo, who was watching over Palmer's red and white bag.

Arnold used his left hand to wipe two beads of sweat from his forehead; he inspected a sweat drop on his thumb and shook it to the ground. Nicklaus putted a bit too aggressively, running his ball two and a half feet past the hole before marking it. Palmer knew Jack wouldn't choke on that one.

He sent his downhiller at the hole anyway, just for the hell of it, and it slipped by on the right side. Palmer walked toward the cup, reached out his putter, and slapped at his ball as if he were a weekend warrior who'd just been told by his fellow member that his next putt was good.

Palmer missed that one, too, tapped in for a six, and then shockingly reached down for Nicklaus's marker, fumbling it on the first try before picking it up on the second. Palmer shook Nicklaus's hand and gave Jack his marker as they headed off the green, Jack wrapping his right hand around Arnold's shoulder while whispering words of consolation.

Joe Dey of the USGA stopped the men in their tracks. As state troopers and Open officials gathered around them, Dey told Nicklaus he needed to hole his ball.

Jack returned to the green, where his caddie, Nick "Topsy" Bugna, pointed to the spot where the ball should be placed. Like Nicklaus, who was wearing his lucky pants from the day before, Bugna had on his lucky shoes and the same foul-smelling clothes he'd worn across those thirty-six Saturday holes.

Jack made his two-footer, and his score of 71 was officially better than Arnold's score of 74. Nicklaus had become the youngest winner of the U.S. Open since his inspiration, Bobby Jones, won in 1923.

Dressed in her white linen outfit, Barbara Nicklaus left Winnie Palmer's side and made a beeline for the winner. She tapped Arnold twice on the back as she passed him without looking his way — Arnold reached out and tapped her three times between the shoulder blades — and then she stepped straight into her husband's hug and kiss.

"I can't play any better than I played here," Palmer said, "and I couldn't win. And that Nicklaus, he won't give anything. He played super."

Nicklaus finished with one three-putt green in ninety holes, or ten fewer than Palmer.

"I just wanted to win so badly," Arnold said.

Three rows of white chairs were stretched across the putting green for the championship ceremony, along with a head table covered by a white cloth. Seated to the left of USGA President John Winters, Palmer was dressed in a white blazer. Seated to the right of Winters, Nicklaus was dressed in a dark blazer.

Some two dozen photographers were capturing the scene, snapping away at the winner and loser. Winters congratulated Palmer and handed him his $8,000 second-place check. When Winters called up Nicklaus, Palmer rose to his feet with an L&M planted between his lips and applauded with the rest of the crowd. Nicklaus accepted the trophy and arched his white eyebrows in mock surprise when handed the $15,000 winner's check.

Jack and Arnold evenly shared in a $5,000 USGA bonus out of the playoff receipts, their only purse-splitting of the day. Palmer posed with Nicklaus for the cameramen, playfully holding his right fist against the champion's chin.

"Now that the big guy is out of the cage," Palmer said, "everybody better run for cover."

The fat boy had grown into the big guy.

Palmer made the longest forty-mile drive of his life back to Latrobe, where he huddled with close friends; theirs was a traditional gathering after big tournaments. They went into the basement of Palmer's white three-bedroom ranch, and the man of the house stood behind the bar between his workshop and pool table and relived the Open as much as he could bear to relive it.

They tapped a keg of Rolling Rock; Joe Tito, Arnold's friend, was a member of the beer's owning family. The alcohol did little to dull the pain.

"It was supposed to be a victory celebration," said Nancy McCormack, wife of Arnold's manager, Mark. "It was a wake instead."

Palmer slipped away long enough to call Dow Finsterwald, whose father had been buried the day before. Sunday night, after Palmer expressed his condolences one more time, they talked about golf and a lost opportunity Arnold would never get back.

"We knew this SOB was going to be a great player," Finsterwald said of Nicklaus, "but you have accelerated his career three or four years by letting him win this."

"Maybe," Palmer responded. "We'll see about that."

CHAPTER 6

Augusta

T HE MORNING AFTER, Arnold Palmer rose to a front-
page story in the *Pittsburgh Press* written by his
friend Bob Drum under the headline "JACK THE GI-
ANT KILLS OFF ARNIE." The story revisited all the painful details of
how the mighty Arnie had struck out.

"Like Mudville," it opened, "there was no joy in Oakmont yesterday."

Palmer's older daughter, Peg, went to her first-grade class at Baggaley Elementary School and was teased by a classmate over her father's U.S. Open loss. All the Palmers were hurting in a big way. Nobody had considered defeat a likely scenario.

The winner, Jack Nicklaus, would go home to a Columbus parade
attended by several thousand people; he rode with his wife, Barbara,
in the back seat of a red convertible along High Street to the state-
house steps, where he accepted the key to the city. Jack's good friend
and neighbor Pandel Savic, the former Ohio State quarterback, hung a
banner across Nicklaus's Upper Arlington Cape Cod that read "WEL-
COME HOME, 1962 OPEN CHAMP."

Nicklaus would make the cover of *Time* magazine, just like Palmer
two years earlier. "The Prodigious Prodigy," *Time* called Nicklaus.
Halfway through his first season Jack had won $43,198, nearly twice
as much as any other rookie had earned in a full year. With Mark Mc-
Cormack, the rep for Palmer and Nicklaus, mapping out the business

plan, Jack's Open triumph was expected to gross him a quarter-million bucks.

Books. TV shows. Exhibitions. Endorsement deals. Jack was representing Glazer Brothers slacks and Revere Sportswear, and he was contracted to play MacGregor golf clubs in the States and Slazenger clubs overseas. Yes, McCormack wanted to turn Nicklaus into another Palmer.

"I'm sorry to say," Arnold said of Jack, "he'll be around for a long time."

As it turned out, the devastating defeat at Oakmont hadn't crushed the Palmer spirit for good; not even close. A few weeks later Arnold defended his British Open championship at Troon, where he played the best golf he'd ever played on foreign soil. His presence helped draw a star-studded field to the British. He beat that field by half a dozen strokes and, of equal significance, blasted Nicklaus into the Firth of Clyde, trouncing him by twenty-nine shots.

Palmer was back. British writers were falling hard for this dashing American with his shirttail flapping about, writing up Arnold the way Grantland Rice once wrote up zigzagging football heroes on Saturday afternoons in the fall.

They loved how Arnold savored every puff of his cigarettes, loved how he elevated the prestige of the Open, loved how he changed the thinking of American players who had never before crossed the Atlantic, loved how he slashed out of a bush at Birkdale in 1961 — against the advice of his caddie, Tip Anderson — and sent the bush and the ball flying en route to victory.

The message in the British papers was the same as the message forever relayed through the American media: this guy was everything you wanted to be.

So fans in the United Kingdom adored Palmer as much as the Augusta crowds did, and they weren't yet sure what to make of Nicklaus, who managed to score a ten on the eleventh hole while flaming out at the 1962 Open. Arnold had reestablished his reign at Troon and had restored the pre-Oakmont pecking order to his relationship with Jack.

The hard feelings lingering from the heated U.S. Open playoff slowly dissolved as Palmer evened the score, and Arnold and Jack and their wives flew together from Troon to the States and played bridge all the way back.

"We did that a lot," Nicklaus said.

But golf and business kept getting in the way, pulling Arnold and Jack apart just when they would move to the fringe of a close friendship. Palmer gave his papal blessing to Nicklaus when Jack asked if he'd let McCormack represent him, and that favor wasn't doing their relationship any favors.

McCormack was a nervous, nail-biting wreck on the golf course when his clients squared off. He would try to mask his rooting interests, though it was assumed he was a Palmer guy first and foremost. After all, Arnold was the one who allowed McCormack to branch out and sign other golfers.

Palmer was in a Baton Rouge motel, rooming with Dow Finsterwald, when the call came in from McCormack, who was on the line asking Arnold if he could take on a young South African named Gary Player.

That phone call, Finsterwald said, "was the start of IMG."

The International Management Group. Once Palmer agreed on Player, he unwittingly opened the door to a new McCormack stable. Nicklaus was the next thoroughbred in line. By the time Palmer and Nicklaus reached the 1963 Masters, "it was a nightmare," said McCormack's wife, Nancy, "because Arnold was very jealous of Mark's attention to Jack."

The McCormacks had dined with the Nicklauses the night before the Oakmont playoff. "Arnold didn't like that at all," Nancy said. The agent was performing a most delicate dance. The year before, after Palmer's collapse at the 1961 Masters, the McCormacks joined a celebration at the Players' home.

"We were so obviously in Palmer's camp," Nancy said, "and then to go over to the Player house and fawn over them, I just felt so hypocritical. I felt terrible."

Arnold wasn't so bothered by the attention McCormack paid to the South African. "[Arnold] and Gary got along," Nancy said, "but Jack was too much of a threat."

So Palmer and Nicklaus weren't playing bridge during Masters week, 1963, when Palmer prepared for the tournament as — what else? — the favorite. He was coming off a Player of the Year season that had earned him more than $81,000, and he'd already won three times on the 1963 circuit.

Palmer was making upwards of $400,000 off the course, as McCormack had him involved in more than fifteen companies and had him endorsing everything from Heinz ketchup to Sunstate slacks to Swing after-shave.

"That Arnold Palmer magnetism!" screamed one Swing ad. "Try Arnie's idea of a real man's after-shave."

He was pictured in the ad blasting out of a bunker in one scene and gazing skyward in another while a smiling woman shot him an approving look.

The camera loved Arnold, and Arnold loved it right back.

"We're all a little jealous of him," said Chi Chi Rodriguez, the Puerto Rican just getting his start at the Masters. "But golf without Arnie would be like *Gunsmoke* without Matt Dillon. There's no *Gunsmoke* without Matt Dillon."

Nobody was calling Nicklaus Matt Dillon, or John Wayne, or Errol Flynn, or Elvis Presley, or any other prominent American character or entertainer who had presence, charisma, and/or sex appeal. Those comparisons were the exclusive property of Palmer.

"Arnold was the King, and Jack was the prince who was more like the ugly duckling," said Frank Chirkinian, the CBS producer of Masters telecasts. "Jack was the baby blimp with big, fat pleated trousers that made him look even bigger. He was no matinee idol."

He had no desire to be one. While Palmer busied himself acknowledging the fans, especially the comely blonds and brunettes and redheads among them, Nicklaus was in a world of his own. He would have been just as happy dueling Palmer and the rest on a deserted island.

Jack's approach was so sterile, he might as well have been playing in a white lab coat. Arnie? He was best suited for a bullfighter's montera and cape, and in the eyes of his fans, Nicklaus had committed the mortal sin of goring him at Oakmont.

"When Jack beat Arnold," Ken Venturi said, "he beat everyone's hero ... He beat Popeye. You can't beat our hero like that."

Nicklaus had his Open title, and by April of 1963 he'd grown less patient waiting for his first Masters title than President Kennedy was waiting for the Soviets to leave Cuba.

Nicklaus wasn't even three months removed from his twenty-third birthday, and already he felt a triumph at Augusta National was long overdue. Jack was a major winner who had claimed a $50,000 first prize the previous September in a World Series of Golf match against

Palmer and Player, his fellow members of what was commonly called the "Big Three."

But the Masters had quickly evolved into the crown jewel of golf's Grand Slam, and Nicklaus's best finish in four previous trips was a tie for seventh in 1961. Despite Palmer's three Masters titles and six Grand Slam crowns, Nicklaus already believed he was the better player. He resented the fact that nobody outside the state of Ohio seemed to share that opinion at the start of the 1963 Masters.

Thursday, April 4, was a sunny, windblown day at Augusta National, which had the look of the last plantation in the South. The men who lugged the bags and opened the doors and served the drinks and lighted the cigars were black. The players, officials, and newsmen were as white as the greenside sand.

Only the day before, the Reverend Martin Luther King Jr. had started a series of sit-in demonstrations in Birmingham restaurants and public facilities, leading to the arrest of King and hundreds of protesters and inspiring demonstrations across the South. But inside the gates of Augusta National, with President Kennedy on the verge of submitting his civil rights bill to Congress, George Wallace might as well have been acting chairman. Old-world order would not be disturbed.

Reporters, fans, and players wanted to talk only about white men hitting a white ball and, specifically, the most talented of those white men, Arnold Palmer and Jack Nicklaus.

Controversy? The only voices of dissent were heard on the subject of Palmer, Nicklaus, and the three-time major winner and reigning PGA champ, Player, the Big Three. Some veterans in the field were weary of all the talk that the 1963 Masters winner was sure to come out of McCormack's high-profile, highly compensated client base.

"It's ridiculous," said Jimmy Demaret. "You would think only three men were playing. In a tournament of this caliber, there are thirty men who could do it."

"The Big Three? Strictly a publicity gimmick," raged Tommy Bolt. "It should be the Big Thirty or the Big Forty."

The first round came and went, and the hot sun and the baked greens and the thirty-five-mile-per-hour gusts made temporary sages out of Demaret and Bolt. Palmer and Nicklaus each shot 74 on the par-72, 6,980-yard course, and they were five shots off the pace set by Mike Souchak and Bo Wininger, who came out of the same Oklahoma high school that would produce Mickey Mantle. Player was the lone member of golf's closed superstar society to stay near the lead, shooting a 71.

"Where are your Big Three now?" Demaret sniffed as the opening round closed.

Nicklaus had been struggling with a case of bursitis in his hip. Palmer had been struggling with his nicotine addiction; some 524 billion cigarettes would be smoked in the United States in 1963, and Arnie was as visible and prolific a smoker as any public figure. He started feeling guilty about that as more and more evidence linked cigarettes to health problems, and as more and more concerned citizens wrote him to request that he stop setting such a bad example for their kids.

Palmer had won in Los Angeles, Phoenix, and Pensacola despite his fight against his nicotine cravings, and he entered Augusta National determined to play seventy-two holes without lighting up a single cigarette, much to the dismay of the L&M executives who had signed him to an endorsement deal.

Arnold couldn't settle into the tournament, not without a smoke to relax him on those tricky six-foot putts. Nicklaus? He'd quit his on-course smoking after watching a USGA highlight film of his victory at Oakmont, a film that showed him throwing down and picking up a smoldering cigarette before and after a putt. Nicklaus thought it looked bad, real bad. He weathered the nicotine urge as easily as he'd weather a Palmer-pumped crowd and limited his smoking to private social settings.

Jack shot a 66 in the second round—the first time he'd broken 70 at Augusta—while Arnold came in with a 73. Palmer was seven shots behind Nicklaus and eight shots off Souchak's lead. After winning in 1958, 1960, and 1962, Palmer appeared ready to lose yet another odd-year Masters. He appeared ready to lose it not to Art Wall Jr. or to Player, or even to Souchak, who didn't know how to close out a major.

For the first time Palmer was preparing to lose his hold on Augusta to the last golfer on earth he wanted to see in a green jacket.

In Saturday's pouring third-round rain, Nicklaus splish-splashed his way to a one-stroke lead and a score of 74 on a day when 74 felt like 67. Some twenty-five thousand fans had decided a good soaking was worth the price of a possible Arnie charge out of the Cherry Hills playbook, but Palmer landed six strokes back of Nicklaus, who was too strong for his playing partner, Souchak.

They were on the thirteenth hole when Souchak completely lost it.

The former Duke football player had smacked a flawless drive into the belly of the par five and had an easy midiron to the green if only he could find a piece of the fairway that wasn't covered with not-so-casual water.

"Why don't we call it off?" Souchak complained to an official. "The fairways and greens are under water; the course is unplayable."

"No, you've got to continue," the official responded. "Mr. Roberts says, 'Play on.'"

Clifford Roberts, co-lord of the Masters. Bobby Jones's more anal and less forgiving half.

"Hell, I'm not going to play," Souchak said after Nicklaus had already placed his ball short of the creek on his second shot. "Here's my ball. Find me a place to play."

This went on for a while until Souchak finally played it safe himself on his way to a closing 40 and a place four strokes behind Nicklaus's lead. Jack had watched Souchak unravel in the rain and made one of his countless mental notes.

"That's when you play a round," said Nicklaus, who would finish with eleven consecutive pars. "I just kept plodding through the mud."

Whenever Nicklaus heard a competitor complain about the weather or course conditions, he instantly dismissed him as a legitimate threat to win the tournament. At the time Nicklaus was deep into his routine of charting every square foot of every hole of every course, this a habit he picked up from Gene Andrews, whom he defeated in the semis of his first U.S. Amateur championship. Nicklaus kept his yardage notes on an index card in his back pocket, and that card was all but ruined during this Masters deluge.

Nicklaus didn't flinch. "You can't complain when you're leading the tournament and the conditions were the same for everybody out there," he said.

As he approached the eighteenth green, Nicklaus peered at the scoreboard and saw nothing but an indecipherable maze. The number two was next to Nicklaus's name, and Jack knew he was two under par. But the ones on the board?

Nicklaus was partially colorblind. He didn't know if those ones were red (under par) or green (over par).

"How many numbers up there are red?" Nicklaus asked his caddie, Willie Peterson.

"Just you, boss," came the reply.

Nicklaus had a three-shot lead that would be cut by two at the completion of fifty-four holes. He wanted this one in a big way because the Masters was Bobby Jones's tournament and Augusta National was Arnold Palmer's house.

On Sunday, April 7, Palmer rose to an unlikely proposition. He wasn't driving the ball worth a damn, and his short game wasn't exactly covering the tab. "I'm the worst wedge player in the world," he whined.

Arnie's Army did its damnedest to get him back in the tournament; a fan on the tenth hole picked up Palmer's wayward drive and threw it back into the fairway. Arnie retrieved the ball, returned it to its rightful place, and proceeded to make bogey.

The "Go Arnie" sign posted in black letters on the scoreboard at eleven didn't reverse the trend; Palmer's third bid to become the Masters' first back-to-back winner died a slow and painful death.

Arnie's stranded fans needed to latch on to an alternate contender, so they offered their broken hearts to Sam Snead. Slammin' Sammy, winner of seven majors and owner of the sweetest swing in golf, was coming up on his fifty-first birthday and, for a time, had emerged from a pack that included Player, Julius Boros, and Tony Lema to pass Nicklaus and take the back-nine lead.

Nicklaus was jeered at the twelfth tee by a packed Amen Corner crowd that was saving its prayers for Slammin' Sammy and lighting candles to the possibility that Fat Jack's tee shot would plunge into Rae's Creek. But Nicklaus only hit into the bunker on the treacherous 155-yard hole and made a critical eight-foot bogey putt to stay two behind Snead.

At twenty-three Nicklaus was trying to become the youngest Masters winner by beating a man more than twice his age. Snead wanted to take out Nicklaus almost as much as Palmer did; Jack had shown up fashionably late to the first tee during an exhibition match the previous fall, and Snead was itching for payback.

He didn't get it. Competing in only his third event of the 1963 season, Snead made bogeys at numbers sixteen and eighteen and then jerked his right arm in disgust as he trudged off his seventy-second green under his straw hat.

Nicklaus regained the lead by nailing a twelve-footer at number sixteen, a birdie he punctuated by swinging his putter through the air in two-fisted, uppercut form. After Lema birdied the eighteenth to get into the clubhouse at one under, Nicklaus needed only a safe par on his seventy-second hole to win the Masters.

His hip wasn't bothering him anymore. After his drive at eighteen landed in the muddy rough to the left, Nicklaus was permitted to move his ball to a dry edge of the fairway, where a six-iron shot stopped thirty-five feet from the cup.

His heart pounding, his thoughts racing ahead to the moment when Jones would meet him in the winner's circle, Nicklaus ran his first putt three and a half feet by the hole. He wasn't taking any chances on the follow-up, ramming it home as Peterson, wearing number forty-seven on his official white Augusta National overalls, lifted his left arm in the air.

"Those three feet looked like eighty-six to me," Nicklaus would say. "I just hit it, closed my eyes, and waited for the sound."

As Nicklaus bent over the hole to fetch the winning ball, his thoughts quickly returned to Oakmont. He'd barely cracked a smile when he finished off Palmer in the playoff, and people couldn't believe how stoic he appeared in the face of a monumental triumph.

So Jack Nicklaus, the charisma-free champ, the anti-Arnie, was going to let down his buzz-cut hair. He grabbed his white cap and fired it into the air before his father, Charlie, wrapped one of his big-bear arms around his boy's shoulders.

"I just knew that Snead was the guy," Nicklaus said, "and then all of a sudden Snead wasn't the guy."

Jack was the guy who held the U.S. Open and Masters titles. Nicklaus was almost two full years younger than the previous youngest winner at Augusta, Byron Nelson in 1937.

During the presentation ceremony Nicklaus handed his ball to Jones, who was growing more infirm by the hour. Palmer did his defending champion's duty and slid the 44-regular green jacket over Nicklaus's shoulders.

"Just think," Arnold said. "He has ten years more to go before he's as old as I am today."

For Arnold Palmer, losing the 1963 Masters made the wait for the next one feel as long as the Mississippi. It was one thing to fall to Art Wall Jr. and Gary Player, quite another to do his Augusta National bleeding on Jack Nicklaus's sword.

Nobody was talking about young Jack's future anymore; his future had arrived. Palmer's prime was suddenly Nicklaus's prime, too, a truth Arnie appreciated about as much as a plugged lie in a bunker.

The game looked and felt a whole lot easier to Palmer when he had to beat Dow Finsterwald, Bob Rosburg, and Mike Souchak. Nicklaus was an entirely different obstacle. To Arnie, Jack was 215 pounds of endgame trouble.

Palmer would say his sluggish 1963 Masters was the result of wearing himself out in too many practice rounds, and he promised not to repeat the mistake. But even though he believed he could extend his good even-numbered fortune, Palmer wasn't the favorite to claim Augusta in 1964.

"The Pack vs. Jack in Today's Masters," read the headline in the *Augusta Chronicle* on the tournament's opening day.

Arnold had been reduced to another face in the pack trailing Jack Nicklaus, and no son of Deke Palmer's was going to stand for that.

The 1964 Masters was the perfect place for Palmer to repel Nicklaus's coup, to end his own slump, and to prove to the doubters he hadn't become a wildly successful entrepreneur at the expense of winning Grand Slam events.

After several unsuccessful attempts by Mark McCormack to end his relationship with Wilson, the sporting goods firm, Palmer was finally free from a contract his rep found all too confining and cheap. He was selling his own clubs and gear. He was marketing his own line of shirts while still endorsing Munsingwear's. He was starting his own miniature golf company and doing ads for L&M smokes. He was calling press conferences to announce his involvement in laundry, dry cleaning, and maid services companies.

The laundry idea was hatched by Sidney Wood, the 1931 Wimbledon champ who figured Palmer's perceived trustworthiness would make him an ideal business partner. Wood sold McCormack on the notion that customers send their clothes only to people they can rely on, and that Palmer was seen by the public as a most reliable man.

Arnold and Wood made their announcement at New York's Town Tennis Club, where Palmer threw an apron over his jacket and tie and posed for photographers in the club's kitchen to set the mood. Palmer estimated that he was involved with twenty-seven corporations, but that the laundry and maid service companies represented "my first investment completely unrelated to golf."

Even before dozens of Palmer dry cleaning centers popped up around the country, Arnold's off-course income was said to have pushed his annual gross up near half a million bucks.

Arnie was hardly the first sportsman to earn money pushing a product. Babe Ruth endorsed Puffed Wheat cereal, Wheaties, Red Rock Cola, Old Gold cigarettes, and Babe Ruth All-American Athletic Underwear, among many other items. Ty Cobb hawked suspenders and cigars.

Long before either baseball great took the field, Harry Vardon, who would win six British Open championships, embarked on an exhibition tour of the United States and Canada in 1900 for the Spalding sporting goods company and did a print ad for a muscle rub called Bell-capsic Plasters.

A parade of prominent golfers followed Vardon's lead. Francis Ouimet endorsed shirts. Walter Hagen pushed Lucky Strike smokes, locker room slippers, and soap. Bobby Jones endorsed Listerine Shaving Cream and Coca-Cola. Gene Sarazen did ads for Pabst Blue Ribbon beer and Bromo-Seltzer. Ben Hogan sold Camel cigarettes, Vitalis hair formula, and Timex watches.

Advertisers recognized the marketing value of golf's self-policing mores. Players called penalties on themselves in this sport, and that honor code bestowed a sense of nobility on golfers that made them valuable product spokesmen.

So with Palmer agreeing to void all vows of exclusivity, McCormack signed up as many name golfers as he could. To Player and Nicklaus he added Doug Sanders and Bob Charles.

"For golfers like Arnie and Jack and Gary and Doug," McCormack said, "this golf explosion we're undergoing in America is leading them to one gold mine after another. It's absolutely incredible the money they can make. And, by gosh, I'm going to see that they make it because they sure deserve it."

None of McCormack's athletes pieced together an endorsement and merchandising empire as vast as Palmer's. Arnold exuded integrity and trust. The poor man could relate to his Depression-era struggle, and the rich man could relate to his successful quest for a more prosperous life. Therefore, Palmer could sell high-end products to the wealthy and ketchup to the masses.

Arnie's marketability made him the number-one get for eager promoters. McCormack had tournament directors approach him and say,

"You bring Arnold Palmer here, and we'll pay him in cash and slip you a little something under the table. And we'll also throw in a blond."

No cash and no blonds, the agent would respond. "We don't work that way," McCormack said.

On an honest platform he built Palmer into the ultimate brand name. Only Arnie's Army was concerned that the agent was wearing down Palmer, channeling his energy away from the fairways and greens and toward Madison Avenue.

When Palmer fans weren't sweating that, they were worried his on-course slump was the result of his decision to stop smoking. The surgeon general had come out with a report linking cigarettes to cancer and chronic bronchitis, and Palmer had fully committed himself to no more nicotine fixes. Some fans encouraged him to give in to temptation and light up as many L&Ms as he needed to shoot 66.

"When a cigarette means a lot . . . ," read the print ad that featured Palmer pulling a club out of his bag while a burning L&M dangled from his lips.

The fans didn't want an old Arnie; they wanted the old Arnie back.

At the 1964 Masters Palmer was ten pounds too heavy, nicotine-free, and desperate to end a losing streak that had stretched across six months. He was only thirty-four years old, and even the lionhearted lieutenants in Arnie's Army were worried he was all washed up.

It didn't much matter that Palmer had finished 1963 as the first man to clear $100,000 in official earnings in a single season (he won $128,230 to Nicklaus's $100,040), or that he'd won seven events to Nicklaus's five in that season, or that he'd beaten Nicklaus in a Western Open playoff, or that he'd captained the Ryder Cup team to a resounding victory over the Brits.

Palmer hadn't made a single Grand Slam event his in 1963. He had lost another U.S. Open playoff, this one claimed by Julius Boros. He hadn't contended at the British Open—a tournament he saw Nicklaus throw away with bogeys on the final two holes—and he'd watched with other noncontenders from the PGA Championship locker room as Nicklaus and Dave Ragan battled for the victory in Dallas temperatures north of one hundred degrees.

"If Ragan thinks he can beat Jack, he's full of shit," Palmer told the players around him that day. "Jack will grind in these four- and five-footers every time."

Jack proved Arnie right, and Dallas hosted its last celebration in the national spotlight before America was changed forever on its watch.

Palmer, the Republican son of a Democrat father, was among President Kennedy's favorite celebrities; truth was, they shared much in common. Looks. Charisma. Bedroom eyes that made women weak at the knees. Like Kennedy, Palmer was very much a product of television.

Like Dick Nixon, Nicklaus wasn't going to win any popular vote with his appearance on TV.

So as the masses kept gravitating toward Palmer, Nicklaus kept making little effort to steal away their hearts. At the 1963 World Series of Golf in Akron, the thirty-six-hole TV event designed to include the season's four major champions, Palmer was invited to join Nicklaus, Boros, and British Open champ Bob Charles (Nicklaus had gobbled up two playing slots with his Masters and PGA titles) by organizers who knew he'd sell a few tickets.

Nicklaus wouldn't let this development go without a comment made only half in jest. He stopped a pre-tournament news conference by saying, "Arnie shouldn't be here. After all, he was an also-ran," before kicking Palmer's chair for emphasis.

"JACK LABELS ARNIE AN ALSO-RAN," read the next day's headline in the *Akron Beacon Journal,* and the national wires picked up the story. Nicklaus took some abuse from Palmer fans, then won the event to spite them.

And that's what Arnie's Army detested the most. At Oakmont, at Augusta, at Akron—Nicklaus proved to be a winning machine that never wavered in the face of human insult.

Somehow, some way, Palmer needed to put Nicklaus down. He had partnered with Jack in the U.S. victory at the Canada Cup in France and in the *Big Three Golf* TV show that would also star Gary Player and send the three McCormack clients off on a ten-episode series of matches. But with the Nicklaus threat becoming more ominous by the round, Palmer was on a singular mission at Augusta.

He needed his fourth green jacket more now than he needed his first one then.

He took a share of the lead in round one, Palmer did, hitting seventeen greens in regulation and firing a 69 to gain a two-stroke edge on Nicklaus. The next morning Palmer showed with a visor meant to protect him from a warm Georgia sun. He had a skin infection on his face, and he'd tried a Hogan cap in the practice rounds, and then a baseball cap in the opening round. "It made him look balloon-headed," his wife, Winnie, complained.

Palmer stuck with the visor. He went out with Chi Chi Rodriguez, all 118 pounds of him, a self-celebrating showman who made Arnie look like a wallflower. Rodriguez's fans — "Chi Chi's Bandidos" their buttons said — made their presence felt in the company of the button-wearing regulars inside Arnie's Army, and Chi Chi waved his straw hat and danced his jigs and did whatever he could to fire them up.

Rodriguez claimed to have given Palmer his nickname, "the King." On this day it didn't matter. Palmer, who thrived on his own connection with high-energy crowds, was getting fed up with Chi Chi. When Rodriguez put his hat over the hole, he'd had enough.

"You shouldn't do that," Palmer told him.

"I wasn't doing it on purpose," Rodriguez would explain. "I didn't know I was bothering him. He shot 68, so he was bothered pretty good."

Palmer shot 68 after a plane flew overhead with a thirty-five-foot banner tethered to its tail that said, "Go Arnie Go." The extra weight Arnold had put on after he quit smoking — the result of his nonstop nibbling — wasn't slowing him down. Palmer was thirty-six holes closer to becoming the first four-time winner Augusta had seen. He had a four-shot lead over Player and a seven-shot advantage over Nicklaus, who was getting roughed up by the Augusta gallery.

Playing with Bob Goalby, Nicklaus heard the jeers pick up on the back nine.

"Jack, goddamn," Goalby said to him. "I don't know how you can take that. I'm ten years older than you and I couldn't take it."

Nicklaus stopped and looked Goalby in the eye.

"Bob," he said, "someday I'm going to have those fans with me."

Only this much was certain: those fans wouldn't be with Nicklaus as he attempted to pitch and putt his way back into the tournament.

For Saturday's third round, customers were turned back at the gates. Clifford Roberts had already cracked down on crowd behavior, which was growing rowdier with every Palmer birdie; he drew up a code of patron conduct — Roberts decreed that fans were patrons, not fans, at the Masters — to be enforced by his police-state henchmen. He also decided to start limiting the crowd. Roberts figured that once ten thousand cars had crammed into Augusta's parking lots it was time to close up shop.

Some forty thousand ticket holders made it through before the 1:00 p.m. lockdown, and they came for the aesthetic pleasures Augusta offered every spring: The pines, dogwoods, and azaleas. The greenest grass and whitest sand. Everything that made this indigo plantation turned tree nursery turned golf course into the cathedral Roberts and Bobby Jones imagined when they bought the property for $70,000 in 1931.

The fans came for Magnolia Lane, graced by sixty-one magnolia trees, and for the giant clubhouse oak, all planted before the Civil War. They came for the sixty-five-foot Eisenhower Tree on the seventeenth hole.

But above all else the fans came to see Eisenhower's friend Palmer reclaim his rightful place at the Masters. And Arnold didn't disappoint. Surging with confidence, his wintertime slump a million miles removed from his thoughts, Palmer kept shooting at the pins and dropping putts.

He signed for a 69, his third consecutive sub-70 round, and stood at ten-under 206, five strokes ahead of Australian Bruce Devlin and a whopping nine strokes ahead of Nicklaus. Palmer was gunning for history. He was shooting for the record Masters score of fourteen-under 274, set in 1953 by Ben Hogan, who had emerged from the crypt on this very day, April 11, 1964, to shoot a 67 at age fifty-one.

Hogan's little walk down memory lane left him in a tie with Nicklaus at one-under 215, which meant he made for an interesting sidebar, nothing more. Nicklaus? He needed to play his best golf to get within range of Arnie during Sunday's final, and after what had transpired at the twelfth tee during the third round, that seemed about as likely as Palmer joining Hogan for a few Saturday night beers.

Roberts and Jones had rumbled out to Amen Corner in their buggy to watch Nicklaus hit his eight-iron to the par-three green. Instead they saw Jack's tee ball whistle over their heads; Nicklaus had delivered quite possibly the worst shot of his career, a shank to the right that would've made a twenty-four handicapper proud.

All these years later and Nicklaus still couldn't play worth a damn while Jones was watching him. His own decapitation averted, Jones decided this near miss was a good reason to spend less time on the course.

Jones was closer to Jack than he was to Arnie, but he understood what Palmer meant to the Masters. Arnie was in his element at Augusta.

He was family. Palmer had this amazing talent of making everyone in the gallery feel as if he or she was the only patron on the grounds.

Arnie's Army kept swelling, and one rank-and-file member was a TV ad salesman named Bert Harbin, who rented his Augusta home to Palmer. Knowing that no golfer had ever owned or repaired more golf clubs than Palmer, and knowing that his houseguest loved reshafting, regripping, and refinishing perfectly functional irons and woods, Harbin installed a workbench and a vise in his garage to make him feel at home.

On the morning of the final round of the 1964 Masters, with Palmer in command of the tournament, Harbin found him blowing off some steam in that garage. Arnold was sawing down some clubs, working out his nerves, when the subject turned to the only golfer in creation who could be nine shots back with eighteen holes to play and still pose a credible threat.

"When that big fat boy comes around in as many Sunday finals as I've been in," Palmer said of Nicklaus, "he's going to have to shit so much he'll lose all that weight."

As it turned out, Palmer was the one shitting in his pants with six holes to play: Nicklaus had closed his deficit from nine strokes to four. Playing with Johnny Pott in the group ahead of Palmer and Dave Marr, Jack was making an Arnie-like charge without the benefit of any Arnie's Army support.

Marr's own charge fizzled when he found the water at number twelve. Up ahead Nicklaus was unleashing a series of booming, nothing-to-lose drives. He eagled the par-five thirteenth with the help of a five-iron and then birdied the 520-yard fifteenth. If Palmer wanted to make Masters history, Nicklaus was going to make him sweat for it.

"Whatever Arnie wants, Jack gets," *Time* magazine had written.

Only Arnie wasn't letting Jack get this one. Dressed in black, normally Player's color of choice, Nicklaus had a twelve-footer at sixteen that would've put serious pressure on Palmer. He missed it by an inch or two to the left and then dropped to his knees in surrender.

As Nicklaus was putting the finishing touches on a 67, Palmer was making birdies at numbers fourteen and fifteen and leaving Hogan's Augusta standard as his only legitimate competition.

Palmer couldn't catch Hogan's ghost. He missed a birdie putt at sixteen, hit a tree on his way to a bogey at seventeen, and that was that. On the eighteenth tee, with the tournament tucked like a glove in his back pocket, Palmer asked Marr if he could do anything to help him.

"Yeah," Marr cracked. "Make a twelve."

Palmer got a kick out of that. He was in the best of moods even though Hogan was staying in the record books. On his stroll to the eighteenth green, with his army trailing him, Palmer basked in the glow of an unlikely rout.

He was tired of all those photo finishes. "I wanted to win the Masters comfortably," he said. "I just wanted to see what it was like to walk up the eighteenth hole with a feeling of satisfaction, and I did it."

Palmer's visor was off when he made it to the final green. He wanted his people to see his world-famous face, the one forever stretched into pained winces on wayward putts. His was a mask of contentment and joy this time. Nicklaus was beaten. Augusta was his.

At 5:26 p.m. Palmer nailed a sidehill twenty-footer and swung his putter with both hands across his body and over his left shoulder, his final-round 70 and twelve-under 276 total good enough even for Hogan.

"You have to consider Arnold Palmer one of the great players," conceded the Wee Ice Mon.

Hogan actually uttered Palmer's name, if not directly to his face. Arnold had won the $20,000 first-place prize and had become the first pro in golf history to clear the $500,000 career earnings mark, because he had one three-putt green the entire tournament.

Nicklaus tied Marr for second, six shots off the winning number. Jack slid the green jacket over Arnie's shoulders, just as Arnie had slid the green jacket over Jack's the year before. Palmer looked over his right shoulder and smiled at Nicklaus, who graciously reached in to shake the winner's hand.

Palmer was on his plane at 9:00 a.m. the next morning, headed back to Latrobe. He was most pleased with himself that he'd finally turned back Nicklaus and that he'd won the Masters without a competitor or two giving him some late back-nine help.

"This one I won," Palmer said. "I won it all by myself."

Arnie had seven Grand Slam titles to his name. He departed Augusta believing he had at least another seven left in his bag.

CHAPTER 7

• Back to Back

JACK NICKLAUS was in the car with his good friend Ivor Young when he made a confession he would have never made for public consumption.

"I'm getting a little tired of wearing the black hat," Jack said.

On just another ride to make just another tee time in just another tournament, Young was surprised Nicklaus was willing to confirm a cold, hard fact about the human condition: everyone likes to be liked, even golf champions who swear they ignore the vile intentions of jeering fans.

For the record, Nicklaus had generally refused to acknowledge that he heard the insults from Arnold Palmer's loyalists, never mind that those insults cut him to the bone.

But when he arrived for the 1965 Masters, Nicklaus yearned for even a fraction of the unconditional love and affection sent Palmer's way. "It had to be puzzling to Jack that he wasn't getting it," Young said. "I mean, 'Why are they picking on me?'"

If Nicklaus were threatening to dethrone Ben Hogan, a grim figure and Garbo-like conversationalist, he wouldn't have been resented any more than the next challenger. Only Nicklaus wasn't threatening to dethrone Hogan. He was trying to tear down the most popular player of all time.

When Nicklaus was paired with Palmer for the final round of the

1964 PGA Championship, right in Jack's Columbus backyard, the fans didn't go after Arnold in an attempt to even an old Oakmont score. In fact, Nicklaus said, "I'd be concerned over how they treated *me.*"

Bobby Nichols won the event, and Nicklaus and Palmer shared second. Arnold became the first man to shoot four rounds in the 60s and still fail to win the PGA, and he established himself as the only player in golf who could steal half the paying customers away from a prominent hometown boy.

"The crowd was fifty-fifty," said Mason Rudolph, who played with Nicklaus and Palmer that day, "or even a little toward Arnold. It was like a football game, like Ohio State–Michigan."

Except that Wolverines fans would never outnumber Buckeyes fans in the heart of Columbus. But that's what Nicklaus was confronting, an opponent who never had to suffer the indignities showered upon the visiting team. "It doesn't make any difference where it is," Jack said of Arnold's chokehold on the fans.

This truth was starting to wear on Nicklaus. That was most evident at Augusta National, always guaranteed to offer Palmer the same reception he'd get if he were playing in the Latrobe Country Club championship.

"Jack felt he was the better player," said Frank Chirkinian, producer of CBS's Masters telecasts, "and everybody was tripping and falling over Arnold's presence . . . If you're human, that has to bother you, and it did bother Jack."

So did fresh suggestions that he was short-changing his golf game as his outside interests expanded, the same suggestions that had long dogged Palmer. Yes, Mark McCormack was in the business of making his clients a lot of money, and business was good.

McCormack was an agent of dramatic change in the endorsement world. In the past athletes accepted almost any condition and restraint written into contracts offered by the corporations they represented, as long as the company checks cleared. Modest salaries and purses had athletes scrambling for whatever extra money they could make on the side.

Draconian captains of industry were like the old-school coaches of the day: they told the athletes what they could have and when they could have it. Judge James Cooney of Wilson railed against McCormack's many attempts to renegotiate Palmer's contract with the sporting goods company once it was clear Arnold's standing in the game had outgrown it. Cooney's harsh stance only helped McCormack persuade his lead client that he needed to go into business for himself once the Wilson contract expired.

The result? McCormack would write in his book *Arnie: The Evolution of a Legend* that a consumer didn't have to settle for buying Palmer clubs or wearing the Palmer clothes made in eight countries. "You can buy your insurance from a Palmer agency, stay in a Palmer-owned motel, buy a Palmer lot to build your home on, push a Palmer-approved lawnmower, read a Palmer book, newspaper column or pamphlet, be catered to by a Palmer maid, listen to Palmer music and send your suit to a Palmer dry cleaner. You can shave with his lather, spray on his deodorant, drink his favorite soft drink, fly his preferred airline, buy his approved corporate jet, eat his candy bar, order your stock certificates through him and cut up with his power tools."

With TV coverage of sports in a major growth spurt, and with advertisers pouring more and more dollars into the games people play, McCormack had helped flip the athlete-corporation dynamic, tugging the power away from the Judge Cooneys and putting it in the athletes' hands. Companies would bid against each other to sign champion golfers whose heroic on-course images were beamed into tens of millions of American households, and the price of star power kept going up.

These were prosperous times for the country, and Palmer — golf's first TV superstar — was a symbol of that prosperity. The greenskeeper's son was raking in an estimated $800,000 annually in investments, endorsements, appearances, and other ventures.

Nicklaus was no Palmer in the endorsement world; nobody was, of course. But Jack had come a long way from his first paid appearance as a pro in December of 1961, a seventy-five-dollar speech in Columbus for the White-Haines Optical Company. He'd come a long way from his first paid exhibition at the end of that month, when he appeared with Palmer, Gary Player, and Sam Snead in Miami and pulled his very first tee shot into the water. "That's a pretty good start as a professional," Nicklaus joked.

Jack would hit it straight enough from there to make himself a wealthy young man. He'd won three major championships in his first two seasons, and off the course his staggering success rate compensated for his lack of charisma.

Nicklaus was hardly the most likable figure around, but he was an undeniable winner, and corporate America liked to associate with undeniable winners. McCormack was able to sell Nicklaus's greatest asset: his talent. Mostly through exhibitions, endorsements, and Big Three TV matches, McCormack was helping Nicklaus bring in half a million bucks a year.

Jack made it a little tougher on the agent than Arnie did. "Arnold was always very prompt and courteous," said McCormack's wife, Nancy, "and Jack used to keep all the CEOs waiting on corporate jets to take him somewhere. Jack was a brash young kid."

A brash young kid who benefited greatly from Palmer's presence. The more Arnie inflated the value of doing business with a star golfer, the more McCormack could play off Palmer's contracts while negotiating deals for Jack.

The Arnie-Jack rivalry put money in Nicklaus's pockets, too. Rivalries had always been the lifeblood of sports, and the matching of Palmer's immense appeal with Nicklaus's immense skill was the perfect vehicle to carry golf from the age of black and white into the age of living color.

Opposites attract—interest, ratings, and corporate sponsors. A Nicklaus-Hogan rivalry would've never captured the public's imagination the same way, not with the Wee Ice Mon viewing the gallery as an unnecessary evil. With his own singular focus, his own habit of icing out the fans, Jack didn't need a rival who was forever auditioning for a role in a silent film. He needed a high-volume action hero in his twosome, and Palmer was all of that.

More than anything Nicklaus needed to keep winning. That's what he brought to the corporate table: the all-American ability to finish first.

Entering the 1965 Masters, Nicklaus was winless for the season, and Palmer—forever dying for a cigarette—hadn't seized a tournament in eleven months. "Masters Provides Key Test for Fading Palmer, Nicklaus," read the headline in the *Washington Post*.

Nicklaus failed to win a major in 1964, and Palmer lost another Grand Slam bid two months later at the U.S. Open, where a familiar foe, Ken Venturi, did a death march to the title in the oppressive heat that gripped the Congressional Country Club in Bethesda, Maryland.

Fittingly, the most intense Palmer-Nicklaus duel between the 1964 and 1965 Masters came in a tournament neither man won. The Cajun Classic in Lafayette, Louisiana, the final event of the 1964 season, decided whether Palmer or Nicklaus would claim the money title; Arnold entered with $111,703 in winnings, Jack with $111,384.

The duel had this backwater event jumping one year after the tournament shut down for a day in the wake of the Kennedy assassination. Nicklaus was in the ninth fairway in 1963 when he got word that the president had been shot, a bulletin leaving an eerie silence to sweep across the course like a midnight fog.

The 1963 Cajun Classic ended on a thirty-six-hole day that nudged Nicklaus past the $100,000 mark, making him the only man not named Arnold Palmer to break the six-figure barrier. The 1964 Cajun was a different kind of money game. It came down to a Gay Brewer eighteen-footer in raw, freezing conditions. If Brewer made the putt, Nicklaus would be pushed down to third place and Palmer, the fourth-place finisher, would win the money title. If Brewer missed, Nicklaus would finish in a tie for second and beat Palmer by a lousy $81.13.

Brewer left his attempt a couple of inches short. "Jack beat me," Arnold said, "and it pissed me off." For once Nicklaus knew people would remember the guy who finished second.

Competitive tensions between the two men weren't eased on their arrival in Hawaii a week later to defend their Canada Cup team championship. Palmer's older sister, Cheech, was living in Hawaii and greeted the golfers at the airport. Cheech had met Nicklaus before, she said, "but certainly I wasn't any friend or admirer."

She placed a lei around Jack's neck as Nicklaus turned to Palmer.

"Who is this now?" he asked.

"This is my sister," Arnold said.

"You have relatives all over the place," Jack responded.

Cheech wasn't amused. "That made me dislike him even more," she said.

In Cheech's eyes, anyway, Arnie shared some of her feelings for Jack. "I don't think he liked him," she said.

But the Palmers and Nicklauses were teammates playing for their country, so all grudges were set aside for the moment. Palmer had a sore thumb and Charlie Nicklaus, Jack's father, was quick to break out some pills from his pharmacy to make the pain go away.

Palmer caught fire and put the Americans out in front, carrying

Nicklaus along the way. The Canada Cup offered an individual title as well (Nicklaus had won it the year before), so with the Americans holding a commanding team lead entering the final round, and with Jack six strokes behind Arnold, Charlie Nicklaus decided there would be no more pills for Palmer's thumb.

Jack shot 70 to come from behind and defeat the player the Associated Press described as "his collapsing teammate," Arnold, who shot 78.

"But the team won," Palmer said. "That's the important thing."

Deep down, neither Palmer nor Nicklaus truly believed that.

At Augusta National, spring of 1965, Palmer was again burning to become the first back-to-back champ of the Masters. He'd destroyed Nicklaus and the field in 1964, only to carry the burden of another slump back to his favorite Grand Slam stop.

On April 8 Gary Player led the first-round attack on Augusta's green monster (the field combined for 252 birdies) with a seven-under 65, taking a two-stroke lead over Nicklaus and a five-shot advantage over Palmer.

The next day, with more than two hundred American warplanes wreaking havoc across North Vietnam, the world was in perfect order inside the Augusta National sanctuary. As the wind conspired with tournament officials looking to tame the scoring through cruel pin placements, Palmer managed a brilliant 68 to join Nicklaus and Player in a tie atop the leaderboard.

The Big Three lorded over the Masters, and the beloved Palmer had the momentum. Arnie's Army had just steamrolled Arnie's rookie playing partner, Raymond Floyd, who followed up his opening-round 69 with an 83 to miss the cut. "Arnold's magnetism and the army; they just blew me out of the ballpark," Floyd said. "I just wasn't prepared for it. To have all that screaming and hollering, the people didn't even know I was there. It was overwhelming."

Saturday morning brought one of the more anticipated weekend rounds in Masters history. Palmer, Nicklaus, and Player all started the day at six-under 138. Nicklaus would tee off with Dan Sikes at 1:01 p.m., Player with Tony Lema at 1:36 p.m., and Palmer with Tommy Aaron at 2:04 p.m.

The son of a Johannesburg gold miner who never made more than one hundred dollars a month, Player had overcome his size with a relentless spirit. He was the Jack LaLanne of South Africa, burning off what little fat he had on his bones through countless pushups and sit-ups. Player was called the "Black Knight," as he dressed accordingly to mimic the cowboys he'd seen wearing black outfits in western films.

Player was fiercely proud of his ability, and he believed he was often overlooked by American fans caught up in the Palmer-Nicklaus rivalry. But he didn't let that feeling stop him from getting closer to Arnie, and closer to Jack, than Arnie and Jack ever got to each other.

Player called Palmer and Nicklaus "different people, vastly different." The South African was the buffer, the peacemaker, the one who helped Palmer and Nicklaus temporarily remove the walls between them.

The Big Three were filming a TV match once in Montreal, sitting around a three-bedroom hotel suite, when they started behaving like the best of schoolboy friends. Palmer was on the phone with his wife, Winnie, and Nicklaus was watching TV. A room service order arrived with big bottles of beer. To break up the boredom, Player removed the cap from one of the bottles, pressed his fingers over the opening, and shook it like mad.

"And then I let Arnold have it," he said. Palmer was covered in cold brew before he could hang up on Winnie, and Nicklaus almost fell over laughing.

"Then Jack grabbed this big chug pot of iced tea," Player said, "and he flung it at me and I ducked and it hit Arnold and went all over the curtain. We made a mess."

Player was chosen to report their food fight to the hotel manager and to make a group offer to pay for the dry cleaning bill. The manager was in a good enough mood to give the Big Three a bigger break.

Palmer, Nicklaus, and Player often traveled together, sometimes with their wives. When Player wasn't around, Arnold and Jack would fly together to exhibitions. Arnie's Army couldn't get between them at twenty-five thousand feet.

But down in the manicured field of Augusta, the army could let loose on Nicklaus. Player realized that Palmer "fell out of bed with cha-risma" yet saw the gallery's past treatment of Nicklaus as "very unfair . . . The public could still love Arnold, but they didn't have to take it out on Jack."

In the end, sticks and stones could break Jack's bones. Player was once walking with Nicklaus on Augusta's third hole, about fifty yards short of the bunker on the left, when Jack decided he'd heard a few too many jeers from Palmer's fans.

"The more they do this to me," Nicklaus told Player, "the more I'm going to beat him."

Off before his fellow leaders in the third round of the 1965 Masters, Nicklaus grabbed Augusta National by the throat and choked it until it fell limp in his hands. His friend Deane Beman had tweaked something in his swing, telling Jack he was aiming to the right and rotating his upper body too quickly in an artificial attempt to keep the ball out of right field.

So on a warm and wind-free afternoon, ideal conditions for scoring, Nicklaus went about converting the Big Three into the Big One. He was well past the hole at number one, barely tapped his ball to get it close to the cup, and immediately realized the greens on this day were just as fast as he liked them.

Nicklaus hit his ball twenty-five yards deep into the woods on the par-five second, blasted a three-iron out of the pine needles, knocked his wedge shot to twelve feet, and made the birdie putt to begin his roll.

He kept landing long, majestic drives into Augusta's velvet fairways, which always played wider than the Atlantic. From under his flop hat, Nicklaus couldn't stop smiling. Fans were actually cheering for him. He kept dropping in birdie putts, and they kept encouraging him to deliver more.

Nicklaus wasn't sure why this sudden shift in sentiment had swung his way; it seemed the gallery couldn't help but celebrate the destruction of a golf course that had never taken such a beating from Hogan, Snead, Nelson, or Palmer.

One of the sportswriters on the scene, a cub reporter out of Baltimore named Ernie Accorsi, was assigned to start with the twenty-five-year-old Nicklaus before jumping over to the thirty-five-year-old Palmer. The future NFL general manager of the Colts, Browns, and Giants, Accorsi was a Pennsylvania boy, a card-carrying member of Arnie's Army, and a graduate of Palmer's Wake Forest.

"When Arnie was winning, he'd march with those forearms out in front," Accorsi said. "He was demonstrative and emotional, with his fist in the air. He brought the game of golf to the real sports fan. At the Masters a birdie cheer for Arnie was totally different than any other cheer. It sounded like the Colts had scored a touchdown."

But Accorsi was too mesmerized by Nicklaus's power and touch to jump over to Palmer's twosome. "I had that sinking feeling that it was all over for Arnie," Accorsi said. "Arnie played on inspiration and confidence and daring, and Nicklaus just took the air right out of his balloon ... Arnie used to out-drive everybody, and here comes Jack with his high fades just blowing it past him. It was a body punch to Arnie, and it wasn't pretty to watch."

Nicklaus's eight-footer for birdie at number sixteen meant he needed only one more bird to break the tournament record of eight-under 64 set by Lloyd Mangrum in 1940. He was smiling, waving, assuming the role of Arnie. If Jack didn't understand this surreal plot twist, he wasn't about to fight it either.

He started his round with an estimated five thousand people in his gallery and ended it with an estimated twenty thousand on his trail. Nicklaus finished with a pair of two-putt pars to tie Mangrum's mark, to set a new fifty-four-hole record of fourteen-under 202, and to make a perfectly fine 69 from Player a moot point. Palmer? His round of 72 seemed like an 82 when matched against Jack's game-changing statement.

On the final hole of a long day in the sun, Palmer watched from the rear as his playing partner, Tommy Aaron, chipped in from forty feet to shoot 71.

"He put his hands on his hips like only Arnold can," Aaron said, "with those huge arms of his, and he locked his eyes on me and glared at me. His look said, 'What the hell are you doing? This is my place, where the army was born.'

"Palmer was a pugnacious tough guy, and he wanted to out-drive everybody and walk right over you. But he couldn't do that to Jack Nicklaus."

Sunday's final round was a walking coronation and a rebuke of the living legend, fifty-two-year-old Sam Snead, who would call Nicklaus "a great pair of golfers." Snead had just won the Greater Greensboro Open for the eighth time to become the oldest man ever to win a tour event. In response to predictions from Byron Nelson and others that Nicklaus was destined to smash every record in sight, Snead was quoted as saying, "Jack has been going full steam since he was fourteen years old. A man can only go to the post so many times under this kind of pressure. He burns himself out, and I don't think Jack will get any better."

The Slammer was a sage in this context: it couldn't get any better for Nicklaus in the towering Georgia pines. At the ninth hole Jack cleared the trees on the left with a drive that amazed his playing partner, Mason Rudolph, and left him with a half wedge to the stick.

The gallery wrapped its forgiving arms around the moment. On the sixteenth hole, after watching the fans stand and applaud for his only son, Charlie Nicklaus turned to his friend Pandel Savic. Jack's father had tears in his eyes.

"He's finally won them over," Charlie told Savic. "Jack's finally won everyone over."

The Masters crowd that once cheered the posting of Nicklaus bogeys on the scoreboards was putty in Jack's hands. "Yay," his wife, Barbara, told herself. "He's a good person. I knew people would find out."

Jack nearly holed out from the fairway on seventeen to move to seventeen under for the tournament. A double bogey on eighteen would still be good enough to do what Palmer had tried and failed to do in 1964: erase Hogan from the record books.

Nicklaus drove through the dogleg on the last hole. The instant he struck his second shot, fans raced across the fairway in front of him as marshals tried in vain to rope them off. Jack removed his flop hat as he approached the green and acknowledged the adoring crowd. He chipped to within two feet of the stick, tipped his hat, and sank his par putt. Nicklaus tugged at the right leg of his dark slacks, retrieved the ball, wheeled toward the fairway, and heaved the ball toward the fans, making like Willie Mays on the back end of his most famous World Series catch. Within six months the practice of throwing the winning golf ball into the gallery would be banned on tour as a potential menace to society.

Nicklaus wasn't about to worry right then and there about plunking some poor soul. He slapped his left arm around Rudolph and headed to the scorer's table. Jack handed his playing partner his card, the one that said he'd shot a 69 for a seventeen-under 271, nine shots better than Palmer, nine shots better than Player. "You know you can't win this thing until I sign this card," Rudolph told him.

Jack laughed. He walked into the club's new Butler Cabin for the CBS presentation of his green jacket and greeted his crippled idol, Bobby Jones. Standing to the right of Clifford Roberts, Arnold Palmer, dethroned champ, shook his head at Nicklaus in disbelief.

John Derr of CBS then turned over the proceedings to Roberts, who announced to millions of viewers that the following year's telecast might be shown in color. "If it works out," he said, "I believe the fans who watch this golf show might find it a little bit more interesting because we have a lot of color, a lot of wonderful plants this time of year, [which] should add quite a bit of beauty to the telecast."

Roberts then turned to his co-lord, Jones, hunched over in a chair as his partner called him "indestructible." Jones thanked Roberts and said, "If Jack Nicklaus hasn't destroyed me this week, it's the only thing he hasn't destroyed."

Jones offered some words of consolation to Palmer, who was seated next to Nicklaus. "Thank you," Arnold said. "First of all, I think I must congratulate Jack on probably one of the finest seventy-two holes of golf that's ever been played."

Palmer looked Nicklaus in the eye, and they nodded their heads on cue. "And I mean that, Jack. With Mr. Jones and Mr. Roberts, we discussed it earlier, and Augusta National is not supposed to be shot like that. Dadgonit, you're not supposed to shoot scores like that. I just can't imagine seventeen under par. I think it's fabulous . . . I'll look forward to next year. Maybe we can do something about it then."

The two men smiled. Jones and Palmer went back and forth a bit before the founder of the Masters directed his attention to the winner. "Jack," Jones said, "I have an aversion to superlatives as a general rule, but I just can't avoid them on this occasion. This was the greatest tournament performance in all of golfing history."

Palmer looked as if he had just swallowed two tablespoons of castor oil when Jones made that declaration. For his part Nicklaus sounded overwhelmed by the magnitude of what he'd done. "I've been sitting here trying to think of something to say," Jack said. "Well, I don't know. I've never played golf like that before."

For the second time in three years, Palmer was asked to do the honor of helping Nicklaus into his green jacket. "I guess I'd like to keep this odd and even going for a few years now," Jack said.

"You know," Arnold responded, "there's nothing I can think of . . . I wasn't going to say it. I'm glad you said it. But there's nothing I can think of that will suit me better."

They laughed, shook hands, and made their way outside for the official ceremony, where Jones would say that Nicklaus "plays a game with which I am not familiar." Jack's idol was saying he would've been no match for Jack.

It was the grandest of Sundays for Nicklaus; his younger son, Steve, turned two, and Barbara was expecting their third child in May. Personally and professionally, the line between reality and fantasy was blurred.

Nicklaus didn't just walk out of Augusta National with Arnold Palmer's tournament. Jack left with a few platoons from Arnie's Army, too.

"It's a lot more fun to wear a white hat," he said.

A rnold Palmer had a brand-new plane, a $750,000 jet colored red, white, and blue that was racing him from boardroom to boardroom, tee to tee. The Jet Commander replaced his old Aero Commander and was marked by the golfer's name and the Arnold Palmer Enterprises logo, the multicolored umbrella, just in case anyone didn't know who was flying it.

Palmer had inspired Jack Nicklaus to buy himself a plane, too, because Arnie inspired Jack to do a lot of things—namely, to take his place as the world's premier golfer.

"Jack was jealous of Arnold in that Arnold was ahead of him in a great many things and ways," said John Derr, the CBS announcer who knew both men.

Charlie Nicklaus, Jack's father, once approached Derr at the Doral Open to ask him for a favor. With Arnold already a licensed pilot, Jack had started taking flying lessons in the hope of buying and piloting his own plane. Charlie wanted the announcer to talk his boy out of it.

"Jack respects you," he told Derr. "You probably have some influence on him, since you've given him some good advice in the past. Can you tell him he doesn't need an airplane or a pilot's license?"

"Charlie, it's really none of my business," Derr answered. "How am I going to tell Jack Nicklaus, 'You have no damn bit of business flying'? I can't go to him and say that."

"Well," Charlie concluded, "if the situation develops, say that."

Sure enough, the situation developed at a tournament reception, where Derr sidled up to Jack.

"Someone said you're taking flying lessons. Why?" Derr asked.

"I'd like to know how to fly," Nicklaus answered.

"You don't need a plane, do you?"

"Yeah, I've got to go on the spur of the moment for business, and I can get a lot more done."

"There's enough commercial planes to get around. I know Palmer's got a plane and he's flying."

"No, no. That's not the reason at all. I just need to go places. But you've got a point. I'll think about it."

A few days later Derr ran into Charlie Nicklaus and told him he had his little cocktail party chat with Jack.

"It worked out great," Derr said. "I may have gotten a spark from him."

"I sure hope you got him straightened out on that," Charlie responded.

The next day Derr's morning paper carried a story under the headline "Nicklaus Buys Jet."

Jack had run down Arnold on the ground, and he decided he would chase him into the heavens.

"If Arnold had a plane," Derr said, "Jack felt he was entitled to have a plane, too."

Palmer maintained he was the one who steered Nicklaus in the direction of buying the plane, even helping him pick out the model. Either way, Nicklaus ultimately dropped his bid to become a pilot but did purchase a twin-engine Aero Commander, starting an arms race with Arnie that would rival the U.S.-Soviet race to the moon.

This is the way it was between Palmer and Nicklaus, who shared a healthy respect for each other's game and a more palpable, big brother–kid brother urge to beat each other to a pulp.

One night in Jacksonville, Palmer and Nicklaus were getting ready to go out when one of them brushed his shoe against the other's leg. In return, the offended brushed his own foot against the offender's leg.

"And we sat there and kicked each other about fifteen times in the shin," Nicklaus said. "It was, 'What do you think of *that!*' 'No, what do you think of *that!*' Both of us left with bruises, laughing like hell."

Their food fight in Montreal was hardly an isolated case. "Oh, we had a lot of those," Jack said. "We did stupid things."

And great things for the sport. Americans were watching and playing golf in larger numbers and identifying themselves as Arnie fans, or Jack fans, with no gray area in between.

In the spring of 1966 Palmer and Nicklaus drove down Magnolia Lane having taken the last four Masters. Only Arnold hadn't won a major since Augusta, 1964. In the summer of 1965 he had a golden opportunity to finally win his first PGA Championship at the Laurel Valley Golf Club in Ligonier, Pennsylvania, where Arnold served as traveling pro a dozen miles from his Latrobe home. But he was hit with a two-shot penalty on the first hole after eager-beaver marshals removed a section of a wooden bridge to give ol' Arnie a clearer crack at the green, a ruling that left Palmer pancake-flat.

Arnold managed all of one victory in the 1965 season, at the Tournament of Champions in Las Vegas, a far cry from his performances from 1960 through 1963, when he captured between six and eight tournaments each year. Arnold started playing cautiously, doubting his gambler's instinct. He wasn't stepping onto the first tee anymore like a hooded middleweight climbing through the ropes.

"I began to think I was afraid to win," Arnold told Mark McCormack. "I would get close, and my hands would begin to shake — don't let anybody ever tell you they don't get nervous out there — and . . . I really didn't know if I was ever going to win again."

Arnold had won the first event of 1966, the Los Angeles Open, giving him reason to believe his game and his confidence were coming around. But Palmer was also growing increasingly distracted by business deals that had nothing to do with playing winning golf.

His name was on products in people's sheds, kitchens, bathrooms, and laundry rooms. When he wasn't doing a TV show with Perry Como, he was doing one with Bob Hope. When he wasn't doing an exhibition in Scotland, he was doing one in Japan. Arnold Palmer was an international brand, and one that wasn't sinking enough putts.

He showed at the 1966 Masters clinging to the flagstick-thin notion that his number always came up in an even-numbered year. Arnold had that on his side, and, of course, he had his army, too.

"There's a lot of people at Augusta who would rather watch Arnie lose than watch somebody else win," said Ray DeBarge, a Masters gallery guard.

DeBarge worked in the Augusta Club Shop run by Colonel Bernie Porter, and Palmer would come in all the time with his Rolling Rock beer and go to work in Porter's shop. Arnold's intense commitment to tinkering with his golf clubs — many of which didn't need tinkering — bordered on an obsession. Porter had gone to Latrobe to deliver clubs to Palmer and returned telling tales of garages full of every imaginable iron and wood.

Palmer never made a bad putt; his putter was responsible for every errant attempt. That's why his clubs ended up in more vises than any player's on tour. The man with the blacksmith arms played the part eight days a week.

Truth was, he needed every club face and shaft and grip to be just right to have any shot at beating Nicklaus, who the year before had reduced Augusta National to a miniature golf course sans the windmill and clown's mouth.

"I feel young and strong," said Palmer, who would turn thirty-seven in September.

Everyone knew Nicklaus to be younger and stronger.

"Any man who beats Jack Nicklaus will win the Masters," Gary Player said.

Player had won the most recent U.S. Open in a playoff with Kel Nagle and had donated his entire $25,000 purse back to the USGA, asking that $20,000 go into youth golf programs and $5,000 into a cancer research fund. The South African was forever overshadowed by Palmer and Nicklaus, but he was too good a player, and too strong a man, to be dismissed as the Big Three's answer to Ringo Starr.

Nonetheless, Player did continue serving as a buffer for the group's John and Paul. He hosted Nicklaus and Palmer for exhibitions in his homeland, only at separate times.

With Player aboard, Arnold once landed his plane on a strip inside a South African game reserve. "You had guys with bushes keeping the elephants and the wildebeests and the wart hogs off the runway," Player said. "As we landed, man, these animals came back on the strip, and I'm thinking, 'Oh, man alive, they see the airplane and they can't all get out of the way.' There are no mulligans there."

Palmer didn't need one. He landed the plane safely and ended up in a gold mine with McCormack and Player, the gold miner's son. They boarded an elevator to go twelve thousand feet down, and when McCormack decided he was afraid to make this trip, Palmer grabbed him by the shoulders and dragged him in.

They came to a massive room in the mine filled with tens of millions of dollars' worth of gold. The tour guide pointed to a gold bar on a table and said that nobody in the history of the mine had been strong enough to pick it up. The guide said that any man who lifted the bar could keep it.

"I've got a friend here from America, sir," Player said. "Do you mind if he tries?"

"Certainly," the guide said.

Palmer walked to the table and lifted the bar as if it were a stray divot, and the guide's eyes nearly popped out of his head.

"Now, now," the guide said, "I only work here, sir."

"You *did* work here," Palmer responded. "You're fired now. I picked it up and you're going to have to pay for it."

Palmer finally laughed, and the guide restarted his own heart.

On a different trip to South Africa with Nicklaus, Player was the one who nearly had a stroke when Jack went off to hunt down a buffalo. This could've been hazardous to Nicklaus's health, as buffalo were known to kill the bush-savvy locals, never mind suburban golfers from Ohio.

Player found two expert hunters to go along with Nicklaus, one to stand in front of him, one to stand to his rear. "Don't you let anything happen to Jack Nicklaus," Player told the escorts, "because [the headline] will be 'Gary Player Invites Jack and He Gets Killed,' you know?"

Nicklaus shot a buffalo and then closed in for the kill. Finishing off a wounded buffalo, Player explained, is a treacherous pursuit. "Their blood drops and you follow," he said, "and they cross over an area where you can't see the blood. Either a little stream or something, and they come around the back of you while you're looking with your spears, and . . . *boom!* They get you from behind."

Nicklaus was supposed to fly to Player's ranch that afternoon but spent the entire day with those expert hunters, successfully tracking down his wounded prey.

"Jack came back with his pants torn, his shirt torn, and blood all over him," Player said. "I was never so happy to see Jack Nicklaus in my life."

He couldn't say the same at Augusta in 1966; Player hadn't won the Masters in five years. Even in the throes of a winless season, Nicklaus was the man to beat.

In his first Augusta round since his seventeen-under 274 from the year before, Nicklaus ignored the gusting winds and reestablished his dominance of the event with a 68, six strokes better than the scores Palmer and Player managed.

Nicklaus had relied on another tip from his friend Deane Beman, who told Jack to quit rushing his downswing. Given the circumstances, the 68 was almost as remarkable as the record-tying 64 in the previous year's Masters. The night before, Nicklaus learned that four friends, Bob and Linda Barton and Jim and Jeretta Long, had perished in a private plane crash on a Tennessee hillside on their way to the Masters.

Bob Barton had organized the homecoming parade in Columbus after Jack beat Arnold at Oakmont. Nicklaus wanted to pull out of the Masters field and relinquish his latest bid to become the first repeat winner at Augusta. His wife, Barbara, talked him out of it. Jack would stay and try to birdie his way through the pain.

On Friday, round two, Nicklaus's touch was gone with the wind. He putted terribly and shot 76 to fall out of the lead and into a second-place tie with Palmer, one shot behind Peter Butler and Paul Harney. Palmer managed a 32 on his front nine and was at his fist-pumping, crowd-pleasing best, before scuffling for a 38 on the back.

Saturday's third round was stolen by Palmer and fifty-three-year-old Ben Hogan, who chipped in from seventy-five feet at the tenth hole and outplayed Arnold by one stroke, 73 to 74, to remain in contention. Hogan had beaten Nicklaus in a practice round before the tournament—a microscopic piece of payback for Jack's record-breaking performance in 1965—and stood only two off the lead shared by Nicklaus and Tommy Jacobs, who posted an even-par 216.

Predictably enough the Hogan-Palmer pairing drew the day's largest gallery, and the Wee Ice Mon didn't sound overly impressed with Arnie's Army. "They're just a bunch of golf enthusiasts and fans," Hogan said. "Arnold takes a lot of chances and they like to see him try things that are nearly impossible."

Much to Palmer's dismay, Hogan joined him at 218. Player had burned to be in their company—"I want to win so badly I can taste it," he'd said—and yet posted a shocking 227.

Sunday's round was shaped by the expectation Palmer would summon the old magic from even-numbered years gone by, pass the plummeting Jacobs, and engage Nicklaus in another indelible duel. Palmer would have a captive CBS audience, too, watching the Masters in color for the first time. To most golf fans the only thing better than watching Arnie charge was watching Arnie charge in color.

Option number three—no Arnie charge at all—was the least desirable alternative. But after a birdie at number nine signaled a back-nine explosion to come, Palmer's putter went south. Every time his ball brushed by the hole, Arnold whipped his head over his shoulder as if he were tracking a speeding bullet and made one of those anguished, face-crunching expressions for which he was getting more and more famous.

The winner in 1958, 1960, 1962, and 1964 wasn't going to win in 1966. It was coming down to Palmer's playing partner, Gay Brewer, and Jacobs and Nicklaus. This appeared to be the biggest mismatch since the second Louis-Schmeling fight.

Having survived a full round in the company of Arnie's Army, Brewer needed only a six-footer on the seventy-second hole to take the outright lead. He missed.

Nicklaus had a better chance on the seventy-first hole, a three-footer to break the deadlock. Jack had never missed a putt this critical in a major. He pulled it left anyway, and the crowd groaned. Nicklaus wasn't the bad guy anymore. The Augusta fans embraced him on his dash to history in 1965, and the tragic pre-tournament plane crash made him more of a sentimental pick in 1966.

Nicklaus had actually built up a following with a frequently referenced name, "Jack's Pack." It wasn't Arnie's Army, but it was proof that Nicklaus was advancing, slowly but surely, behind enemy lines.

Jacobs failed to birdie eighteen, and so he settled for a share of Brewer's clubhouse lead at even-par 288. Nicklaus had one last chance to avoid a three-man playoff, a birdie attempt from forty-five feet above the cup. The hole was cut into its customary position on the left front, and the putt was a right-to-left breaker, moving fast.

Three-quarters of the way home it looked dead center. Jacobs was sitting behind the green with Hogan when the Wee Ice Mon said, "Well, that silly shit has made that putt."

Jacobs was telling himself, "Come on, baby, break," just as the ball broke below the hole and missed by a single blade of grass. Nicklaus made a small circle with his lips, as if he were whistling. He was booked for a Monday playoff, but he had some homework to do before he got there.

Nicklaus saw a CBS replay of his short birdie miss at seventeen and realized his eyes were too far out past his ball. He went to work on the putting green and made the one adjustment he needed to become the first back-to-back champion in Masters history.

Nicklaus finished off the 1966 Masters in the twilight hours of April 11, after a marathon playoff every witness knew he'd win. For the first time an Augusta champion had to put the green jacket on himself. Nicklaus posed for photographers whose flashbulbs threw light across the gathering darkness, and Bobby Jones — smoking with the aid of a cigarette holder — looked up adoringly at the man who played a game with which he wasn't familiar.

"There is no reason to think that 26-year-old Jack Nicklaus won't win every Masters championship from now until the year 2000," *Sports Illustrated* wrote.

"Jack William Nicklaus the great, conqueror of all men," the *Augusta Chronicle* called him. The master of the Masters needed a new challenge, a new frontier. He was all done claiming Arnold Palmer's old Augusta home.

CHAPTER 8

• Master of Disaster

D EKE PALMER TOLD his boy he should always help others, including opponents, whenever he could. This direct order inspired Arnold Palmer to encourage the rookie Jack Nicklaus on the last hole of the 1962 Phoenix tournament Arnie would win by a dozen strokes.

No, Arnie would never help an opponent claim a victory at his expense, not knowingly anyway. But if a kid needed a little boost to finish second instead of third, why the hell not?

So when Palmer had the 1966 U.S. Open zipped inside his golf bag with nine holes to play at the Olympic Club in San Francisco, Deke's voice was back in his son's ear.

Billy Casper wants that second-place check and you're seven up with nine to go? Shoot, if you don't help a man in that position, what kind of man are *you?*

Casper was afraid of being beaten out of the runner-up spot by the one player Palmer couldn't escape. Arnie couldn't go anywhere or do anything without the magnitude of Jack Nicklaus framing the day.

Palmer was trying to claim his eighth major championship and the first since Nicklaus decided to make Augusta National his. Casper was the measuring stick of the moment, another charisma-free golfer trailing the sexiest man in spikes. He didn't want Nicklaus climbing up the leaderboard any more than Palmer did.

"Arnie," Casper said at the final turn, "I want to finish second."

"I'll do everything I can to help you," Palmer responded.

They continued their conversation in the tenth fairway.

"I gotta make some birdies," Casper said. "Gotta finish second."

"Just keep plugging away," Palmer said. "You'll make some putts and you'll be fine."

No, it wasn't the kind of support Ben Hogan or Nicklaus would've given a down-on-his-luck foe. Most Open leaders, in fact, wouldn't have offered more than a grunt and a shrug in that position, before walking as far away from the poor sap as possible.

But Palmer figured that not helping Casper would've been akin to not helping a motorist with a flat tire on a remote country road.

Palmer was one of the good guys. Where most found a grudge, he found a friend. Jimmy Cannon, the famous New York sports columnist, used to mock the suggestion that golfers are athletes, enraging the most athletic and masculine of the breed, Arnold Palmer himself.

Arnie ended up drinking with Cannon at Toots Shor's. "He and I became good friends," Palmer said.

Arnie never turned down autograph requests, never slid out the back door of the clubhouse to escape his adoring fans. Palmer wanted to be everything to everyone. On a trip to the Philippines with his manager, Mark McCormack, Palmer was approached by a stranger who asked the golfer to send something to his brother in Buffalo when he returned home.

On arrival in the States, Palmer hopped into his plane and personally flew the gift to the man's house.

So at the 1966 Open, Casper was playing with the right leader: Palmer was going to pep him up. At the same time Palmer was going to win the Open, and he was going to break Hogan's Open scoring record, too.

Palmer had failed to erase the Wee Ice Mon's Augusta National record at the 1964 Masters, but he wasn't about to go 0 for 2. If he could pull it off and help Casper beat out Nicklaus for second, it would be worth an extra champagne toast at the victory bash.

It had already been a tough tournament for Nicklaus. The USGA was enforcing two rules at Olympic designed to make life less pleasant for slow players, and Jack was as slow as they came. Players were asked to putt continuously until they holed out, and they were allowed to lift and clean their golf balls only once per green.

Palmer was one of many who stewed in their own juices while Nicklaus was laboring over his birdie and par attempts. Sometimes Jack took so long to pull the trigger, it appeared he was engaging the hole in one of those let's-see-who-blinks-first contests.

Palmer had once told Nicklaus to pick it up, and when asked to reveal what Jack had said in response, Arnold said, "Nothing. Same thing he always says. Nothing."

Only Nicklaus had plenty to say after the second round of the Open, after his threesome was told by a USGA official to play faster. Jack was grouped with Tony Lema and Bruce Devlin, but he took this as a personal warning despite his strong relationship with the Open's governing body.

The USGA didn't want any round to exceed four hours. Nicklaus didn't want anyone to tell him how to play national championship golf.

"I can't remember when I've been so mad," he said, claiming that the warning was responsible for four consecutive bogeys. Nicklaus allowed that he'd received only one warning, "but from then on, the USGA had one of their policemen with a watch walking along right beside us. You can't play with someone on your back all the time."

Nicklaus was five strokes out of the Palmer-Casper lead, but it was surprising to hear him complain about the Open's rules and playing conditions. In the days before this ocean-side tournament, pros had bellyached over the ultra-penal length of the rough; the small greens; the tight fairways; the thousands upon thousands of eucalyptus, pine, and cedar trees; and the oppressive heat.

Nicklaus was never one to cry at a Grand Slam event. "You arrive at the golf course [at a major]," he would say, "and you hear guys say, 'The rough is too deep. Aw, the greens are too hard. Aw, the greens are too fast. The fairways are too narrow.' Count them out. Everybody's yelling about something, and first of all, they aren't good enough to play it anyway. And they just go by the wayside."

But at the 1966 Open Nicklaus was going by the wayside. He hadn't contended at the Open since beating Palmer at Oakmont in 1962, and with nine holes to play on Sunday, June 19, he was out of it one more time.

That is, until Casper brought him into it and used Nicklaus as one of his two sources for back-nine inspiration. The other source was harder to believe than the golf that was to come over the next ninety minutes.

Casper was much like Nicklaus — doughy and colorless, a living study in caution. In short, he was everything Arnie was not. "[Casper] didn't do too much talking," said the pro Bob Goalby. "He wasn't well liked."

He wasn't one of the boys. During a practice round at Olympic, Casper found himself playing with Chi Chi Rodriguez while Chi Chi was listening to Juan Marichal pitch on the radio. Casper cut the round short after nine holes.

He was a damn good golfer, though, even if he didn't impress anyone with his power off the tee. Casper once played with Palmer and Nicklaus at Doral and spent the round with his back turned to both when they were driving their golf balls: he was afraid he'd get spooked by their tape-measure homers.

Casper won the tournament anyway. He never choked under pressure and always played to let his opponent make the deciding mistake.

He was the 1959 Open champ, a three-time Ryder Cup member, a thirty-time winner on tour, and a guy who had already pocketed nearly half a million bucks in earnings, second to Palmer on the all-time list. He thought the Big Three should've been called the Big Four and believed that his association with McCormack's former business partner, Dick Taylor, ensured that he'd never get promoted like McCormack's Palmer, Nicklaus, and Gary Player.

He was right, but Casper wasn't one to fret over publicity and endorsement deals lost. He was in a good place. Casper had dropped fifty pounds after a doctor diagnosed his many allergies to food and put him on an exotic diet of buffalo meat and organic vegetables. He was the best putter on tour, a consistent winner, and a man who had found peace in his recent conversion to the Mormon church.

Casper also found something else on a goodwill trip to Vietnam sponsored by the State Department: a surreal vision that would compel him to hunt down Palmer at Olympic.

"They were like lions that were basking in the sun," he said of the troops he visited, "and when they got hungry, they did things. And when the situation presented itself over there, they took care of it, see. And I envisioned [the troops] as these lions, and I envisioned myself as these lions and these people … So on the back nine I took care of the situation."

Once a fat man who somehow melted into a chubby man on a diet of buffalo meat, Casper had become a lion fixing to eat a king.

Casper studied Palmer with predatory eyes from the tall grass. Arnold was nearly flawless on the front nine, going out in 32 to Casper's 36 to extend his lead to seven. On the way in Palmer needed to shoot one-over 36 or better to beat the Hogan standard. Mass hysteria had raged across the golf course, and a simple Palmer bogey at number ten did nothing to tame the crowd.

They each parred number eleven, and they each birdied number twelve. Palmer held a six-shot cushion with six holes to cover, and his body language reflected the sunny day. He felt so good, he figured he could lock in on Hogan's Open scoring record of 276, set at Riviera in 1948.

Palmer missed the green on the 191-yard thirteenth and bogeyed to cut his lead to five. He was far more concerned that he'd lost a stroke to Hogan than he was that he'd lost a stroke to Casper. Palmer and Casper each took a four at number fourteen, and a five-shot advantage with four to play felt like a six-inch putt.

Then something funny happened on the fifteenth tee. Casper, who made a comfortable living aiming for the middle of the green, played a typically safe shot, the kind of shot you'd see from a man with a five-shot lead rather than a five-shot deficit. Palmer? He'd never met a flagstick he didn't want to hit on the fly.

Arnie went for broke at the most absurd time, firing his seven-iron at a pin guarded by a bunker. An inch this way, and it's all over the stick. An inch that way, and it's in the sand. It went an inch that way. Palmer was going with the all-out blitz when a prevent defense was the obvious call. He couldn't get up and down out of the bunker, and he watched as Casper advanced his considerable reputation on the greens by sinking a twenty-foot downhiller.

Casper wasn't worried about holding off Nicklaus for second now. He was only imagining himself as a soldier, or a lion, or both, and his prey was standing right next to him on the sixteenth tee.

"I can win this tournament now," Casper told himself.

He sensed a seismic shift in the gallery, a mass desertion inside Arnie's Army.

"They left because they wanted to go watch him on television," Casper said. "And when I started catching up, this was the feeling of the American people. They root for the underdog, and I was the underdog. They became converted to Casper. It really was a weird feeling."

Palmer had forgotten all about Hogan, just as Casper had forgotten all about Nicklaus. Arnie was incredulous that his playing partner, the stranded motorist on the side of that country road, had turned out to be a thief. Palmer would later confide to his friend and fellow pro Bob Toski that he was angry Casper stopped talking to him when it became clear he no longer needed or wanted encouragement to finish second.

"Arnold," Toski told him, "I can't understand how you got trapped like that."

Palmer fell into his own trap as well, working himself into a tizzy over Casper's play-it-safe strategy. Who was the leader? Who was the chaser? Palmer didn't think it was very manly of Casper to charge by not charging at all.

"This is a very demanding course," Casper had said. "I feel you can't charge it. Instead, you have to romance it . . ."

Palmer wasn't romancing anything; he was going out in a blaze of glory. Arnie had worked on Nicklaus-like fades before the Open to better his chances on Olympic's left-to-right holes, but the 604-yard sixteenth was bending the other way, favoring the old Arnie draw. He chose a driver over the safer iron or three-wood and snap-hooked his tee shot into the trees.

In the deep rough Palmer made another wretched choice: a three-iron. He would've had better luck using an old maid's broom. The ball traveled all of eighty, ninety yards and plunged deeper into the shit.

Out in Hawaii Palmer's two sisters were driving around with their mother, absorbing the shocking Open call on the radio. "We got half-way around the island and all of us were sick," said Cheech, the older sister. "So we turned it off and didn't even listen to it."

With a lump in his throat the size of the Goodyear blimp hovering above him, Palmer chopped a nine-iron shot into the fairway, finally making a wise percentage choice. From there he smoked a three-wood into a greenside bunker. He blasted out to within four feet of the cup before Casper dropped a right-to-left thirteen-footer for birdie, cutting the deficit to one. Palmer needed to sink his putt to salvage a bogey six and to cling to the last remnant of what had been a seven-shot lead. He made it, scooped up his ball, and walked off, shaking his head and exhaling through lips forming a perfect lowercase *o*.

Palmer set fire to a cigarette on the seventeenth tee; a whole carton of L&Ms couldn't have relaxed him then.

"I'd never, ever seen him feel the pressure like he felt the pressure then," Casper said. "He couldn't make a swing . . . He'd lost the chance of breaking Hogan's record, and then the little fat boy crept up on him, and he panicked. And that's the only thing it was, a panic."

In his bright blue sweater and light gray slacks, Palmer was starring in his own Greek tragedy for millions of ABC viewers. He sent his penultimate drive into the rough and knocked his second shot across the fairway and into the opposite rough. Palmer was literally playing like a hopeless weekend hacker. He stopped his third shot seven feet from the pin, and Casper pitched over a bunker and got inside Arnold, to five feet.

A huge pine was casting ominous shadows across the green, and into those shadows stepped Palmer, facing a straight-on, easy-to-read par saver that felt like a triple-breaker from a hundred feet away. He measured the line, jabbed his blade at the ball, and watched it quit rolling one precious inch short of the cup. Palmer waved his putter and threw his head backward. He never, ever left a putt short.

Casper drained his par attempt and the U.S. Open was all tied. Six years after overcoming a seven-stroke deficit to win at Cherry Hills, Palmer had squandered a seven-stroke lead at Olympic.

The turnabout was more stunning than Hogan's playoff loss to Jack Fleck at this same club eleven years earlier. Up ahead, before his last putt of the tournament, Nicklaus heard a cheer go up as the Palmer-Casper scores were posted on the board. Nicklaus finished at five-over 285 and stood off the green with his playing partner, Dave Marr, watching the bizarre scene of Palmer and Casper heading for home.

"A few holes ago," Byron Nelson told his ABC broadcast partner, Chris Schenkel, "everyone thought that the championship was over. Golf is the strangest game in the world."

Casper hadn't hit the eighteenth fairway in the first three rounds; of course, he hit the fairway in the fourth. Palmer used a one-iron off the tee, but he was too deep into this manic and epic collapse to turn back now. His ball banked hard to the left, and Palmer retreated from the point of impact and grabbed his club with both hands as a look of sheer horror distorted his face. His ball was heading for a familiar spot. It settled into the rough as if it were a homing pigeon landing in its nest.

The frenzied gallery broke through the ropes from behind the tee box and chased after Palmer and Casper, who were two under for the tournament. The game of golf, Schenkel told America, "can often make you feel awfully tiny and humble, and it has done that to Arnold Palmer."

Arnold wasn't thinking about Hogan's record on the seventy-second hole; he was thinking about Hogan's infamous Olympic loss to Fleck. With his brain gone to mush, with his heartbeat pounding in his ears, with his veins bulging from his reddening neck, Palmer acted on muscle memory. He was the carnival strongman again, trying to ring the bell with his mallet. He let it rip from the rough with a nine-iron, digging out an obscene patch of grass. His shot barely cleared a bunker, crash-landed on the green, and quit rolling thirty feet from the pin.

"Greatest shot I've ever seen," said his caddie, Mike Reasor, dressed in a red windbreaker marked by the Palmer name and wearing a tee behind his left ear, a pencil behind his right.

Casper wedged to seventeen feet, and it seemed a predetermined fate that Arnold would two-putt and lose the Open to Casper's bird.

Nicklaus was watching from a greenside knoll as Palmer left his downhill putt four feet short and to the right. Arnold was afraid he'd step into Casper's line on the next attempt. "Should I putt, or do you want me to mark it, Cas?" Palmer asked.

"Go ahead and putt, Arnie," Casper responded. "You're warm."

Staring down an unholy end to a hell-on-earth day, Palmer thought to himself, "Everything is on the line here. My pride. My business. My livelihood."

He slapped his ball toward the target. It broke to the right, then plunged like a field mouse into the hole.

"Biggest putt I've ever made," Palmer said.

Overcome by relief and embarrassment, Arnold shook his head and exited the scene of his certain demise. Casper, the short-game magician, wasn't holding a putter anymore but an instrument of euthanasia. The whole world expected him to put Arnold Palmer to rest.

And for the first time across the most mind-boggling closing nine in U.S. Open history, Casper let up. With Palmer crying uncle, he released him from the headlock. "You've picked up seven shots on one of the greatest players the game has ever known," Casper thought to himself. In other words, "Don't blow it now."

Casper didn't. He lagged his putt short and tapped in for the playoff-clinching par, forcing Palmer back for another gut-wrenching day.

"We didn't talk after we finished," Casper said.

What was there to say? Arnold's implosion, wrote Arthur Daley of the *New York Times*, "was the equivalent of galloping toward the wrong end zone." Palmer and Casper signed their cards — "Two of the most garbled signatures you ever saw," Reasor said — and went their separate ways. Palmer headed to the nearby home of his friends Ed and Rita Douglas; Ed was an Olympic member and the Pennzoil executive who would ultimately help Arnold land his signature endorsement deal. The Douglases had befriended the Palmers at Olympic in 1955, when Arnold and Winnie were just kids.

"They were staying in a bum little old motel down the road," Rita Douglas said, "so we took them home."

Eleven years later Rita walked every step of that fateful back nine at Olympic with Winnie. "Oh, that poor little face," Rita said. "She didn't want to watch ... She was always smiling, but on that back nine, she stopped smiling. I'll never forget her face as Arnold started to go downhill."

The Douglases and Palmers shared a quiet dinner after Arnold's collapse and kept the golf talk to a minimum. The Palmers would stay with the Douglases whenever they were in town for the Lucky International, and Ed and Rita would insist that Arnold and Winnie take the master bedroom. On the night of June 19, 1966, that master bedroom was little more than a hideout.

Meanwhile, Casper was attending a fireside service at the Church of Jesus Christ of Latter-Day Saints in Petaluma, talking to fellow Mormons until 11:30 at night. He didn't eat his dinner — a full plate of pork chops, sliced tomatoes, and string beans — until 1:00 a.m.

The next day Casper devoured Palmer whole. Arnold actually carried a two-stroke lead into the back nine, only to confront the same demons and doubts from the day before. Casper took the lead for good on a forty-footer at the par-three thirteenth, a birdie that inspired him to raise both hands in the air and to swing his putter like a helicopter blade around his head.

On the final hole, with Casper up three, Palmer made his par putt — the fortieth stroke of his second nine — for a 73 and nodded over and over to the applause. Casper dropped his birdie putt for his 69, waved to the crowd, and put his right hand on Palmer's left shoulder.

"Arnold," he said, "I'm sorry."

Casper hugged his wife and kids and pledged 10 percent of his $26,500 check—including a $1,500 playoff bonus—to the Mormon church. Palmer ended up in the locker room, sitting next to his caddie, Reasor, a Brigham Young player who landed Arnold's bag in a club lottery—Palmer drew his Ping-Pong ball from a sphere.

"You can live a long time and never see a man's guts right in front of you like that," Reasor would tell *Sports Illustrated*'s Rick Reilly years later. "It was the darnedest thing, the whole last day, like water running through your fingers."

Like tears running from your eyes. Palmer and Reasor grew emotional in the deafening clubhouse silence, before the player threw his arm around the caddie.

"Sorry, Mike," Palmer said.

"Time will pass," Reasor said. "You'll get over it."

Palmer could never get over this, his third defeat in an Open playoff, a blow more crushing than his loss to Nicklaus at Oakmont.

"You lost the tournament," Arnold's friend Bob Toski told him, "because you're too nice of a guy."

Too nice a guy for talking up Casper in his bid to beat out Nicklaus for second place.

"Bob," Palmer said, "I never realized if I encouraged him like that it would cost me the tournament."

Palmer met the press, took his medicine like a man, and went back to the Douglas home to be with his wife. Winnie was in the upstairs bedroom when Arnold came through the front door, finding ten close friends sitting quietly in the living room, as if they were waiting for their turn at the casket.

Palmer walked into the kitchen and found Rita Douglas preparing some hors d'oeuvres. He leaned his head against the wall, trained his glassy eyes on his friend, and released a barely audible breath.

"Oh, Rita," sighed the master of disaster, "I could cry."

CHAPTER 9

• Baltusrol

B Y THE MIDDLE of the 1967 season, Arnold Palmer could no longer stake a credible claim to the title of world's best player. He was still winning tournaments, still winning money, and still convincing bookmakers that he represented a fairly safe bet.

In fact, one year after he left his broken heart in San Francisco, Arnie was made a 6-to-1 favorite to take the U.S. Open.

But in golf and tennis, the heavyweights all kept score the same way. Major championships determined who was king and who was not.

So Palmer was the King in name only. In the eighteen majors leading up to the 1967 Open at Baltusrol Golf Club in Springfield, New Jersey, Arnie had captured only one title while Jack Nicklaus had captured five.

Jack had won the career Grand Slam; Arnold was still missing the PGA Championship from his mantle. More than ten years younger than Palmer, Nicklaus already had a chance at Baltusrol to match his rival's career sum of professional major victories (seven), and to advance the notion that Arnie would never again rule the landscape as he did before Jack showed up.

Palmer's fans were growing more desperate by the bogey. Nicklaus might have earned the respect of the galleries at Augusta National, but the army that assembled at Baltusrol hadn't won a big one in forever.

This wasn't spring in Augusta, either. This was a humid and stormy part of June in congested, ill-tempered New Jersey, where the Open was being staged ten miles away from the Newark riots that would unfold in a month's time.

With Nicklaus and Palmer paired together in the third round, it was no surprise that Jack needed relief—and not the kind he would get from casual water. Nicklaus needed a place to hide from the crowd at Baltusrol, where Arnie's Army was as hot and bothered as it had ever been.

By then, Nicklaus was accustomed to the jeers and fat jokes that worshipers of the bronze golfing god would fire his way. But in making what felt like their last Grand Slam stand, Palmer's fans were pumping up the volume, using Jack's eardrums as their vehicles of retribution.

The army wanted its pound of flesh, and with Palmer holding a one-stroke lead over the other half of his twosome, Nicklaus, the loyalists on the front lines opened fire. "And it hurts you," Jack conceded. "Absolutely it hurts you."

The fans mocked his weight, and they rooted for his ball to find the deepest patch of available rough. They were finally penetrating Jack's impenetrable shield. Not since Oakmont had Nicklaus confronted a pro-Palmer gallery that, in his words, was so "blatantly partisan."

Some thought the unruliness of the mob was a byproduct of the heat—temperatures soared into the mid-nineties. Others thought the unruliness of the mob was a byproduct of the drought—Palmer hadn't won a major since the 1964 Masters.

It was a combination of both, of course, partnered with the omnipresence of Nicklaus on a Grand Slam leaderboard. Jack had seized the 1966 Masters and the 1966 British Open, his first British victory in five attempts, and he was even growing familiar to the public by a nickname, "the Golden Bear," that rivaled Palmer's, the King.

An Australian sportswriter named Don Lawrence came up with the pet Nicklaus name, citing Jack's blond hair and grizzly physique. The notion of a growling bear sat well with Jack, who was self-conscious about his high-pitched voice.

The Arnie's Army hard-liners weren't impressed. Nicklaus would never be Palmer to them.

His appeal was limited to his game: Jack could hit fairways and greens in his sleep. Arnie's Army didn't see the fun in all that when

Palmer was playing out of the same forests and wetlands its members hacked out of at their local munis.

At Baltusrol, the army hardly cared that Palmer and Nicklaus had teamed up to win their third Canada Cup championship, this one in Tokyo the previous November, or that they came together the following month in Palm Beach Gardens to claim the PGA team title. Jack Nicklaus was back to being the enemy. His forward march had to be stopped.

Palmer actually had the momentum entering the 1967 Open, as he'd won in Los Angeles and Tucson and contended almost everywhere else. Off the course, business was just as good. Palmer sold five of his eight companies to NBC in a deal that included exclusive rights to Arnie's TV appearances and allowed the golfer to continue to manage Arnold Palmer Enterprises.

Nicklaus? He had no such network partnership, and his golf game was in a state of disrepair. Jack had taken the Bing Crosby at Pebble Beach in January, but he had missed the cut at the Masters and had slumped until the moment he ran into his friend, Deane Beman, on the Baltusrol practice green, where Beman flashed a Bulls Eye putter that caught Jack's eye.

Beman had a buddy pull a nearly identical putter from the trunk of his car — the blade on this one was painted white to combat the glare from the sun — and offer it to Nicklaus. The putter was given a name, "White Fang," and it helped Jack shoot 62 in a practice round at Baltusrol's Lower Course.

Asked if that Nicklaus score had tested his faith, Palmer said, "I can't imagine how a 62 in practice can shake anyone up but Jack because he didn't have it [in the tournament]."

Jack didn't appreciate that remark. "I think I'd rather have my 62 than what Arnold shot in practice," he said.

The two men survived the oppressive early-round heat to meet face to face in Saturday's third round. In making an unfortunate comparison, Palmer would write that Nicklaus's gallery "met mine in a collision of hopes and emotions that could only be matched by the outbreak of war in the Middle East."

Most players, Nicklaus included, believed Arnie did what he could to control his fans. But one fellow Mark McCormack client, Bob Charles, believed Palmer could've done more.

Charles complained to McCormack that Arnie wasn't always considerate of his playing partners, telling the agent that Palmer "would hole out and walk off the green to the next tee and take the gallery with him when it wasn't really necessary."

Arnie couldn't have tamed his army at Baltusrol even if he tried. The Nicklaus gallery—whatever there was of it—got steamrolled from the start. Those hopes and emotions on the Palmer side were fueled by the result of the 1966 Open, a humiliating loss with one positive spinoff: it humanized Arnie more than any other defeat.

"Arnold wasn't a Nicklaus," Ken Venturi said, "but Nicklaus wasn't a Palmer, either. Palmer didn't know what the hell a lay-up meant, and that's why [the fans] loved him ... What's not to like about Arnold Palmer? Olympic Club—I mean, Ray Charles could've won there, but that's what Arnold was."

Palmer was easily distracted—by a new business venture, by a pretty face in the crowd, by this and by that. Nicklaus's blind on-course focus was simply a club Palmer didn't carry in his bag.

With a score of 137, thirty-six holes deep into his first post-Olympic Open, Palmer had reporters asking him if he could make another run at Ben Hogan's record 276. At the time, the haunting Billy Casper—Casper the not-so-friendly ghost—was two shots back at Baltusrol. "Why don't you let me get into the position and then worry me with it?" Palmer said.

He'd just endured a second-round day that saw the temperature hit one hundred degrees at noon. Palmer shot two-under 68, and Nicklaus shot 67 and lost seven pounds doing it. On Saturday, June 17, when Palmer and Nicklaus stepped onto the first tee, no thermometers were needed to measure the heat between them.

"The fans there were just as bad as they were at Oakmont," said Nancy McCormack, wife of the players' manager. "They were ruthless ... They had big cardboard cutouts of Arnold that they carried around on sticks."

The crowd was louder and rowdier than Nicklaus had imagined. He wasn't ready for the intensity of a New Jersey gallery that had been all but airlifted out of the foothills of western Pennsylvania.

"It was a brutal environment," said Put Pierman, a Nicklaus friend and business associate. Pierman had to stop himself from going for the Adam's apple belonging to a Palmer fan.

Neither Jack nor Arnie played inspiring golf. They were too busy running their own two-man game, too busy getting swallowed up by thousands upon thousands of ornery, sweat-soaked fans to realize they were opening the door to the rest of the field.

"Let's stop playing each other and play the golf course," Nicklaus told Palmer on the eighth tee.

Easier said than done. As Jack had stood over an earlier putt, one Palmerite shouted, "Miss it, Jack." The U.S. Open had devolved into a cross between the New Jersey Match-Play Championship and rush hour on the Garden State Parkway.

Nicklaus and Palmer got caught up in the traffic. "They both got lost in that a few times," Barbara Nicklaus said, "and forgot that there were seventy other people in the tournament trying to beat each other. And all of a sudden they're four shots behind."

And all of a sudden a Texas amateur and Byron Nelson protégé named Marty Fleckman slipped into the fifty-four-hole lead with a 69. Palmer and Nicklaus shot 73 and 72, respectively, to join Casper in a three-way tie for second, one stroke back of Fleckman at 210.

The cruel forces of fate had conspired against Palmer and Nicklaus one more time: they would be paired again for Sunday's final round. For Nicklaus, this was the worst possible scenario. For Palmer, this was a favorable option only when measured against a possible alternative — another final round spent in the company of Billy Casper.

At 3:08 p.m., it would be Jack versus Arnie, Arnie versus Jack. ABC wanted the late start time for the benefit of ratings, and, despite the possibility of rain and the protests of golfers and print guys on deadline, ABC got what it wanted. It was a "craven capitulation to the space cadets," wrote Arthur Daley of the *New York Times.* Palmer had helped create the TV monster that was about to devour them all.

This was one duel that needed no buildup. The USGA program had this to say about Arnie: "Palmer is, by all accounts, the outstanding golf personality of our time and perhaps the first man of his profession to be just as much a national idol as the baseball and football celebrities."

It had this to say about Jack: "With the exception of Bob Jones, no golfer in history has made such an indelible impression at such an early age."

The heavyweight championship of golf came off on June 18, two days before Muhammad Ali was sentenced to a five-year prison term for refusing to be drafted into the United States Army. Palmer was the knockout artist trying to reclaim his belt. Nicklaus was the counter-puncher trying to retain his title on points.

USGA officials didn't want too much dancing around the ring; they'd warned Jack at Olympic about his stalling tactics. In the weeks before he arrived at Baltusrol, Nicklaus was penalized by the tour for his snail's pace in Houston. The USGA had officials in carts stationed at every Baltusrol hole to ticket the tortoises, but Jack wasn't about to blow a major championship just because an official, or Arnold Palmer, wanted him to speed it up.

Nicklaus adored the 7,015-yard Lower Course and its monstrous 623-yard seventeenth, longest hole in Open history. The fairways were wide enough to keep the driver in play, and they provided landing areas so perfect that approach shots wouldn't have been any easier to strike if the golf balls were sitting up on tees.

Jack could manage the course; there was no question about that. But could he manage the army that would be rumbling through the evergreens and oaks?

"I am used to it," Nicklaus said. "It has become part of the game ... You expect yelling, screaming, and banners when you play with [Palmer]."

Banners? Yes, banners. Palmer's people had brought in bed-sheet-size signs that invited Nicklaus to land his shots in a bunker or in the rough. One such sign that read, "Right Here, Jack," would be mistaken by ABC's Jim McKay as a show of support for Nicklaus.

At least McKay was right about the mood of the big-event Sunday crowd. "I've been in a lot of Arnold Palmer and Jack Nicklaus galleries," he told his viewers, "and I've never seen one with a tremendous enthusiasm and vitality to it that this one has."

This matchup was also colored by a sense of finality. One of the sportswriters at Baltusrol, Ernie Accorsi, the old Palmer fan and future NFL GM out of Pennsylvania and Wake Forest, wrote a piece for the *Philadelphia Inquirer* suggesting this could be the last of the epic Arnie and Jack wars. "I could tell Arnie was hanging on," Accorsi said. "It was a mood ... We all knew it was happening. [Nicklaus] was like Bill Russell taking over the NBA. You could see him dominating the league, and there was nothing you could do about it."

Later, Nicklaus would come to see similarities between his rivalry with Palmer and Russell's rivalry with Wilt Chamberlain. "Chamberlain would've been the more popular player," Jack said, "and Russell would've been the technician. And Russell just got in Chamberlain's ... head."

Nicklaus didn't need to clarify which player was golf's Russell and which was golf's Wilt. But if Palmer was looking for a good omen, Chamberlain had just given him one in the 1967 playoffs. After losing five postseason matchups with Russell, Wilt the Stilt had finally eliminated the Celtics.

Palmer's uniform for this latest clash of titans included a white shirt and light blue pants; Nicklaus's included a yellowish shirt, brown pants, and a visor. They were playing for a first prize of thirty grand, but neither man wanted the money as much as he wanted the other guy's hide.

Just as they did at Oakmont, the players' wives would walk together for these eighteen holes, Barbara Nicklaus and Winnie Palmer side by side. "I mean, obviously she wanted Arnold to win and I wanted Jack to win," Barbara said. "I think the public wanted it to be a rivalry. I don't think they ... wanted them to be friends. They wanted them to want to kill each other and continue off the golf course ..."

With the forecast calling for afternoon thunderstorms, Nicklaus and Palmer teed off in front of Fleckman and Casper, and the entire gallery went right with them. Arnold started with a string of steady pars, while Nicklaus went par-bogey-birdie. Jack nailed a flawless three-iron shot at the par-three fourth that died three feet from the cup to make birdie and take the lead, then followed up with a fifteen-footer at the fifth to give him three consecutive birds and a two-stroke lead.

Palmer continued playing consistent Nicklaus golf, making his sixth straight par at the next hole while Jack continued playing up-and-down Arnie golf, making a bogey to shave his lead in half. The battle was tense but civil, or civil but tense. Palmer and Nicklaus conducted themselves as they normally did in these matchups, exchanging small talk here and there but keeping it short and semisweet. If they didn't give each other the Wee Ice Mon treatment, they didn't act like neighbors at a barbecue, either.

Palmer and Nicklaus usually talked a bit as they left the tee boxes, but they'd shut it down and return to their private thoughts some thirty or forty yards away from their golf balls.

The fact that they'd won team championships together helped contain the hostility, at least on the players' side of the ropes. "We appreciated what we had begun [as teammates]," Palmer said. "We kind of practiced the fact that we respected each other …"

At day's end, that mutual appreciation and respect didn't dull each man's desire to conquer the other. "We wanted to beat each other's brains out," Nicklaus said.

They had their chance at Baltusrol. Behind Jack and Arnie in the final round, Fleckman had already sprayed his way out of the tournament. Nerves drove the amateur to play some amateur-hour golf, and the defending champ, Casper, surprisingly faded along with him, much to Arnold's relief.

Nicklaus was one ahead of Palmer when they arrived at the forbidding 470-yard seventh, where the length of the hole and the dogleg (to the right) prevented players on the tee from seeing the green. Bunkers guarded the dogleg corner and the front and sides of the green, which dropped off in the back, and even a sturdy drive would leave the best of pros with a long iron to an elusive target.

Palmer started with a blast into the fairway, and Nicklaus answered with the same, his drive a couple of paces past Palmer's, of course. Arnold's weapon of choice was the one-iron, only the hardest club in the world to hit, and he fired his approach straight at the stick, his ball coming to a stop a dozen feet by the hole.

The army erupted. Arnie was on his game, hitching his pants and puffing out his chest. He was thirty-seven years old and looking very much like the younger man who made himself an iconic sports star with his 1960 comebacks at Augusta National and Cherry Hills.

Nicklaus landed his two-iron shot twice as far from the cup as Palmer's had landed, and he got half the applause. "Everybody just wants Arnold to win," Nicklaus said. If he didn't understand why at Baltusrol, the reasons would become evident over time.

"Here's this big, fat kid who came along and beat Mr. Adonis," Jack would say.

The big, fat kid was away on the seventh green, and he understood that a miss preceding a Palmer make would tie the ball game and allow Arnie and his fans a sudden leap of faith.

Nicklaus carefully surveyed the slight right-to-left line. He moved as close as he could to his ball, leaned his head over and behind it, and placed his White Fang putter into striking position as Palmer watched intently from the side. The longer Jack stayed over a putt, the more witnesses knew he was going to make it.

When he finally sent his birdie attempt on its way, Nicklaus thought he might've given it too much of a pop. Only the ball was running on a perfect line from the start, and Nicklaus started walking after it five feet from the cup, a clear sign it was going down. The ball dropped into the heart of the hole as easily as a nickel drops into the slot on a vending machine.

Palmer shot Nicklaus a stunned look. "It was like, 'Are you ever going to let me do something?'" Jack said. Arnie nearly fell over, his expression suggesting he was growing more flabbergasted by the second. Palmer, Nicklaus said, "had a look on his face like, 'Oh, God, now what do I do?' That was where I think the tournament ended for Arnold."

Palmer barely missed his eleven-footer, staggered to the eighth tee, and followed Nicklaus's position-A drive on the short hole with his worst tee shot of the Open, a ball that sliced to the right and nestled behind a tree. Nicklaus birdied, Palmer bogeyed out of a greenside bunker, and the four-shot margin left Arnie and his army emotionally crushed.

The game was over. The game within the game, anyway. Palmer wasn't going to beat Nicklaus. He wasn't going to break his own streak of major championship futility.

It was all playing out as the Arnie-adoring sportswriter, Accorsi, had feared. Nicklaus was putting Palmer behind him for keeps. He was breaking the collective spirit of the man and his followers, leaving most observers believing that Arnie could never again launch a serious major championship assault on Jack's reign.

The King was dead, long live the king.

Jack still had to win the tournament, of course, and still had to weigh the reward of breaking Hogan's Open scoring record against the risk of repeating Palmer's collapse at Olympic in pursuit of it.

"Seven shots, nine holes to play," Nicklaus said of that collapse. "Good gracious."

On the par-five eighteenth, Nicklaus did his damnedest to block out thoughts of the record and everything else. He could've had a lot on his mind. His wife, Barbara, was pregnant again. His new career as a golf course designer was just starting to take shape as he planned to build a tour-worthy club and course in the Columbus, Ohio, area.

Only Nicklaus's power of concentration trumped his power off the tee. Somehow, he was focusing exclusively on Palmer, who had finally made birdie at the seventeenth to cut his deficit to four. Nicklaus was worried that a double bogey coupled with a Palmer eagle would force a reenactment of their Oakmont playoff.

Jack was the only man, woman, or child at Baltusrol who thought Arnold was still a threat. Nicklaus needed a birdie four to beat Hogan's 276, and he only cared to take nothing worse than a bogey six.

"I'm not going to try to break a record here and blow this tournament," Nicklaus told himself on the tee box. "There's a creek over on the left, and I'm staying as far away from that as I can."

Jack chose a one-iron on the 542-yard finishing hole, astonishing some observers. "I mean, would Babe Ruth bunt in the bottom of the ninth on the last day when he had fifty-nine home runs?" asked Jim Murray of the *Los Angeles Times,* who also likened Nicklaus's choice to Ara Parseghian's decision to play for the tie in Notre Dame's infamous game with Michigan State the year before.

Even playing it safe, Nicklaus sent his ball into the right rough. "But I couldn't lose the tournament in the right rough," he said. "I knew how Arnold had thrown it away the year before and . . . I had no interest in Hogan's record whatsoever. The only interest I had was in beating Arnold Palmer."

His drive settled near a TV cable drum. Nicklaus was granted a free drop—he required a second drop after his first trickled closer to the hole—and chose again to play conservatively and short of the water hazard with an eight-iron off an uncomfortably barren lie. "A horribly fat shot," Jack said.

He was sitting two, 238 yards from the hole. Nicklaus went back to his one-iron, uphill and against the wind. He tore into it with a vengeance, carrying a bunker by inches and landing his ball on the putting surface. Nicklaus was certain then that he'd won his second Open title. He removed his visor as he walked up to the green and waved it twice to the cheering fans, people who had been worn down to the nub by Nicklaus's brilliance one more time.

The large electronic scoreboard near the eighteenth green reported that Jack had twenty-two feet to cover to score a 65 and a record-breaking 275. With its lighted foot-high letters and numbers, the IBM scoreboard was something new at the Open, and fans gawked at it as they would an alien spacecraft that had just touched down.

The otherworldly Nicklaus was the commander of this ship. He was about to match Palmer's total of seven major titles at the age of twenty-seven.

Dusk was closing and closing hard. Nicklaus had played faster on the back nine, not to appease the USGA or Palmer, but to beat the expected rain. Only Jack wasn't in a rush anymore. For the first time all tournament, he wanted a piece of Hogan as badly as Palmer had wanted the same the year before.

Nicklaus made sure his putt wasn't short. As the ball was about to fall, Jack stepped forward and swung his right hand back and over his head like a softball pitcher. As his ball disappeared, Nicklaus whipped his right hand forward and kicked the air with one of his tree-trunk legs. Palmer stood to the side, right hand on hip, leaning on his putter, wearing a look that could kill.

Jack accepted another round of congratulations from Palmer, by then an almost forgotten prop. Nicklaus had just played a U.S. Open like no man ever had.

Jim McKay grabbed Jack and Arnie for an ABC interview, and started asking his producers if they had the tape of Jack's birdie at the fourth. Nicklaus was standing to Palmer's right; Palmer was standing to McKay's right, head down, eyes glued to his shoelaces. On camera, McKay announced that they were about to look at Nicklaus's putt when Palmer did something he almost never did: he bailed on a request in full public view.

"Jim," he told McKay, "I've looked at these things all day. I think I'm going to excuse myself and go to Latrobe. Thank you very much."

With that, Palmer grabbed McKay's hand, grabbed Nicklaus's hand, and left the two of them to bask in the camera lights. Nicklaus would later throw a not-so-subtle jab at Palmer for taking his eye off the Olympic prize while recklessly chasing Hogan.

"Records are accidents; they just come," he said. "Nobody tries to break a record. How silly can you be to lose sight of winning the tournament?"

Palmer returned to his Latrobe workshop, slapped on his gloves, and hammered and chiseled away at the golf clubs that had failed him, sawing down his emotions in the process.

Nicklaus left Baltusrol feeling his game had returned, and believing that he'd never lose a meaningful duel to Palmer. "I just felt like I was the better player," Nicklaus said. The box scores backed him up.

"Arnold was the best player in the world for about seven years there," Jack would say, "but then he ceased being so."

The *Sports Illustrated* headline out of Baltusrol read like this: "Jack Delivers the Crusher." Nicklaus would tell *SI* about his third-round experience at the eighteenth hole, where he out-drove Palmer by thirty yards.

"'[Palmer] hits a 4-wood toward the green. Crowd goes wild,'" Nicklaus said. "'I hit a 4-iron. Silence. Nothing from the crowd. I figure his is close and mine must be long, into the pro shop or down the driveway. Turns out I'm 15 feet from the hole, he's just over the green, yet the crowd cheers his shot.'

"[Pause] 'Big deal.'"

Part II

CHAPTER 10

• Transformation

T HE KIDS IN LATROBE were like kids everywhere; their teasing could be downright cruel. Some classmates would mock Arnold Palmer's daughters when their father blew a tournament.

Some would remind Peg and Amy that Jack Nicklaus was the superior player.

"Arna" was the nickname they reserved for Peg, Arnold's older daughter.

The small-minded among the small-town residents resented the fame and fortune that had found one of their own. There was a saying in Latrobe among those jealous of Arnold's success: The Palmers always come out smelling like a rose.

"It was horrible," Peg said. "When he lost, going to school the next day was hell ... Everyone's official position was that my father was a native son, 'and we're all so proud of him.' But behind the scenes it was different.

"In the battle they were rooting for him. It's afterward, when the victory happens and all the good stuff goes to the victor, that's when the jealousy kicked in for people who used to be close and then felt pushed aside."

As a teenager Peg was an ace swimmer and straight-A student, and she said her success coupled with her father's "just pissed everyone off."

Sure, Arnold Palmer was revered in the region, the state, the country, around the world. No other golfer was ever supported by a more vocal crowd than the one Palmer found in his Oakmont backyard.

And Arnie always made sure to declare his hometown as Latrobe, not Pittsburgh, when he traveled about. But inside a town of eleven thousand residents, one slight — real or imagined — can quickly turn a working-class hero into a man who has forgotten his roots, a man who has grown too big for his britches.

"A very ethnic and competitive place," Peg said of her home community. "I would've given anything . . . not to have a famous father."

"My dad thought I wasn't proud of him and didn't appreciate him, but really it was so painful that people didn't root for him."

The resentment cut across class lines. If some of the blue-collar locals felt snubbed, some of the white-collar members of Latrobe Country Club were also put off by the rise of the laborer's son.

"They tried to diminish him," Peg said.

Away from his hometown people still rooted for Arnold Palmer as they rooted for no other figure in sports. It didn't matter that Arnie wasn't winning major championships anymore.

It only mattered that he showed up and made the fans feel as if he was playing solely for them.

On May 3, 1970, six years after he claimed his last major title, Palmer's enduring star power was on full display at the Byron Nelson Classic. He was playing that morning with John Schroeder, a rookie on the PGA Tour, and Jack Nicklaus.

Schroeder was the son of the former Wimbledon and U.S. Open champ Ted. He grew up around Jack Kramer and other big sports stars and celebrities, so no, he was not easily flustered or awed.

But a little before 8:00 a.m. Schroeder couldn't believe the sound Arnold Palmer generated on his first hole of a thirty-six-hole day. Schroeder and the thirty-year-old Jack Nicklaus were on the par-five green in two as they watched the forty-year-old Palmer play from a Preston Trail Golf Club bunker, his ball nestled in the sand to the left of the stick.

Arnie wasn't telling himself to get it close; he was telling himself to do exactly what he did: knock it in for eagle.

"And the crowd made the goddamnedest noise of my life," Schroeder said. The cheer was as thunderous as a Sunday roar at Augusta on the back nine.

"It startled me," Schroeder said, "so early in the morning."

Arnie's Army was back on the march, trying to hunt down its Public Enemy Number One, Nicklaus, while the twenty-four-year-old rookie from Texas took his front-row seat. They started on the back nine on this Sunday morning as tournament officials scrambled to make up for Thursday's rainout, sending threesomes off both tees.

At the twelfth Nicklaus ran his approach right up the flagpole, and his ball stopped dead on the lip. The huge early-bird gallery released a barely perceptible ripple of applause. Palmer? His second shot didn't scare the hole at all, and the crowd reacted as if he had dunked another eagle.

Still incredulous after all these years, Nicklaus turned to Schroeder. "See what I have to put up with out here?" he said.

It only got worse from there. Palmer and his camp were long obsessed with Nicklaus's talent for beating him, one way or another. Three months after their last major championship duel—the 1967 Open at Baltusrol—Palmer held a small final-round lead over Nicklaus at the Thunderbird in Jersey as he paced and fidgeted for seventy minutes in the locker room, certain that Jack was about to catch him.

Palmer was watching a Cowboys-Giants game on TV as he received scoring updates from a tournament official with a walkie-talkie. The man kept telling Palmer that Billy Casper was fading, and Palmer kept asking the man the same question: "Where's Jack?"

Palmer handed two balls to his pilot, Darrell Brown, and told him to keep them handy in the event of overtime. Finally the official with the walkie-talkie informed Palmer that Nicklaus was on the eighteenth green, facing a nine-foot birdie attempt that would force a playoff.

Arnold had seen this movie before.

"He missed!" the official shouted. "He blew it."

"Ask again," said a stunned Palmer.

"No, he missed it," the official responded.

Palmer smiled over the endgame revisions in a script he was sick of living. He would win only four tournaments between that 1967 Thunderbird and these thirty-six holes with Nicklaus at the 1970 Byron Nelson, none a Grand Slam event. In 1968, the year he became the first golfer to clear a million bucks in earnings for his career, Palmer had a crack at the one major he'd never won, the PGA Championship, but followed up a remarkable three-wood out of the rough with a missed eight-footer that would've earned him a playoff with Julius Boros.

Arnold was forced to qualify for the 1969 U.S. Open, and two months later he shot an 82 in the first round of the PGA, equaling his worst number as a pro. Palmer withdrew from the tournament when the bursitis in his hip started bothering him more than his score. His slump was met with a tidal wave of fan mail offering exotic treatments for his bad hip and worse short game — pads, liniments, gimmicky putters. One fan sent some radioactive plutonium and advised that Arnold should sleep with it.

Palmer was the million-dollar golfer with his own jet and an endorsement portfolio to die for. He was being asked to declare himself a Republican candidate for governor of Pennsylvania, and an Associated Press poll had named him Athlete of the Decade, picking him over Bill Russell, Sandy Koufax, Johnny Unitas, Willie Mays, and Mickey Mantle.

But Arnold would've given back every shiny trophy, every political endorsement, and every red cent he'd won on the course if it meant seizing his first major in six years. Arnold's only consolation was Nicklaus's parallel dry spell: Jack hadn't won a big one since Baltusrol.

The 1970 Byron Nelson wasn't a big one, but the Palmer-Nicklaus duel down the stretch made it big enough. "They were trying to kick each other's ass," Schroeder said. "They weren't talking a lot to each other; both were talking more to me. There was not a whole lot of conversation between them other than 'You're away,' or 'Nice shot,' or 'Is it my turn?'"

On the seventy-second hole of the tournament, their thirty-sixth of the day, Arnold was one shot behind Jack (Schroeder was two back) and dead tired. Those ten years and change he was giving away to Jack were showing up: Arnold had spent much of the closing eighteen sitting on his golf bag while Nicklaus and Schroeder fired away.

When Nicklaus drove left and behind a TV tower on the final hole, cheers were heard from the crowd. Jack had finally shed some weight and let his buzz cut grow out as part of a makeover that was in its early stages, but he still couldn't touch the magnetism of Palmer.

Nicklaus got relief from the tower and smacked his eight-iron approach long and into the crowd; Palmer was on the fringe in two. Jack chipped short, then just missed a twenty-foot par saver that would've won the event.

After running his birdie try six feet past the cup, and after watching

Arnold Palmer, walking on air at the 1960 Masters.

In the Palmer household Arnold's tough-love father, Deacon, was the one who always called the shots.

Charlie Nicklaus, nurturing father and pharmacist, congratulates his thirteen-year-old son after his victory over sixteen-year-old Stan Ziobrowski at the U.S. Junior Amateur championship.

John Dominis/Getty Images

When he needed to blow off some steam, the ultimate "equipment freak" went to work in his shop.

John Dominis/Getty Images

Other than playing golf, Palmer enjoyed nothing more than smoking his cigarettes and flying his planes.

John Dominis/Getty Images

Arnie congratulates Jack at Oakmont in 1962, where Nicklaus broke all of western Pennsylvania's heart.

Arnie and Jack staged a fierce heavyweight battle for control of their sport.

Arnold's parents thought Winnie was "Grace Kelly come to Latrobe."

Barbara Nicklaus was always there to seal her man's victories with a kiss.

In 1964 Nicklaus puts the green jacket on Palmer, the king again at Augusta.

Palmer puts the green jacket on Nicklaus after Jack's record-shattering victory at Augusta in 1965.

Nicklaus and Palmer blazed a trail of greatness at the British Open.

Fat Jack almost always had a leg up on Arnie and his army.

Palmer's duels with Nicklaus were never any day at the beach.

At the end of another gamble gone wrong, Arnie hands Jack a fifty-dollar bill.

Fat Jack transformed himself into a dashing figure, and the crowds rewarded him in kind.

Arnie and Jack, cheek to cheek after Palmer's victory over Nicklaus at the 1973 Hope. It was Arnold's last dance; he never won again on the PGA Tour.

The eagle lands for Nicklaus at the 1986 Masters, as his son Jackie takes flight.

In 1994 Palmer says goodbye to his final U.S. Open at Oak-mont, where he first lost his crown to Nicklaus.

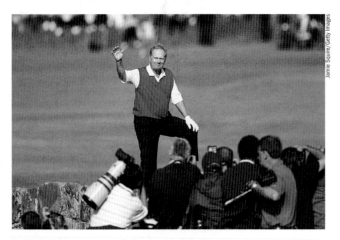

In 2005 Nicklaus says goodbye to major championship golf at St. Andrews, where he won two of his three British Open titles.

Nicklaus bogey, Palmer had a sudden spring in his aging step. He was looking at this six-footer as a gimme.

"He was so confident and cocky," Schroeder said. "He looked at Jack and he looked at me. He lined up the putt and banged it in and just looked at Jack and grinned at him. Arnold just slammed it into the back of the hole, like it was automatic ... I'll never forget the way he hit that putt to tie Jack. It was like, 'Why are we even wasting our time? Let's go right to the playoff hole.'"

Palmer and Nicklaus thanked Schroeder for his company and then headed for the par-five fifteenth, a 555-yard sudden-death test. The hopes of many in the crowd of fifteen thousand were immediately deflated when Nicklaus out-drove Palmer by a good twenty yards.

Arnold was short on his second shot, and Jack was pin-high and just off the green. Palmer chipped to eighteen feet; Nicklaus chipped to eighteen inches. Arnold missed, Jack made, and the Golden Bear had once again overcome the anti-Nicklaus sentiment in the crowd.

Byron Nelson, the tournament host, told Nicklaus he was a little embarrassed by the gallery's behavior and thanked him for conducting himself with ample grace.

"I was very proud of Jack," Nelson said. "It was very evident the people were pulling for Arnold, but I give Jack credit for how he handled it. I developed more of a feeling for him. If anyone criticized him, he never looked at the guy or acknowledged him. He just played."

With his winning scorecard signed, Nicklaus went into the clubhouse to take a victory call from Vice President Spiro Agnew.

"Hello, this is Nicklaus," Jack said after pressing the phone to his ear.

The vice president asked for Palmer.

"Palmer? What do you want him for?"

Agnew had played a recent round with Arnold and wanted to chat.

"When I found out it was for Arnold," Nicklaus would tell reporters, "I went back out and picked up the trophy."

The victory at the Byron Nelson was the first for Jack Nicklaus since the death of his father and very best friend, Charlie, ten weeks earlier.

Charlie was fifty-six when he died. He'd been at a football game with his wife, Helen, when she thought her husband was turning a shade of yellow. She thought hepatitis, maybe, until the doctors told her she wasn't that lucky.

Cancer of the pancreas and liver.

As they wheeled Charlie into the operating room, he waved to his family and said, "Don't think it ain't been charming." The doctors came out of surgery and reported that Charlie had six weeks to three months to live.

On his last Christmas Day, Charlie received an unannounced visitor at his home. Woody Hayes rang the doorbell at three in the afternoon and told his friend that his relationship with his boy, Jack, "is the best father-son relationship I've ever seen."

Charlie succumbed to the cancer on February 19, and his boy was broken in half. On so many levels Jack was the spitting image of his old man.

They loved to needle others with the straightest of faces. Charlie had been very competitive, just as competitive as Jack. Neither one could ever sit still. They both loved to talk sports as much as they loved to eat.

Charlie was different in one regard: he wasn't half as straight-laced as his son. Before Jack's 1960 U.S. Amateur match with Phil Rodgers, Charlie told his boy that Rodgers had stood on the clubhouse roof and announced, "The bigger they are, the harder they fall."

Jack was foaming at the mouth when he destroyed Rodgers on the course, only for his battered opponent to tell him later that Charlie's tale was a complete fabrication.

Yes, the pharmacist was a good-time Charlie. He was the opposite of Arnold's father, Deke, who retreated from public view and remained adept at finding hiding places on golf courses.

Charlie was up front and center, and he was often helpful in smoothing over Jack's jagged edges. The Palmer family might've had little use for Jack, but Charlie was an easier figure to embrace.

"He and I had a lot of fun together," Arnold said. Palmer and Charlie were known to share a drink or two in the clubhouse bar.

"Jack's father was a great guy," Arnold said. "Matter of fact, he was a better guy than his son."

Phil Rodgers aside, Charlie Nicklaus had a way with opponents. At Jack's first pro event, the 1958 Rubber City Open, Charlie bought cigars for his son's pairing mate, Charlie Sifford, the pioneering black player who had outscored Jack in the first round.

"Be careful," Jack's father told Sifford through a smile. "Jack didn't like what happened yesterday. He's going to be mean today."

Sifford got a kick out of it, at least until Jack put it to him in the second round.

Jack liked telling the story of the time he was a fifteen-year-old passenger in Charlie's car when a young driver cut off his father and beat him to a parking spot. Ol' Charlie hopped out, tore into the young man's car, reached under the dash, and ripped out whatever wiring he could grab.

"What are you doing?" the parking-spot thief asked.

"I'm doing what I want to do," Charlie said. "If you want to come stop me, come stop me."

Jack and his father went straight from that confrontation to dinner, and Charlie never said another word about it.

"My dad actually was a gentle giant," Jack said. "But don't get on the wrong side of him. Don't do something against his kid."

Charlie's kid, the winner of the Byron Nelson Classic, wanted to do something in his father's name. Jack had slacked off since defeating Palmer at Baltusrol. He was trying to get by on talent more, trying to grind it out in practice less. Having beaten back Arnie and his army, Nicklaus couldn't find another source of motivation to drive him to a new level of achievement.

Charlie's death would be that source.

"I was playing sloppy golf," Jack said. "I knew I wasn't working out the way I could ... I think my dad lived for what I did; that was his greatest thrill and pleasure, and I think I let him down. And I said, 'Well, he would've wanted to kick me right in the rear end and tell me to go out and do what I had to do.' And that's what I did."

Jack went back to work on his game, just as he'd gone back to work on his weight, his hairstyle, and his clothes. He wanted to be a new man for his old man.

The extra blood, sweat, and tears finally paid off at the 1970 British Open, where Nicklaus won a playoff from the Texas playboy Doug Sanders, who hung out with the Frank Sinatra–Sammy Davis Jr. Rat Packers and who claimed he hit his ball so straight that he left the fairway only to secure a young lady's phone number. Sanders choked on a two-and-a-half-foot putt at the close of regulation, and Nicklaus flung his putter toward the heavens at the close of the playoff.

That one was for Charlie. At thirty, Jack had passed Palmer with his eighth professional major triumph, but Arnie wasn't on anyone's mind at the time. Nicklaus walked into the press room at St. Andrews and heard Bob Green of the Associated Press say, "Jack, that's ten major championships. You've only got three more to tie Bobby Jones."

Green was including Nicklaus's two U.S. Amateur titles in his math.

"I'd never counted them before that," Jack said.

It was a hard claim to believe, given his stated goal of becoming the best player of all time. Either way, Nicklaus had a clear target in Jones. To get there he would continue working on his diet and conditioning, a commitment he made after fatigue set in at the 1969 Ryder Cup at Royal Birkdale, where Nicklaus — as a show of sportsmanship and goodwill — famously conceded a putt to Tony Jacklin to allow Great Britain to halve the match.

But Nicklaus would make another fundamental change to honor his father's memory. As much as people suggested Jack was changing his appearance to improve his image and to be more like Arnie, Nicklaus decided to get as far away from Palmer as he could in a different arena.

Charlie had wanted his son to break away from Mark McCormack's Palmer-centric International Management Group, and Jack was finally acting on his father's wish. With Palmer and Gary Player in the McCormack stable, Charlie felt his boy wasn't getting the proper attention and respect from IMG reps. McCormack had landed deals for Nicklaus with Pontiac, Coca-Cola, and Gates Learjet, among others, but he was spending most of his time and energy on Palmer; he'd handed Jack over to one of his underlings, Jay Lafave.

"Arnold got the Cadillac, Gary got the Buick, and Jack got the Pontiac," said Put Pierman, Jack's friend and business associate. "That was distressing to Charlie. Jack was beating the both of them on the course."

Palmer thought it was a mistake for Nicklaus to leave IMG, as McCormack had earned Jack hundreds of thousands of dollars in endorsements and exhibitions. But no, Arnie wasn't all that broken up about it. Nicklaus's departure meant that a clear and present threat to Palmer's in-house standing was walking out the door.

And Jack wasn't turning back. "They represented me for nine years and I made no money," Nicklaus claimed. "That's why I left. Arnold was most important to them, and I won all these tournaments, and my net worth wasn't any more, barely, than when I started with them. And so I said, 'Well, the only way I'm going to do this is to do it myself.'"

McCormack contended that Nicklaus had blown through his money and was merely using him as a scapegoat. The agent was used to acquiring big-league talent, not losing it, so he was stung by Jack's defection.

Truth was, their marriage appeared doomed as early as 1963. Jack had committed then to a Cincinnati pro-am run by a friend, Mort Olman, when he was told that McCormack had exhibitions scheduled for him in France and Japan that conflicted with Olman's event.

"No way," Nicklaus said. "That's what McCormack thinks. I'll be in Cincinnati. He's not sending my ass all over the world."

Nicklaus ultimately filed for divorce from IMG and started his own marketing company. He traded in McCormack for Pierman, who was already supporting Jack in the building of his golf club in Dublin, Ohio — Muirfield Village. Pierman and Nicklaus met with McCormack at his home in Pepper Pike, Ohio, outside Cleveland, and told the IMG founder that they were unhappy with the company's treatment of Nicklaus and wanted out.

"Mark McCormack did in fact have a loyalty to Arnold," Pierman said. "Arnold was his first client. So how the hell else was Mark going to handle the conflict of interest [with Nicklaus], other than undoubtedly when the best deal came in it went to Arnold irrespective of what happened on the golf course?"

Pierman was in the heavy-construction industry, and he became something of a personal adviser to Nicklaus. It was his Weight Watchers diet — Pierman lost thirty-three pounds in thirteen weeks — that Nicklaus used to drop twenty-five pounds.

They put together a team under the name of Golden Bear, Inc., and the business plan was as subtle as a skulled one-iron.

"It was sort of an unspoken fact: we were going to beat the hell out of Arnold Palmer," Pierman said. "Our goal was to kick Arnold Palmer's ass in business like we were kicking it on the golf course."

Palmer was the much wealthier man; Jack had next to nothing socked away. "Arnold was really beating him in endorsement money at the time," Pierman said. "It was no contest with Jack."

The grand plan was to change all that. Nicklaus didn't just want to be a greater golf champion than Palmer. He wanted to be the smarter executive, the more successful product spokesman, the better manufacturer of golf equipment and clothing, and the superior course designer.

From scratch, Nicklaus also wanted to create a country club out of an Ohio bog that put to shame Palmer's Bay Hill Golf Club in Orlando.

"Make no mistake about it," Pierman said. "Any endeavor that Arnold was involved in or had an interest in, Jack was going to be better at."

Nicklaus had already done some work with course designers Pete Dye and Desmond Muirhead, and the Muirfield project had become his obsession. With Palmer entrenched as proprietor of Bay Hill — Arnie simply bought a preexisting club — Jack desperately wanted a place to call his own. He wanted to create another Augusta National near his hometown, and he risked financial ruin to pull it off.

McCormack had pleaded with Jack to bail on his Muirfield dream, another reason why Jack hired a new business manager. "You can't do it," McCormack had told Nicklaus. "You don't have the money, and I can't find it anyway. There's no way I can continue to fund land purchases, and I think you've overstepped in your ambition."

Nicklaus wasn't going to be denied his own Shangri-la; he thought it could enhance his legacy in the game. Back when he first looked at this Dublin site, a site discovered by his friend Ivor Young, Nicklaus was taken by the natural creeks cutting through the valleys.

He asked Dye for his opinion. "Curly," Dye said, using the nickname he gave the buzz-cut kid, "this is the best damn site you're going to find without an ocean or mountains. Go for it."

So Nicklaus did. When the project looked doomed because of a lack of financial support, Nicklaus turned to a prominent Columbus family, the Wolfes. John W. Wolfe was in publishing, TV, banking, and real estate, and he had an equities firm called the Ohio Company. Nicklaus and his executives met with Wolfe, made their pitch, and sat there waiting anxiously for his response.

"Well," Wolfe said, "that's as easy as a bear shitting in the woods."

Wolfe would deliver a firm underwriting of $7 million, and the Golden Bear would forge ahead with his goal of building a course and real-estate development worthy of landing a pro tour event.

But to establish Nicklaus as an endorser and businessman the equal of Palmer, Pierman needed to make Jack more user-friendly. It wasn't an easy task. Palmer was the ultimate schmoozer, a performer who thrived on human contact, a man who sucked the energy out of a crowd. Nicklaus? The crowds sucked the energy out of him.

Palmer, Nicklaus said, "will be the first one at a cocktail party, and he likes it. And I'm trying to figure out how I can get to the last end of the cocktail party so I'm doing my obligation to spend fifteen minutes with the sponsor. Now, I'll stay for dinner and I'm very happy to do it. But Arnold's gone because there's no more socializing."

For Nicklaus, people skills needed to be practiced like bunker shots. He was abrupt and bluntly honest to a fault, and Pierman told him he was an incredibly rude speaker on the phone.

"You're kidding me," Nicklaus said.

"No, I'm not kidding you," said Pierman, who pushed Nicklaus to soften his act and call his corporate backers to let them know how much he appreciated their support.

"Are you serious?" Jack said. "I don't talk to these people."

"You're going to start now," Pierman shot back. "You're endorsing them. They're showcasing you, not me, and they need to talk to you."

The personality transplant wasn't any one-hour procedure. Nicklaus was a spokesman for a charity benefiting handicapped children, and one day he was running late for a meeting at his North Palm Beach offices with a twelve-year-old girl who was "just buckled up in braces like you couldn't see," Pierman said.

Nicklaus was being photographed plowing balls out of a sand trap near his Lost Tree Village home when a furious Pierman arrived.

"Jesus Christ, what the fuck are you doing?" Pierman shouted at Nicklaus. "Do you realize you're now an hour and twenty minutes late to meet this poster child? If you don't get out of that bunker, I'm going to screw you up. You're going to be in braces."

Nicklaus raced to the office and made the young girl's month.

With Charlie gone, Pierman was among the few people around Nicklaus who wasn't afraid to put him in his place. Pierman and his son once accompanied Nicklaus and his boys to a Miami Dolphins game and watched as Jack treated his walk through the parking lots like a walk up the thirteenth fairway at Augusta.

Jack was coldly brushing past well-wishers and autograph seekers as if zoning in on his next shot. When Nicklaus blew past one man in a wheelchair hoping for a few seconds of his time, Pierman grabbed him by the arm and yanked him to a halt.

"Shake this guy's hand," Pierman barked.

Nicklaus followed the order, then got his comeuppance anyway. Another ten paces later, a woman ran up to Jack, threw her arms around him, and then stepped back in eye-popping awe.

"I can't believe it," she cried. "It's *Arnold Palmer!*"

Nicklaus couldn't get away from Palmer. After he'd slimmed down and grown his blond locks to hip, early seventies length, many observers saw it as a case of Jack imitating Arnie.

The Golden Bear batted away any suggestion that Palmer had something to do with it. He had his story, and he was sticking to it. He told Barbara on the plane ride back from the 1969 Ryder Cup that he was going to heed his doctor's advice and take the fatigue as a sign he needed to lose weight.

He'd take four or five clubs out onto the course and jog between shots. He'd call his clothing supplier, Hart Schaffner Marx, and schedule a tailor to come and measure him for some threads to fit his soon-to-be-sleeker body.

Barbara encouraged him to trash his army pants and painfully dull black-and-white outfits and add some color and flair to his wardrobe. The hair change? "It just happened," Barbara said.

One day she woke up and her husband's blond stubble had sprouted wings and covered his ears.

"It had nothing to do with trying to change my image," Jack swore. He said he was just going with the times, but it was clear he didn't want to be known as Fat Jack the rest of his life.

As Nicklaus grew easier on the eyes, and as Palmer stopped winning on a consistent basis, the TV cameras turned more and more toward Jack. "I don't know if [the transformation] was truly inspired by Arnie," said Frank Chirkinian, the CBS producer, "but it worked . . . Jack became a damn near movie idol. It was a metamorphosis right before our eyes."

Jack Nicklaus as Robert Redford—who would've thunk it? With the summer breeze making his blond hair dance across his forehead, Nicklaus had stepped in Palmer's line. He'd become sexy, of all things, and the women noticed in a big way.

"My God," Jack told Pierman. "I can't believe all the young girls in my gallery."

The young girls would sidle up to Pierman and Nicklaus's caddie, Angelo Argea, and ask them to pass along their phone numbers to Jack. "The tournament was not complete if he didn't get at least one," Barbara said.

Wife and husband laughed about it. Barbara trusted Jack, and after all these years of watching her husband act as a barely animate prop on Arnie's stage, she was happy for him.

One attractive, well-known woman was most eager to test that happiness. She was a member of a prominent hotel family, and she asked Pierman to hand Nicklaus the number of the room where she was staying.

"I'd love to be able to meet and talk with Jack," the woman said.

"Excuse me," Pierman responded, "but the quickest way for you to make that happen is to go five yards away from me and speak with his wife, Barbara. She'll be seeing him before I do."

The blood drained from the woman's face, and she disappeared into the crowd.

Jack Nicklaus still wasn't Arnold Palmer. He still wasn't able to convince the masses that he was trying to win for them the way Arnie did.

But at the start of the seventies, the period Tom Wolfe would describe as the "Me Decade," Nicklaus was coming into his own as a man. He'd bypassed Palmer in the game of golf, and now he was closing the gap in the game of love.

"The adulation? Yeah, absolutely, I liked that," Nicklaus said. "Here you are a little fat boy and all of a sudden you've got a different image. Sure, of course you like that. Why wouldn't you?"

CHAPTER 11

• Pebble Beach

B Y THE SUMMER OF 1972, Arnold Palmer and Jack Nicklaus had their routine down pat. Half the time they acted like big brother and kid brother. The other half they acted like Muhammad Ali and Joe Frazier.

Big brother/kid brother moment: They came together to win two more PGA team championships at Palmer's Laurel Valley Golf Club, and at night they'd join Dave Marr and a few others for quiet get-togethers around the pool. "They even swim nice together," Marr said of Arnie and Jack.

Ali/Frazier moment: Palmer was once playing in Charlotte when he was in the locker room with John Derr of CBS, looking for a sports section from that day's paper. Someone handed him a copy of the *Charlotte Observer,* and Arnold headed straight for the men's room. "I'm going in to take a Nicklaus," he announced.

Big brother/kid brother moment: Palmer and Nicklaus won again as a team, this time at the 1971 Ryder Cup. "I think we were a little imposing on who we were playing to start with," Nicklaus said. "I mean, they said, 'We may be able to handle Arnold Palmer. We may be able to handle Jack Nicklaus. But the two of them together, we're not going to be able to handle.' I don't think we ever got beat at much of anything."

Ali/Frazier moment: Nicklaus often celebrated his January birthday during the Bing Crosby at Pebble Beach, and prior to Jack's split with

IMG, Mark McCormack would want to take him out to dinner. "But Arnold wouldn't go," said McCormack's wife, Nancy. "So we didn't go to dinner with Jack . . . With the tension with the Nicklauses and all that, it's not what I'd call a holiday."

Nicklaus won the Crosby in 1972, and five months later he was back at Pebble Beach for another crack at his third U.S. Open title. Using his father's memory as inspiration, Nicklaus was playing the best golf of his life.

In 1971, when he won nearly a quarter-million bucks on tour, Jack took the PGA Championship (played in February that year) in Palm Beach Gardens while allowing Gary Player, his closest contender, to stay at his home.

Jack then lost the Masters by two shots to Charles Coody and was so upset he'd blown his chance at the calendar Grand Slam that he told his wife he'd go fishing rather than play in his next event, the Tournament of Champions.

"They're going to think you're a big, spoiled baby and that you're pouting," Barbara told him. "You made your plane reservations, and you're going."

Nicklaus won the Tournament of Champions, and that was the first and last time Barbara told Jack what he would and wouldn't do with his playing schedule.

Nicklaus would claim his second consecutive Byron Nelson, then lose a U.S. Open playoff to the new star on tour, Lee Trevino. Jack would rebound the following spring to seize the 1972 Masters, the first played since the death of Bobby Jones, who was sixty-nine when the syringomyelia finally claimed him in December. Nicklaus hadn't just honored Jones: he'd matched Palmer's record total of four green jackets.

Entering the 1972 Open at Pebble, Palmer had less reason to be hopeful. Age was becoming a common theme in pieces written about the forty-two-year-old Palmer, who had been around long enough to see Mike Reasor, his caddie during the Billy Casper Olympic collapse, join the tour and outscore his old boss, 66 to 73, in the first round of the Dow Jones tournament in Jersey a couple years earlier.

Around the same time the army that had failed so many times to rattle Nicklaus was failing to rattle even the likes of Dave Stockton, who held off Arnie at the 1970 PGA despite the best attempts of at least one Palmer loyalist. Stockton had the lead when he three-putted early in the final round and heard a fan shout, "You've got him now, Arnold."

Stockton was furious. "As soon as [the fan] shouted it," he said, "I said, 'Aha, Arnold's really got me. We'll see.'"

Stockton won the tournament by two shots. This was the same Stockton who was spooked by his pairing with Palmer at the 1966 Los Angeles Open, where a thunderous ovation for the eventual winner, Arnie, left the twenty-four-year-old "absolutely petrified . . . I looked down at my shoes and my toes were shaking."

Palmer wasn't the same fearsome figure anymore. He had never been a strong chipper around the greens, and his putting touch — once regarded among the finest of all time — had stopped delivering him the usual supply of thirty-footers. Palmer followed up a winless 1970 season with three nonmajor victories in 1971 and then a winless first half of 1972 that included a thirty-third-place finish at the Masters, fourteen strokes behind Nicklaus's crowning 286.

Arnold actually had a ruling go against him in the 1972 Masters, another sign that Augusta National was no longer his stage. At the ninth hole of his second round, Palmer landed his approach in a depression left by a chair and requested a free drop. He didn't get one. He was forced to take a bogey on his first ball instead of the par he scored on a provisional while the rules committee deliberated, and then an enraged Palmer slashed his way out of contention while Nicklaus rolled on.

The gap between the game's two biggest names was widening. "Jack just grabbed [Palmer] by the throat," Stockton said, "and strangled him to death."

As Nicklaus tightened his grip on the sport, Palmer's biggest victory was scored a long way from the pro tour. He purchased Latrobe Country Club, the very place where his father had taught him that blue collar should always defer to blue blood.

"You're crazy," Deke Palmer told his boy. "What do you want to buy that place for? It's nothing but a money pit."

Arnold wanted to buy it for the sake of his old man, and for the sake of the members who thought Deke's boy was destined to be a ditch digger. "You could see [the pride] on my father's face," said Arnold's younger sister, Sandy. "Whether he thought it was a good idea or not, no question he was very, very proud."

Arnold fixed up the place and, of course, kept his father on as head pro. "I think Arnie has made good," ol' Deke said, in a rare compliment for his own flesh and blood. The father wasn't about to let the new owner of Latrobe get too full of himself.

"I still bawl out Arnie whenever he needs it," he said.

Palmer needed someone to light a fire under his ass as he arrived at Pebble Beach in June of 1972, and the sight of Nicklaus, the favorite to win his third Open championship, was a good bet to do the trick. At the Open the year before, three months after Ali and Frazier fought an epic battle in Madison Square Garden, Palmer and Nicklaus traded verbal haymakers in the press.

Arnold was fed up again with Jack's slow play and decided to go public with his beef. Palmer told reporters he thought the Merion layout was a fair Open test but added, "What is unfair is to play in the afternoon and wait at every tee for two or three groups ahead of you to hit.

"That's ridiculous. We took five hours to play because play was not moving earlier in the day. I heard that Nicklaus and his pairing mates got twenty-three or twenty-five minutes behind the group ahead of them. They should have been spoken to and moved up. What's good for the goose is good for the gander."

The following day Nicklaus returned fire on Palmer. "I've got my ammunition," he said. "When we played in the morning, Arnold on Thursday and myself on Friday, I finished two minutes sooner than he did. And when we played in the afternoon, he was eleven minutes quicker."

The dichotomy of the Nicklaus-Palmer relationship was on full display. Jack would claim that he "kidded" with Arnold about the controversy on the Merion putting green, and five weeks later they were back at Palmer's Laurel Valley Golf Club as teammates looking to win another PGA team title.

"Jack can play as slow as he wants," Arnold said then, "as long as he makes birdies."

They played their gentleman's game like gentlemen, never exchanging harsh words with each other in public view. Opponents said they never saw Arnie and Jack engage in even one shouting match behind closed clubhouse doors, although Jack was known to spend little time in the locker room while Arnie loved sharing a beer and a joke with the boys.

When Palmer and Nicklaus were on the circuit, Palmer's older daughter, Peg, would occasionally babysit the Nicklaus children, Jackie, Steve, and Nan. Winnie and Barbara kept in touch, writing and calling as often as they could. Their friendship ensured that the competitive tension between their husbands never completely burned the bridges between the two camps.

But with the careers of Arnold and Jack heading in opposite directions, the Palmer-Nicklaus buildup to a major championship just wasn't what it used to be. Truth was, on the eve of the 1972 Open at Pebble, Nicklaus didn't view Palmer as a serious threat.

He was now focusing on five-foot-seven Lee Buck Trevino, the reigning British Open champ and former thirty-dollar-a-week caddie and shoeshine boy who beat Nicklaus at the 1968 Open at Oak Hill and again in the playoff at the 1971 Open at Merion.

That victory at Merion, wrote Dave Anderson in the *New York Times,* "projected [Trevino] as a threat to supplant Arnold Palmer as golf's most appealing competitor." Trevino was a nonstop talker and jokester, a self-described street hustler from Dallas who grew up in a home that had no electricity or indoor plumbing but did have a close-up view of the emerald Glen Lakes Country Club fairways, where Trevino first saw how the other half lived.

The grandson of an immigrant gravedigger from Mexico, Trevino was an eighth-grade dropout who ended up in the marines and later on the pro tour with his own army of fans known as "Lee's Fleas." Trevino was a driving-range pro with a homemade swing, and he made himself tournament tough by winning five-dollar bets with two dollars in his pocket.

Trevino hated the Masters; he hit the ball too low, and his humble Mexican American roots didn't jibe with the WASP-y elitism that was as much a part of Augusta National as the azaleas. But everywhere else the guy was a hell of a closer, and Jack Nicklaus was having a devil of a time trying to beat him.

Nicklaus's regular caddie, Angelo Argea, the Korean War vet who kept a silver-haired Afro, would stand with his man before the leaderboard of an event Jack was winning and rattle off the names of contenders they didn't have to sweat. Argea never thought Palmer stood a chance against Nicklaus, not in the seventies, but the caddie rarely passed one familiar name on the leaderboard without warning Nicklaus, "We've got to watch Trevino."

Jack was watching when Trevino heaved a rubber snake his way before the playoff at Merion; Nicklaus had waved for Trevino to throw it and took no offense. Jack was listening the day before, after missing a fourteen-footer for the win, when Trevino lived up to the "psych artist" label Nicklaus had given him.

Trevino was asked how he thought he'd fare in an eighteen-hole one-on-one with the world's best player.

"And I looked at the guy," Trevino said, "and I said, 'Listen, Jack and I just played seventy-two holes. We just shot 280. I know you already have your headlines ... But I am playing in a playoff with Jack Nicklaus. Whether I win or lose, I have won. He has nothing to win.' And I looked right at [Nicklaus] and said, 'He's got everything to lose. So I'm not going to have any pressure on me.' And I know [Nicklaus] thought about that the whole time."

Trevino captured the playoff by three strokes.

He used an open stance and a flat baseball swing, and yet opponents considered him the purest ball striker since Ben Hogan. When Lee won the 1968 Open, Nicklaus said, "I didn't know Trevino from a load of coal." Jack knew him well enough four years later to believe that Trevino's hospitalization for bronchial pneumonia wouldn't keep him from teeing it up at Pebble Beach.

Trevino had a putting carpet slid into his El Paso hospital room to practice before the Open, and he spent time in his bed sketching the Pebble Beach layout with multicolored pencils. Four days before the first round, he was already trying to psych out Jack. "I think Nicklaus is going to be stale," Trevino said. "I think he's overtrained. He's been playing [the course] every day since last Wednesday. I think the only way to train myself is under competition."

On antibiotics, a pallid Trevino made it to Pebble, shot 74 in a practice round, and declared himself ready to defend his national championship.

The next day Nicklaus got the jump on him by shooting 71 to share the lead with five others, none named Trevino or Palmer. Lee managed another 74 on seventeen antibiotic pills, while Arnold stumbled to a 77 completely healthy.

Nicklaus was in his element on the rocky shoreline of Pebble Beach, where he'd won his second U.S. Amateur and a couple of Crosbys. This heaven-made piece of the Monterey Peninsula was his favorite

American course, and it wasn't likely that anyone in the Open field would be able to stay with him across four windswept rounds.

But on the second day Palmer came raging out of the past like an old lawman barreling through the swinging doors of a saloon. He neutralized the damage from his opening-round 77 with an improbable 68 and landed one stroke behind Nicklaus and five others at 144. Trevino was hanging in there at 146.

Palmer played a young man's game on this day, yet the salt was overtaking the pepper in his retreating hair and his slightly swollen jowls betrayed his age. Arnie had changed, his smoldering sex appeal diminished by time. No more dramatic flicks of a cigarette to the fairway grass: he'd quit smoking for good at a holiday party in 1970, when he promised to pay fifteen friends five hundred dollars a pop if he ever put another cigarette to his lips. Meanwhile, Nicklaus would still sneak a smoke here and there inside the Port-A-John at the turn.

In the third round, with the army out of mothballs and all revved up to go, Palmer's putter — one of the twelve hundred he was estimated to have in storage — hit the brakes on the charge. He actually left a four-footer short on the fourteenth hole.

"I only made one putt of any length," he complained.

At even-par 216, Nicklaus was alone in the lead after fifty-four holes, one ahead of Trevino, two ahead of Palmer. This wasn't Oakmont in 1962 or Baltusrol in 1967. Nicklaus had no doubt who would present his stiffest challenge in the last round, and his name wasn't Arnold Palmer.

"The reason I tormented Jack," Trevino said, "was because he knew if I ever got my nose out in front, I wasn't ever going to bogey a hole." At least Nicklaus would be able to monitor Trevino's every step; they were paired together for Sunday's closing eighteen.

The sun was out, the wind was strong, and the blue Pacific water was sending white waves crashing against the black rocks. The greens were fast and the stakes were high. ABC was using twenty-three color cameras and a blimp to broadcast images from thirteen holes, the most ever televised in a golf tournament.

Nicklaus came to the cliffs above Carmel Bay in full Golden Bear splendor, cutting the kind of dashing figure only Palmer was supposed to cut. The new Jack could've passed for a movie star who had taken a wrong turn north on the way to his Hollywood set. Nicklaus was dressed in a white shirt, a bright yellow sweater, and powder-gray slacks. The gusts made his blond hair snap heroically like the flag on a stick.

He held a four-shot lead over a tired Trevino after nine holes but went wide right on his drive at number ten, sending his ball over a bluff and sixty feet down into the beachfront sand. Jack's double bogey (Trevino made bogey) put one scuffling contender right back into the mix: Arnold Daniel Palmer. Arnie had an up-and-down front nine, but he did sink a thirty-five-footer on the third green and did jab his putter to the ground and pump his right fist to get the army believing one more time.

With Nicklaus at the twelfth and Palmer at the fourteenth, the spread between them was one lousy shot. Nicklaus sent his three-iron tee shot over the par-three hole, flubbed a wedge, and ended up with an eight-footer for bogey. At the same time Palmer was facing an eight-footer for birdie.

If Arnold made and Jack missed, Palmer would own the outright lead in the U.S. Open with four holes to play. They putted almost simultaneously, Jack pulling the trigger first. As Nicklaus's ball approached the cup, Trevino cried, "Get in there."

The ball listened, leaving Palmer with a chance only to tie. Arnold hunched over his ball, struck his classic knock-kneed, pigeon-toed pose, and stabbed at his birdie attempt the way he always had. His father, Deke, often complained that Arnold never followed through on a putt. This stroke was no different.

The ball slid by the hole to the left, and Palmer dropped into a squat as if ducking a hurled stone, raised his putter above his head, and whipped his shoulders to the right, his face clenched in a gruesome knot. Palmer was crushed. He bogeyed the next two holes and faded like a setting sun into the sea.

The clincher was the Nicklaus one-iron at the 218-yard seventeenth, a tee shot that hit the pin on a single bounce and nearly fell for an ace. The vanquished Trevino was right there to absorb the majesty of this stroke, one of the greatest he'd ever seen.

"Nobody was Jack's equal," Trevino said.

Nobody except Bobby Jones. Including his two U.S. Amateur titles, Nicklaus had thirteen major championships to his name, the same number Jones had before retiring at age twenty-eight.

Jones won his calendar-year amateur Grand Slam in 1930, and forty-two years later Nicklaus was halfway to the pro version he so coveted. In the manic moments after winning at Pebble, Jack was told he had a call coming in from the White House—just as he was told at the Byron Nelson two years earlier.

Only this time it wasn't Vice President Agnew asking for the loser, Arnold Palmer. On the day after five men were arrested for trying to break into the offices of the Democratic National Committee at the Watergate Hotel, President Nixon was calling to congratulate Jack Nicklaus on a job well done.

CHAPTER 12

• Last Dance

O N THE COURSE, Arnold Palmer kept losing ground to Jack Nicklaus at an alarming rate. Off the course, the scorecard was flipped upside down.

Palmer remained the most visible corporate spokesman in all of sports, protecting his lead over Nicklaus on the endorsement front. Mark McCormack's strategy with Palmer — market him as a successful man, not as a golf champion — was paying huge dividends.

McCormack didn't want to sell the image of Arnold celebrating tournament victories for a very simple reason: he knew the winning wouldn't last forever.

Arnie's Everyman likability? His earnestness? His appeal to consumers on both ends of the economic spectrum?

McCormack could sell those for a lifetime.

But even as the agent was making Palmer a fabulously wealthy man, "Mark and Arnold were always confrontational," said McCormack's wife, Nancy.

She described a tense business relationship that allowed for little leisure time. McCormack and Palmer would go out with their wives, "but socially I wouldn't say the four of us really had a good time together," Nancy said. "Mark was always on guard . . . I know each one meant the world to the other, but they didn't relax around each other and get drunk together. Mark didn't do that. He felt he had to be perfect."

In Palmer's eyes the agent fell short of perfection. "Arnold really didn't like sharing Mark and having him go off in all these other directions," Nancy said.

McCormack wasn't representing just golfers anymore. For starters he signed tennis star Rod Laver in 1968 after Laver sent him a handwritten letter requesting his help. McCormack also landed the Olympic skiing champ Jean-Claude Killy and the racing driver Jackie Stewart.

Palmer gave McCormack the go-ahead to sign Gary Player and Nicklaus years earlier and was having some regrets over his choice to allow the agent to break the marital vows they sealed with a handshake.

"He and I had meetings, a lot of meetings," Palmer said, "and we talked, and there were a lot of disagreements."

Palmer would write testy letters to McCormack, letters Arnold would give to his own aide, Doc Giffin, a former newspaperman and tour press secretary. Palmer said sometimes he would write McCormack "telling him how he didn't stick to our agreement or something else."

Those letters never made it to the mailbox.

"[McCormack] said, 'Don't ever write me a letter. If you have something to tell me, tell me right to my face,'" Palmer said. "Which I did. The letters never got sent."

Arnold kept doing ads for Cadillac, Coca-Cola, Holiday Inn, Aero Commander, Allstate, Arnold Palmer cardigans, and dozens of other brands, and his fans kept wondering if all these time-consuming business deals were adding strokes to Arnie's rounds.

Palmer wasn't about to decline the lucrative offers McCormack brought to him. Arnold's major championship play had turned stone cold, and he appreciated the fact that his nonstop TV and print ads allowed him to finish first in some public forum.

But he also harbored a Depression-era mentality, a belief that he needed to earn every nickel that was there to be earned.

"He never liked digging into principal," said his daughter Peg, "and he needed to pay for his airplane, which was one very expensive habit ... But then I think [endorsements] evolved from money into something to keep him in front of people."

Palmer wanted nothing more than to stay in front of people. The people were his inspiration, his motivation to perform. He wanted to achieve for them more than he wanted to achieve for himself.

That's what made his play in the 1973 Bob Hope so special: the smiles on the fans' faces, the sparkle in their eyes, as a forty-three-year-old Arnie charged through the California desert like the indomitable young golfer he used to be.

Palmer had won this tournament four times, including the inaugural event in 1960. He loved mingling with the celebrities who were attracted to the Hope like moths to a flame, and he loved how the Palm Springs sun kissed his wintered bones.

Sure, even his most ardent fans feared this bid for a fifth title was some kind of cruel mirage, a hoax, someone's idea of a practical joke. Palmer hadn't won a golf tournament in eighteen months, and yet he was one shot down entering the final leg of this ninety-hole marathon.

Arnie was trailing the latest hotshot kid on tour, Johnny Miller, and a man by the name of Jack William Nicklaus. On truth serum, every Arnie's Army member who had shouted, "Miss it, Fat Guts!" or "Hit it in the bunker, Fat Jack!" on one tee box or another over the years would concede that Nicklaus had something over Palmer, something that went beyond power and skill.

Jack was Arnie's kryptonite, and the feeling of weakness and inferiority that swept over Palmer in Nicklaus's presence wasn't one that sat well with the golfer cut out of the western Pennsylvania hillside.

Of course, Jack was the younger man by ten years — "almost eleven," Arnold said, taking liberties in rounding up from ten years, four months, and eleven days. That clear Nicklaus advantage probably wasn't brought up enough when Jack was measured against Arnold. "No," Palmer said, "it hasn't been ever."

Palmer was sensitive to the notion that he couldn't beat Nicklaus in a head-to-head confrontation on a tournament's final pressure-packed holes, that he could beat him only the way he did in his last tour victory, an easy triumph at New York's Westchester Golf Classic in July of 1971, when Nicklaus had to shoot 67 just to finish five strokes back.

Fifteen months later, after losing the U.S. Open to Nicklaus at Pebble Beach, Palmer was so desperate to beat anyone, even a rookie the likes of Lanny Wadkins, that he hit into Wadkins's group on the par-five seventy-second hole of the Sahara Invitational in Vegas.

"He wanted to win," explained Wadkins, who had gone to Wake Forest on an Arnold Palmer scholarship.

Playing with Art Wall Jr., Wadkins was standing over an eight-footer for birdie when Palmer ran his second shot up the false front of the green, drawing shouts from the crowd and forcing the rookie to back away from his putt.

Wall was furious. "It's just like Arnold to do something like that," he said.

Wadkins was ahead by one at the time, and he accepted Arnold's maneuver as "just gamesmanship." He missed his birdie attempt but secured his first tour victory when Palmer failed to make his own four.

Wadkins ended up playing regular money games with Palmer; it was usually Lanny and Bert Yancey against Arnie and Tom Weiskopf. Wadkins marveled at Palmer's way with the fans, at how a simple "hello" from the King made the average fan feel as if he or she had made a famous friend for life.

From their regular gambling games, Wadkins also saw how dearly Palmer missed his place atop a sport Nicklaus was dominating. "He did not like his skills diminishing," Wadkins said of Arnold. "He didn't take easily to going downhill."

Nicklaus knew that better than anyone. He captured the first two majors of 1972, nearly won the British, and set an earnings record of $316,911 (Palmer won only $81,440), becoming the first man to break the single-season $300,000 barrier. The more Jack won, the more Arnold became a living, breathing monument to a bygone era.

Palmer was still the man most responsible for the fact that more than eleven million Americans were playing golf in 1973, almost triple the number playing the game when the Arnie phenomenon gained steam in 1960. He was still the man most responsible for the expanding TV coverage and swelling TV rights fees and the $7.5 million a year in prize money being awarded on the pro tour, more than four times the sum doled out ten years earlier.

But he didn't just want to be the greatest statesman or ambassador. He was dying to be the greatest player, too.

"He *hated* to lose," Nicklaus said. "Gary [Player] and I always thought we were pretty good at shaking somebody's hand when we lost. Arnold would shake your hand, but he wasn't very enthusiastic about it . . . It just *killed* him to lose."

On the morning of February 11, 1973, Palmer rose to the overwhelming feeling that he did not want to lose another tournament to Jack Nicklaus.

In his colorful polo shirts, their busy patterns announcing the New Jack for those who hadn't been paying attention, Nicklaus was on his way to a seven-win season. He'd come off a 1972 campaign that nearly saw him win a third consecutive major at the British at Muirfield, where he made up six strokes on Lee Trevino in the final round before Trevino, appearing beaten at the seventeenth hole, rushed an indifferent wedge shot that made an undeserved beeline for the bottom of the cup.

"A give-up shot," Nicklaus said.

And one that ended his Grand Slam bid.

"I'm not giving back the trophy," Trevino said at Muirfield, "but everybody knows who is the greatest golfer in the world."

Nicklaus wore that label proudly a month before facing Palmer at the 1973 Hope, when he took part in "Jack Nicklaus Day" at La Costa Country Club. The attending writers and sportscasters gave him the title "King of Golf" and slapped a crown on his blond head while photographers snapped away. Jack played along and had some fun with the whole thing, a testament to how far his relationship with the press had come.

In the early days Palmer owned the Fourth Estate. He charmed the print guys with his aw-shucks demeanor. He drank with them and took them in as confidants. Palmer worked the press the way he worked the fans.

"When Jack came out and whipped his ass every time they were paired together," Don January said, "the media didn't like it much ... They were just merciless on him."

At first Nicklaus didn't help his own cause with the media. "He considered them an adversarial force," said his business partner, Put Pierman. "A lot of guys in the media were big Arnold fans, saying, 'Who the hell is this fat kid who looks like the Michelin Man coming in here and whipping our man?' They didn't like it, and Jack felt the animosity and just shut down."

Just as he wore down some of his hecklers with his overwhelming power and precision, Nicklaus ultimately wore down the press with his accessibility and candor. He had an intellectual curiosity Palmer didn't have, and his answers to news conference questions ran deeper than Arnold's.

Jack would take off with almost any question on almost any subject, offering enough theories and opinions to fill any reporter's notebook. Arnie? He had an exceptional talent for faking it. In an attempt to stay clear of any potential trouble, he avoided direct answers like the plague.

"Arnold loves riding the fence," Nicklaus said. "He just never says anything."

But Arnie had such a charming way of deking and dodging.

"When Palmer came into the press room, he'd already established his rapport with you and you loved him," said Edwin Pope of the *Miami Herald,* who covered his first Masters in 1947 as a nineteen-year-old sports editor of the *Athens* (Georgia) *Banner-Herald.* "With Nicklaus it was like, 'Hey, you're the guy who's taking Arnie's place. Show us what a good guy you are.'

"Jack had a much tougher battle than Arnie. Palmer had a friendly air about him, and Jack was a gruff fat boy. Arnold looked like a halfback out of the NFL, a Frank Gifford, and Nicklaus looked like the guy who was in the office all week. But in the long run, and considering everything he had to face, Jack was a much better interview than Arnie."

The appreciative writers at La Costa gave Nicklaus a standing ovation at his "King of Golf" ceremony, this after Jack answered their questions for more than an hour. The following month the King of Golf went one-on-one with the King for the sake of old times.

The Bob Hope was a pro-am played over four Coachella Valley courses for the first four rounds, before the pros squared off in a fifth round at Bermuda Dunes. In the CEO and celebrity portion of the event, Palmer played with Lawrence Welk, Dean Martin, Andy Williams, and Efrem Zimbalist Jr. Nicklaus was paired with the host, Bob Hope.

Like the Crosby, the Hope wasn't a garden-variety tour event. Its host had done as much as anyone to promote the game. Hope often used a golf club on stage as a prop; he found a role for Palmer in one of his films; and he talked up golf on his programs, *The Tonight Show,* any broadcast that would have him. In the end, winning his tournament meant winning a measure of prestige not found at the Greater Milwaukee Open.

Coming off his playoff victory over Ray Floyd and Orville Moody at the Bing Crosby, Nicklaus was fully expected to claim his second Hope title. He ripped off a 64 on the first day, and Palmer was left to play catch-up from there. Jack held at least a share of the lead at the end of each of the first four rounds, but he couldn't shake Arnold, who rode a new putting style — a friend had suggested he use more wrist in his otherwise stiff-armed stroke — to shoot 68 in the fourth round and stay within one of Nicklaus and Miller.

"I changed [putting styles] because I wanted to be Superman," Palmer said. "I didn't want to sink just a few putts; I wanted to sink them all."

He was putting better than he had in five years, and he was eager to try out his newfound accuracy on Nicklaus across the closing eighteen holes. With the pro-am complete, the singers and comics and executives were thanked for their time and asked to leave the premises. The desert party was over. The fifth and final round would be for real golfers only, and for the real fans who wanted to see Palmer versus Nicklaus one more time.

Did Arnold have it in him? Did he still know how to win a tournament, or were his nerves and short game too frayed from natural wear and tear to present a credible challenge to Nicklaus?

"It's no secret that Arnold's lost more golf tournaments than he's won," Lee Trevino would say. "And the reason for it is Arnold never knew how to back off. When Arnold got ahead by one stroke, he wanted to be ahead by two. And when he got ahead by two, he wanted to be ahead by three. If Arnold came to a hole and pulled out a nine-iron to lay up . . . the gallery wouldn't let him. 'Oh, go for it, Arnie,' and that's what he had to do."

At forty-three, Arnie wasn't about to temper his go-for-it style. Jack? His strategy for the fifth round of the Hope was simple: demoralize Palmer by grabbing the early lead. Arnie would play these eighteen holes burdened with doubt, as he entered them unsure if he'd ever win another tour event.

That Sunday, February 11, with Palmer and Nicklaus and John Schlee grouped together, the craziest thing happened: the skies opened wide over the desert, the first time the tournament had seen rain for a weekend round. This wasn't any passing shower, either. For Palm Springs the cold, steady rain qualified as a violent storm. The advantage would naturally go to the younger, mentally tougher Nicklaus, who never wavered on a muddy track.

But through his aviator glasses speckled with raindrops, Palmer saw good omen after good omen sprouting up before him. Umbrellas.

Multicolored umbrellas. The official Arnold Palmer logo, thousands of them, lined the playing arena and marked it off like stakes around a hazard.

Arnie's Army had Jack Nicklaus surrounded. Palmer was wearing sideburns down to his earlobes, a visor, a sweater, and those tinted shades. This was a New Arnie look in search of a New Arnie ending.

Palmer had tried contact lenses to improve his vision but decided his extra-large set of glasses worked better on the greens. "[The glasses] scare me to death," he would say. "I can see too well, every blade of grass and every impediment. It's frightening."

Nicklaus blinked first on the opening hole of the 6,778-yard Bermuda Dunes course. He sent his tee shot into the rough and eventually three-putted from thirty-five feet for bogey. Palmer nailed an eight-footer for birdie, and Arnold's one-shot deficit was suddenly Arnold's one-shot lead.

Palmer went up two on a twenty-footer at the fourth hole, and Nicklaus kept struggling to navigate the driving rain, the gusting wind, and the jeering fans. "The Army was in its usual form," wrote Shav Glick of the *Los Angeles Times*, "cheering mistakes by Nicklaus and the other leaders, chatting and running while other players shot, and roaring every time Arnie hitched up his pants."

Palmer kept hitting fairways and greens, making pars, and forcing Nicklaus's hand. Arnold hit the first fifteen greens, mocking the bad weather, while twenty-five-year-old Johnny Miller, among other contenders, completely lost his focus.

"I kept thinking the round was going to be rained out," Miller said. "The greens were almost unplayable and I couldn't keep my mind on playing because I expected [officials] to stop play any time."

Play was never suspended, and the mobile army of umbrellas marched on. At the sixteenth hole, where Palmer missed his first green of the day, he wedged out of a bunker and faced one of the defining par savers of his career. Through his fogged-out, rain-splashed glasses, Palmer dropped it in from eight feet out.

Nicklaus had a three-footer to cut the Palmer lead to one, and if these two had been playing a practice round for a few bucks a hole, Arnold would have told him to pick it up.

Jack missed. At forty-three, Arnold would end up on the ninetieth tee box of the tournament with a two-shot lead.

The 501-yard, par-five eighteenth at Bermuda Dunes was easily reachable in two for the big hitters, but the right side of the fairway bled into tall palms and a large lake. Nicklaus figured he needed an eagle to force a playoff, so he railed against the elements, hammering his drive into the fairway and landing his approach eighteen feet from the cup.

Palmer's drive wasn't nearly as impressive; it had been a long five days for the older man. But he stayed out of the palms and away from the water and hit his three-wood just short of the green, in comfortable par range. With Jack already on in two and in legitimate eagle position, Arnold chipped his ball to within eight feet of the hole.

The umbrellas circled the green, choked it off, locked the Golden Bear in a cage. More than twenty thousand fans had put up with a raw rain all day, and many of them were in position to watch this breathless drama unfold.

Schlee, the third member of the group, might as well have been a marshal for all the fans cared. He was out of contention and out of mind. Schlee would call it the most stirring duel he'd ever witnessed and would acknowledge his place in the threesome as nothing more than "the best seat in the house."

Nicklaus would go first. Palmer's resurgence and ability to protect the lead had to come as a complete surprise; Jack had always been able to pass him in these situations. In fact, wrote Jim Murray in the *Los Angeles Times*, "Jack Nicklaus couldn't have been more shocked if Amelia Earhart came walking out of the woods."

The pilot in front of him, Palmer, would need only a two-putt to win if Nicklaus failed to deliver an eagle. Every Arnie fan watching on TV had the same wretched thought swirling inside his or her head: Jack would make, Arnie would miss, and Jack would win the playoff.

Nicklaus lowered himself over his putt; shot the cup that icy, blue-eyed, you'd-better-not-let-me-down stare of his; and then sent his last arrow Arnold Palmer's way. "I was sure it was going in," Arnold said.

So was everybody else.

The ball missed going in by two or three dimples, and Nicklaus tossed his putter into the air, end over end.

"What are you trying to do?" a winded Palmer asked.

"Trying to beat you," Nicklaus answered.

Palmer allowed himself a winner's smile. Jack settled for birdie, and Arnold needed only a par to take the Hope for a fifth time.

The rain was still coming down in the desert, and the umbrella-wielding army was still standing guard for the legend with the umbrella logo. The King was back, eight feet away from the winner's circle. "He is to the game what Gable, Cagney, Grant and Bogart were to movies," Murray wrote.

Palmer could've lagged it, played it safe, let Nicklaus die a slower, more painful death. He could've rolled an eight-foot putt seven feet and then tapped in for his first victory in eighteen months.

But then he wouldn't be Arnold Palmer. And his opponent wouldn't be Jack Nicklaus if he didn't feel good, in a strange way, for the old rival who was about to defeat him.

"Did I think he was going to be a force to beat me at that point in his life? No, probably not," Nicklaus would say. "And I suppose if it had been ten years earlier and he would've been in the prime of his career, I wouldn't have felt as good about it, because I would've been wondering whether he was going to be drumming me.

"But I felt good for him. He hadn't played very well recently. When your competition sort of disappears, your competition with somebody you spent your whole life beating your head against, all of a sudden you feel good when it comes back, because it sort of revives you a bit, too. That was the feeling. That's why I felt good for him."

Palmer felt better for himself. He enjoyed Nicklaus's missed eagle, and then he did what Arnold Palmer was born to do: he went for the birdie. He made it, too, and then ripped the visor from his head and fired it toward the crowd, just as he had thirteen years earlier at Cherry Hills.

Arnie's Army let out a thunderous roar from under the umbrellas. Palmer had shot 69 against Nicklaus's 72. Defeating Jack, Arnold would say, "meant so much to me."

Nicklaus congratulated Palmer and wrapped his right arm around Arnold's shoulders as they headed off the green and toward the scorer's tent.

"We were having a battle, one of our classic battles," Palmer would say. "[The last putt] made me very happy."

Arnold found Bob Hope later and told the tournament host he couldn't stop shaking. "I feel pretty damn young right now," Palmer said. He was tired of playing golf, tired of cleaning the rain from his glasses. He was dripping wet and in no rush to find himself a nice, warm bath.

"I thought it was a hell of a day, really," Palmer said through a smile. "The sun shone all day."

It rained only on the Golden Bear's parade. The more this defeat sank in, the less thrilled Nicklaus was about the prospect of things to come.

"I guess after putting up with Arnie's Army for twelve years," Jack said, "I'll have to try and put up with it a few more."

Nicklaus and Palmer had just been voted among the top five golfers of all time in a national poll of writers—Hogan and the late Bobby Jones and Walter Hagen were also named—and were eight days away from receiving their awards in New York. But in the post-tournament delirium that gripped Bermuda Dunes, Arnie and Jack were most concerned about getting something hard to drink.

They went separately to a party at Indian Wells, one of the Hope's courses; it was a jam session for players, celebrities, and sponsors. Nicklaus was already seated at a table when Palmer entered and approached with several friends.

In his haste to get to his newly vanquished rival, Palmer bumped into a woman and knocked her wig to the floor. *"Ohhhh!"* the mortified woman shrieked.

Arnold bent over to retrieve the hairpiece. "I was going to put it back on her head," he said, "and I thought, 'That won't help the situation.' So I put it on my head."

Nicklaus saw the bushy blond wig on Palmer's head, its locks covering his eyes, his ears, and half his nose, and blew Arnold a kiss.

"Would you like to dance?" Palmer said.

Old Jack never would've left his chair or blown the kiss in the first place. New Jack left his seat and walked right up to the man who had requested his presence on the floor.

When Nicklaus arrived, Palmer pulled the unruly wig from his head and slapped it on Jack's. "And I put my arms around him and danced with him," Arnold said.

"It was after the tournament, and everything was irrelevant except that we were friends and we were having a good time."

A photo of the dance showed a beaming Palmer taking Nicklaus's right hand with his outstretched left, in tango form. Jack was laughing from under the wig and pressing his nose against Arnold's right cheek, as if ready to whisper a sweet something in his ear.

The King and the Golden Bear were having the time of their lives, rekindling the shared glory days of the sixties, when hotel food fights with Gary Player were a common theme in the Big Three script.

Arnold was dreaming big again, believing he could win another major. Of all the thoughts swimming through his head on this giddy night at Indian Wells, none approximated the reality of the moment.

This tango with Jack Nicklaus would be the last dance. Arnold Palmer would never again win a tournament on the PGA Tour.

CHAPTER 13

Oakmont Revisited

J ACK NICKLAUS was weeping in front of his TV. He had just watched the running of the 1973 Belmont Stakes, and Secretariat's thirty-one-length victory to complete the Triple Crown left him looking the way men often looked after they watched *Brian's Song.*

Only Nicklaus wasn't shedding tears of sadness. He was weeping over another living being's pursuit of perfection.

"I just like greatness," he said. "Here you won the first two and all of a sudden you're coming down and you just blow the world away the third time out."

Nicklaus had never won three straight legs of the Grand Slam, but in the immediate wake of Secretariat's victory he was on the verge of his own historic feat. He needed one more major victory to break Bobby Jones's record of thirteen.

Oakmont, the site of his first major triumph, was a most appropriate forum for Nicklaus to claim number fourteen. The place hadn't changed much since Jack defeated the hometown hero, Arnold Palmer, in the 1962 U.S. Open, but Nicklaus was playing much better golf in 1973 than he was as a winless rookie in 1962. He'd already taken the Crosby, the Greater New Orleans Open, the Tournament of Champions, and the Atlanta Classic. He'd nearly stolen the Masters from Tommy Aaron with a final-round 66, and, of course, he'd nearly beaten the resurgent Palmer at the Hope.

The night he left that tournament and that showstopping dance with Arnold at the Indian Wells jam session, Jack might've felt good for Arnie that the old man proved he could still win on tour. The sentiment didn't last very long. At an appearance in Chicago the following week, Nicklaus was asked about his latest battle with Palmer.

"It was fun doing it again," Jack said, "but believe me, there were no mixed emotions. There is no one in the world I want to beat more than him, and I especially didn't want to lose that one.

"Yes, if it had been Grier Jones or Joe Blow or most anyone else, I'd have been happy for them. But not him."

Him. Arnold Palmer. The opponent whose first shot at the 1973 Open sounded like a two-iron aimed straight for Nicklaus, who was changing his pre-major routine by playing rather than practicing. The Philadelphia-area tour stop, Whitemarsh, offered Oakmont-like fairways and greens, Jack believed, so competing in this tune-up made sense.

"There's no similarity," maintained Palmer, who was skipping the tour stop. "Whitemarsh is a good course, but Oakmont was designed as a links similar to a Scottish course. It has few trees compared with Whitemarsh. Its bunkers are famous, although they are no longer furrowed. It has magnificent greens and it has no water holes, while Whitemarsh has creeks and ditches.

"I just don't agree with Jack at all."

As Gary Player said, they were "vastly different" people. Palmer and Nicklaus were vastly different personalities at vastly different points in their vastly different golfing careers.

Jack was in the middle of his prime. Arnold was just trying to hang on long enough to experience one last magical major Sunday.

He wanted that Sunday to be this Sunday, at Oakmont, to even an eleven-year-old score. Tee to green, Palmer spent five days hitting the ball about as well as a man could hit it in 1962, and still he lost to Nicklaus in a playoff.

His putter failed him, and in turn, Palmer felt he'd failed all of western Pennsylvania.

In the official 1973 Oakmont program, Kaye Kessler authored an advance piece that said Nicklaus's victory over Palmer "was the start of 'Operation Wipe-Out' for the amazing youngster who had uncommon problems winning devotees if not influencing people with his prodigious game.

"Palmer agonized as he watched Nicklaus hover over putts, paced the greens like a caged lion, but never shook his young adversary, who later calmly explained, 'On my putts, I just took my time. I putted when I was good and ready because I missed too many rushing them in other tournaments.'"

In the 1973 program Palmer appeared in a full-page ad for natural gas companies serving the Pittsburgh area. He was a man for all reasons and seasons.

Oakmont was giving him a mulligan this time around, and Palmer carried to the Open a feeling he hadn't experienced in a long time. He knew he could beat Nicklaus. He had the Hope trophy for proof.

The first three rounds did nothing to change Palmer's mind. He knew Oakmont like the back of his meat-hook hands, knew it so well, in fact, that he didn't bother to wear his glasses or contact lenses during the tournament. Palmer's eyesight was strong enough to allow him rounds of 71, 71, and 68, good enough for a share of the fifty-four-hole lead.

He was tied with John Schlee and Jerry Heard and with fifty-three-year-old Julius Boros, who wasn't the biggest surprise of the tournament: that distinction belonged to Nicklaus, who was four strokes back after a barely adequate round of 74.

"It's Jack Nicklaus Against Field of 149," read the headline in the *Pittsburgh Post-Gazette* the day the Open began.

Jack had been everyone's pick to win. And if it wasn't going to be Jack, then it was going to stay in the Ohio State family.

"This course is so much suited for Nicklaus and [Tom] Weiskopf," Billy Casper said of the Golden Bear and his fellow Buckeye and potential heir apparent, "that starting out they're ten shots better than the rest of the field."

Those ten shots were buried somewhere in the cruel Oakmont rough. Weiskopf was one back after three rounds, in better shape than his idol. "Four strokes is not too much to make up," Nicklaus maintained.

Jack considered the leaders vulnerable. Boros was practically a relic; he couldn't possibly take the Open, could he? Heard was a fine young player who'd won a few tournaments, but he hadn't finished higher than fifth at a major. Schlee? He had only one tour victory to his name, and as an amateur astrologist he seemed more eager to read the stars than the greens.

"Mars is in conjunction with my natal moon," he said.

And then there was Palmer and his home-court advantage.

"I think Arnold's going to be the man to beat," Lee Trevino said, "because he knows the course so well."

It was an interesting call, and not one Nicklaus took all that seriously. Gary Player looked as if he'd run off with the tournament when he started 67-70 before blowing up with a 77, and Nicklaus figured Palmer might have a high number in him as well. Arnie hadn't won a major in nine years, after all, and nobody was confusing the U.S. Open with the Bob Hope.

On Sunday morning, June 17, this much was clear: someone on the board would have a chance to shoot a hell of a number. The course had been hit hard by rain, and an apparent glitch in the watering system had the sprinklers running all Saturday night.

Water had reduced Oakmont to a toothless tiger, easy prey for a King or a Bear. But nobody counted on a dark horse to come storming out of the formless pack to play a round of golf as no U.S. Open golfer ever had.

Johnny Miller first made his name as a teenage caddie turned qualifier at the 1966 Open, where he finished tied for eighth on the day of Palmer's implosion. Miller had shot 76 in the third round to fall six strokes off the Oakmont pace; he was playing the course like a blind man after leaving his cherished yardage card — a bible he consulted as religiously as Nicklaus consulted his own — in another pair of pants.

He didn't forget his book for the fourth round. Out ahead of the field, his moppy blond hair bouncing all about, Miller made like an expert dart thrower standing five feet from the bull's-eye. His irons crisper than his tight black-and-white-checkered slacks, Miller went on a tear that made USGA officials cringe.

He birdied numbers one, two, and three. "Son of a gun," he told himself, "I'm at even par. Maybe I've got a chance to get back in the tournament."

He birdied number four, too.

Maybe the stranger who had approached him before the Open was right. Miller asked her if she wanted an autograph, and the woman said no, she didn't. She just wanted to tell him he was about to win the U.S. Open.

After each round the woman would tell Miller, "You're right on track; don't worry about it." Sunday morning, following his Saturday blowup, Miller was worrying about it. He received a letter at his locker from Iowa that said, "You are going to win the U.S. Open," and Miller didn't believe it.

That morning the former Brigham Young star had left his wife, Linda, and infant daughter, Kelly, back at the hotel with instructions for Linda to pack up and prepare for an early flight home. Miller figured he was out of contention, and yet here he was birdieing up a storm on the front nine at Oakmont and hearing voices in his head telling him to "open it up."

So Miller opened it up with a nothing-to-lose fury. Soon enough he realized he had a chance to win the national championship, and he was proud that he was proving himself wrong.

"You have to understand," he said. "I played with Arnie the first two rounds."

Arnie's Army had taken a toll on Miller. The Palmer loyalists didn't call him fat; Miller was built like a flagstick, after all. But the steel-town toughs did move enough and talk enough and cheer enough for their man for Miller to get a small taste of what Nicklaus had confronted his entire career.

"If I had a twelve-footer and Arnie had a fourteen-footer that he made for birdie, the gallery was gone," Miller said. "I had to putt through everybody leaving the green, leaving to run to the next tee or the next fairway to get in position for Palmer's next shot. I mean, the gallery was going crazy for Arnie."

The Open leaderboard on this day was among the best of all time. Palmer, Nicklaus, Player, Trevino, and Boros were all there, as was Weiskopf, in the middle of a breakout five-win season.

As Miller made his charge from the rear, he looked at Palmer more as an oddity than as a contender with a real shot to win the Open.

"An equipment freak" Miller called Palmer. "There's never been a guy who's enjoyed golf equipment more than Arnold Palmer. It was, 'I won the Open because of that putter,' or 'I lost the Open because of that wedge.' It wasn't that he was bad; it was always the club was bad or good. He's the only guy I've ever seen who goes to a putting green with as many as twelve putters every day. And literally when they were calling his name, he'd grab one of them and go and leave the rest behind."

On this fourth-round day at Oakmont, Miller didn't count on Palmer grabbing the right putter from that pile.

"He stopped making those two [thirty-footers] a day he used to make," Miller said, "and two times four is eight strokes. And losing those eight strokes puts you nowhere.

"Arnie was still one of the greatest drivers of the ball in the game; he actually became a better driver of the ball later in his career . . . But once that short game leaves you, you're just another player."

Palmer hardly looked like just another player early in the final round. Under an overcast sky Arnie went to the first tee feeling a whole lot differently about his game than the cocky Miller did.

"I thought I had a pretty good chance to win," Palmer said, "and I felt good about it . . . I beat Jack in the last round [at the Hope] . . . Why can't I go win now?"

At the top of the board, sixteen players started the round within half a dozen shots of each other, and it was Palmer who birdied the fourth hole to take the Open lead. This time around the Oakmont crowd was more intent on supporting Arnie than on assailing Jack, who was fortunate enough to stay out of Palmer's pairing but who was caught up in the pack, playing a more benign game than the one he used to conquer the army in 1962.

The fans wanted their happy ending and they were going to do what they had to do to get it. So Schlee, the astrologist, would find his natal moon eclipsed by Arnie's Army. He repeated Miller's claim that a pairing with Palmer meant a two-stroke handicap per round.

"This is no knock on Arnie, because none of us would be here if it weren't for him," Schlee would say. "But I just couldn't settle down out there."

A vast majority of the twenty-three thousand fans in attendance were walking with Palmer. Playing in relative solitude, Miller would cool off before erasing a bogey at number eight with another birdie at number nine. With nine holes to go in his Open, and with Palmer in stronger position than Nicklaus behind him, Miller still figured Arnie was more likely to crack than Jack.

"Arnie would play a little bit to the gallery, where that was not Jack at all," Miller said. "Jack was all about playing his game plan. He had tremendous ability to eliminate temptation, and golf is all about temptation.

"If Arnie had just bogeyed the last hole, he would hit driver every time. He would submit to temptation every time, where if Jack had just made a double [bogey], it wouldn't matter. He would still hit the one-iron. There was no, 'Well, I've got to catch up.' Arnie? Golf seduced him all the way."

But Miller did learn something from Palmer that was helping him ride this tidal wave of momentum across Oakmont. Miller's father had told him that if he wanted to be the best player in the world, he had to have a little Arnie in him. He had to try shots nobody else was willing to try, something Palmer did eight days a week.

If everyone else is playing for the middle of the green, Miller's father told his son, go for the stick. Go for broke, just like Arnie.

Behind Miller the lead was being passed around like a basket of dinner rolls. Palmer was in a tie for first at the turn, and the fans were trying to will him to an improbable victory with constant shouts of "Come on, Arnie!" and "Let's go, Arnie!"

Only Miller kept stringing together red-on-white birdie numbers as his name made a serpent's climb up the leaderboard. "Just three or four more and you've got this tournament," his playing partner, Miller Barber, was telling him. The mobile scoreboard in the hands of this group's standard-bearer read as if it were announcing one player's full name rather than both players' surnames.

MILLER
BARBER

Johnny Miller was off the charts in every literal and figurative way. As word of this remarkable run spread, fans on both sides of the Pennsylvania Turnpike — at least those who weren't Arnie's Army loyalists — went scurrying off to find Miller late in his round. By the time Palmer made it to the eleventh green, Miller was an absurd eight under for the day and five under for the tournament after birdies at numbers eleven, twelve, thirteen, and fifteen.

He was leading the Open at last. He was doing to the Oakmont field exactly what Palmer had done to the Cherry Hills field thirteen years earlier.

Tucked under a white visor, Arnold was oblivious to the storm he'd have to weather. He had a five-footer at eleven to get to five under, which he assumed would leave him in sole possession of first place, ahead of Weiskopf, Boros, and his own playing partner, Schlee. Ahead of Jack Nicklaus, who wasn't waking up any echoes of 1962.

Palmer slid his five-footer by the hole. Miller was right: Arnold had picked the wrong putter from his pile.

As painful as that body blow felt, Palmer never saw the vicious right hook to come when he glanced at the leaderboard.

Arnold shot a stunned look at Schlee. "Where the fuck did he come from?" he asked of Johnny Miller. "How much under par is he?"

Five under, he was told. One better than Palmer, whom Miller believed to be out of the Open.

"There was no way Arnie was going to play twelve to eighteen in one under par," Miller said. "It was not going to be done."

Palmer unleashed a drive toward the left side of the twelfth fairway, almost precisely where he wanted to put it: balls that landed there usually kicked right, into position A. An Oakmont member named John Fitzgerald was working with the USGA camera crew that pulled up to the twelfth hole as Palmer headed off to find his drive. Fitzgerald saw Palmer stop to take another look at the scoreboard, slap his hands on his hips, and shake his head.

"As if to say, 'Oh, my God,'" Fitzgerald said. "Arnie was too much of a hero to put that on film."

Or to record his reaction when he discovered his ball's resting spot. When Palmer came upon the one ball that was sitting upright in the short grass, he discovered it was Schlee's; Arnold's drive had taken an uncommon hop into the rough.

"They could have stuck a fork in me," Palmer said, "because I was cooked."

He went bogey, bogey, bogey from there.

"The crowd turned into a morgue," Schlee said. "I've gotten more claps than that playing a practice round."

Palmer was beaten at yet another Open in front of his hometown fans. It was a surreal afternoon that saw Weiskopf make birdie after landing his ball between the bread and mustard on a hot-dog stand, that saw Schlee make the most serious charge at Miller, this after he hit three balls off the first tee on the way to a double bogey.

When Miller was done thrashing the 6,921-yard beast, he signed a scorecard showing nine birdies and one bogey for a 63, the lowest score in the seventy-three-year history of the Open. "Finest round of golf I've ever seen," Miller Barber told him as they walked off the eighteenth green.

Many writers on the course never saw a single brilliant shot Miller hit. "I followed Arnold, thinking he was going to win," said Dave Anderson of the *New York Times*. "With Miller, I told myself, 'This guy has to cool off.' I figured, 'Hey, how could Palmer lose? He's minutes from Latrobe, it's his course, his fans, and Nicklaus is kind of out of it, so the great specter of Jack isn't there.'"

Palmer hobbled in with a 72, and Nicklaus came home with an irrelevant 68. Arnie and Jack ended up exactly where they had after four rounds of the 1962 Open at Oakmont—dead even.

Only there would be no playoff this time. Nicklaus failed to break Bobby Jones's record of thirteen major titles, and Palmer failed to break anything but western Pennsylvania's heart.

In the clubhouse Arnie was mulling what might have been when a reporter asked for his thoughts the second he realized Miller was running away with his Open.

"I saw the scoreboard," Palmer responded, "and I nearly shit."

Miller's 279 was four strokes better than Ben Hogan's winning Oakmont score in 1953 and four strokes better than the Palmer-Nicklaus regulation score in 1962. Funny how things work out, but Billy Casper, the ghost of Palmer's Open past, had worked with Miller, his friend and fellow Mormon. Casper had told Miller that he shouldn't try to play finesse shots under pressure, that he should take a shorter club and hit it hard.

In effect, Casper had coached Miller to beat Palmer. "It was fun to watch him play the last nine holes at Oakmont," Casper said, "and every time he made a good hard swing he put it right against the flag. That's something he adopted into his game, and he was always grateful to me for that advice."

In 1962 Palmer's friend Dow Finsterwald told Arnold he'd accelerated young Nicklaus's career three or four years by letting him win at Oakmont. Eleven years later the world was telling Palmer the same thing at the same place about another young buck.

"I took it away from Arnold," Miller said.

"I just pulled the carpet out from under him."

CHAPTER 14

• Gamesmanship

B OB MURPHY WAS TAKING his turn in the rotation as the invisible man. He was playing with Arnold Palmer and Jack Nicklaus at the 1975 Jackie Gleason Inverrary Classic and marveling over how badly the two titans wanted to take each other down.

On the front nine Nicklaus had knocked one of his drives into the fairway, and Palmer and Murphy had sprayed their balls to the right. Jack was up first. He hit his approach short of the green, and the unmistakable sound of a fat shot—*thwaaaaaap*—echoed in Murphy's ears.

Problem was, Arnold didn't catch it: he was already suffering from the early stages of hearing loss. His caddie, Creamy Carolan, was a nonstop talker who didn't hear the sickly sound of Nicklaus's second shot, either.

Jack figured as much. He put his hand over the bottom of his club face, the area that identified the misfiring weapon as a four-iron, and handed it to his caddie, Angelo Argea, while loudly saying, "I hit that three-iron pretty good."

Palmer was out ahead of Nicklaus, and he fell straight through the trapdoor. He pulled a four-iron from his bag and promptly sailed his ball twenty-five yards over the green.

"You could see how absurd Arnold's four-iron was," Murphy said.

"The people behind the green just turned around and started looking behind them."

Murphy laughed to himself and hit a comfortable seven-iron shot that stopped two feet from the cup. Murphy made birdie, Nicklaus made bogey, and Palmer made double bogey.

"It was a perfect example of them fighting each other," Murphy said, "and they did that all the time ... They were fighting it out, fighting it out. It was incredible."

Later, Nicklaus confessed his not-so-venial sin to Palmer.

"You asshole," Arnold said. "Why would you do something like that to me?"

It was all in good fun.

"That Creamy," Palmer said, "he can't get anything right."

Late in the round, as soon as it became clear Palmer wasn't going to catch Murphy, some Arnie's Army hard-liners started backing the Brooklyn-born Irishman. If Arnie couldn't win the Gleason, they sure as hell didn't want Jack to win it either.

"Here we go," Nicklaus had said when he first heard he was being paired with Palmer for the final round. "I thought we were done with that ten years ago. I just gotta stay out of the way of his gallery, I guess."

Only there was no getting out of Arnie's Army's path. Nicklaus lost to Murphy, too.

"Thousands of disciples came out to Inverrary this afternoon to see the two gods of golf," wrote Gerald Strine in the *Washington Post,* ". . . and a very mortal, portly little Irishman beat them both."

Palmer, for one, wasn't the least bit surprised. "It seems every time Jack and I have led on the final day of a tournament, and played against each other," he said, "the third guy wins."

Nicklaus left the Gleason shaking his head. Even as the Golden Bear remained dominant and the King reluctantly assumed the role of elder statesman, they couldn't keep out of each other's hair.

Fate was their relentless matchmaker, pairing them as opponents and teammates. After all the Canada Cup, World Cup, and PGA team titles they won together, Palmer and Nicklaus partnered again at the 1973 Ryder Cup, going 1-1 for the victorious U.S. squad. Palmer had also been chosen captain of the 1975 team that would feature Nicklaus as its star member.

But Arnold and Jack never seemed more appropriately coupled than they did in Augusta, Georgia, where they had each won a record four green jackets before ending up—where else?—in the same pairing for the third round of the 1975 Masters.

Nicklaus returned to Augusta National as the holder of more Grand Slam titles than any other golfer in history; he'd broken Bobby Jones's record of thirteen at the 1973 PGA Championship at the Canterbury Golf Club in Cleveland, where Palmer missed the cut in the only major he'd never won.

Nicklaus also returned with a business empire estimated to be worth $200 million, though money was never his primary source of motivation. As far back as age fifteen, Nicklaus had said he wanted to be "the greatest golfer who ever lived." Eighteen years later, writers were calling him just that.

Nicklaus finished the 1973 season as the first man to earn $2 million in official winnings; Palmer was at $1.63 million when his rival hurdled the big-bucks barrier.

The following June, despite the fact USGA officials had turned New York's famed Winged Foot Golf Club into a penal colony, their way of avenging Johnny Miller's 63 at Oakmont, the forty-four-year-old Palmer threatened again to win something more valuable than a money title. He held a share of the three-over, thirty-six-hole lead in the national championship and rose the following day to this first paragraph in John S. Radosta's *New York Times* story on the Open:

"Well, hello, Arnie. It's so nice to have you back where you belong."

Palmer shot 73-76 over the weekend and finished five back of Hale Irwin's winning seven-over 287.

So Arnold returned to Augusta in April of 1975 with the same number of professional major titles he had when he left Augusta in April of 1964—seven. If he could never approach Nicklaus's record, he could at least stop the Golden Bear from becoming the first player to win five Masters titles. And the surest way for Palmer to do that was to become the first player to win five Masters titles himself.

He'd have some heavy lifting to do over the weekend to make it happen. When he greeted Nicklaus on the first tee box of Saturday's third round, Palmer was tied for second with Billy Casper and Tom Watson, five strokes behind Nicklaus's nine-under 135.

Before leaving the putting green to make his 2:10 tee time, Nicklaus spoke with Palmer about their pairing. "The ordinary way to pair up is the first and third man," Nicklaus said. "But this was a one-two pairing. I asked why, and a man said, 'They do things a little different here.'"

Nicklaus was told by Masters officials that they preferred one oversized gallery with the final group, rather than back-to-back oversized galleries following Palmer in one group, Nicklaus in the other. It was their way of saying, "We want great theater at the Masters, and Arnie and Jack make for great theater."

Palmer and Nicklaus grounded everyone at Augusta National, a place where Old South customs were maintained as carefully as the greens. The world was changing outside the gates of the 1975 Masters — President Nixon had resigned in the Watergate scandal seven months earlier, and the fall of Saigon was only three weeks away — and the white men lording over the tournament never wanted their club touched by evolving social mores.

So Clifford Roberts and his underlings were hardly thrilled that the first two rounds revolved around the presence of Lee Elder, the first African American to compete in the Masters. Augusta National had long resisted calls from House of Representatives members and from prominent newspaper columnists to invite a black man to play; Roberts altered policy whenever he saw fit but refused to adjust his qualifying standards for the sake of a broken color line. Elder finally forced his way into the field by winning the Monsanto Open and made history at the Masters twenty-eight years after Jackie Robinson debuted at Ebbets Field.

Elder missed the cut, exited stage left, and, much to Roberts's relief, handed the tournament back to Arnie and Jack.

"The P. T. Barnum Pairing" read the headline in the *New York Times*.

The circus turned into a most predictable act, as Palmer and Nicklaus ignored the other highly capable men in the tournament and turned their portion of the Masters into a match-play stare-down. They simply couldn't resist. Even in a major, even with both in contention to win that major, Palmer and Nicklaus could never be on the same fairway or green without burning to outplay each other above all else, regardless of the consequences.

And yes, there were consequences.

This pairing, said Dan Foster of the *Greenville* (South Carolina)

News, "had the nightmarish effect on their galleries of two guys staging a fistfight while their boat was sinking."

Arnie shot 75 and Jack shot 73, this while Tom Weiskopf fired a 66 to take the lead and Johnny Miller ripped off a record 30 on the front nine to move into contention.

Walking up the seventeenth fairway, Nicklaus turned to Palmer. "Well, we did it again," Jack said. "We played each other rather than play the golf course."

A recipe for near disaster.

"We never seem to play well when we play together," Palmer said. "I can't explain it, but I know we just don't play well together. If we had our druthers, we would rather play with someone else."

Jack was quick to agree, though the pro-Palmer gallery was nothing like it was in the early sixties, when Nicklaus was welcomed to Augusta about as warmly as Sherman was welcomed to Atlanta.

Arnie's Army was good and loud, but the verbal abuse aimed at Nicklaus had been on the decline at the Masters since his record-shattering performance of 1965, when the applause moved Charlie Nicklaus to tears. On this day ten years later, the army was nearly matched in size by the pro-Nicklaus group known as Jack's Pack.

"The galleries are more objective now," Palmer said. "But they're still just as involved in the rivalry."

The rivalry. It was very much alive and kicking.

"I don't like to be beat by Arnie," Nicklaus said. "I never have and I never will."

The following day Nicklaus didn't have to worry about losing to Arnie. He only had to hold off Miller and Weiskopf in what was likely the most exciting final round in Masters history. Miller shot a 66 on top of his Saturday 65 for a record weekend total and still was left to watch helplessly with Weiskopf from the sixteenth tee as Nicklaus put down the hammer at the par three.

Dressed in a green-and-white-striped shirt and white slacks, Nicklaus had just birdied the par-five fifteenth on perhaps the purest swing of his career, a 246-yard one-iron that nearly holed out for double eagle. He hung forever over his forty-foot birdie try at sixteen before turning it loose. With the attempt on its way, Nicklaus lifted his putter with both hands toward his right shoulder, like a cleanup man getting ready in the batter's box. His caddie, Willie Peterson, raised his right fist and then jumped as the ball dropped into the cup. Nicklaus spun toward the water behind him and jumped himself, defiantly shooting his putter toward the sky and taking a victory lap around the green.

Ahead of the mass hysteria, Palmer was finishing up to his standard ovation. His more-salt, less-pepper hair was boxed in by a white visor, and the disappointment in his eye was muted by his large glasses. It was, the *Augusta Chronicle* reported, "a dark moment for the man who put the word 'charge' in golf's lexicon."

Nicklaus had made off with another piece of Palmer's legacy, becoming the Masters' first five-time champ. During the championship ceremony Nicklaus leaned over to Miller and said, "I just want to thank you for making that so much fun for me."

A light went on in Miller's head.

"That's why this guy never runs away with tournaments," he said to himself. "He wants it to be this close; that's his ticket to ride . . . He wanted Johnny Miller to shoot 65 and 66, and he wanted Weiskopf to be right there."

Nicklaus wanted to be tested. He wanted to be pushed to the outermost fringe of his ability.

Jack had achieved every imaginable goal in the game of golf, other than the calendar-year Grand Slam, and at thirty-five, Nicklaus knew his time to claim that one was running short.

He had thrown away other seasons after losing the Masters, his desire tempered by the first-leg surrender of his Grand Slam bid. But he'd won again at Augusta, and he was dominating golf the way Muhammad Ali was dominating boxing.

"I think Jack can do it this year," Johnny Miller said.

As it turned out, Jack nearly pulled it off, missing the Grand Slam by a handful of shots. He won the PGA Championship later that year with help from one of the great par-saving escapes of his career, a penalty drop followed by a 137-yard nine-iron over a thirty-foot tree with water guarding the sixteenth green. "As soon as I heard Bob Rosburg tell them on television I was dead," Nicklaus said, "I knew I had a chance."

Between his Masters and PGA triumphs, Jack finished one stroke out of a British Open playoff after ending his failed U.S. Open run in another pairing with Palmer at the Medinah Country Club. Nicklaus bogeyed numbers sixteen, seventeen, and eighteen to shoot 72 at Medinah and finish two behind Lou Graham and John Mahaffey, while Palmer shot 73 to land one behind Nicklaus.

In their post-round interview session, after Nicklaus whined about his un-Nicklausian performance on the closing three holes, Palmer said, "Why don't you just sashay your ass back out there and play them over?"

Nicklaus appeared taken aback before Palmer eased the awkward moment by throwing an arm around Jack's neck. Neither had the trophy. Both had each other.

Three months later, at Palmer's Laurel Valley Golf Club in Ligonier, Pennsylvania, Nicklaus chose a strange forum to perform another act of gamesmanship. As captain of the American Ryder Cup team, Palmer had written a letter asking all of his players to be in town on a certain day.

"Jack didn't show up until [the day after]," said Hale Irwin, a member of the team. "Not a big deal, but to me, it's my first time. I'm there at eight o'clock, sir, ready for duty, and Jack didn't come in until a day later . . . [Palmer and Nicklaus] knew what was going on. I didn't at the time, until I got to know them better."

Palmer decided against ripping into Nicklaus for showing up late. "I think Arnold fully expected it," Irwin said.

Whether it was a dose of front-nine deception at the Jackie Gleason, or a declaration of independence at the Ryder Cup, Nicklaus was forever trying to show the King who was boss.

Beaten down by his life of hard Pennsylvania labor, Deke Palmer cherished his golfing getaways at his son's Bay Hill Golf Club in Orlando. On his last such retreat Deke played twenty-seven holes on his son's course and mentioned to his friends he was going to his room for a nap. He told Arnold's aide, Doc Giffin, that he'd join him for dinner and a late night of playing gin.

Giffin and Deke were staying in adjoining rooms at the Bay Hill lodge. When Giffin returned to his room, he saw the connecting door open and walked through to find Deke. "He was probably dead when he hit the floor," Giffin said.

At the time Arnold was in contention again at the Bob Hope, battling it out with the likes of Jack Nicklaus and Billy Casper. Crushed, Palmer withdrew from the tournament and headed home. Deke's body was flown from Orlando back to Latrobe in his son's private plane, and

Arnold's father was cremated, his ashes scattered near the eighteenth green of the golf course he built with his bare hands.

Deke was immensely proud of his older son, though he was loath to show it. He played his taskmaster role to the hilt, and Arnold's feelings toward him were always found at the intersections of respect and admiration, love and fear.

Arnold's mother, Doris, was the soother and protector, the one who got her boy from tournament to tournament, tee to green. "The soft part of the team," said Arnold's sister Sandy. Doris was also the parent who would edge up to the ropes and get as close as she could to the action; she enjoyed the spoils of being a celebrity's mom. "One time we were shopping in Augusta," Sandy said, "and the saleswoman said, 'Are you here for the Masters?' And my mother said, 'Yes, I'm Arnold Palmer's mother.' My father would never do that."

Doris was a vivacious, athletic golfer before the late arrivals of Jerry and Sandy reined her in. She was ultimately crippled by rheumatoid arthritis, and Arnold would lose her a few years after he lost Deke.

Between the devastating losses of his parents, Palmer devoted himself to the building of Bay Hill into a tour-worthy site. He fell for the place the first time he saw it in 1965, signed a five-year lease with an option to buy four years later, and took ownership in 1974.

His vision of a peaceful nature reserve was stamped out by the Disney Corporation, which opened its Walt Disney World Resort on October 1, 1971. At first upset by the magnitude of the theme park and the very real possibility it could run roughshod over Bay Hill's tranquillity, Palmer eventually resigned himself to the reality of the tourist attraction and the real estate rewards it could bring Bay Hill.

Orlando had become a big-league town, and Palmer figured he might as well have a big-league event for his club. By the mid-1970s Palmer wanted the kind of tournament his rival, Nicklaus, had landed for his Dublin, Ohio, club, Muirfield Village, which Jack had finally opened after years of financial problems and construction delays.

On May 27, 1976, a thousand miles from Bay Hill, 96 golfers competed in the first round of the first Memorial, an invitation-only tournament that irritated the tour veterans who would've preferred a full-field event of 144. The purse was $200,000, and the goal was to create a spectacle worthy of the major that inspired it, the Masters.

Nicklaus had taken the lead over Palmer on a new front, and Arnold was hell-bent on catching up.

CHAPTER 15

• Reunion

ARNOLD PALMER AND JACK NICKLAUS were a combined thirty-one shots behind Seve Ballesteros's lead when they were told their misery would love each other's company for the final round of the 1980 Masters.

"I'll whip his ass," Palmer pledged.

He wasn't talking about Seve.

Palmer had hit fifty, old enough for the inaugural year of the senior tour but young enough to want to settle a regular-tour tab. Nicklaus, who was running his own tour event at Muirfield Village, which he won in 1977, had bypassed Palmer's Bay Hill Classic in 1980 after playing in the first Bay Hill event the year before.

The indignities didn't start there. In 1976, after winning the Tournament Players Championship at Inverrary in Fort Lauderdale, Nicklaus took some heavy divots out of Palmer's stated goal of luring the TPC to Bay Hill.

"The only choices in Florida are Doral and [Inverrary], or build your own facility," Nicklaus said. "I haven't played Bay Hill in years. It's a good golf course, but I don't think it's that good ... I don't remember a hole on it."

It would be a long par five before Palmer would forgive and forget that one.

Nicklaus played Bay Hill in 1979, finished ten strokes off the pace, and then ripped the course again on NBC, suggesting that Palmer should improve it. Arnold privately seethed, and Nicklaus realized after the fact he should've fibbed for the public record.

"He wouldn't have been happy with my quotes, no," Jack conceded. "That's something where you wish you could bite your lip before you say it."

But Nicklaus said it because he believed Muirfield Village — his own personal Augusta National — and the Memorial were superior to Bay Hill and Palmer's Classic. "Yeah, but I shouldn't say that," Nicklaus said. "That's my point. I shouldn't come out and say I believe that. The guy's my friend; I shouldn't say something about his golf course."

If this love-hate relationship never ascended to a state of true love, it never descended into a state of true hate either. The Arnie-Jack grudges were never permanent, though Palmer and Nicklaus competed ferociously in everything.

They both wanted the most prominent date on the tour calendar for their clubs. They both wanted the best playing fields in their events and the highest ratings for their host courses. They both wanted the most endorsements, the fastest and biggest airplanes, and the heftiest course design contracts — a business that was taking up more and more of their time.

Jack was beating Arnold in the design field, commanding higher fees and building more elite courses. Arnold was beating Jack in endorsements, just as he had been beating every other athlete in endorsements every year since 1961. By the end of the seventies Palmer was clearing nearly $4 million a year in his role as America's most likable corporate spokesman, though Nicklaus was also in seven figures by way of hundreds of print and electronic media ads.

Palmer was a United Airlines man; Jack was with Eastern. Palmer was a Cadillac man; Nicklaus was with Lincoln.

They were fighting too many border wars to count. But for all their tense clashes and snippy comments, Arnie and Jack often forgot why they were annoyed at each other to begin with.

Less than a year after his harsh assessment of Palmer's Bay Hill layout, Nicklaus received a phone call during his fortieth birthday party.

"Jack, this is A.P.," the caller announced. "You know, your young buddy, Arnold Palmer. I see you're forty going on fifty. How does it feel?"

"You'll be sixty before I'm fifty," Nicklaus answered. "How does that feel?"

Truth was, Nicklaus had the leverage in their relationship, because he was the younger, better player with a few prime years left in him. He suffered his first winless season in 1979 after seventeen straight with at least one victory, but Jack wasn't far removed from his near-miss loss to Tom Watson at the 1977 Masters, his epic loss to Watson at the British Open at Turnberry three months later, and his victory at St. Andrews the following year.

Jack Nicklaus was still Jack Nicklaus, and with Barbara and their five children at home, he would pick and choose his tournament appearances as he saw fit. His general rule of thumb was to play no more than two consecutive events so he could spend more time with the kids.

Palmer? He wasn't balancing Grand Slam contention against back-yard baseball catches with the boys. His two daughters were older than the Nicklaus children, and he hadn't won a tour event in years. His championship golfing career was, in effect, complete. So Palmer had turned to other pursuits, like the round-the-world speed record he set in his Learjet in 1976, completing his flight in less than fifty-eight hours and smashing by more than twenty-eight hours the old standard set by the entertainer Arthur Godfrey.

If Palmer couldn't win on the ground anymore, he would win in the clouds.

But that didn't count for much in Nicklaus's eyes; he had two full-time pilots fly his plane for him. And with Arnold no longer a competitive factor in mainstream golf events, Nicklaus wasn't about to lose sleep over Palmer's decisions to appear, or not appear, at Muirfield Village.

Arnold did make regular stops at the Memorial, "but Jack didn't care whether or not Arnold was in his tournament," said one prominent professional who had played with both. "Jack knew he'd have a good tournament anyway. Jack didn't need Arnold, but Arnold needed Jack to have the best possible field."

Arnold also needed Jack to get fired up for a Masters he was bound to lose by twelve to twenty strokes.

Nicklaus had a far easier time in Grand Slam events than did Palmer; at the start of the 1980 season, Jack had captured fifteen to Arnold's seven. Jack would later tell Johnny Miller, among others, that majors were actually the easiest tournaments to win.

Another light went on in Miller's head.

"The tournament makes 99 percent of players totally choke, and then [Nicklaus] will make the other 1 percent choke," Miller said. "The longest lines of the year are doing number two at the toilet at the U.S. Open on Thursday. The bottom line is everybody's got the Hershey's squirts ... and then Jack would just hang around playing a game of chicken, a percentage game, and he'll just wait until the end. He would just finish off the rest of them by being Jack Nicklaus."

It didn't always work that way. For a stretch of time Lee Trevino tormented Nicklaus in every major but the Masters, the tournament Nicklaus persuaded Trevino to play against Lee's better judgment. The gap-toothed, auburn-haired Watson, once regarded as a serial choker, held off Nicklaus at Augusta and then beat him at Turnberry in the most spectacular British Open duel of all time.

With five holes left in a 65-65 weekend finish that beat Nicklaus's 65-66, Watson even had the nerve to initiate a Wild West exchange with Jack that captured their duel in the Scottish sun.

"Fourteenth tee," Watson said, "waiting for the crowd to clear the crosswalk in front of us. Dusty, looking back into the sun. It looks very foggy because of the dust in the air. Very dry and hot that day. We were both just sitting up there waiting for [the fans] to cross. Standing on the tee looking out to the west, and nothing was being said. And I just really felt the moment and said, 'Jack, this is what it's all about.' And he said, 'You bet it is.'"

Watson and Trevino had cracked the Nicklaus code that Palmer couldn't crack. Why?

"That's a good question," Watson said. "Jack just had Arnold's number the whole time, and why I don't know."

Palmer suffered as many mental breakdowns at the close of majors as anyone, starting with the 1961 Masters, where he needed only a par on the seventy-second hole to win, a bogey to get into a playoff with Gary Player. He drove his ball into the fairway and then walked over to a friendly golf hustler and self-styled putting expert named George Low, who told Palmer, "You won it, boy; great going." His mind wandering, Arnold hit into the bunker, double bogeyed, and lost the tournament.

"A great disappointment," Palmer said. "I violated all my own rules. [Low] didn't walk across the fairway and shake hands; I did ... I was the master of my own fate, and that's the way it works out.

"I made a mistake. Are you going to tell me that Babe Ruth never made a mistake? Or Hogan never made a mistake? Or Nicklaus? ... We all make mistakes. We go to the '66 Open, and I could go to four Opens where I didn't make the same kind of mistakes; I made mental errors in playing, and that's the way it is.

"If I hadn't won Cherry Hills [in 1960], and this is something that haunts me all the time, I probably would've won the other four [Opens] that I didn't win, that I should've won, if I didn't have that U.S. Open title in back of my name. I might've won at Oakmont. I might've won at [Brookline]. I might've won back at Oakmont again. I might've won at Baltusrol ... The good news is Sam Snead never won an Open. If anybody in the world had a right to win an Open championship, it was Sam Snead ... Here's one of the great swingers of the golf club of all time."

In the end Palmer's major championship disappointments shaped him more than his triumphs. "Losing," he said. "You've just got to learn from losing."

Palmer had learned a lot from losing to Nicklaus. He learned that he hated it, for one. And he learned that no matter how crisply he hit the ball in Jack's presence, it was probably going to happen, for two.

On Sunday, April 13, 1980, Palmer promised himself it wasn't going to happen again at Augusta National. He was sixteen strokes behind the dashing twenty-three-year-old Spaniard, the Arnie-like Ballesteros, who had fifteen strokes on Nicklaus. Arnold and Jack would have their own Masters tournament a couple of hours before the real contenders went off.

They teed it up at 11:32 a.m., and Bob Jones IV, grandson of the club founder, was among those in the gallery. "Everyone on the planet was following them," Jones said. "I don't care if they were in leg braces with seeing-eye dogs, if Arnold and Jack showed up on the first tee it was going to be five thick the entire hole."

A guest visiting the Masters for the first time would've assumed this had to be the final pairing of the day. Some prominent figures had come and gone at Augusta National—Bobby Jones, cofounder, had succumbed to his disease in 1971; and Clifford Roberts, cofounder, had shot himself in the head on club grounds in 1977, right alongside the pond named for his friend Dwight D. Eisenhower—but Palmer and Nicklaus were the constants, the men who made the Masters the Masters.

They had ten green jackets between them, and it didn't matter to Palmer that number eleven wouldn't be awarded to the winner of their little intramural competition in 1980. Arnold wanted blood.

Jack wanted to go home.

Dismayed over the fact he hadn't won since 1978, depressed over his performance in the first three rounds at Augusta, Nicklaus had no use for a pairing with Palmer that would be no more relevant to the championship than a two-dollar Nassau.

"I treated it like it wasn't much of a game," Nicklaus said. "If I wasn't in contention to win, I was very unenthusiastic about what I was doing."

But since they were keeping score, Nicklaus figured he might as well shoot a lower number than Palmer's. This was one round where it would be OK for the two to play against each other and not the golf course.

"Hell," Nicklaus said, "if we're going to compete at something, we want to win. I want to beat him; he wants to beat me. That's fun. That's human nature."

With Arnie's Army and Jack's Pack jostling for position behind the ropes, Palmer struck first with a couple of early birdies. Colonel Joe Curtis, an Arnie's Army veteran, was stirring up the troops along with his friend from Palmer's school, Wake Forest, a riotous cheerleader named Doc Murphrey. Curtis and Murphrey tore a red bandanna in half and kept waving it in the air as Palmer scrambled out of trouble to save par and make birdies, just as he had in the old days.

"Give him hell, Arnie!" they shouted.

Nicklaus couldn't gain any momentum, and Curtis and Murphrey only got louder as the round wore on, waving their red bandannas in warpath form.

"Arnie saw it; he couldn't miss it," Curtis said. "Seve was winning the tournament and there's absolutely no doubt that more people were watching Nicklaus and Palmer than would watch Seve later."

Curtis and Murphrey didn't bother to watch Ballesteros hit a single winning shot that day. Their tournament ended when Arnie and Jack marched up eighteen to their last thunderous ovations.

The forty-year-old Nicklaus putted out for a 73. The fifty-year-old Palmer putted out for a 69.

"The old boy finally got Jack," Curtis shouted.

Nicklaus and Palmer shook hands and headed off to do a dual news conference. "They wouldn't let us in on the interviews inside," Curtis said, "but we were all outside hollering anyhow . . . The greatest thing that ever happened for Arnold was to beat Jack Nicklaus in the final round of the Masters."

When he stepped into the press room, Palmer glowed like a man who has just pitched a two-hit shutout in Game Seven of the World Series. Nicklaus was all but rolling his eyes.

"Today," Jack said, "I had about as much enthusiasm as zip . . . It's very difficult for anybody to get pumped up when you're twenty shots out."

Palmer didn't find it difficult at all. Only three times in his previous twenty-five Masters had Arnold broken 70 in the last round.

"I don't think Jack and I have ever played when we didn't compete," Palmer said, "whether it be at Palm Springs, the Masters, or for last place at Hazeltine. We've always competed, and we always will, until he gets too old."

The reporters belly-laughed; Nicklaus forced a chuckle. He was sitting next to Palmer in the Masters interview room, wishing he could be anywhere else in the world.

"I guess I had a little more incentive to play better," Arnold said.

He was asked by a reporter to spell that out.

"I don't think I have to elaborate," Palmer responded.

When Arnold left the interview session and stepped outside, Curtis and Murphrey and other Arnie's Army loyalists gave him a rousing cheer. "Talk about a grin from ear to ear," Curtis said of their man's reaction.

They all knew it wasn't going to get any better than this for the fifty-year-old Palmer. Curtis and some fellow army members went out for their annual tailgating party in the parking lot, and Arnie went out to join in the fun.

He had taken Augusta National back from Jack for one glorious Sunday spent a million miles from the leaderboard. Palmer finished tied for twenty-fourth at the Masters and it felt first-place good, thanks to the man who finished tied for thirty-third.

Two months later Jack Nicklaus would put the Augusta embarrassment behind him. He was walking toward the eighteenth green at Baltusrol, the club where Arnie's Army had blitzed him with taunts and banners in 1967. Jack broke Ben Hogan's U.S. Open record then, and he was about to break his own U.S. Open record now.

Only thirteen years later the boisterous New Jersey fans were treating Nicklaus like Palmer. They rushed up behind him, blowing past a marshal and clipping Nicklaus by the heels, making Jack wince and hop as he approached his ball.

Nicklaus couldn't have cared less. Some strangers were rapping him on the back, and it was the best feeling in the world.

Jack made birdie on Baltusrol's seventy-second hole to finish off Japan's Isao Aoki, just as he'd made birdie on Baltusrol's seventy-second hole to finish off Latrobe's Arnold Palmer. Only the forty-year-old Jack's 272 was three strokes better than the twenty-seven-year-old Jack's score to beat Palmer and Hogan's record in less popular times.

Nicklaus pumped his fist when his final putt dropped, and Angelo Argea, the caddie in the silver Afro and yellow jump suit, joined the circle of state troopers who closed in around the Golden Bear. Nicklaus hugged Argea, hugged Aoki, then held off everyone so his Japanese opponent — his playing partner for all four rounds — could attempt to break the old Nicklaus record of 275, too.

Aoki made his putt for 274 and then fired his ball into the crowd. But Nicklaus was a tournament winner for the first time in nearly two full years. He had done some short-game work with his old friend Phil Rodgers, and so he joined Hogan, Bobby Jones, and Willie Anderson as the Open's only four-time champs. Nicklaus did it for an ABC telecast that reached an estimated ninety million homes.

The old Baltusrol signs asking Nicklaus to land his ball in a bunker or a particularly thick patch of rough were replaced by a scoreboard statement in the column reserved for gallery messages:

JACK IS BACK

When the fans began chanting those three words, it sounded nothing like "Go, Arnie, go." Nicklaus had been shown love and respect during the British Opens at Muirfield (1972) and St. Andrews (1978) — he was never Fat Jack in the United Kingdom, just a brilliant golfer — but he'd never been so touched by an American crowd.

Jack walked into Baltusrol as an underdog, as a champion written off as washed up. He left Baltusrol feeling a bit like the kid American hockey players who had defeated the Soviets' Big Red Machine in Lake

Placid. "You know," Nicklaus said, "the Olympic chant, all that kind of stuff."

Fans were reaching down from everywhere, trying to touch him. At the trophy presentation, with a healthy portion of the twenty-seven-thousand-strong crowd in attendance, Nicklaus told the fans, "If you don't mind, I'm just going to stand here for a minute and enjoy this."

He'd won on Father's Day again. Nicklaus dialed up his oldest son, Jackie, who had just finished playing a tournament in Palm Beach County. Before Jack could relay the big news, Jackie launched into a review of his own round.

"And he listened to the whole thing," Jackie said. "Listened to me talk about every shot I hit or missed, before he finally goes, 'OK, well, I just called to let you know that your dad won the Open.'"

Nicklaus won it with a record-tying 63 to start and a record-breaking 68 to close. In his post-tournament news conference Nicklaus told reporters that he felt "this old body's still got one or two more wins in it."

He would easily win that season's PGA Championship at Oak Hill Country Club in Rochester, matching Walter Hagen's collection of five PGA titles. Nicklaus had his seventeenth victory in a professional major.

He had no idea he'd go nearly six years before living the last and greatest of his Grand Slam Sundays.

CHAPTER 16

• Separation

ARNOLD PALMER WAS WALKING out the clubhouse door at Augusta National, out toward the old oak tree where golf's movers and shakers kibitz every April, when he suddenly stopped dead in his tracks.

Moving his way was a large and animated circle of people — reporters, autograph seekers, assorted sycophants — making a fuss over Jack Nicklaus. The Golden Bear was still a threat on the tour, a threat at the Masters.

The King? He'd been reduced to a golden oldie, a noncontender who was well on his way to full-fledged ceremonial star.

Palmer was frozen by the moment, paralyzed by the choice: Keep walking, alone, and ignore the big-shot treatment being afforded Nicklaus? Or make a spin move back through the clubhouse door before anyone realizes that nobody was making a similar fuss over him?

Arnold thought he was deliberating in private. But the IMG rep assigned to him by Mark McCormack, a dashing young Scot named Alastair Johnston, was quietly watching Palmer when Arnold made a very human choice.

"I saw him turn around," Johnston said. "He didn't want to go out there because it would appear Arnold went out there and there was nobody around him, and there were all these people walking up [with Nicklaus]. And Arnold never said a word, but I saw it."

Johnston saw an ego as big as the eighth hole.

The agent took over Palmer's business interests in 1976, as McCormack busied himself turning IMG into a global superpower. No, Arnold was never comfortable with the fact that McCormack had moved on to bigger and better things.

"Being represented by this immigrant Scotsman as opposed to Mark McCormack, the leader of the industry," Johnston said, "was not something Arnold was going to take to real easily for quite a while."

Johnston won Palmer's faith by jogging with him at six in the morning, by drinking beer with him until ten at night, and by earning the trust of Palmer's closest advisers and friends.

"I might not have had the same vision as Mark," Johnston said, "but I had more time and patience. And the thing that really bugged Arnold was that Mark was always going somewhere. 'Arnold, I've got fifteen minutes and I've got to go.'

"I'd go to Arnold and he'd say, 'How long are you here for?' And I'd say, 'Until you kick me out.'"

Johnston advanced McCormack's strategy of marketing Palmer as a successful and genuine man, and not as a champion golfer. Johnston didn't want any company that employed Arnold as a spokesman congratulating him in an ad for winning a tournament or skins game.

"People can relate to success," Johnston said. "They can understand success more than they can winning."

Palmer's only winning was done in competition with other Sunshine Boys. He'd won the 1980 Senior PGA Championship in a playoff with Paul Harney, and then he'd won the 1981 U.S. Senior Open, scoring a small measure of revenge against Billy Casper, the master of Arnold's disaster at Olympic in 1966 and, along with Bob Stone, a playoff loser to Palmer fifteen years later.

Palmer was giving the senior tour the kind of jolt he gave the regular tour in 1960. But in his early forties, Nicklaus was a long way from conceding he was done as a Grand Slam force.

In June of 1982 he was minutes away from becoming the first man to win five U.S. Opens. Nicklaus was standing by the eighteenth green at Pebble Beach, among his all-time favorite courses, and he was waiting for Tom Watson to finish fouling up the seventeenth hole.

Dressed in blue slacks and a bright green sweater bearing a Golden Bear logo the color of his hair, Nicklaus did a greenside interview with

Jack Whitaker of ABC. The brief give-and-take had the unmistakable air of certainty to it.

"Well, Jack," Whitaker concluded, "we're going to wait here with you, and you're on the edge of your fifth Open win. And it's a pleasure to be in your time, I'll tell you."

A pleasure to be in your time — Nicklaus liked the sound of that about as much as he liked the sight of Watson in the shit at seventeen, facing a near-impossible chip.

Ten years earlier Nicklaus bounced one against the flagstick at seventeen with his one-iron to punctuate his Open triumph over Arnold Palmer and the rest. This was his hole, his course, his tournament.

Nicklaus was long past his Open battles with Palmer, who was visible on the final day only in a Pennzoil ad running between live shots of Jack and Watson. Arnie was planted on his tractor at Latrobe, dodging the sprinklers and cutting the grass. "This old tractor and I are a lot alike," he said in the ad. "We're both still using Pennzoil, and we're both still running."

Palmer had missed the Pebble Beach cut, and the Open gallery had shifted to Nicklaus, who had become more likable — improved image and looks aside — now that he was routinely losing big events to a younger foe.

Watson had Jack's number just as Jack had Arnie's, but he'd never won the Open and he believed no great golfer's career was complete without at least one national championship trophy on his shelf. Watson didn't want to go down as another Sam Snead. He'd been wishing upon this U.S. Open star since he was ten years old, and this scene at seventeen didn't look promising for a man trying to realize any boyhood dream.

Watson had beaten Nicklaus at Augusta in 1977 and 1981 and at Turnberry in 1977, but with his ball in the Pebble Beach rough, logic said he didn't stand a chance.

"Now comes, well, possibly, the decisive shot of this championship," said ABC's Jim McKay.

"This is a shot of [Watson's] that he generally plays very well," said McKay's broadcast partner, Dave Marr.

Watson's caddie, Bruce Edwards, ordered his man to get it close.

"I'm not going to get it close," Watson shot back. "I'm going to make it."

He opened up the blade of his sand wedge, measured the surprisingly accessible position of the ball, and slid his club underneath it to produce a soft pop-up. The moment his ball landed on the green, Watson knew it would find the bottom of the cup.

"Looks good, looks good!" Marr cried on ABC. "Do you believe it? Do you believe it?"

"What can you say?" McKay shouted as Watson triumphantly danced about the green, pointing to his caddie in I-told-you-so form. "Tom Watson, pitching into the hole for a birdie, has taken the lead of the U.S. Open. One more par and he's finally won it."

Watson had just delivered one of the greatest shots ever struck in major championship play. The camera flashed to Nicklaus, who was absorbing the roar as he watched the Watson celebration on a TV monitor. Jack's arms were folded, and the color had drained from his cheeks.

This was a familiar look to Nicklaus, the one he'd always seen on Palmer's face. Now it was on his face, this look that Palmer gave him on the seventh green at Baltusrol in 1967, the one that said, "Are you ever going to let me do something?"

Watson had become Jack, and Jack had become Arnold.

"When Watson hit his tee shot at seventeen," Nicklaus said, "I didn't think there was any way that I would lose the golf tournament. Not any way on this earth."

The man who had fainted for the births of all five of his children looked ready to pass out. At home his daughter, Nan, was crying in front of her TV.

"That was a time in his career when Dad really needed to win that," she would say. "It was a time when people were saying, 'Jack's old. He's this and he's that.' He really needed it more than [at] any other time."

And he wasn't going to get it.

"Nicklaus watching our coverage on a monitor," McKay said on ABC, "now knows that he can't do a thing. A man like Jack Nicklaus doesn't like to stand there helpless."

Whitaker was hovering near this helpless man, watching Watson on the same screen. Nicklaus would say that Watson could've set down another thousand golf balls in the very same spot at seventeen and not holed a single one of them.

"It was like Jack just took a tremendous body punch and sagged," Whitaker said.

Watson made another birdie at eighteen, then wrapped his caddie in a liberating hug. "He wins it by two from the greatest golfer of them all, Jack Nicklaus," McKay told America.

His windblown hair swept across his forehead, his thin smile failing to mask the pain of a colossal defeat, Nicklaus walked up to the winner with an extended hand. "You little son of a bitch," he said, "you did it to me again. I'm very proud of you. Congratulations."

Their rivalry should've intensified from there. Lee Trevino, another Nicklaus foil, hadn't won a Grand Slam event in eight years, and Palmer was off on the senior tour; the week before Pebble Beach, Arnie had won the Marlboro Classic for the fifty-and-over set.

But Nicklaus wouldn't be a factor in the final two major triumphs of Watson's career — the 1982 and 1983 British Opens — and wouldn't finish in the top five in thirteen of his next fourteen majors, the one exception being his second-place showing behind Hal Sutton at the 1983 PGA.

Watson-Nicklaus had seen its best day. So Jack's new rival would be his old rival.

Arnold Palmer was still the man to beat, only in different arenas and under different rules.

At fifty-three, Arnold Palmer had challenged the regular tour boys at the 1983 Glen Campbell Los Angeles Open, briefly taking the lead in the final round before Arnie did what he often did in those situations: he got distracted by his twenty-four-hour, seven-days-a-week role of goodwill ambassador.

At the tenth tee a fan threw him a commemorative coin carrying the image of a shamrock and shouted, "Luck of the Irish." Palmer caught the coin, thanked the fan, and proceeded to bogey numbers ten, eleven, and twelve.

He'd learned little from his premature handshake with his friend and putting guru, George Low, on the seventy-second hole at the 1961 Masters. Jack Nicklaus would've never walked over to George Low on the first hole of the Masters, never mind the seventy-second, while holding a one-shot lead. Nicklaus would've never acknowledged the fan on the tenth tee at the L.A. Open.

But that's why Arnie was Arnie, and Jack was Jack. That's why the L.A. Open crowd headed for the exits when Palmer was done and didn't bother to stick around to see who'd actually win the tournament (Gil Morgan would).

"I think Arnold wanted to win because everybody wanted him to win so badly," Alastair Johnston said. "And he felt like he let them down. He always wanted to perform for them, whereas Jack wanted to win for himself."

Palmer wanted to win, but only if he could make a legion of friends along the way.

One of those friends, a dentist named Howdy Giles, was a fanatic who wore Arnold Palmer pants, shirts, and sweaters while swinging Arnold Palmer clubs. His lifelong dream was to meet Palmer and become his dentist. Giles was the equivalent of a college basketball fan who paints his body and face in the colors of his alma mater.

Palmer didn't just make Giles his dentist; he made him his neighbor, his fellow Bay Hill member, and one of his very best friends.

Howdy Giles would not have existed in Jack Nicklaus's world.

Palmer was an autograph machine who never dismissed a stranger approaching him between bites of his porterhouse to ask about that wedge he chunked at the Thunderbird. Once he was walking down the fairway with Orville Moody when a fan yelled out, "Hey, Arn, remember me? I played with you in the '72 pro-am at Pebble Beach. My name is John."

Palmer shouted back to the man, "Hey, John, sure I do. Good to see you again."

A couple of paces later Moody sidled up to Palmer.

"Arnie, did you really remember that guy?"

"No, but I just wanted to make his day."

Jack Nicklaus wouldn't have made that guy's day, not when he was busy stalking a golf course.

Nicklaus was doing some consulting work for CBS in the early eighties when he found himself at a meeting of affiliate representatives who wanted a piece of his time. A very senior CBS executive asked Nicklaus to do what the network was paying him to do: mingle and sign autographs.

"I'm having lunch," Nicklaus said. "I'll come over when I'm done."

Arnie would've left his half-eaten club sandwich and never made it back for the kill. He was as friendly and agreeable as his fellow Latrobe native Fred Rogers, of *Mister Rogers' Neighborhood.*

"When Arnold looks into a grandstand of several thousand people," said Gary Koch, the tour veteran who won Palmer's tournament at Bay Hill in 1984, "you bet every single one of them goes home and says, 'He looked right at me.' Arnold played it to the hilt, too. He just loves being with people, whereas Nicklaus is the exact opposite."

Koch first played with Nicklaus in the Tournament of Champions in 1977. "That was difficult because it was a twosome," he said. "Jack was very cordial, but he wasn't outgoing at all. There was no conscious effort made to try to make me feel comfortable. You just kind of shook his hand on the first tee and that was that. He's not going to go out of his way to make you feel more at ease, where Arnold does."

That approach also applied to the locker room, where players rarely saw Nicklaus hanging out with the boys the way Palmer did.

"Arnold was the guy and Jack dethroned him," Koch said, "so there were a lot of people who didn't like Nicklaus. They really didn't . . . From a locker room situation, you never really saw [Palmer and Nicklaus] talk. There was a mutual respect kind of thing, but I never got the impression they wanted to have much to do with each other."

Nicklaus wasn't out to renew clubhouse acquaintances in the hours before his tee time. He separated himself from the garden-variety tour players, as his intimidating aura was as valuable a weapon as his driver and putter.

Nicklaus would just appear on the practice range, said tour veteran Jay Haas, "and you never saw where he came from. But Arnold, you knew where he was. He was in the locker room. Two totally different personalities. Not only did Jack not interact with Arnold; he didn't interact with a lot of players."

As the seasons passed, and as Palmer spent more time on the senior tour, Arnold and Jack saw less and less of each other.

"I don't think the friendship ever went away," Palmer said. "It was just the nature of the times and what we were doing individually. When I started playing the senior tour, the whole thing changed and . . . there was no communication really . . . We just separated naturally, and I was doing something different than he was. It had nothing to do with . . . anything other than the fact that we weren't around each other a lot."

Nicklaus was quick to agree. "People didn't understand that Arnold and I were playing side by side and spending a lot of time together ... and then he started to play the senior tour," Jack said. "Well, we didn't see each other. So when you're not spending a lot of time together and you don't see him, all of a sudden that was a rift. It wasn't a rift. We just didn't spend time together."

But when Jack didn't play in Arnold's Bay Hill event in 1980, 1981, and 1985, and when Arnold didn't play in Jack's Muirfield Village event in 1981 and 1985, it was hardly a coincidence.

The business competition between Palmer and Nicklaus was growing teeth by the hour, and the fate of David Harman, a six-foot-six, three-hundred-pound, laugh-a-minute golf course builder, illustrated the gulf between the game's two walking conglomerates.

Harman was a dirt mover and course shaper whose father worked for Nicklaus. "David grew up with us as a kid," Jack said.

He was a valued member of the Nicklaus business team, a guy who could mold eighteen challenging and aesthetically pleasing holes out of the mud and make you laugh while doing it. "A nice guy," Nicklaus said.

But then that nice guy started signing contracts to build courses for Arnold Palmer.

"When a guy is doing business with you," Nicklaus said, "and all of a sudden he starts doing business with the other guy, you sort of [leave] that guy alone ... David did several golf courses with us ... and the next thing, I turn around and he's working for Arnold."

Harman was no longer a valued member of the Nicklaus team.

Jack was also fond of using Toro products for the courses he was designing, at least until he came across an ad with Palmer endorsing Toro. "Soon as Jack saw that," said Jay Morrish, a Nicklaus course designer, "it was over."

When asked to confirm that he dropped Toro because Palmer picked it up, Nicklaus said, "No, that probably happened. Probably."

Nicklaus figured you were either with him or you were with Palmer. No double dealing allowed.

"If there was a strain in the friendship," said Doc Giffin, Palmer's trusted aide, "it was more brought about by business. I think the business got personal."

And the less time Palmer and Nicklaus spent together, the fewer opportunities there were to reminisce about their bygone team victories and food fights and shin-kicking contests—the experiences that softened the rough edges of their relationship.

Nicklaus was the one who left IMG and started his own Golden Bear, Inc. By the mid-eighties Golden Bear, Inc., had upgraded to Golden Bear International. Put Pierman was long gone and Chuck Perry was the executive responsible for making as much money as Nicklaus could make without a golf club in his hands.

Perry was a publishing man and former educator who had built Florida International University out of an abandoned airport, and by 1985 he had helped Nicklaus expand his design company to the point where Jack could command a fee of up to $750,000 per course, a figure Palmer couldn't touch.

"Golf course design was something Jack liked," Johnston said, "because he wasn't as good with people as Arnold was." Jack could get away from the masses in an open pasture or field, playing God with the land. He liked the isolation and the power.

"And therefore he wasn't nearly as enchanted by doing the spokesman stuff," Johnston said.

Perry had gotten rid of unnecessary investments in a radio station and car dealership, but he also persuaded Nicklaus to get involved in everything from oil and real estate to shrimp farms. The markets turned against Jack, and two golf community developments in which he had invested heavily—St. Andrews in Westchester County, New York, and Bear Creek in Murrieta, California—were devolving into money pits, inspiring investors to run for cover and leaving Nicklaus to pick up their slack.

By the time a pair of Golden Bear executives informed Nicklaus of his dire financial straits, Jack was facing the fall of his empire.

"I basically had the obligation probably of over a hundred million dollars," Nicklaus said, ". . . which I had no way in the world of ever repaying."

Estimates actually put Nicklaus's debt at $150 million and his annual revenue at $6 million. His company overextended and overstaffed, Nicklaus was overcome by the terrifying thought he'd just thrown away everything he'd worked for since turning pro in 1962.

Jack was furious with himself. "I'm not a good businessman," he told his wife.

"You are a good businessman," Barbara said. "You have too much common sense. We'll be fine."

"I learned some great lessons," Jack would say. "Some things I'm not proud of in there because I was stupid enough to get myself in that position. But I was very proud of the way I finished."

Nicklaus approached Chemical Bank of Manhattan, which had poured tens of millions into St. Andrews, and told bank officials the Hastings-on-Hudson project was falling apart. Bear Creek units weren't selling either, despite the fact Nicklaus scored a highly promoted Skins Game for the new course that included Palmer, Tom Watson, Fuzzy Zoeller, and himself.

Jack didn't want to declare bankruptcy. He wanted to work out a deal with Chemical and his other lenders, and on this front Nicklaus's luck hadn't run out.

Bankers with twenty-two handicaps were far more willing to cut a break for Jack W. Nicklaus than they would have been for John Q. Public. Nicklaus ultimately paid $12 million to settle his $150 million tab.

"Perry got me in trouble by guaranteeing ... some stuff I didn't know he guaranteed," Nicklaus said of the executive he would fire, "but I did it. And that was to the tune of a lot of millions of dollars, but it got paid off."

Nicklaus stayed with the St. Andrews project until it was complete.

"I'm very proud of it," he said. "[Chemical Bank] came back to me and said, 'Look, we've never had anybody who has ever stayed with a project through its conclusion after a workout. Would you come and do some work for us?' I didn't do it, but it was a very nice compliment ... Am I proud that I stood up like a man and took it? Damn right."

Nicklaus had hired too many employees and chased too many rainbows. The conservative golfer, Nicklaus, had nearly gone bankrupt by being a reckless businessman. The reckless golfer, Palmer, had protected his fortune by being a conservative businessman, by keeping a relatively small payroll and limiting his exposure in most of his ventures.

"I suppose there's something to be said for that," Palmer said. "Jack was raised at a country club, and you know my background ... That reflects into our business acumen."

Palmer was a child of the Depression, and Nicklaus was not. The poor little rich kid had almost lost his shirt, and at age forty-six, nearly half a dozen years after he'd last won a major championship, Nicklaus knew there was only one place to launch his comeback.

Augusta.

CHAPTER 17

• King for a Day

ON APRIL 13, 1986, Jack Nicklaus was staring at the fifteenth green at Augusta National, beholding the most inviting pin he'd ever seen. He was 204 yards away on a cloudless Sunday, and the flagstick might as well have been five feet in front of him.

On most holes at the Masters, a man got himself in big trouble when hitting to the wrong side of the green. But at fifteen Nicklaus didn't see a wrong side from the fairway. His piercing blue eyes saw nothing but a chance to make an eagle and win the tournament.

Nicklaus's waistline was spilling over his belt again, only not as conspicuously as it did in his Fat Jack days. Middle age was taking hold of his body, that's all. He was a champion golfer running out of time.

"How far will a three go here?" he asked his son Jackie, whose white caddie overalls carried the number eighty-nine on his left breast.

"I think it will go a long way, Pops," Jackie said.

The kids never called Nicklaus "Pops," but they did during this week, if only because it was a week when up was down and down was up. Jack's seventy-six-year-old mother, Helen, had made the trip to Augusta for the first time since 1959, the first year her boy was invited to play. She would sit at the piano with her daughter and daughter-in-law every night that week in Augusta, singing church hymns.

Her Charlie had been gone sixteen years, she had some health problems, and she lived her post-Charlie life assuming her end was near.

"I just want to go to the Masters one more time before I die," Helen told her daughter, Marilyn.

Helen was where Jack got his bluntness; if you asked her a question, you got an answer. Helen didn't take kindly to wayward golf shots, either. If Jack hit one, she'd end up behind a tree, afraid to watch.

On this Sunday Helen had nothing to fear. She watched her son take a four-iron from her grandson on the fifteenth fairway so Jack could send the golf ball on the ride of its life. Nicklaus pressed his right hand against his forehead and squinted while tracking its flight, and the deafening roar told him he was back in the ball game.

Jack had birdies at numbers nine, ten, eleven, and thirteen to overcome his one stumble at the par-three twelfth — thanks to a vile, parbusting spike mark — and get to five under. But if he made the eagle putt at the fifteenth, he would be considered a serious threat to win for the first time.

He made the eagle putt. His son Jackie jumped for joy as Nicklaus pumped his fists. "My goodness," the CBS analyst Ben Wright told his viewers. "There's life in the old bear yet."

Jackie had tried to time his leap so his father wouldn't see it; the caddie had gotten overly excited during a birdie barrage at Pebble Beach in 1982, right before Nicklaus bogeyed and ultimately lost on Tom Watson's chip-in. Jackie didn't want to jinx the old man this second time around.

Only there was no jinxing Nicklaus on this day. At the ninth hole he had heard the eagle roars behind him for Seve Ballesteros and Tom Kite, sounds that actually made him relax and let down his straw-colored hair.

Nicklaus twice backed away from his eleven-footer, then turned to the gallery in true Arnold Palmer form. "You know what," Nicklaus said, "let's make some noise up here."

The fans laughed and cheered, Nicklaus sank his birdie, and off they all went on their carpet ride across the back nine.

That morning, with his father four strokes off the lead, Nicklaus's son Steve had phoned with a question.

"What number do you have in mind?" Steve asked.

"I think 65 to win, 66 to tie," his father answered.

"That's exactly what I'm thinking, Pops. Go shoot it."

On the sixteenth tee Nicklaus had that winning 65 dead to rights. It made no sense. He was 160th on the money list with a lousy $4,404 to his name. He hadn't won a major since 1980, hadn't won a tournament since his own Memorial in 1984. In 1985 he'd missed the cut at the U.S. Open for the first time since 1963 and then missed the cut at the British Open for the first time ever.

Viewers around the world were transfixed. A fifteen-year-old South African and junior world champion, Ernie Els, stayed up late with his father to see if Nicklaus could pull it off.

"It was kind of like watching an old boxer like Muhammad Ali fighting Larry Holmes," Els would say, "and you hope he's going to beat the guy, but you think he's going to get the crap beat out of him."

Nicklaus was fighting the younger lions of the day, Ballesteros and Greg Norman, and he was inspired by a noble cause. His wife, Barbara, had suggested a yellow shirt that morning as a throwback: Jack used to wear that color on weekends in honor of a boy who died of bone cancer in 1971.

Craig Smith was the thirteen-year-old son of the minister who presided over the church where Jack and Barbara were married. If Craig couldn't be a golfer, he was going to be a doctor. In the boy's dying days, Nicklaus phoned him whenever he could. Craig told him once that yellow was his favorite color, and Nicklaus kept a promise to wear yellow in every tournament, his private hello to a child who was watching on TV.

Fifteen years later, Craig's mother, Mary Lou, was working in a Victorian museum a couple of days before the 1986 Masters started when she blurted out to her coworkers, "This Sunday Jack is going to win and he's going to wear yellow."

So Mary Lou and her husband, the Reverend Dr. William E. Smith, were already choking up as they watched the final round of the Masters, as they watched Jack Nicklaus grab his five-iron on the sixteenth tee. The man in the yellow shirt was aiming for the right of the stick, figuring the ball would bleed down to the hole. With the ball airborne, Jackie pleaded, "Be the right club."

His father was too busy reaching for his tee to watch. "It is," Jack assured his son as he winked at him.

It was the cockiest thing Nicklaus ever said or did on a golf course. The ball landed to the right of the pin, kicked left as planned, and missed the hole by half a foot.

The crowd erupted. "That's my boy," Helen Nicklaus kept telling the cheering fans. Nicklaus's mother was practically floating at this point, keeping up with the giddy masses, tapping strangers on their shoulders to let them know the Golden Bear was her cub.

Nicklaus birdied sixteen, and Ballesteros hooked his second shot at fifteen into the creek. "And the foreign invasion is reeling under the Bear's attack," Ben Wright said on CBS. The Bear and the Spaniard were tied for the lead at eight under, and the gallery sounded like a sold-out Ohio State crowd in the fourth quarter of the Michigan game.

Nicklaus was running the table. Ohio Fats had become Minnesota Fats, and the old Quonset hut turned press room was all abuzz. "It was almost like Palmer had come back," said Edwin Pope of the *Miami Herald*, "because by then Nicklaus had become almost like Arnie. He was a radiant guy. He'd gotten past the pudgy, smoky image he had. He was now a lovable old guy instead of a brash intruder. He'd generated so much goodwill, just like Arnie, and Jack loved it."

No writer gave Nicklaus a shot, not with Ballesteros and Norman high on the board. On the eve of the tournament Ballesteros was quoted as saying this Masters "is mine."

But that wasn't the newspaper story that boiled Nicklaus's blood. Tom McCollister of the *Atlanta Journal* wrote what nearly every other golf writer wrote. "Nicklaus is gone, done. He just doesn't have the game anymore. It's rusted from lack of use. He's 46, and nobody that old wins the Masters."

John Montgomery's son, John Jr., happened to read McCollister's advance, and John Montgomery and his wife, Nancy, happened to be sharing an Augusta home with Jack and Barbara Nicklaus.

"Dad, this article is terrible about Jack," John Jr. told him. Montgomery had an idea, because he always had an idea. He was a former FBI man who left the bureau to run the Jacksonville tour stop, and his big, strapping frame was a perfect fit for his extra-large sense of humor.

His pranks were legendary. Montgomery once dumped five tons of horse manure in Nicklaus's driveway and planted a golf pin in the pile with the words "Happy Birthday, Jack" written on the flag; Nicklaus returned the favor by having the manure stuffed inside Montgomery's new Cadillac Eldorado. The ex-FBI man once had a donkey tied to the rearview mirror of Jack's Pontiac and once had one hundred small chickens left on Jack's lawn.

So to Montgomery, taping a demeaning paragraph to the refrigerator door was little more than a knock-knock joke. He picked the fridge for McCollister's piece, he said, "because I knew Jack would see it there. The only thing you can count on every day is Jack going to the refrigerator about four hundred times." For good measure Montgomery highlighted the offending words.

"I don't have to guess who put this on the refrigerator," Nicklaus said the first time he opened the fridge door. "It's not a very good article, is it?"

"Well," Montgomery said, "it's not exactly complimentary, Jack."

They had a good laugh over it, the way they always did.

"But every day Jack had to look at it," Montgomery said. "He read it every day."

When Jack and Jackie got to the seventeenth tee on Sunday, their ears were ringing. Nicklaus hit that green in regulation and had an eleven-foot birdie attempt to take the outright lead. He was making a statement for a new generation of players and fans, showing them just how great he was in the sixties and seventies.

"A love-in," Dave Anderson of the *New York Times* called it. "That was the way Arnold used to win, coming from behind, and Arnold was no longer Arnold, even at Augusta. Jack had his own army, so to speak, and it was incredible to watch it come together."

The idea that Nicklaus could win a sixth green jacket, at his age, "was too fictional to be real," Ken Venturi said. But CBS had a fairy tale come to life in the Augusta pines, and the network was riding it like a midnight train to Georgia.

"It was a stampeding," said Gary McCord, the player turned analyst, "and the yells weren't a slow eruption. It was a giant fucking eruption going right to the top of the ladder. It kept going and kept going and you kept thinking, 'This can't happen. There's no way this can happen.' And it kept happening."

As Nicklaus headed for the seventeenth green, Verne Lundquist, the CBS announcer at that hole, told himself, "Don't clutter this up. Don't get in the way of this."

In front of a TV on the campus of Southern Methodist University, Nicklaus's only daughter, Nan, was watching with some friends she was visiting. Nan was a student at the University of Georgia. Her choice for the weekend was SMU over Augusta, and she was as mad at her friends as her father had been at that spike mark on number twelve.

"I'm going to kill you guys if he wins this tournament," Nan told them.

Nicklaus tugged at his yellow shirt and crouched over the putt, his thighs bursting through his tight checkered pants. Jackie thought the putt would break to the right. His father thought it would break a bit to the right but then straighten out at the hole.

Father decided he knew best. He had this oversized putter, a Response ZT 615 from MacGregor, that had evolved into a sorcerer's wand. The first time Nicklaus used it in a tournament, the wind swept his blade into the ball and a four-inch putt traveled only two inches.

He decided to stick with it anyway, and with the silent crowd at seventeen frozen in time, Nicklaus sent his birdie attempt on its way. Up in the tower, with the ball two-thirds of the way home, Lundquist said, "Maybe."

Maybe.

Don't clutter this up. Don't get in the way of this.

With the ball a revolution or two from dropping, Nicklaus stepped forward with his left foot, raised his Response ZT 615 with his left hand, and stuck out his tongue as if he were the Chicago Bulls' new sensation, Michael Jordan, in midair.

The Golden Bear — mocked as the Olden Bear — had a near-satanic look in his eye a second before he'd break his tie with Ballesteros and Tom Kite and grab the lead by the throat. A moment after his ball disappeared, Lundquist cried, "Yes, sirrrrrrrrr!" just as Nicklaus pumped his arms.

A CBS executive next to Lundquist, Neal Pilson, screamed so loudly in celebration he was afraid he'd been heard on the air. Pilson was ashamed of himself, a journalist cheering in the press box. But he couldn't help it. Nobody could.

In South Africa young Ernie Els and his father were awestruck. They had fully expected this heavyweight fight to end with Nicklaus looking like Muhammad Ali, not Larry Holmes. "We couldn't believe what we were seeing," Els would say.

A forty-six-year-old man was making all witnesses feel half their age.

Nicklaus rolled his eyes and shook his head while his playing partner, Sandy Lyle, prepared to putt. In the press room, on the course, every credentialed reporter had the same reaction as Art Spander of the *San Francisco Examiner*.

"Holy Christ. Jack Nicklaus is going to win the Masters."

Nicklaus's eyes turned red and moist. Back in Columbus, Craig Smith's parents were crying, too. The people who had walked away from this scene two hours earlier, thinking Nicklaus wouldn't win, were kicking themselves silly.

Jack's Uncle Frank and Aunt Rachel had left Augusta National after nine holes. Jack's close friend Pandel Savic left in the middle of the thirteenth hole to catch an evening flight home. He walked into an airport bar and was stunned to see Jack's score at seventeen, but his bags were checked and his flight was boarding. Savic and his wife watched the eighteenth on a portable Sony a fellow passenger carried onto the plane.

Fighting back the tears and waving to the fans, Nicklaus walked up that final fairway to an ovation Palmer would've envied.

It was the culmination of a long journey. At the Masters, Nicklaus was the King for a day.

"A great piece of Americana, forty-six years old, coming in with the lead," said Pope of the *Herald*. "People were pathetically exuberant. There was a huge amount of people crying, and they were ashamed of themselves for crying. They were just so happy to see this happen, for Jack to end up like Arnold at Augusta. I think Jack felt as good about that part of it as he did about being in the lead."

Nicklaus had to work on this connection, this bond, as much as he ever had to work on his chipping and putting with his teacher, Jack Grout, and that's what made this endgame reception so rewarding.

Jackie grew emotional on eighteen, thinking about the way his father had won over these fans across the years. The Golden Bear had dabbed at his own tears and told himself to cut it out, to concentrate on finishing the tournament. He had composed himself in time to land his ball on the seventy-second green, a gust of wind leaving his second shot forty feet short of the cup.

Nicklaus would've been content with a two-putt par, but he damn near holed the forty-footer. He marked his ball so Lyle could finish first and avoid the avalanche to follow Nicklaus's tap-in.

At that point Lyle couldn't hear himself think. This riotous celebration of all things Nicklaus had left him numb. "It was something you never hear," Lyle said. "It was more than stereo. It was coming from behind you, sideways, forward, echoing all around you. It was surreal. It just raised the hair on the back of your neck."

Lyle missed his putt and then pressed his right thumb against the tip of his nose and wiggled his fingers at the cup, his own "screw you" to the course for being so accommodating to another man in his company. Nicklaus was about to follow with his tap-in when Jackie said, "Keep your head still."

The old man had told Jackie to give him that order on every putt, but this time Nicklaus grinned at his son, his expression saying, "I think I can handle this one."

Nicklaus made his par for a 30 on the back nine and a 65 for the round, the very number he'd assured his son Steve would win the Masters. This was why players and friends often called Jack "Carnac," the all-knowing Johnny Carson character on *The Tonight Show*.

Nicklaus raised his arms above his head and exchanged pleasantries with Lyle and Lyle's caddy. He turned to Jackie, and father and son embraced. They walked off the green arm in arm, a scene that would encourage a year's worth of letters and telegrams from touched fans.

Nicklaus waited anxiously in the Bobby Jones cabin to see if anyone would tie him or beat him on the final hole; no one did. Ballesteros finished two back. Tom Watson, the Nicklaus slayer, finished four back. Kite missed a twelve-foot birdie putt to finish one back. And Greg Norman, who needed only a par to force a playoff, choked on a wild second shot into the gallery and failed to get up and down.

"It's OK," Norman said, "because I know one of these days I'm gonna break his record of six Masters anyway."

As night descended on Augusta, Nicklaus wasn't thinking about his record collection of green jackets. He was merely basking in his triumph over the next generation, the one that had allegedly passed him by. The youngest man ever to win the Masters was just happy he'd become the oldest man ever to win the Masters.

Nicklaus would see Tom McCollister, the *Atlanta Journal* writer whose work graced Jack's refrigerator door. "Thanks, Tom," he said through a smile. "You just write the same article next year and put forty-seven in it."

The next day Mary Lou Smith reported to work at her museum and handed out an endless supply of "I told you so's." The man who won in honor of her lost son, Jack Nicklaus, reported to his own office in Florida and began fielding reports that suggested better financial times ahead.

MacGregor was already selling Response ZT 615s to weekend warriors faster than Augusta National could sell its shirts and caps in the gift shop. By the end of 1987 MacGregor would sell 350,000 of those Nicklaus putters, or 344,000 more than the company figured it would sell.

Nicklaus would call the notion that the 1986 Masters and its first-place prize money pulled him from the poorhouse "rubbish ... You don't win $144,000 and have that make up for $100 million. And selling a couple hundred thousand putters, you don't make that up."

Either way, the victory was priceless. Congratulatory notes came in from entertainers, sports stars, politicians, and fans. To Nicklaus, one stood out from the mountainous pile.

"That was fantastic! Congratulations. Do you think there's any chance for a fifty-six-year-old?"

It was signed by Arnold Palmer.

Part III

CHAPTER 18

• Cold War

C HI CHI RODRIGUEZ was sitting with Arnold Palmer and Jack Nicklaus on a plane, Nicklaus's plane, when he appointed himself mediator in the ongoing conflict between golf's two superpowers.

"Hey, guys," Rodriguez said. "It's over."

Over? From appearances nothing needed to be over. Palmer and Nicklaus were traveling together, playing the senior tour together, and, as always, behaving cordially toward each other in public view.

They played practice rounds together. They even staged unlikely revivals together — they each opened up with rounds of 68 to contend briefly in the 1989 PGA Championship. Their wives, Winnie and Barbara, had been good friends for thirty years, writing notes to each other and occasionally catching up on the phone.

Was there a problem here?

Rodriguez had been in enough locker rooms to know that yes, there was a problem. This was around 1991, and Palmer and Nicklaus hadn't played in each other's tournaments since 1984. Arnold and Jack were still competing fiercely for course design contracts and endorsements — Arnold was still winning on the endorsement front; Jack was still winning on the design front — and for the unofficial title of golf's chief elder.

"We're seniors now," Rodriguez told them. "You guys can't still be acting like this."

Arnold and Jack listened. Thousands of feet above the ground, they were told to get their heads out of the clouds.

"We can't have this animosity between us anymore," Rodriguez continued. "We've got to let it go."

Chi Chi turned his attention to Palmer.

"Don't worry," he told Arnold. "Someday you can have an airplane that you can stand up in like Jack does."

If Palmer found that funny, he didn't laugh.

"Jack had a bigger plane then," Rodriguez would say. "It was intense, their relationship. They were such competitors. The King never wanted the prince to get the crown."

Rodriguez always saw Palmer and Nicklaus as larger-than-life figures. At an outing during the Bay Area earthquake of 1989, Arnold stood under a tree that was shaking like a candle's flame in the wind, and Chi Chi ran to his side. Rodriguez thought the safest place in an earthquake would be the place right next to Palmer, the man who would never die.

"Arnold's the type of guy, if you're in a war, that you want to be your leader," Rodriguez said. "If he was there when the *Titanic* went down, he would've put scuba gear on and [gone] down after it."

Nicklaus wasn't the same heroic character, but Rodriguez was in awe of his otherworldly powers on a golf course all the same. In their 1991 U.S. Senior Open playoff, Nicklaus had a piece of mud on his ball when Chi Chi turned to his caddie and said, "Mr. Jack's in trouble here."

Mr. Jack landed his next shot squarely on the green and won the tournament.

"That's why he's Jack Nicklaus," Rodriguez told his caddie. "Can you believe that shot? I thought he'd go a hundred yards away from the flag, and he put it twenty feet from the hole."

Rodriguez envied Nicklaus's talent and Palmer's charisma, and he wanted to broker a truce between Jack and Arnold for two reasons: he was a friend to both men, and he thought it would be good for the game if its most significant figures presented a completely unified front.

The golf landscape was big enough for Palmer and Nicklaus both, but they had a hard time seeing it that way. They were so dedicated to being the best, and so conditioned to believe that second place was no better than last place, that their competitive juices boiled when they were in the same arena.

Palmer and Nicklaus were opposing gladiators on the course, so they would be opposing gladiators away from it, too. "We've both conducted our business and our lives in our own way," Palmer would say, "and they weren't necessarily the same. They were probably different."

Jack struck first in 1985 by declining an invitation to play the Hertz Bay Hill Classic, and Arnold fired back by declining a spot in the Memorial. That started a vicious cycle both men were too proud to break.

"There were a couple of times when I was a little upset when he didn't come and play, but not as a general rule," Palmer said. "I'd just ask him to come and play and he had something else on his schedule. It wasn't convenient to play."

Their wives, Winnie and Barbara, remained close, but Palmer said even though he considered Nicklaus a friend, "we just didn't spend a lot of time together. We had different points of view."

The chill could be felt from Dublin, Ohio, to Orlando and back. "I don't know whether it was so much a frost as a lack of warmth," said Bev Norwood, who worked with Palmer at IMG.

"There was a frost, and pure competitiveness was the reason," said Put Pierman, former head of Golden Bear, Inc. "Arnold wasn't a threat at the time, as he was not challenging Jack on the course. He was always challenging Jack as it relates to that senior-most ambassadorial position in golf."

Plenty of back-channel sniping was going on between the Palmer and Nicklaus camps as Jack consistently snubbed Bay Hill and Arnold consistently snubbed Muirfield Village.

Palmer was known to refer to the Golden Bear logo on Nicklaus merchandise as a pig. A member of Arnold's inner circle, *Orlando Sentinel* columnist Larry Guest, was among those who had the misfortune of wearing a Nicklaus shirt in Palmer's company when, according to Guest, Palmer would grab the Golden Bear logo "and with a good helping of skin as well, he'd pinch and twist and say, 'What are you doing wearing that pig on your chest?'"

Asked about Palmer's mocking of his logo, Nicklaus said, "I hadn't heard that one . . . A lot of people have said that kidding around. That wouldn't be anything."

Only Nicklaus was said to have ordered a redesign of the logo to give the bear in the image longer legs, and to give Palmer and his people less reason to keep referring to it as a pig.

The pig references, said IMG's Alastair Johnston, were "as close as you'd get to trash talk [between Palmer and Nicklaus]. And Arnold was embarrassed by that."

Johnston maintained that Arnie and Jack never lost their respect for each other, not even for a fleeting moment. "Envy on both sides? Absolutely," Johnston said. "Competition? Absolutely. Lack of respect? Never."

But at times the rivalry had a second-grade feel to it.

"It's one of those things," Johnny Miller said, "where I hit you, and you're my brother and you hit me back, and then I hit you. It wasn't that [Palmer and Nicklaus] both hit at the same time. One didn't play in the other guy's tournament, so it's like, 'If you're not playing in mine, I'm not going to play in yours.' And, of course, he didn't play in yours, so you're not playing in his. So it never stops.

"It's like the back seat of a car when your father's driving. It's like, 'Who's going to stop hitting first?'"

The gallery represented the third brother in the back seat, egging them on. During the 1987 PGA Championship at PGA National in Palm Beach Gardens, where Nicklaus, Palmer, and Tom Watson were grouped together in the stifling heat of the day, Arnie's Army gave Jack another hard poke to the ribs.

All three men had knocked their balls into the water, all three took drops, and all three hit approaches that failed to scare the hole. Nicklaus walked up first to a nice round of applause, and then Watson received the same warm welcome.

"But when Arnold got up there the place went apeshit," said Ed Seay, Palmer's course designer. "You could see Jack; he was just about opposite me and Jack's wife, Barbara. He just shook his head like, 'What in the hell is going on?' This is after twenty-five years of competition. Barbara looked at me and said, 'Jack will never understand, Ed. He'll never understand.'"

Golf had great personality contrasts in Hogan and Snead, Hagen and Jones, but this rivalry between Palmer and Nicklaus trumped them all. The public fascination with their relationship never waned like the public fascination with their eroding games.

The sport was built around a culture of respect and civility, so the notion that golf's most prominent stars squabbled constantly represented a delicious twist to a vanilla plot.

"Golfers are pussies," said Paul Azinger, winner of Palmer's tournament in 1988. "We don't fight, and if there's a rift in the press it's some-how always smoothed over. There's never this open animosity between players, and if open animosity happens, then you do everything you can to smooth it over.

"Basketball players fight. Baseball players charge the mound. Hockey players fight. Football players grab your face mask and pull you to the ground. Golfers don't fight."

Palmer and Nicklaus didn't trade haymakers with their balled-up fists, but they did indeed fight.

By 1992 Nicklaus had 184 golf courses that he had either built, or was building, or was about to start building, and he was getting as much as $1.25 million a pop.

Palmer's course design company was happy to secure a little more than half that sum, but Arnold made money by playing off of Nicklaus's exorbitant fee. In 1992 Palmer also beat Jack in the game of corporate sponsorship, riding Pennzoil, Hertz, Sears, United Airlines, and Ca-dillac, among countless other benefactors, to a payday of $11 million, according to *Forbes*, which reported that Nicklaus had earned an esti-mated $9 million.

Palmer was a pitchman without peer. Arnold had teamed with O. J. Simpson in popular Hertz ads, though he had no use for the Juice, who was a favorite of Hertz CEO Frank Olson.

In the commercials Palmer had America believing he was O. J.'s best bud. Yes, Arnie could sell anything. That's why nearly thirty years af-ter he last won a major championship, Palmer was still the most highly compensated golfer in the world and a man whose face, voice, and name could earn in one year more than three times all the money his woods, irons, and putter won in his entire golfing career.

Arnie also had one other ace in his hole: a 10 percent stake in the In-ternational Management Group, which had grown from that Palmer–Mark McCormack handshake into a juggernaut about as popular with its enemies as the Soviet Union.

"Mark was smart enough to give Arnold a piece of the action," said Nancy McCormack. "I think Arnold forced that. He said to Mark, 'You have a piece of me, I should have a piece of you.' Arnie used to joke that he was pimping for Mark."

From his humble Palmer-Player-Nicklaus days, McCormack built up a remarkable stable of clients. Rod Laver, Jackie Stewart, and Jean-

Claude Killy grew into Chris Evert, Greg Norman, Nancy Lopez, Mario Lemieux, Andre Agassi, and Nick Faldo. Another client, tennis star Betsy Nagelsen, would become McCormack's second wife in 1986 after the agent was divorced from Nancy, the mother of his three children.

IMG didn't just stick to the business of representing athletes and entertainers; it promoted events and negotiated TV deals. Clients included Wimbledon, the USGA, and the Vatican.

The founding father, Palmer, never got lost in the hustle and bustle. IMG helped make him the number-one athlete endorser for three full decades before Michael Jordan knocked him off the mount in 1991.

"Arnold never had any aspirations to be . . . way up at the top of the market like a Greg Norman," Johnston said. "Arnold still lived in the same house he always had [in Latrobe] and had a condo at Bay Hill. Arnold Palmer is value priced for America; he was affordable for America. The demographic skewed all the way up and all the way down.

"Arnold's also on a stage where he didn't have to retire. As soon as an athlete retires there's this perception that you're finished. I don't care if your name is Jordan or Montana or whatever. But Arnold could still come out and play."

Though Palmer played more conservatively than Nicklaus in the business arena, and though he was among the more trusted spokesmen in America, he did have to weather his own financial and public relations storms.

He signed off on the $48 million sale of Bay Hill to a Japanese firm, angering World War II vets in the Orlando area and inside Arnie's Army (the deal fell through). Palmer lost millions when his good friend and business partner James O'Neal failed in his grandiose bid to expand the Arnold Palmer Automotive Group and take it public. The six dealerships had made a killing in the past on a deal with Palmer-centric Hertz, which bought one hundred thousand cars a year from APAG before collapsing under the weight of O'Neal's ambitions, a disastrous buyback deal with Hertz, and a mile-high stack of lawsuit documents.

Finally, Palmer's own personal Disney World — the Isleworth golf development — went up in smoke when local Lake Bessie residents sued Palmer and his development partners over the Isleworth drainage that was allegedly flooding and polluting the lake, a move inspired by the drowning death of a resident's dog. A noted dog lover and owner, Arnold lost the protracted legal fight, the Lake Bessie residents were awarded a $6.6 million judgment, and Palmer — who had limited financial exposure in the deal, as always — surrendered a sliver of his good name.

"I don't think Arnie will ever get over the situation at Isleworth," said his sister Cheech, "because he put his heart and soul into building that golf course and clubhouse. His office there had leather floors. It was just something that he created."

And something that he lost. Palmer did sell O'Neal's Isleworth estate for $4.5 million as part of the APAG settlement, but a series of lawsuits and loan defaults had sheriff's deputies literally storming the Isleworth compound armed with foreclosure papers and orders to confiscate whatever they could.

Palmer's friend Joe Tito helped Arnold's wife, Winnie, and younger daughter, Amy, frantically gather as many of the King's trophies and mementos as they could before the deputies grabbed them. Winnie scrambled to move a grand piano back to Bay Hill. The stress of it all took a toll on Amy, a mother of four young children and a woman fighting breast cancer and facing a grim prognosis.

"It was just a devastating time of our lives," Amy said. "The whole thing was ludicrous . . . It was fairly frightening to think you had to gather these things collectively and do it before they confiscated everything. It was an unbelievable scene to watch them carting things off."

Amy's father sold his two lots, kept his design fee, and retreated to the peace and tranquillity of Bay Hill. Isleworth would recover and become a gated sanctuary for some of the biggest stars in sports.

The Palmers would recover, too. Amy would beat the cancer, and Arnold would continue to hold the public's trust and rake in millions by doing commercials and licensing his name in the United States and Japan, where Palmer was almost as big as he was in the Allegheny foothills.

Arnold Palmer would also receive a most unexpected honor. In the middle of the 1992 season, the host of a PGA Tour event phoned Palmer to tell him his career would be celebrated at the following year's event.

The caller's name was Jack Nicklaus.

CHAPTER 19

• Honoree

ACH YEAR the Memorial Tournament celebrated a titan from golf's past. The committee that made those decisions was known as the Captains Club, a cartel of Jack Nicklaus friends and associates advising the Golden Bear on the running of his event.

The Captains Club selected figures no longer active on the course. Bobby Jones, Gene Sarazen, Byron Nelson, and Sam Snead were among those already honored. At the time the committee was sorting through candidates for its 1993 event, Arnold Palmer remained an active player at the Masters and on the senior tour.

But despite the tension that colored his relationship with Palmer, Nicklaus pushed the committee to make an exception.

"The debate was, 'Was Arnold really an active player?'" Nicklaus said. "I kept saying, 'Guys, if you're going to honor him [when he's not active], he's never going to quit. You're never going to get a chance to honor him.'

"So they took the position that he was no longer a viable force as it related to winning, and that's why they agreed to go ahead and do that."

The Captains Club went ahead and asked Nicklaus to give his blessing to his own suggestion.

"Jack was anxious to do it," said his wife, Barbara. "And he was hoping Arnold would accept and come."

That was no gimme putt, either. Neither Palmer nor Nicklaus had attended the other's tournament in eight years.

Nicklaus had gone on the record about his feelings for Bay Hill, which he didn't see as a layout worthy of playing in Muirfield Village's league. Nicklaus also frowned on Palmer's course design philosophy. Known as an extreme micromanager, Jack saw Arnold as a detached ribbon cutter who would lend his name and fame to projects and little else.

"But even though they weren't real close friends," maintained John Montgomery, a Memorial elder, "they still respected each other."

Memorial protocol had Nicklaus approving or rejecting the Captains Club's pick and then contacting the approved candidate with the good news.

"So the night we selected Arnold," Montgomery said, "Jack got up and left to call him."

After Palmer answered the phone and absorbed Nicklaus's invitation to attend the following year's Memorial as its first honoree from the modern era, Arnold told Jack he'd have to check his schedule. It was thought to be a joke. Palmer finally accepted, and Nicklaus was credited with making the first significant move in securing a cease-fire between the players' camps.

"I was flattered," Palmer said. "I considered it a great honor."

The eighteen voting members of the Captains Club saw Palmer as the logical next choice in its fairly chronological celebration of the game's champions and dignitaries. Though the committee didn't pick Palmer for the cause of world peace, "I know for a fact that was the beginning of their friendship renewing," Montgomery said. "I don't think everybody really understood that Arnold and Jack had differences. Most of the Captains Club did, and I know I did. But ever since then it was a different ball game."

Soon enough, Nicklaus committed to playing Bay Hill in 1993, and Palmer committed to playing the Memorial in the days after his ceremony two and a half months later.

Arnie and Jack were a tandem again, and nobody was sure how long it would last.

"I sometimes think the two of them can't quite remember when or why they hated each other's guts," Put Pierman said. "Time does heal all wounds . . . They'll trivialize that. They'll say, 'Yeah, we did kind of jaw back and forth, but that was good for golf.' But, hey, come on. It was a lot more serious than that."

The reunion tour started in March of 1993 at Bay Hill's Nestle Invitational, where Palmer and Nicklaus sat side by side in leather chairs for a joint news conference, "looking a little like Churchill and Roosevelt," wrote George White of the *Orlando Sentinel*, "or the way you would imagine Olivier and Fonda, or maybe Ruth and Cobb."

On the dais Nicklaus repeated his oft-stated line that "I always had Arnold's gallery to fight, but I never had to fight Arnold," a line nobody took seriously, not even Palmer.

Arnold was asked if the man-to-man rivalry still burned bright. "Damn right," he said. "Jack and I will always compete. We always have and always will."

Palmer and Nicklaus kept score on trophies collected, money won, commercials made, equipment manufactured, sportswear sold, courses designed, and licensing deals cut.

So when Arnold and Jack opened their morning newspapers, they each turned to the business and sports pages and went straight to the other guy's box scores. "I always looked to see what Arnold was doing," Nicklaus said. "It was a habit."

And one that was impossible to break.

"Arnold has his feelings on different issues and I have mine," Nicklaus said. "They're not always the same. But if Arnold ever needed something or wanted something, as a friend, I'm there."

Palmer said much the same. And then they went out and played the wind-whipped 7,114-yard Bay Hill course in the first and second rounds of the Nestle Invitational. As it turned out, the course had gotten meaner since the last time Nicklaus had dismissed it.

Jack shot a 78 in the second round to finish at six-over 150, one stroke too many to make the cut. Palmer double bogeyed the seventeenth hole of his Friday round but parred the eighteenth after receiving a rousing standing ovation and made the cut at 149.

When the crowd stopped cheering, one fan seized upon the silence and shouted, "At least you beat Jack, Arnie." That was the only cut Palmer cared to make.

Eleven weeks later Lee Janzen and Rocco Mediate were playing Jack

Nicklaus and Arnold Palmer in a practice round at Nicklaus's Memorial Tournament when Palmer nailed a twenty-footer on the eighteenth hole that had Jack's fans sounding like an Arnie's Army platoon.

Palmer was wearing a hearing aid, only he didn't need it for the noise the gallery was making. Arnie and Jack and their opponents waited for the crowd to settle before Janzen attempted his fifteen-footer: professional pride wasn't all that was on the line.

The four men had a little wager going, and the Janzen-Mediate twosome had pressed on the final hole. If Janzen made his putt, his team would win about eighty dollars. If he missed, the teams would break even.

After taking the gallery's temperature, Mediate approached Janzen. "Why don't you just make sure this doesn't go in?" he said.

"What?" Janzen responded. "Are you kidding me? I'm trying to make it."

He missed. Once again, Palmer and Nicklaus couldn't lose as a team.

The Memorial fans were most generous to Arnold, treating him as if he were Dublin born. But there was no mistaking that this was a Nicklaus-first crowd. Jack had twice won his own event, and in 1986, after Nicklaus had claimed the Masters at age forty-six, Peter Jacobsen was among those to bear witness to the Bear's popularity among his own kind.

Nicklaus had ripped off a string of back-nine birdies to move into contention in the final round when he walked up to Jacobsen on the fourteenth green and asked him if he wanted to putt out. Jacobsen had been in the bunker and had blasted his ball inside of Nicklaus's; golf protocol would have Jack try his fifteen-footer first.

Jacobsen asked Nicklaus why he was making the offer. "Because when I make this putt," Jack said, "these people are going to go apeshit."

Of course, Jacobsen thought to himself. Nicklaus was only trying to help him avoid a gallery stampede while he was trying to putt. Jacobsen politely declined the offer, told Jack he needed to learn how to deal with adversity, and then watched the old man putt.

Nicklaus nailed his birdie attempt. "And the people went nuts," Jacobsen said. "Jack did his obligatory wave, then he backed off the green, and now I've got a three-footer. You've been in sporting events where the din is so loud you can actually feel the pressure on you, and that's what I was feeling."

Suddenly Jacobsen was desperate for help on his short par putt. He turned to his caddie, Mike "Fluff" Cowan, who was standing only five feet away. "He was looking up into the crowd and I was trying to get his attention to confirm my read," Jacobsen said. "I was screaming so loud and he couldn't hear me. He was looking like he just saw a UFO drop out of the sky into the fucking front bunker."

Muirfield Village was Nicklaus country. Jack told the community locals that the club and the tournament were his gifts to the game, his gifts to them. Nicklaus wanted Muirfield and the Memorial to represent a significant part of his legacy.

Sometimes it seemed the golf gods were dead set against that ever happening.

Like most events at the Memorial over the years, the ceremony to install Palmer as the tournament's honoree on June 2, 1993, was met by bad weather. A steady, chilling rain couldn't stop the Ohio State band from playing, or the assembled VIPs from speaking, or the reunited rivals from setting aside their 24/7 competition to savor a moment in time.

"Let's face it," said Russell Meyer, a close Palmer friend and head of Cessna Aviation, "we're all members of Arnie's Army, and on this day at the Memorial, that army also includes Jack Nicklaus."

Thousands of fans gathered on the Muirfield grounds to watch the Golden Bear kiss the King's ring, and many of those fans closed off the ceremony with a circle of multicolored umbrellas, Palmer's logo. This was a scene stolen from Arnold's last victory on the pro tour, his rain-soaked triumph over Jack at the 1973 Bob Hope in the hours before the winner and loser danced cheek to cheek.

Nicklaus carried an umbrella over Palmer's head as the two walked to the podium area. "Arnold Palmer has meant as much to golf as anyone who ever played the game," Nicklaus said at the ceremony. "Everyone who has ever played knows that. He's a man who needs no introduction."

Jack introduced Arnold anyway. Palmer thanked the fans for everything they'd given him, and he thanked Nicklaus for testing his ability and fortitude like no other foe.

"I've had a good career," Palmer said. "I've had a lot of fun. I've had a lot of competition. But . . . if [Nicklaus] hadn't given me that competition, maybe my career might have been a lot different. It might not have been so much fun."

On their reunion day, a day of forgiving and forgetting, the mood was warm and fuzzy. But at dinner that night, with their wives and close friends present, Palmer and Nicklaus were moved to discuss a delicate piece of business that could've imperiled their truce.

Larry Guest of the *Orlando Sentinel* had a book due out in the coming weeks, titled *Arnie: Inside the Legend,* that would include a chapter detailing the friction that existed between Palmer and Nicklaus. Guest wasn't just another newspaper columnist looking to sell a book; he was a Palmer friend and insider, a man who socialized with Arnie, flew on his plane, and shared dozens of golf rounds with him.

"I was very much a confidant of his," said Guest, who was also a member at Bay Hill.

Palmer didn't want the book written. In fact, when Guest and Palmer's former pilot, Darrell Brown, told him years earlier about their intentions of writing an inside-Arnie book, Palmer threatened to kick Brown's ass right then and there.

"Arnold went absolutely berserk about it," Brown said.

"They were on the inside," Palmer said, "and I didn't think it was fair."

So the former pilot grounded the project, only for Guest to revive it on his own. Nicklaus wasn't a fan of the columnist; Jack saw Guest as an FOA — Friend of Arnie — which meant he wasn't an FOJ — Friend of Jack. Whenever Palmer was angered by a Nicklaus snub of Bay Hill, Guest was his go-to print guy.

Back in 1980, when Nicklaus declined a Bay Hill invitation because he wanted to see one of his sons play in a high school basketball tournament, Palmer told Guest he might take a pass on the Memorial, too. "[Nicklaus] doesn't give a crap whether I'm there anyway!" he told the columnist. "And you can quote me on that!"

In his book Guest quoted Palmer taking shots at Nicklaus. The columnist was also critical of IMG representatives, who were worried that Guest's book could damage Palmer's image. Before the book was released, Guest said, Palmer "cornered me in the Bay Hill parking lot and said, 'You'd better be careful there. I've got some friends in Korea. They'll do anything for me. Anything. You understand?'"

Asked about this encounter, Palmer said, "I deny all of that." Believing he'd been threatened, Guest reported the exchange to the editor of the *Sentinel,* John Haile, who met with Palmer. Arnold told the editor he was merely joking around, according to Guest, and the matter was closed.

But the book remained open. As a courtesy Guest allowed Palmer to read an edited draft in the weeks before it was released. Arnold knew Nicklaus wouldn't appreciate some of the reported anecdotes, such as Palmer claiming the Golden Bear in the Nicklaus logo looked more like a Golden Pig.

So over dinner at the Memorial, after a full day of alpha-male bonding, Palmer had some explaining to do. "I need to tell you about Larry Guest," he told Nicklaus. Arnold proceeded to give a brief outline of the negative comments attributed to him.

"I don't know if I said it or whatever," Palmer said. "If I did, I feel badly."

Alastair Johnston, Palmer's IMG rep, was at the table when he heard Nicklaus respond this way:

"Arnold, I don't like Larry Guest. I don't care what Larry Guest says. I'm never going to read it . . . so let's just get on."

Johnston said that exchange and that dinner altered the dynamic between Palmer and Nicklaus. "Then they really started getting together, enjoying time together . . . They started having fun."

On the Nicklaus side of another Jack-Arnie dinner table that week, John Montgomery, a member of the Captains Club that voted in Palmer as that year's honoree, saw the same melting of polar icecaps between the game's two overlords.

"Whatever was between them in the negative was slowly going away," Montgomery said, "and I mentioned that to my wife and she agreed. They were talking like good friends, talking about airplanes mostly, talking about remember this, remember that. You could tell the camaraderie there was really smoldering. They were like old friends who'd met again after a long time. Like old soldiers."

Palmer and Nicklaus weren't fighting their cold war, not for the time being anyway. Jack had used his Memorial platform to build a bridge across to the enemy's side, and Arnold was gracious enough to follow his lead.

For a few days in Dublin, Ohio, Palmer and Nicklaus were presenting the unified front on the ground that Chi Chi Rodriguez had asked them to present in the air.

Jack Nicklaus was back at Oakmont in June of 1994, back in contention for the U.S. Open championship that he had won on this mighty course thirty-two years earlier as a rookie, beating the hometown hero, Arnold Palmer, in a playoff.

Nicklaus was fifty-four years old going on twenty-three, and for good reason. On the morning of the first round of the 1994 Open, his wife, Barbara, cast a spell over him. "It's nineteen sixty-twooooo," she said, wiggling her fingers in bewitching form. "You're twenty-twooooo."

Palmer's wife, Winnie, could summon no such magic. Like Jack, Arnold was a grandfather, only ten years older. He shot 75 the first day and was busy working on a higher number in the brutal heat the second.

But this wasn't just another missed cut for Palmer. This would be his last appearance in a U.S. Open, and it would come on a course he first played as a twelve-year-old after his father, Deke, drove him there in a 1939 Chevrolet. Arnold shot 82 that day, and fifty-two years later he shot 81.

The USGA had granted Palmer a special exemption after he'd missed ten consecutive Opens, and the move drew the ire of Seve Ballesteros and former USGA executive director Frank Hannigan, who didn't believe a washed-up player — even one the magnitude of Palmer — deserved a spot in the field. But as he walked up the eighteenth hole on Friday, the final hole of his Open career, Palmer was given the ovation of his amazing golfing life.

He cried and waved his straw hat to the masses, and soon enough fans in the bleachers around the green were acknowledging the King's majesty with a "we're-not-worthy" bow. On the very day his partner in Hertz TV ads, O. J. Simpson, was in the white Bronco evading police, Palmer was creating his own surreal scene.

He tapped in for bogey, did a brief but emotional interview with ESPN, and then the man who believed he should've captured more Open titles than Ben Hogan ever sniffed walked off as the one-and-done winner at Cherry Hills. As Palmer walked out of the camera shot, ESPN flashed to the Oakmont leaderboard.

Jack Nicklaus was in first place at five under.

Palmer stepped into his news conference with a towel around his neck, looking like a boxer who'd just done twelve grueling rounds. He kept choking up, kept shaking his head, kept burying his sun-drenched face in the towel.

"I haven't won all that much," Palmer finally said, his voice quaking, his lips quivering. "I've won a few tournaments. I've won some majors. But I suppose the most important thing is the fact that [golf] has been as good as it has been to me. I think all this is a little bit of just being a little sun-whipped and tired and ready to take a little rest. Hopefully a few more golf tournaments along the way. And I think that's about all I have to say. Thank you very much."

His eyes spilling over, Palmer rose from his seat as some two to three hundred reporters rose with him. Arnold exited the interview tent, and many journalists in attendance applauded for a sports figure for the first and last time of their careers.

Palmer gathered Winnie and went home to Latrobe. Two days later, after Nicklaus blew up in his weekend rounds, the phone rang in the Palmers' home.

Jack and Barbara wanted to know if they could stop by on their way out of town. Thirty-two years after Arnold's crushing hometown defeat, thirty-two years after Jack was first assailed by Arnie's Army at Oakmont, the Palmers and the Nicklauses shared a drink and some laughs.

Arnie and Jack were advancing a relationship that had been renewed the year before at the Memorial, getting past their petty feuds.

"Why do you think that happened?" said Palmer's sister Cheech, who offered the answer to her own question.

"Winnie and Barbara."

CHAPTER 20

• Winnie and Barbara

I F THE ACCORD between golf's most prominent figures required a system of checks and balances, Winnie Palmer represented the checks and Barbara Nicklaus the balances. The wives first assumed their roles at Oakmont in 1962, when they walked together during the U.S. Open playoff that saw an overheated mob of Arnold Palmer fans try and fail to unnerve Jack Nicklaus.

Arnie and Jack were getting along relatively famously more than thirty years later, but the story of David Chapman illustrates why Winnie and Barbara had to stay on their peacemaking toes. Chapman was an accomplished amateur golfer from North Carolina who would sell real estate for Nicklaus's development company and who later partnered with Jack on a course known as Bearpath in Eden Prairie, Minnesota.

Nicklaus had brought him into the deal, and Chapman cherished his association with the Golden Bear. Only he couldn't shake his boyhood fascination with the King. On the courses of his Durham youth, Chapman would putt like Palmer, march like Palmer, even dangle a tee in his mouth as if he were smoking an L&M like Palmer.

"I wanted to be just like him," Chapman said.

Nicklaus found out the hard way the time he walked into Chapman's office and found his walls covered with framed pictures of Palmer. One story that made the rounds had Nicklaus asking Chapman, "Who in the hell is that old man?" before ordering him to remove the photos.

Chapman would say Nicklaus never ordered the pictures off the walls, but confirmed that the tale wasn't entirely apocryphal. "Jack walked in and said, 'What's all this business with Arnold?'" Chapman said. "I said, 'Jack, he's still the King,' and that's how I left it . . . That probably was not the smartest thing to say . . . He did make the comment, 'What the hell are all these pictures with Arnold doing up?'"

That encounter wasn't the half of it. Nicklaus had learned that Chapman purchased a piece of land in La Quinta, California, to build what would be known as the Tradition Golf Club. On the 1996 day Bearpath opened in Eden Prairie, Nicklaus approached Chapman and asked if they would be working together on the Tradition project.

"No," Chapman answered. "I'm going with Arnold."

Nicklaus's blue eyes turned ice cold.

"You're a traitor," he said.

Chapman felt bad that he'd angered Nicklaus, but he had long ago befriended Palmer's son-in-law Doug Reintgen and Arnold's older daughter, Peg. As a teenager Chapman found himself playing golf at Bay Hill. "It was everything Arnold," he said.

When his dream of working with Palmer was a signature away from reality, Chapman couldn't stop himself from closing the deal. "Jack felt like there should be some loyalty to him," Chapman said, "and he's right, there's no doubt about it."

Nicklaus didn't forget this alleged double-cross, either. He would acknowledge Chapman in future meetings, but with a fraction of the old warmth.

"I can tell the way he acts toward me," Chapman said, "that he's kind of peeved I went on to be such an Arnold loyalist.

"I like Arnold's management style. Arnold gives his people room . . . Jack makes you feel nervous. Jack's not the kind of guy at the end of the day to come over and say, 'Let's have a drink.' Arnold says, 'Hey, do you want to have a beer or a Ketel One?' You feel like you're sitting with a friend, and Jack never makes you feel that way. Arnold's non-judgmental, very relaxed, and with Jack you're scared to say anything wrong. You're on pins and needles all the time."

Arnie used the buddy system to motivate; Jack used fear. Each thought the other had it all wrong.

A line of demarcation separated the Palmer and Nicklaus bunkers. Even in peacetime a struggle over a design contract or an endorsement deal could boil over in a heartbeat and send members of both camps scurrying to their battle stations.

"I think Jack was an easy lightning rod for my father's desire to be perceived as the best at everything that had to do with golf," Peg Palmer said. "I don't think it was really personal, but there were things about Jack's personality and character that were irritating to my dad."

And to his entire family. This, of course, went back to Palmer's playing days. In Arnold's household, from the middle to the back end of his prime, family members fretted over the challenges posed by the Gary Players, Ken Venturis, Tony Lemas, and Billy Caspers.

But Nicklaus represented something far more ominous.

"I was aware of Nicklaus because I felt threatened by him for my dad," Peg Palmer said, "because he was so much better. It was not like Player or Casper. The tournaments my dad lost to the other guys, I saw him having a bad day. The tournaments I saw Jack winning felt more threatening."

So the residue of golf's greatest rivalry trickled down to the next generation. That this tension never completely destroyed the relationship between the two families was a tribute to the two mothers who bonded like sisters against the odds.

Barbara Bash was the daughter of a high school math teacher, Stanley Bash, who never made more than $6,300 a year. Stanley and his wife, Helen, had a girl and a boy, just like Charlie and Helen Nicklaus, but the Bashes lived a greater day-to-day struggle.

Stanley and Helen never bought each other birthday or Christmas presents because they couldn't afford them. Their girl, Barbara, grew up assuming this was standard operating procedure and believing that gifts were exchanged only at weddings.

"But I never wanted for anything," she said. "I had as many sweaters as the next person . . . I don't know how my parents did it. They were really wonderful people."

Barbara Bash was a freshman at Ohio State, on her way to becoming a homecoming queen candidate ("A Ballot for Barb!" would be her campaign slogan), when she stopped walking across campus one day to say hello to a young woman she knew from high school. That old classmate happened to be dating the young man standing next to her, another freshman named Jack Nicklaus.

Barbara was introduced to Jack, the old high school friend headed off to class, and Jack walked the tall, blond, and attractive stranger to the bacteriology building, where she held down a job to work her way through school.

Jack called that night and asked for a date, and Barbara gave him the Arnold Palmer answer — "I have to check my schedule." Truth was, Barbara didn't know a driver from a putter. "I didn't even know golf existed," she said. "Anyone who was on the high school golf team just didn't do anything else. It wasn't like a football player or basketball player."

She agreed to date Jack anyway, and to take a phys ed course in the winter quarter that had her hitting golf balls out of a Quonset hut and playing five surprisingly efficient holes with her impressed boyfriend. They broke up, got back together, and got engaged on Christmas of 1959. They were married during the July week of the 1960 PGA Championship, as Jack, the amateur, wasn't eligible to play in that major.

Barbara immediately became the doting golf wife, spending part of her honeymoon at the Hershey (Pennsylvania) Country Club and the famed Winged Foot Golf Club in Mamaroneck, New York, where she trudged along as Jack played eighteen holes in a driving rain. Jack also took in a round at New Jersey's ultra-exclusive, males-only Pine Valley Golf Club, where he was politely informed his new bride would not be setting foot on any tee boxes or greens.

Barbara was the anti-Jack, a warm, friendly, and outgoing mate who could disarm anyone who found her husband to be cold, blunt, and unapproachable. The Palmers adored her, especially Arnold's mother, Doris. Barbara softened up Jack, helped him improve his appearance and image, made him more user-friendly over time. "An absolutely wonderful, wonderful woman," Tom Watson said in echoing the consensus among players and spouses on the tour. "Barbara's been able to make Jack do things that Jack would never want to do."

She bore Jack four boys and a girl and remained conscious when Jack fainted after all five births. Barbara suffered a miscarriage the night after the third round of the 1967 Sahara Invitational and didn't wake her husband until 8:00 a.m. because she felt he needed his rest for the final round. Jack took Barbara to the hospital, made sure she wasn't in any danger, and then won the tournament before ordering her never again to put his golf ahead of her health.

"She handled me and she handled [the kids]," Jack would say, "and that allowed me to go ahead and do what I had to do because I didn't have a conflict, a deterrent . . . I was a very fortunate guy.

"I look at a lot of guys I started with at the same time who came out of the college or amateur ranks, and were probably as talented as I was, maybe more talented than I was, but they were not married. They didn't have the support I had. They didn't have something to play for . . . They sort of went by the wayside."

Barbara was the soccer mom on the go and the perfect hostess at the Nicklaus's waterfront home at Lost Tree Village in North Palm Beach. Pandel Savic, Jack's close friend, often referred to Nicklaus's wife as "Saint Barbara." She met you once, Barbara did, and she'd remember your name in a chance meeting six years later.

"I don't know how you'd ever match Barbara Nicklaus as far as being a representative of you in business and as a parent," said Ivor Young, another close Nicklaus friend. "[Barbara and Jack] both had the same goal in mind when they entered the relationship. They didn't know they were going to be famous. They wanted to raise good people and be a presence in the lives of their kids."

With his private plane and two full-time pilots at the ready, Jack returned home from the tour for his children's birthday parties, graduation ceremonies, and high school games. He returned home to be with Barbara, the wife who kept him grounded, the woman who provided him the stability he needed to become the greatest player in the world.

Arnold Palmer was not good enough for Winnie Walzer. This was the opinion of Winnie's father, Martin Shubert, or "Shube," who wanted a doctor or a lawyer for his only girl, even if she was madly in love with a greenskeeper's son.

Shube was a canned-food salesman who started his one-man company after World War II, bouncing around eastern Pennsylvania in a station wagon selling his goods to restaurants and hospitals. His wife, Mary, was a teacher. They had three kids and little money, but they'd both attended college and made sacrifices so their children could enroll in the best schools.

Their sons, Marty and John, went to Cornell and Yale, respectively, and Winnie went to Pembroke, the women's college of Brown University. Her parents didn't secure Winnie an Ivy League education so she could run away with a golf pro.

But at age twenty, a figurative fifteen minutes after meeting Palmer at the 1954 Waite Memorial tournament at Shawnee on Delaware, an event run by the bandleader and TV personality Fred Waring, Winnie did just that.

"I met him on Tuesday; he asked me to marry him on Saturday," Winnie would say.

"They eloped and came down to my house," said Palmer's sister Cheech, who lived in Virginia.

Early on Cheech didn't have much use for Winnie, the pixie-nosed brunette whom she incorrectly perceived as a poor little rich girl. Arnie didn't care. He was playing in a tournament near Cheech's home when he told his sister to cancel all the blind dates he'd originally asked her to set up.

"I met the girl I'm going to marry," he told Cheech.

Arnie and Winnie figured on going through a justice of the peace, but Cheech would have none of that. She arranged for a minister to marry them and confessed to him that Winnie wasn't yet twenty-one years old. Cheech asked him if the union was legal, "and [the minister] said, 'Oh, yeah, I think it's OK.' It wasn't, but he didn't say anything about it.

"He married them. Actually, my mother and dad arrived; I don't know how they found out about it. Winnie's parents didn't find out about it until after it was over, because I don't think her father wanted her to marry that wild golfer."

He didn't want her to leave school either. But Winnie was an instant hit in the Palmer household. Cheech became her surrogate sister, and Winnie's new in-laws came to see her as a living doll.

Deke and Doris, their granddaughter Peg would say, "thought my mother was Grace Kelly come to Latrobe. They thought she was the most beautiful, most refined, most brilliant, most wonderful, most perfect person.

"My dad . . . could never be worthy of her in Deacon's eyes. And my dad lived to win his father's approval."

Raised in a strict Moravian household, the only girl among an extended family of boys, Winnie was a traditional wife who embraced her supporting role. She was barely twenty-one when she started her own family. She bore Arnold two daughters, Peg and Amy, and when the girls were young, Arnie would fly his plane to and from tournaments — between rounds — to spend as much time as he could with his family.

He'd jet in from Akron or Cleveland or Washington, DC; land at Westmoreland County Airport; drive three-quarters of a mile to his home off the Latrobe Country Club course; and fly back in the morning to catch his next tee time.

"Part of my philosophy was to give [Peg and Amy] some of the things I didn't have," Palmer said.

He meant the outward love and affection Deke Palmer never afforded him.

The second-born, Amy, was the one more like Winnie. She was more willing to defer, "much more subservient" than Peg, said Winnie's brother Marty.

Peg was the headstrong and rebellious one, as outspoken as the day was long. She thought her father was tough on her, too tough, as if he felt the need to raise his daughter the way Deke raised him.

Peg would argue with her dad and sometimes use language a young girl shouldn't use. "He would say, 'If you were a boy I'd pick you up and throw you across the room,'" Peg said.

On vacations at Bay Hill, Peg and Amy would feel their father's wrath if they left their room a mess after rushing off to be with friends. Once Arnold responded by barging into the girls' room, ripping every drawer out of their dresser, dumping all their clothes onto the floor, and then sweeping his arm across the tops of nearby tables so the rest of their possessions could join their clothes.

"There were definitely times we were nervous for his arrival," Amy said.

From a distance it might have appeared the Palmers were living a Rockwellian American life. Arnold and Winnie came across as an adoring couple who kept a modest ranch home often filled with the pleasing sounds of their daughters playing the piano.

But Peg said, "Every holiday we ever had was a nightmare." She blamed Deke's drinking for the fact his wife and daughters and daughter-in-law would often end up in Yuletide tears.

"He and my dad would get into it over the greens, the rough, whether it was too wet for carts," Peg said. "But that wasn't the issue. My grandfather felt my father was eclipsing him ... They were always squabbling.

"My father and I fought in much the same way. That's one of the reasons I went away to [boarding] school. We always fought. My mother would hide in the closet."

Peg would leave behind Latrobe and attend the Masters School in Dobbs Ferry, New York. Arnold was upset by her decision. Peg wasn't just running from the arguments but from her classmates' teasing.

"I told him, 'You just don't know what it's like when they make fun of me,'" Peg would say. "It hurt his feelings so much to think I couldn't rise above the insults."

Unlike her older daughter, Winnie was one to internalize her problems, keep them locked in a private box. And one such problem, in Peg's eyes, was a source of considerable dismay for her mother.

Arnold Palmer was a sex symbol; there was no mistaking that. "He's like a rock star, only he doesn't need any music," said his friend and fellow pro Bob Toski. "All he does is hitch his pants up and glance over his shoulder. When he puts that swashbuckling look on women, they melt . . . We spent a number of very eventful evenings together."

Life-on-the-road temptations were never in short supply for the average touring pro, and Palmer was hardly an average touring pro. Arnold didn't retreat from the notion that he was an Elvis or Errol Flynn in spikes: he was known to make extra-long eye contact with the prettiest women in his gallery.

"Someone said to him once, 'You're not the best-looking guy in the world, but there's something intriguing about you,'" Toski said. "And Arnold said, 'Yeah, I've got sex written all over my face.'"

Fact or fiction, part of the Palmer legend was his reputation as a ladies' man extraordinaire. Bob Rosburg, another Palmer friend and fellow pro, would be quoted once telling the tale of an enraged husband trying to hunt down his roommate, Palmer, for allegedly spending time with the man's wife.

"Goddamn," said Al Besselink, the pro who played money games with Palmer, "he loved the broads."

Out to dinner Arnold wasn't afraid to greet a golf writer at another table with a comely blond at his side. He was out on the town in Denver once when a bunch of newspaper guys walked in to find Palmer and another prominent player in the back lounge in the company of three women. The second player waved his arms at the group as if he were a football referee signaling an incomplete pass, and the writers knew enough not to approach.

"It was none of our business," one of the scribes said. "I suppose the tabloids would've loved something like that and obviously the British papers would've gone crazy for something like that, but we ... weren't writing that sort of thing."

Some in the golfing community thought the reason was obvious.

"The press loved Arnold," Toski said. "They protected him like they protected JFK."

To Arnold's older daughter the analogy was appropriate. "Jackie Kennedy had nothing on my mother," Peg said. "She painted a picture like Jackie Kennedy ... My mother painted a fairy tale for us that was absolutely seamless."

Winnie and Arnold dearly loved each other, there was no question about that. But Palmer rarely passed on an opportunity to flirt with an attractive waitress or cart girl, even in his wife's company. Winnie often responded by ignoring her husband's behavior, letting him know that she could rise above his bad-boy playfulness.

"A lot of times I wanted to punch Arnie because he'd be paying more attention to the other women around him than [Winnie]," Cheech said. "It never bothered her. In fact, she'd say, 'Go ahead and sit beside him.'"

Peg Palmer saw it differently. She believed her mother was troubled by the rumors—well-founded or not—and annoyed by the flirtations with others. Peg believed that Winnie's willingness to let her husband act frisky and single in her presence—without a rebuke—was her own way of hitting back.

"I think my father was hurt that she rose above it and wasn't jealous," Peg said, "and she was determined not to be [jealous]. And I think it was really just an indication of how very hurt she was."

Arnold could joke about his appreciation for the opposite sex. Asked about Mark McCormack's long-ago bid to reach an exclusive agreement with him to handle his business matters, Palmer responded with a wink, "I said [to McCormack] the only person that has exclusivity with me is my wife, and I'm not sure she had it, totally."

Arnold Palmer, lady-killer. Was it myth or reality?

"People talked," Palmer said. "I suppose that I had, what the hell would you say? I knew a lot of ladies, but I didn't, I wasn't one to ... That was more the talk than it was an action. It was a myth ... I think I knew a lot of people and I was nice to them and that's how this all got construed as something that was more than what it was."

As far as the rumors troubling Winnie, and whether he felt the need to reassure his wife, Palmer said, "No. No, she was very good about that, I would say."

Winnie Palmer was very good about a lot of things. She was as sweet and friendly and caring as Barbara Nicklaus.

"I don't think you can find a person to talk to about Winnie that would ever say a bad word about her," Cheech said.

Winnie was a meticulous records keeper and a prolific letter writer, as organized as anyone could be. Winnie liked structure. She could occasionally suspend her cheery disposition for those who operated outside that structure.

During Arnold's Bay Hill tournament, food in the players' lounge was free for all those in the field but not free for their wives. Winnie was big on keeping the free food away from the wives. When she saw one player sneak a sandwich and apple to his spouse, she grabbed the food right out of the woman's hands and fired it into the trash.

Like her husband, Winnie was frugal. She kept one camel-hair coat for ages, long enough for it to turn threadbare, before Arnold convinced her they could afford a new one. He threw away the old jacket, and Winnie proceeded to dig it out of the garbage can.

She craved consistency and order in her world. "I always had so much respect for her," Barbara Nicklaus said. "I think Winnie handled her life, Arnold's life, and their life better than anybody. One of the things she said to me early on was, 'If I get mad at Arnold on Tuesday, I'm certainly not going to get in a fuss before Thursday when the tournament starts. By Sunday, when the tournament's over, I'd forgotten what I was mad about and it worked out really well.'"

Winnie was the keeper of the Palmer flame. She corrected her husband's grammar, protected his image at every turn, and kept a closet full of gifts bought far in advance for friends and family members, just so she wouldn't miss anyone's birthday.

Winnie wasn't one ever to forget someone special to her, even when burdened with a personal crisis of her own. So it was no surprise that the news of a violent storm approaching the Nicklaus home in North Palm Beach compelled Winnie to check on her dear Barbara, to keep the delicate interfamily bond intact, even as the cancer in her body was only weeks away from taking her life.

. . .

By the end of the decade mortality was closing like a freight train on the Palmers and Nicklauses. Statues and plaques honoring Arnold and Jack in Augusta were up or in the works, reminding the two icons that time was flying by.

Nicklaus had witnessed the emergence of the first young prospect he believed to be his equal, or perhaps his superior, in Tiger Woods, who blasted the 1997 Masters field in a record rout only a year after Nicklaus walked away from a practice round with the prodigy and Palmer saying the following:

"Arnold and I both agree that you could take his Masters and my Masters and add them together, and this kid should win more than the both of us."

That would be a prediction of eleven Augusta National titles for Mr. Woods, the first black champion at a club once viewed as the last plantation in the South.

Nicklaus looked at Woods the way Bobby Jones and Ben Hogan had looked at Nicklaus. Jack was the first great golfer to combine mind-boggling home-run power with the skill and precision required to bat .400. Tiger would be the second.

"The kid is the most fundamentally sound golfer I've ever seen at almost any age," Nicklaus said.

So at fifty-eight, with his belly bulging and his hip and knee barking at him, the Golden Bear took great pleasure in outplaying the twenty-two-year-old defending champion by two strokes at the 1998 Masters and in threatening to take a share of the lead on the front nine of the final round. But whatever fresh life that remarkable showing pumped into Nicklaus's creaky game was snuffed out in 1999 when hip-replacement surgery forced Jack to miss the Masters for the first time in forty years.

Arnold Palmer? Even prostate cancer couldn't stop him from appearing in his forty-third consecutive Masters in 1997, the year of the Tiger. Not three months after his successful cancer surgery, a silver-haired Palmer showed up at Augusta a hunched figure with his wash-board abs a distant memory. He didn't quite do what he'd done the year before — shoot the same 150 over thirty-six holes that was shot by Woods, a player forty-seven years his junior — but his two-round total of 176 was the winning number to the thousands whose love for the King was unconditional.

Two years later Palmer was cancer-free, back at his beloved Masters, and — despite his noncompetitive game — savoring what appeared to be a charmed golden-years existence. He was an invaluable spokesman for the cause of convincing men to get prostate checkups. He was the honorary national chairman of the March of Dimes, and his Arnold Palmer Hospital for Children and Women had been serving the Orlando community for ten years. Arnold's 1995 innovation, the Golf Channel, was going strong. Palmer was about to purchase the Pebble Beach course with Clint Eastwood, former baseball commissioner Peter Ueberroth, and a group of investors for the price of $820 million; and four years after *Forbes* estimated that Palmer and Nicklaus were worth half a billion dollars combined, the magazine reported that Arnold was taking in $16 million in one year's worth of endorsements.

Palmer was rated the third greatest endorser of the twentieth century, trailing Michael Jordan and Woods and beating out Muhammad Ali, Babe Ruth, and Jack Nicklaus. And in another sign that his relationship with his chief rival, Nicklaus, was improving with age despite the inevitable flare-ups, Arnold actually agreed to co-design a course with Jack at the World Golf Village in St. Augustine, Florida.

But for all his charity and prosperity, Arnold Palmer was living a nightmare. His wife of forty-five years, Winnie, was fighting a losing battle with peritoneal carcinoma, a cancer of the tissue that lines the abdomen. Their daughter Amy had beaten breast cancer after one doctor gave her a 15 percent chance to live another five years, and now the family was left to hope for back-to-back miracles.

When Arnold was playing golf, Cheech and her husband, Ron, would remove the phone from Winnie's ear — she loved talking on the phone — and take her for quiet rides in the country. "She was writing notes on things she was thinking about the whole time we were going," Cheech said. "And she'd sit in church and write the whole time we were in there, notes to herself about what was happening or something she thought she wanted to do."

Winnie wanted to go to the Masters in April of 1999, and she was struck by a hopeful thought: she wanted Barbara Nicklaus to go, too.

Jack was out of the tournament after his hip surgery, but Winnie placed the call anyway. "We were friends for thirty-seven years," Barbara said, "and if I didn't hear from her for two or three months and she picked up the phone, or I picked up the phone, it was as if a day had never gone by."

Barbara told Winnie she didn't think she'd be going to Augusta. Jack was scheduled to attend the annual Masters champions' dinner and then ride around the course a bit with the club chairman, Hootie Johnson, before heading back to their North Palm Beach home. Winnie persisted. "You have to come," she said. "You come up and we'll spend the day and we'll have dinner."

Barbara gave in. "I don't think it was anything Winnie knew," she said. "But you know, there was something in her voice when she said, 'You come up.'"

With Winnie's daughter Amy tagging along, they went shopping and then went to dinner. Arnold and Jack met them later at the restaurant, and a grand Augusta time was had by all.

"That's the last time I ever saw Winnie," Barbara said.

The first time they spent quality time together, during the Oakmont playoff of 1962, set the tone for their lifelong friendship. If they could get along while the pro-Palmer mob attempted to lynch Jack, nothing would ever divide them.

They had fun in the early days traveling around the world on Big Three junkets with their husbands and Gary and Vivienne Player. They shopped, hit museums, and played countless hours of bridge. "But once the tournament started," Barbara said, "that was a different ball game, and you just kind of did your own thing."

If there were no food fights among the women, Winnie and Barbara did engage in some mischief later on at the 1993 Memorial, where Arnold was honored by Jack.

During yet another Muirfield Village rain delay, Winnie told Barbara that an alleged curse placed on the tournament by a disgruntled (and deceased) Indian chief upset over the proximity of the course to his burial ground could be eased by placing a shot of gin on the chief's tombstone.

Barbara gathered Pandel Savic, the tournament's general chairman, and drove out to Leatherlips's gravesite and left a full shot glass. It stopped raining within half an hour, and the weekend skies cleared. But when word about the stunt got out, some newspaper columnists and Native American residents didn't see the humor in it.

"It's Winnie's fault I got in all that trouble," Barbara said through a laugh.

She didn't hold a grudge. In the end the wives' friendship prevented the Arnold-Jack rivalry from ever getting to DEFCON 1.

"Even if Arnold and I did have a question," Jack said, "there was no way in the world we could ever be mad at each other because the girls always wanted to spend time together."

In September of 1999, after Hurricane Floyd hit, a dying Winnie reached out to her dear friend. It was the first phone call Barbara Nicklaus received in the wake of the storm, and she was overcome by the caller's grace.

"Winnie was having trouble breathing," she said. "She could hardly even talk."

Winnie would take care of others even when she could no longer take care of herself. While Winnie was very sick, a good friend of hers and Arnie's, a surgeon named Tom Moran, was having a terrible time with his throat and was proving to be too stubborn to do anything about it.

Until Winnie Palmer got in his face.

Winnie and Nancy McCormack persuaded Moran to go to the Cleveland Clinic, where he was diagnosed with throat cancer. "Winnie was quite sick; she was hurting," said Moran's wife, Mary. "And yet they came up to the house and said, 'Mary, we want to talk to Tom without you.' By God, Winnie helped save his life."

She would be powerless to save her own. Winnie spent her final days decorating a guest home on the golf course, taking rides into the woods with one of her housekeepers to heighten his appreciation of flowers and trees, and planning Arnold's seventieth birthday party down at their renovated barn. "She did it with a grand flair," said Arnold's brother Jerry.

On November 20, 1999, Winnie was in bed inside her Latrobe home while Arnold's sister Cheech and the woman hired to care for Winnie, Kathy Merrill, watched over her.

"I was sitting there listening to every breath," Cheech said, "wondering which one would be her last."

Arnold and Winnie's doctor, Harry Speedy, had gone to the country club for lunch. Twenty minutes after Arnold and the doctor left her side, Winnie took her last labored breath.

Palmer was enraged over this devastating turn of fate. "He didn't want her to go," Cheech said. "He thought he'd done everything he could. He took her all over the country [for treatments], and he did everything anybody could possibly do to make her well. He was used to, if he wanted to do something, he did it, and he wasn't able to do it that time. He was mad. He cried a lot of tears."

Some twelve hundred miles away Jack and Barbara Nicklaus were at the qualifying school tournament at Doral, watching their thirty-year-old son, Gary, try to earn his tour card after eight failed attempts. Mom and Dad had tracked Gary's every shot in the six-round marathon. When the phone call came, Barbara and Jack immediately knew the right thing to do.

Gary would have to make the tour on his own.

Arnold tried convincing Jack that he should stay with his son, but that was another argument with Nicklaus that Palmer couldn't win. Jack and Barbara would attend Winnie's service at Unity Chapel with former president George Bush, who held up the start of the ceremony by having his Secret Service detail stop at a local Kmart so he could buy himself a belt.

The service was simple and understated, just the way Winnie drew it up. She'd left specific instructions that asked for no eulogy to be read, no tears to be shed.

Beethoven's *Ode to Joy* was played at Winnie's request, along with a few other arrangements, "and that was that," said her brother-in-law Jerry. "We all came back over to the club."

During the reception Jack was on a cell phone with his son's coach, Rick Smith, to get updates on Gary's endless pursuit of his tour card. Arnold walked over to him and asked how Gary was doing.

"He's got a couple of holes to play," Jack said, adding that the updates were encouraging.

"Well, come on, let's turn on the TV," Arnold suggested.

"You don't have to do that," Jack responded.

"I would want to know," Arnold said.

So Palmer and Nicklaus watched the boy Jack named after Gary Player finish his sixth and final round, a round of seven-under 63.

The Golden Bear's own son was a member of the PGA Tour. Overcome by joy and sadness, Jack Nicklaus and Arnold Palmer fell into each other's arms and cried.

CHAPTER 21

• The King and the Bear

ED BIGNON FELT LIKE nearly everyone else in the development business when he heard his former boss, Arnold Palmer, was collaborating with Jack Nicklaus on a course design.

"I figured it would be a disaster," Bignon said.

And why not? Palmer and Nicklaus had design philosophies that were as different as their swings.

They had worked on more than four hundred courses around the world between them, and there was good reason why this project at the World Golf Village, site of the sport's Hall of Fame, would mark the first time they ever worked together on one.

Arnie preferred right-to-left holes; Jack preferred left-to-right. Arnie built courses for the masses; Jack built them for the elite golfer. Arnie favored greens that could receive low liners; Jack favored greens that demanded high flies. Arnie tried to keep construction and maintenance costs reasonable; Jack would do what he had to do in the pursuit of perfection and bill the owner accordingly.

Arnie was a delegator who relied heavily on his chief design man, a colorful ex-marine named Ed Seay. Jack was a hands-on manager who wanted intimate details on every grain of sand in every trap. Arnie loved playing golf and flying his plane; Jack loved moving hundreds of thousands of yards of dirt to fit his design visions.

At the end of the day, Palmer said, "Jack and I are similar in that we both have two arms and two legs."

Their opposite approaches to architecture, golf, and life fueled speculation this joint arrangement was destined for trouble—that and the one-upmanship forever shaping their business rivalry.

"One of them had a golf club company, the other had a golf club company," Bignon said. "One had a car dealership, the other had a car dealership . . . They just mirrored each other."

Tim Finchem, tour commissioner, had approached Arnie and Jack about the possibility of coming together in St. Augustine, Florida, for the good of the game. Finchem wanted them to create a layout to complement the Slammer & Squire, a World Golf Village course designed under the guidance of Sam Snead and Gene Sarazen.

The new course would be called the King & Bear, and not the Bear & King. The legend with seven major championships got top billing over the legend with eighteen.

"It was the way it rolls off the tongue," Finchem said. "It was a few people sitting around, and as they phrased it, everyone said that sounded better."

No, Nicklaus wasn't consulted on the naming of the course. "Arnold's older than I am, and he's the King," Jack said. "That's fine."

In the early stages of the project, Palmer and Nicklaus found themselves comforting each other over deep personal losses. They were seen embracing and crying on what would be the seventeenth tee in the final days of Winnie Palmer's life. The previous month Bruce Borland, a senior Nicklaus designer and a man charged to see the King & Bear to fruition, died in the private plane crash that claimed Payne Stewart's life.

A memorial was planned and the project was continued. Meanwhile, Nicklaus was rebounding from another huge financial setback, this as a result of his decision to take some of his Golden Bear International holdings public. Jack merged his golf course construction company, his golf centers, and his apparel and licensing companies into Golden Bear Golf, which traded on NASDAQ, and it was a spectacular bust of Hollywood proportions.

Unbeknownst to Nicklaus, executives in his construction company, Paragon, cooked the books to hide more than $26 million in losses from shareholders. When the fraud was disclosed, company shares—which once sold at eighteen dollars—plunged as low as twenty-five cents. The executives, John Boyd and Christopher Curbello, were ultimately found guilty on federal fraud and conspiracy charges, and shareholders were left with an estimated $50 million in losses.

"I had about $27 million worth in debt," Nicklaus said. "It was my fault . . . I thought [going public] would give me an opportunity to put some money away for my kids, which I didn't think I could get done otherwise.

"[Boyd and Curbello] were conspiring to cheat, and they kept giving us numbers that were incorrect, and they could never achieve those numbers. They were saying they were making a million, and they were actually going to lose a million. We had shareholder lawsuits and . . . I just went about my business and decided to pay it off."

Nicklaus had made one wise choice in going public: he kept his course design business private. That business was booming, as he was commanding more than $1.5 million for his services after producing layouts (Valhalla in Kentucky, Shoal Creek in Alabama) worthy of landing the PGA Championship.

Nicklaus had come a long way from his first brushes with design work in the sixties and from his first full project—a collaboration with Pete Dye—at Hilton Head's Harbour Town. Jack had created one of the tour's most admired sites, Muirfield Village. Muirfield's Augusta-like ambiance had elevated the Memorial Tournament into a place on the tour's uppermost tier.

In fact, the Memorial was battling the tour's Players Championship at the TPC at Sawgrass for unofficial honors as the game's fifth major. At least one prominent golf official not named Arnold Palmer wasn't celebrating that development. Back when Deane Beman was commissioner of the tour, Nicklaus felt his old friend and de facto coach wanted the Memorial to fail.

"Deane hurt me," Jack said. "I fought that with Deane the whole time. He would try to get no credit for what we did here."

Beman denied feeling this way, but there was no denying the fact Nicklaus never wanted him to get the job as commissioner in the first place. Jack thought Beman's vision of an ideal tour was one that catered to the average players, the journeymen grinders, which was a concept Nicklaus and Palmer railed against when the tour players split from the Professional Golfers' Association in 1968, and again in the eighties when Beman's tour cut design and marketing deals that Arnold and Jack saw as competition for their own big-name interests.

Though Nicklaus didn't forget all those pre-tournament tips Beman offered to help him win more than one major, business was business. "Deane worked as hard as he could to have a socialist state; the stars were knocked down," Nicklaus said. "He created a tour in his own image ... Deane came up with a great idea with the Players Championship ... but you can't buy a major championship, and that was sort of the effort being made. [The Memorial] was his only competition, and we weren't trying to be a major championship. But everything he could do to put one ahead of the other he would do, and that's always stuck in my craw."

His unhappiness with Beman aside, Nicklaus was flattered by comparisons between the Memorial and the Players Championship. He was less flattered by comparisons between the Memorial and Palmer's invitational at Bay Hill.

"We don't really look at what [Arnold] does," Nicklaus said. "But out of courtesy to Arnold I would do it that way. He's a friend of mine. I don't want to belittle his tournament. That's one of the reasons I went back and played quite a few times; it was for him ... I mean, it's a flat piece of Florida property that's been manufactured a little bit. It's a nice golf course. It's a tough golf course, a really tough golf course, but it's been made tough by basically length and fairly bland ways to do it."

Nicklaus made one other important distinction between the Bay Hill tournament and his Memorial.

"Arnold's has been a commercial event," he said, "and [the Memorial] has not been a commercial event."

Like the people who ran the Masters, Jack wanted to keep the corporate presence at his tournament as inconspicuous as possible. He wanted fans to see Muirfield Village as something of a shrine, a sanctuary for the respectful appreciation of the game.

He didn't want to be another Bay Hill Invitational Presented by Cooper Tires.

Nicklaus also didn't want to be known as a celebrity designer who did a few meet-and-greets and hit the ceremonial first drive. "I hate doing the promotional part of it," Nicklaus said. If Palmer didn't fit his description of a celebrity designer, it was clear Nicklaus thought he came within a short par three of it.

"I don't really look at Arnold as a competitor in the golf course design business," Jack said. "Arnold really doesn't get into the design of the golf course. Arnold gets involved in the promotion of the golf course and does a damn good job of it . . . If somebody's interested in having a name on a golf course and the strength of the promotion in it, Arnold's a good guy to have.

"But if they're interested in the quality of the facility and what they're trying to do with it, then they're looking at me."

Palmer didn't quite see it that way — surprise, surprise. Though he acknowledged that he gave heavy responsibility to his designers, Seay and Harrison Minchew, and that Nicklaus "works harder at it and . . . puts more of a hands-on effect to his golf courses," Arnold said, "I've set policy for all mine and worked with my guys pretty closely. I may not have gone on the job as much as he did, but other than that, we weren't that much apart."

The King & Bear's ground rules called for Palmer to do the routing and for Nicklaus to work on strategy. Arnold and Jack didn't spend much time together on the pastureland site. By their own accounts the disagreements were minor and the deliberations benign.

Arnold didn't like a Jack idea on the driving range, and Jack went along with Arnold's revision. Jack didn't like to go as heavy on artificial mounding as Arnold did, and Arnold went along with Jack's suggestions.

"We let Arnold's people do what they wanted to do within reason," Jack said.

"We agreed pretty much on the entire golf course," Palmer said. "There were some compromises but they were not major confrontations. Jack was usually late getting there and that was always something, and I was always on time. I think that was probably the biggest disagreement that we had."

Others on the site came away with a different read. Jason Kubel, the course superintendent, said there were plenty of arguments over how the bunkers should be built.

"I remember being around either group and they'd say to do this or do that," Kubel said. "And I remember plenty of times them saying, 'I don't care what the other guy says. We need to do it this way.'"

Kubel was there when Palmer decided the fifth hole, a dogleg-right par five, was too easy. Arnold asked that the tee box be moved back.

A couple of weeks later the Bear was prowling the premises. He got to the fifth hole on his site tour and asked Kubel to stop the truck.

"Something's different," Nicklaus said. "What changed here?"

Kubel told him the tee was moved back "when Arnold was here."

"What do you mean 'when Arnold was here'?" Nicklaus responded. "Is this my golf course or his golf course?"

Kubel told Nicklaus that Palmer lengthened the hole to make it more difficult.

"Was this Arnold's decision or that Minchew guy's?" Nicklaus asked.

"Arnold's," Kubel answered.

"Well, he plays golf and Harrison doesn't. So I guess I'm OK with that."

At the second hole Nicklaus thought he noticed something else that didn't agree with his discriminating eye. He asked his own design co-ordinator, Kurt Bowman, to identify the width of the fairway.

"Thirty-two yards to spec," Bowman answered.

Nicklaus wasn't buying it, so Bowman hopped out of the truck and started pacing it off. As he walked from one end of the fairway to the other, Kubel and others in the truck counted the paces to themselves, knowing that any number other than thirty-two might make Mount Nicklaus erupt.

When he was done pacing, the men in the truck lowered their heads. Bowman called out, "Yeah, it's thirty-two."

"Bullshit," Nicklaus barked. "It's thirty-five. I counted, too."

Soon enough, three yards were shaved off the second fairway.

In contrast to Palmer's cheerful, take-things-with-a-grain-of-salt approach, Kubel said, "Mr. Nicklaus was a ball-buster. He was all business. When he's on a golf course, the integrity of the design is of the utmost importance to him."

On the tee at the par-four fifteenth, a short dogleg right bordered by a lake on one side and loblolly pines on the other, Palmer suffered a rare moment of exasperation. He peered out at the most aesthetically pleasing hole on the course, a hole Nicklaus had worked on, and then turned to his designer, Minchew, and said, "Harrison, why can't we do a hole that looks like that, nice and simple?"

Nicklaus got the biggest kick out of that one.

Later, the front lines were moved to the sixteenth green. "Every time one guy came out," Bowman said, "he changed what the other had done. They kept changing that green. I forget who won."

Palmer did, more or less. Arnie and Jack worked a design project the way they played golf: Palmer was fast, and Nicklaus was slow. Arnie made snap decisions, and Jack had to sketch everything out between his hems and haws.

Four times Nicklaus changed his plans for the sixteenth green. In Palmer's presence, after he finally settled on a strategy for number sixteen, Nicklaus turned to Arnold's designer, Ed Seay.

"Eddie, can you live with this now?" Jack asked.

"Jack, I could've lived with it the first time," Seay answered. "Normally when we do something, we do it right the first time."

"Shut up, Ed," Arnold ordered.

Nicklaus was known to joke about Palmer's knowledge of his own projects. In fact, Arnold's people did little to disguise the fact their man wasn't nearly as engaged as Nicklaus was in on-site minutiae.

"Arnold loves to play golf," Seay said. "We never showed Arnold a pile of dirt or a hole in the ground ... He hired us to make sure it drained and would grow grass. Arnold was there to make it fun and playable and beautiful."

While they were standing on the sixteenth green at the King & Bear, Seay asked Arnie and Jack to name their favorite holes on the course.

Jack picked number sixteen, and Arnold picked number fifteen.

"Do you even know what fifteen is, Arnold?" Jack asked.

"Yeah," he answered. "It's the one right before this one."

Stories of Arnie-Jack jousting at the King & Bear became the source of amusement in golf circles. Finchem, the tour commissioner, heard back from his lieutenants on the scene that Palmer and Nicklaus each kept asking the same question about the other: "He wants to do *what?*"

The general manager of the King & Bear, Louie Bartoletti, a former player at UCLA, believed the philosophical and personal gaps between the two design camps were considerable.

"I really don't think they liked being on the property at the same time," Bartoletti said of Palmer and Nicklaus. "I think they knew each guy wanted to take control a bit."

Palmer and Nicklaus were together one day at the course-to-be when Arnie told Jack, "I need to speak with you," and walked him off to the side, out of earshot of their aides. The meeting lasted no more than ten minutes, but it was a one-way conversation.

"Arnold was telling Jack what to do and how to do it," Bartoletti said, "and Jack was just listening."

It was a role reversal for both. Palmer was usually the listener, Nicklaus the talker.

One day, with Jack elsewhere, Arnold was talking to Kurt Bowman about Nicklaus's nickname, Carnac. "Kurt," he asked, "do you know who's buried in the tomb of the unknown soldier?"

"No," came the reply.

"Well, ask Jack," Arnold said. "He knows everything."

Nicklaus believed he knew everything about how to make the King & Bear a course the Hall of Fame would be proud of. He wasn't afraid to walk that talk, either.

"Jack has to come in and take charge," Seay said. "Arnold's never been that way. He'll sit back and listen and say something if asked . . . Jack came in and said, 'Da-boom, da-boom, da-boom, and what do you think, Arnold?' And Arnold would say, 'That's fine.'"

Only Palmer wasn't about to let Nicklaus turn this project into Muirfield Village South. Arnold snuck in some of his own touches without running them by Jack, who had a sixth sense when it came to locating them.

While competing in the Liberty Mutual Legends of Golf event at the Slammer & Squire, Nicklaus dropped by the King & Bear site. He wasn't happy with what he saw.

"He said, 'I want my name off it,'" Bartoletti said. "Jack had [already] rerouted the golf course the first day he came . . . It took forever. I think they ended up using Jack's land plan; they were all mad as hell at him. My boss was saying, 'That son of a bitch; who does he think he is?'"

Palmer might've been mumbling something similar on the occasions Nicklaus showed up late for appointments at the site. Seay, the Palmer designer, kept telling Bartoletti and others that Nicklaus was intentionally tardy.

Jack showed up so late once that Arnold greeted him with an outstretched hand and this jab: "Where have you been? I'm on my third nine."

Palmer had come to expect this as par for Nicklaus's course. For one 9:30 a.m. walk-through, Nicklaus showed up after noon. "We're finished," Seay said, "and he shows up with the normal entourage, and he comes up and Arnold ribbed him a little bit. 'Nice going, Jack; late as usual.'

"Jack was so embarrassed he was so late, he threw a map out there and said, 'I've gone over this, Arnold, and there's some things I have to discuss.' Jack was making a big show of spreading the maps out, which was typical ... 'Here I come, boys. Open the doors.' Yes, he's late on purpose. You wonder why people have to do that, but he did."

Somehow, some way, Palmer and Nicklaus finished the 7,247-yard, par-72 golf course in time for its November 15, 2000, grand opening. Bermuda grass, saw palmetto, and large coquina rocks were among the features. Nicklaus was said to have enjoyed greater influence on the closing holes; number eighteen, a par five, would be called "Bear's Claw."

An estimated ten thousand fans showed up for the big day. Before Palmer and Nicklaus did a clinic and played a round to entertain them, they sat for a news conference to field questions on their unlikely collaboration.

It was immediately clear which man had logged more hands-on hours. "Arnold said, 'We've got a nice collection of holes, doglegs left and right, and the greens are neat,'" Bowman said. "He could've been describing any course he's ever done. Nicklaus went second and said, 'Thirteen is a 563-yard par five, and if you could hit it 265 over the left side,' all sorts of detail.

"Jack is a control freak. If you pay him his fee, you're going to get *him,* not his guys."

After they were done with their news conference, Palmer and Nicklaus started their hourlong clinic on the range. They threw cute verbal jabs at each other, following their usual public routine in such settings. "It was like watching Laurel and Hardy," Bowman said.

They closed the clinic on a time-honored Arnie-Jack gag, with the help of a pair of five-irons. Arnie hit his patented draw at the same time Jack hit his patented fade, and both men swore their golf balls collided in mid-flight.

Palmer and Nicklaus each hit two ceremonial tee shots with persimmon woods from their glory days, and then one with a modern souped-up driver. They played a casual round together and joked that their first shared project in the world of golf course architecture would also be their last.

They announced they would be teammates again at the Liberty Mutual Legends of Golf tournament, scheduled for the King & Bear. They also revealed that four days before the March 30, 2001, Liberty Mutual event, they would meet at the course for a one-on-one match as part of the *Shell's Wonderful World of Golf* series.

And on that day, in a made-for-TV exhibition, a seventy-one-year-old Palmer and a sixty-one-year-old Nicklaus would compete as if they were playing for the U.S. Open title.

Entering the match at the King & Bear, Nicklaus wasn't taking Palmer seriously as a golfer. Arnold had missed seventeen consecutive cuts at Augusta National, whereas Jack had missed only one cut in thirty-three years and had nearly won the tournament three years earlier as a fifty-eight-year-old on one good hip.

Jack thought Arnie had been a ceremonial figure for years. Above all else that was the one thing Nicklaus vowed he'd never be:

Ceremonial.

So Jack expected a blowout victory on March 26, a chance to fine-tune his game for Augusta while Arnie hacked away to the fans' delight. Seven years earlier, in another installment of *Shell's Wonderful World of Golf*, the series that had featured 130 TV matches since 1961, Nicklaus beat Palmer by seven strokes at Pinehurst No. 2, punctuating the victory by draining a seventy-footer at number eighteen.

This time around Gary Player would walk with his fellow Big Three-ers as an ESPN commentator. The winner would get $100,000; the loser, $50,000. But this had nothing to do with cash, everything to do with the possibility it would be the last time Palmer, in the maroon sweater, and Nicklaus, in the yellow sweater, met in a man-to-man competition.

Under a clear blue sky they did a coin toss on the first tee. Arnie called heads, and when heads came up, he gave the honors to Jack, who drove into the left rough before Palmer split the fairway.

Arnold ended up with a nine-footer for birdie, and Jack blasted out of a bunker to leave himself with a six-footer for par. Palmer missed his bird to the left.

"Did you design this green?" he asked Nicklaus.

"I'll let you know who designed this green after I make this putt," Jack answered.

Nicklaus missed.

Seay was carrying Arnold's bag and savoring the back-and-forth needling. "They're much better friends than people know they are," Seay said. "But they'd cut each other's throats in competition. Their sole purpose in life is to beat each other, and there's no doubt about that."

Seay had a good relationship with Nicklaus, but he saw him as an Arnie copycat. Jack's image makeover in the early seventies, Seay said, "was absolutely Arnold-inspired . . . Normally when Arnold would do something, Jack would be right behind . . . It's recognized by everybody. It's a matter of, 'I can do that, too.'"

But when Nicklaus surpassed Palmer in the design field, securing bigger fees and building courses out of the mud that received higher ratings than Palmer's, "absolutely it bothered Arnold," Seay said.

It bothered Arnold nearly as much as Oakmont in 1962 and Baltusrol in 1967.

In their *Shell's* exhibition match at the King & Bear, Palmer and Nicklaus were even entering the fifth hole, a par five called "Fader's Delight," a dogleg right that had the Bear's paw prints all over it. Palmer smoked his drive over the beach bunker and the corner of the bordering lake and left himself 213 yards to the front of the green.

With Nicklaus in the bunker, Arnold shocked Seay by pulling out a lay-up club, a three-iron. "How much fairway do we have up there before the green?" he asked his caddie.

"I think this is the largest green on the course," Seay responded.

Palmer shot him a look that said, "You're an asshole," and then returned his three-iron to his bag and whipped out a five-wood. Arnold Palmer was going for broke.

He launched his second shot, barely cleared the water, and landed on the green to the roar of the crowd. Palmer was twenty feet from the cup, or sixty feet closer than Nicklaus was after his third shot. Jack made a nice two-putt par, but Arnie drained his eagle putt to take a two-shot lead.

Nicklaus was so stunned he gave Palmer a high-five. Jack managed to square the match before the turn, but the momentum swung back to Arnold at the par-three eleventh, where Nicklaus lipped out his birdie attempt before Palmer nailed his from nine feet away.

Arnie had thought a lot about his putting entering the match. "I tried to remember what made me such a good putter thirty years ago," he said. Palmer went back to his knock-kneed, pigeon-toed stance and stayed still over his ball as he hadn't in a very long time.

He also decided to attack the hole. He wasn't leaving anything short, just as in the old days. Never up, never in. At the thirteenth Palmer sank a left-to-right twenty-footer that might've run twenty feet past the hole if it hadn't rammed against the back center of the cup, popped up, and dropped right in, inspiring Nicklaus to tell him, "I've always said you were the best putter I've ever seen."

Unnerved by Palmer's putt, Nicklaus blew his short birdie try to fall three behind Arnie. Palmer sensed the Bear was wounded and moved in for a fatal stab. Arnie was savoring the role of the Bull, as some of the tour pros called him. He charged at a monstrously long downhill putt that snaked through the shadows, into the sun, and nearly into the cup. "I got robbed," Arnie shouted to Jack. They both parred the hole.

At the fifteenth Nicklaus missed another makable birdie putt, this time from twelve feet. On the verge of losing to a seventy-one-year-old man, Jack was growing desperate.

He hit a tree on his approach shot at the 467-yard sixteenth and suffered another bogey to fall four back of Palmer. At the seventeenth, with the match slipping away, Nicklaus missed another par putt to give Palmer a five-shot advantage.

Arnie crushed his final drive into the fairway and smiled wide as he handed his driver back to Seay. Game, set, match. As he hobbled toward his own drive, Nicklaus wrapped an arm around Palmer and pulled him close.

"Well, you dusted me, Arn," Jack said. "You played very well today. I'm very proud of you."

It was a great scene on a great day.

"If you play golf against your brother," Arnold said, "you want to beat him because he's your brother. Same thing with a friend."

Brother. That word was thrown around a lot in conversations about the Arnie-Jack relationship. Arnie, the big brother trying to protect his standing. Jack, the kid brother trying to assert his will.

If they had been raised in the same household, with only a few years of age separating them, they surely would've bloodied each other's noses in pickup basketball games gone wrong, only to go back to being good buds within the hour.

Jack won more than his share of battles as the kid brother, but he was put in his place, too. Once at the Senior PGA Championship in Palm Beach Gardens, Nicklaus was getting his lunch in the grill room when a fan started banging on the glass door and screaming his name. Jack didn't want to get caught signing autographs for an hour, but the man wouldn't relent.

Finally Nicklaus opened the door and reached for the stranger's photo and pen. But the guy made no move toward Jack. "Is Arnold Palmer in there?" the man asked Nicklaus. "I want his signature."

Jack was frozen for a moment with his hands outstretched as the fan pulled back his photo of the King. "Well," Jack said when he returned to the lunch line, "can you believe that?"

Palmer would savor these precious tales when they were relayed to him.

"Arnold looks at Jack like he's a young kid whom he brought along," said Kurt Bowman, the Nicklaus design coordinator. "I heard him say, 'I showed that kid the ropes. I brought him up.' He finds delight in Jack's development."

To a point, anyway. Palmer was thoroughly enjoying this ass-kicking he was giving Nicklaus for an ESPN audience that might've included viewers young enough to believe Tiger Woods was golf's founding father. On the final hole, a par five, Palmer hit his chip close, handed his club to Seay, and slapped him on the shoulder while wearing an ear-to-ear grin. Arnie looked like he was about to win his fifth Masters title.

Nicklaus had putted horribly all day, failing to record even one birdie, so it was fitting that he rimmed out a five-footer on the eighteenth green. "I don't believe it, Jack," Palmer said in a consoling tone. Nicklaus forced an anguished smile and shook his head. "Incredible," he said. "An incredible day of putting."

Palmer made his par to shoot his age, 71, five full shots better than Nicklaus, who needed thirty-six putts to the winner's twenty-four. "Congratulations, Jack, on a great golf course," Palmer said as he shook Nicklaus's hand. The two of them laughed, hugged, and grabbed each other hard around the neck like college frat boys at a kegger.

"You're damned right I wanted to beat him," Palmer said. "When we're out there, I hate him and he hates me."

Palmer was driven by the fact that Nicklaus helped him build this course, and by the memory of Nicklaus beating him at Pinehurst No. 2 in 1994. "That was a lingering thought," Arnold said. "I just felt that I had lost the first one and I needed to win the second one."

They had a dinner at the Hall of Fame that night, and Gary Player was back at the mike. He called Nicklaus the greatest winner of them all, and the greatest loser, too. Player meant it as a compliment—Nicklaus always showed remarkable poise in defeat. But Jack didn't like being called a loser in any context, and eventually he'd ask Player to knock it off.

With the dinner winding down, Nicklaus grabbed an associate, stepped outside, and gazed into the starry night. He looked around to see if any stranger was within earshot, or if Palmer or one of his staffers had quietly stepped out behind him.

The coast was clear. After a long day and evening of playing the good sport, of being the good loser in the company of his chief rival, Jack William Nicklaus was finally free to say what was on his mind.

"Dammit," he sighed.

"I cannot believe I lost to that guy."

CHAPTER 22

• Ceremonial

J ACK NICKLAUS was some kind of pissed off. For the second consecutive year the people who ran the Masters had decided to group him with Arnold Palmer and Gary Player for the sake of the crowd.

Nicklaus wasn't happy the first time around in 2000, only two years after he threatened to write the greatest golf story of all time by nearly winning the Masters at fifty-eight.

Following his opening round in 2000, Nicklaus decided to practice rather than join Palmer and Player for a TV interview and a news conference; he later appeared for both alone, once Arnold and Gary were done. "A childish performance," wrote the author John Feinstein for America Online.

Jack didn't want to cause too much of a stir; he'd just been honored at the Georgia Golf Hall of Fame with a statue depicting his victorious, post-putt pose on the seventeenth green at the 1986 Masters. But he couldn't understand how a player who had outscored Tiger Woods two years earlier could be lumped in with the older, noncompetitive tandem of Palmer and Player. Especially Palmer.

On the final hole of their second round, Arnold needed multiple swings to get his ball out of a bunker. "Hit it harder," Jack barked at him. "I want to play."

Nicklaus missed his par putt from seven feet but shot two-under 70 to land six strokes off David Duval's lead. Palmer, meanwhile, finished his tournament at sixteen over and trudged off the green without shaking Nicklaus's hand.

"Arnold never said he enjoyed playing with me and Gary, never shook our hands," Jack said. "That was probably the most irritated I ever was at Arnold."

Nicklaus ultimately fell out of contention and landed in a tie for fifty-fourth. The following year Jack was even more irritated with the Augusta National elders who arranged for another Big Three reunion.

Nicklaus was coming off missed cuts at the U.S. and British Opens and the PGA Championship the previous summer, which marked the final time he'd play in all four majors in a calendar year.

Jack's missed PGA cut at the Louisville course he designed, Valhalla, had little to do with his age and his pairing with Woods and plenty to do with the death of his mother on the eve of the tournament. In the middle of his practice round, Nicklaus was given the news by Kaye Kessler, the Columbus sportswriter who first wrote about him when he was ten years old.

Jack quietly granted autograph requests on his walk to the clubhouse. He flew back and forth from Columbus to play with Tiger, the eventual winner, because he knew his mother would've insisted he stay in the field. The day after the tournament, Helen Nicklaus was buried on her ninety-first birthday.

Eight months later, at the 2001 Masters, Nicklaus was itching to prove he could still compete in the one Grand Slam event he'd dominated more than any other. The Golden Bear was fiercely proud of his place in the game's history. Asked how he would have fared against Tiger in his prime, Nicklaus would say, "I'd get my share of wins and he'd get his share."

Jack still wanted to play for real. When informed of his Augusta National pairing, Jack couldn't believe he was viewed as the same thanks-for-the-memories figure as Palmer.

Nicklaus hated the notion that he'd been reduced to a ceremonial golfer. He was thoroughly embarrassed by it, as he was forever saying he wouldn't keep playing if he couldn't compete.

"I don't want to go out there, walk around, shoot 85, and wave to everybody with a false smile on my face," Nicklaus would say. "That's not me."

This was always Nicklaus's way of saying he would never do what Palmer was doing every April at Augusta.

Jack always enjoyed Arnie's company in practice rounds at the Masters; that much was clear. Before the bell rang on Thursday mornings, Nicklaus was willing to play along with the routine.

As an amateur, Tiger was a firsthand witness to the show. Arnie and Jack asked him to join their practice round.

"You don't normally have a little kid tagging along," Woods said. "It was pretty incredible that they even asked.

"I just sat back and watched them work. I don't remember much about the practice round itself; it was more about them telling me stories. I'll never forget Arnold unwrapping his fucking driver going down number ten, and Jack says, 'Well, there's Arnold for you.'"

Nicklaus wasn't so interested in Palmer's obsession with equipment once the tournament began. So in 2001 the Big Three Reunion, Part Two, didn't go any more smoothly than the original, even if the gallery couldn't get enough of Arnie and Jack and Gary—the men who had won a combined thirteen green jackets.

On the fourteenth green of the second round, with Nicklaus and Player still harboring reasonable hopes of making the cut, Palmer decided to do his Kingly duty with his adoring fans.

Done with his par, Palmer walked across the green and ducked under the gallery ropes and into a vacant foldup golf chair, causing the fans to laugh. Nicklaus was trying to measure his birdie attempt when the commotion forced him to back away from his ball. He looked at Palmer, then at his son and caddie, Jackie, and then back at Palmer, who tipped his white cap.

Nicklaus didn't crack a smile. "That's what Gary and I were getting so mad about," he would say. "Gary and I both got irritated with him that week."

To different degrees Nicklaus and Player were both overshadowed by Palmer, and Player wasn't any happier about that truth than Nicklaus. In fact, the South African was annoyed by his insignificant presence in a Golf Channel film on Palmer's life.

"All they did was speak about Arnold and Jack," Player said, "and they said, 'There's Gary lurking in the background.' I won more majors than Arnold. More money. More tournaments around the world. More senior tournaments. More majors on the senior tour . . . You've got to be fair in life."

Life is no different from golf: it's rarely fair. Player and Nicklaus spent enough time together to commiserate over their place in Palmer's all-encompassing shadow.

"[The media] would just never realize what my record was," Player said. "Maybe it's the pride of the American journalists; I don't know what it is. I'm not bitter about it at all, because when we're all dead and gone they're going to look at the record book. Yes, they're going to look at the record book."

The book that said Player had won two more Grand Slam events than Palmer, his nine titles placing him halfway to the Golden Bear's mark.

Player and Nicklaus loved to spend time in the outdoors together and to do the silliest of schoolboy things: they would even stage flatulence contests. "I think there's a lot of synergy between Gary and my dad that Arnold and my dad didn't have," Jackie Nicklaus said.

Jackie believed his father looked up to Palmer, admired what he did for the growth of the game, and envied his popularity with the fans. "That's always been a want of my dad," Jackie said, "to be accepted by the galleries as Arnold has been accepted."

But another Nicklaus want was Palmer's acknowledgment. "In all the years of competition," Jackie said, "[Arnold] never walked up to him and said, 'Jack, nice playing. Congratulations.' Not once. And my dad did that every time.

"I mean, Arnold made my dad and my dad made Arnold, there's no question about that. But it obviously bothered [my father] because he would make comments to me. He'd say, 'Well, Arnold was his old self. He never shook my hand.' . . . I've never witnessed a bad moment between them, and the only comment my dad ever said was, 'I wish Arnold would've said, "Nice going."' My dad's never said anything derogatory to me about Arnold ever."

Nicklaus missed the cut at the 2001 Masters, just like Palmer and Player. He didn't blame it on the pairing, but he promised he would lobby hard against a Big Three Reunion, Part Three.

"We're put on now as a sideshow," Nicklaus complained. "I hope they don't do that again."

For the record, Player and Palmer said they had no problems with the golden oldie lineup. Jack said the grouping wasn't fair to the young players who yearned to play with the legends; he cited letters he received from those kids.

But this wasn't about any rookies in the Augusta National field. This was about Nicklaus believing he deserved better than a legends-on-parade spectacle at the Masters.

"It was a contrived thing for publicity for the tournament," he would say, "and I thought the Masters was beyond that . . . I still felt that I was competitive. I was . . . cocky enough to still feel that."

Before he left the club grounds in 2001 for a rare April weekend off, Nicklaus was sure to hammer home his Big Three point.

"We've played seven thousand rounds together," he said. "I hope they don't do that every year. I know Gary feels the same way.

"I haven't asked Arnold."

CHAPTER 23

• Opportunity Lost

HOOTIE JOHNSON, chairman of Augusta National, needed some help. As the 2003 Masters approached, Johnson called on two of his most prominent club members, Arnold Palmer and Jack Nicklaus, to offer him counsel in the midst of a roiling public relations crisis unlike any the National had seen.

Palmer came with his grandson Sam Saunders, and Nicklaus arrived with his son Michael. They played a round of golf, and Hootie and Arnie and Jack sat down to discuss a most pressing concern.

Martha Burk, chairwoman of the National Council of Women's Organizations, had launched a crusade against the club's all-male membership, whipping up a media frenzy around the unwritten ban on female members that had corporate sponsors scattering like roaches surprised by a light.

A protest was planned. News-side reporters who wouldn't know a double bogey from a double cheeseburger were preparing to fly into Augusta to cover the battle of the sexes forming outside the gates of this latter-day He-Man Woman Haters Club. The circus was coming to the National, and for the sake of Clifford Roberts's and Bobby Jones's legacies, Hootie didn't want to be the one who ended up wearing a clown's nose.

But when he summoned Palmer and Nicklaus to his office, Hootie talked about an issue he believed to be of greater consequence. The chairman confessed he had erred the year before when he announced an end to the tradition of inviting all past champions to compete in the Masters. Johnson told Palmer and Nicklaus that his new age limit of sixty-five was no more, reopening the tournament door for every former winner who wanted to shoot 88 in Tiger Woods's field.

Arnold and Jack were thrilled. The year before, Palmer shot 89 in his first round and then disclosed the following day's round would be the last he ever played at the Masters. Johnson had sent out letters to former champions Billy Casper, Gay Brewer, and Doug Ford, urging them to play the tournament no longer because of their unsightly scores, and in declaring that his forty-eighth consecutive Masters would be a wrap, Palmer said, "I don't want to get a letter."

So he sent one instead. Palmer and Nicklaus wrote to Johnson, asking him to rescind the age limit and return the automatic invitation to Masters champions; Palmer and Nicklaus felt it was an element of the tournament that made it special and unique. Arnold wanted to meet his goal of fifty consecutive Masters, and ol' Hootie buckled at a place where buckling was about as popular as Martha Burk herself.

In their news conferences on the eve of that 2003 tournament, Arnold and Jack were happy to talk about their roles in persuading a Masters elder to heed their words of wisdom and drop a misguided policy before it could take effect. Yet when they were asked to offer an opinion on the club's refusal to allow women into their closed circle of Fortune 500 CEOs, Palmer and Nicklaus decided their considerable clout would be better applied somewhere else.

"I've said all I'm going to say on it," offered Jack.

"I'm sorry it's happening," Arnold said. "And I think about all the things that are happening in the world today and we have got enough controversy outside this golf tournament to be concerned about and shouldn't have to be concerning ourselves with such things as this."

That same day Hootie Johnson said enough for both of them. After stating months earlier that he wouldn't be pressured into admitting women "at the point of a bayonet," Johnson closed his combative news conference the way an old University of South Carolina blocking back should.

"If I drop dead this second," Hootie said, "our position will not change."

Tiger had already asked for that change in position, outscoring Palmer and Nicklaus on this front. At twenty-seven, Woods was a three-time Masters titleholder, the two-time defending champ, and the first black winner at a club that didn't have a black member until 1990. He had already won eight major championships, one more than Palmer, and was well on his way to challenging Nicklaus for the distinction of greatest player of all time.

Sure, Woods needed to consult his IMG reps and his Nike benefactors before forming his public opinion, but at least he took a stand right on the Augusta National grounds, with a club official, Billy Payne, sitting next to him. "Should [women] become members, or should they be members?" he said into a microphone. "Yes."

Hootie, the old fullback, would hit Woods, an honorary member, the way he would a blocking sled. "I won't tell Tiger how to play golf," Johnson said, "if he doesn't tell us how to run our private club."

While Palmer and Nicklaus were sitting this one out, burying their heads in the sand trap, their fellow Big Three member, Gary Player, was taking the fight to Augusta National. Player was the first prominent golfer to assail the club's policy on women; he'd also ripped Johnson's age mandate before Palmer and Nicklaus piled on.

This came as no surprise. Player, the product of South Africa's apartheid system, was always more willing to address third-rail social and political issues than the King and the Golden Bear, who spent much of their careers missing golden opportunities to speak out against golf's shameful exclusionary ways.

Those missed opportunities started with Palmer, who spent seven years on the pro tour before the Professional Golfers' Association rescinded its vile "Caucasian clause" on November 9, 1961, more than fourteen years after Jackie Robinson made his big-league debut for the Dodgers. As the biggest star in golf, and as the son of a man who earned his nickname for helping a black deacon in need, Palmer might have been expected to decry a PGA policy that required its members to be "professional golfers of the Caucasian race," a policy that would compel *Los Angeles Times* columnist Jim Murray to call the PGA "the recreational arm of the Ku Klux Klan."

Palmer never did. He never backed the cause of Stanley Mosk, the California attorney general who fought the PGA on Charlie Sifford's behalf and eventually had the clause thrown out. Palmer would later

write in his book *A Golfer's Life* that he wanted the PGA's racial policies to "evolve with the times, but I didn't want to throw the baby out
with the bathwater, so to speak."

No sports organization was slower to "evolve with the times" than
the PGA. As far back as 1948, black players such as Ted Rhodes and
Bill Spiller — restricted to the United Golfers Association, golf's answer to the Negro Leagues — were filing lawsuits against the PGA and
clubs hosting tour events for denying them a chance to participate.
Four years later former heavyweight champion and accomplished amateur golfer Joe Louis was initially denied his application to play in the
San Diego Open by PGA president Horton Smith.

Louis pressed the PGA into a corner, and the governing body decided it couldn't turn away a beloved icon. The PGA allowed Louis to
become the first black man to compete in a PGA event as an "exempt
amateur" but kept its ban on black pros in place.

By 1960, when he was perhaps the most popular athlete in the land,
Arnold Palmer could have made a difference for the likes of Sifford,
who would be subjected to death threats and racial slurs and clubs that
forced him to eat and dress in the parking lot, and who once found human excrement waiting for him in the bottom of the cup at the first hole
in Phoenix. Palmer could have made a difference for the young black
businessmen who couldn't aspire to join the memberships of the tour's
all-white country clubs.

He chose not to make that difference and risk losing friendships and
endorsement money because of it.

Even thirty years later at the PGA Championship, where the founder
of Birmingham's Shoal Creek, Hall Thompson, was quoted saying his
club didn't "discriminate in every other area except the blacks," remarks that ultimately forced Augusta National and other hosting clubs
on tour to admit at least one black member, Palmer remained silent on
the sidelines.

"If he was playing with Charlie Sifford, he probably felt bad," said
Palmer's daughter Peg. "But do I think he spent a minute of his time
really thinking of the plight of the American black man? No."

Sifford put it this way: "It's pretty hard in this country for a white
man to stand up for a black man."

He liked Arnold Palmer, Sifford did. He thought Palmer treated
him with respect. And he never asked Palmer to speak out on his behalf

when Clifford Roberts and Bobby Jones wouldn't extend him an invitation to the Masters.

Sifford didn't feel right asking a white player to take up his fight. He became the first black winner on tour at the 1967 Greater Hartford Open, and then he won again in Los Angeles in 1969, and he charged that Roberts and Jones kept changing their qualification rules to keep him out of the field. Jim Murray lobbied on his behalf, as did Art Wall Jr., the 1959 Masters champ, who was the only player to vote for Sifford when Masters winners were allowed to fill one spot in the field.

"Art Wall, he was just a real man," Sifford said. "He figured I deserved to play in the Masters, and that I was a good enough golfer to play ... But that's one out of a million. You're not going to find everybody doing that. He told me out of his own mouth that he caught hell from a lot of champions."

When tour winners became automatic invitees to the Masters, Sifford was past his prime. Lee Elder secured his place in history as the Masters' first black competitor in 1975 by virtue of winning the Monsanto Open. Years later, even after Woods started tearing down tournament records, Sifford would pledge never to set foot on Augusta National ground.

"It ain't nothing but a hateful spot," he said. "It's a bunch of prejudiced rich white people down there ... I bet Cliff Roberts is turning over in his grave fifty or sixty times [over Tiger]."

By declining to put pressure on golf and country club officials who discouraged—or flat-out blocked—black participation in the game, the stars of the sport were quiet enablers of a discriminatory enterprise. But just as Sifford didn't assign any blame to Palmer for his plight, he didn't blame Jack Nicklaus either.

Sifford liked Nicklaus, too, and the feeling was mutual. "I love Charlie Sifford," Jack said. Charlie Nicklaus, Jack's father, bought Sifford cigars and treated him with respect. That support from the Nicklaus side never flowered into any progressive stand to get Sifford or another black player into the Masters.

Jack turned pro two days before the PGA erased the "Caucasian clause" from its bylaws, so he never entered an event that officially banned black players from competing. He did, however, spend nearly thirty years on tour playing at all-white country clubs without using his public forum to denounce them.

Nicklaus figured he was speaking loudly enough with his actions. At his own Muirfield Village in the seventies, Nicklaus ensured that his first ten members included a black man and candidates of different nationalities and creeds. "Long before it was popular," Nicklaus said. "Absolutely I did it on purpose."

When the course Nicklaus designed at Shoal Creek became engulfed in the racial controversy inspired by Hall Thompson's quotes, PGA Championship officials considered moving their event to Muirfield Village because it didn't have a whites-only membership. And when his friend Arthur Ashe asked him to stop playing in South Africa, Nicklaus obliged.

In later years Jack also would devote his time to the First Tee program, which was established to provide opportunities in golf to children who wouldn't otherwise have the means to play it.

But during his winning days Nicklaus didn't make equal opportunity in golf a chief part of his agenda. His only agenda was winning as many tournaments as he possibly could.

"I wasn't a crusader," Nicklaus said. "In other words, I did what I thought was right. Could I have probably gotten on a bandwagon and said, 'You guys need to do this, too'? I didn't think that was a way to live life. I think you [lead] by example, and if people wish to follow that example . . . and know that you have done this, 'Well, Jack did this over here,' it should be all right.

"I do believe in inclusion. I think that's the way it should be."

In 1994 Nicklaus was addressing the dearth of black players in golf when he was quoted as saying that black athletes have "different muscles that react in different ways." He has maintained ever since the quote didn't reflect his true belief that environment often determines the sports white and black athletes choose to play.

Pressed on his comments, Nicklaus said, "I think my record speaks for itself . . . I hated racially segregated clubs. I solved that problem in my own place."

Only he never thought it was his business to use his stature to help solve that problem in other places.

So with the civil rights movement exploding around their primes, Palmer and Nicklaus let pass an opportunity to expedite change in their separate-but-unequal sport.

"A lot of people looked up to them," Lee Elder said. "People pretty much looked and followed their pattern. And I think had they been a little more outspoken in the way of saying, 'Hey, we're going to have to do something to maybe change the situation for the minority player,' it would've [helped] . . . Their voice was something that I think almost every sponsor and every tournament director would have listened to."

Like Sifford, Elder said Palmer and Nicklaus were a pleasure to play with. He said both men were courteous enough to stay on the greens when they were done putting so the swelling crowds wouldn't move and distract him. He said Palmer was good enough to give him a few rides to tournaments.

But Elder was often mistaken for a caddie when he'd show up at those tournaments. The culture of professional golf encouraged such assumptions, and that was a culture Elder wished Palmer and Nicklaus were more willing to attack.

"They never voiced their opinion about it," Elder said. "If they had voiced their opinion a little more, they were right in that era where it could've made a big change . . . With them being the name superstars, I can pretty much see it, because when you're a top player or you're the number one, you don't want to set yourself to doing something. But if you want it to happen and you want to help somebody, then you show your true colors.

"[Golf officials] want the general public to think that they have been really great guys, have been the champions of the causes and they have helped out. And they really haven't."

Elder said there was one big-name player who did champion the cause of black players. He was the star raised in a society that enforced the separation of black and white as eagerly as the United States enforced the separation of church and state.

Gary Player of South Africa.

Palmer and Nicklaus were never charged to answer for racism in America, but Player was harassed and threatened by demonstrators who saw him as a symbol of apartheid. In the summer of 1969, just weeks after Neil Armstrong landed on the moon, black and white activists disrupted his play at the PGA Championship in Dayton.

During Player's third round someone heaved a souvenir program the size of a telephone book at him during his backswing. A group of fans shouted, *"Miss!"* in the middle of Player's putt on the ninth green, causing him to botch a gimme. Another protestor threw a cup of ice into Player's eyes on the tenth tee. On the tenth green some black and white fans ran onto the green; one of them headed for Jack Nicklaus, who wielded his putter like a cleanup hitter and said, "If you come at me, I'll knock your head right off."

The fan stopped and fell on his rear before police rushed him and the other demonstrators off the course. Another fan threw Nicklaus's ball into a greenside bunker. Three holes later a woman rolled a ball through Player's legs as he was about to putt. In the end eleven people were thrown in jail and Gary Player was thrown for a loss—by one shot to Raymond Floyd.

"I'll go to my grave knowing I won ten majors," said Player, who won nine.

"Every day for two years [activists] were going to kill me. Every day the phone rings: 'We're going to kill you tomorrow.' I said, 'Why are you going to kill me? Because I love people? I have respect for people, and I ain't going home. I'm going to be a champion.'"

Player was a champion whose world travels compelled him to see the evil in his homeland's apartheid system, and yet he absorbed as much verbal abuse as Charlie Sifford had in the "Caucasian clause" days. At a tournament in Australia, Player was met with a "Racist Go Home" sign, and fans taunted him from the first tee forward.

They had picked on the wrong guy. Player would advance the integration of South African sport by persuading the prime minister, John Vorster, an apartheid hard-liner and former Nazi sympathizer, to allow Elder to compete in his country.

"I was called a traitor at the airport in Cape Town many times," Player said. "They'd ask, 'Why did you invite a black to come down and play on our white tour?'"

He told them it was the right thing to do.

Elder would call Player "the greatest humanitarian I ever met." Elder would say that Player "did more to help black golfers ... than any other player on tour." Sifford would have Player introduce him at his Hall of Fame induction ceremony. Nelson Mandela would write in *Golf Digest* that "few men in our country's history did as much to enact political changes for the better that eventually improved the lives of millions of his countrymen" than Player.

The diminutive champion kept standing tall in the face of discrimination. He pierced the deafening Big Three silence by blasting Augusta National on its refusal to consider women for its three-hundred-plus membership.

"I believe [women] should be member[s] because they're human beings," Player said. "They are our wives, the mothers of our children. That's what I believe. If I'm condemned for that, so be it."

Player said he felt a cold shoulder turned his way by Augusta's elders after he first criticized their stance on women. "Yeah, there's a certain feeling [from them], and that's fine," Player said. "Because I've known I've been the best ambassador they've ever had outside of Arnold and Jack."

Arnold and Jack. Over the years they used their fame and standing in the sport to engage in political fights of their choosing.

In the sixties, believing the PGA was catering to club pros, Palmer and Nicklaus helped the touring professionals break away from the organization and form the PGA Tour. "Their involvement was crucial," said Tim Finchem, who became commissioner of the tour in 1994 and who characterized Arnold and Jack as the tour's "founding fathers."

Palmer and Nicklaus also battled Finchem's predecessor, Deane Beman, over the tour's marketing and course-designing aims. They lobbied against cart use and testified against Casey Martin—a golfer with a rare and serious leg disorder who required a cart to compete—in a case that ended in a Supreme Court victory for Martin. They successfully fought Augusta National on a proposed age limit for Masters competitors, and they would blitz Finchem on the subject of high-flying golf balls in a Captains Club meeting on the eve of Nicklaus's Memorial Tournament.

"Boy," said John Montgomery, a Captains Club member and witness, "the two of them got on Finchem like you wouldn't believe ... Jack and Arnie jumped him big time."

Arnie even battled the USGA over his endorsement of Callaway's ERC II driver, which didn't conform to the governing body's standards. The USGA temporarily excommunicated the honorary chairperson of its membership program during the dispute.

So Palmer and Nicklaus weren't hesitant to wield their power and prestige like sabers when their interests were on the line. And in the end, discrimination against African Americans and women didn't represent any impediment to their own pursuits.

Asked later if he regretted not being more outspoken on discrimination in golf, Nicklaus said, "You know my own policies. When I'm out playing golf, I'm out there to play golf. I'm not crusading. I'm going to walk into the pro shop and, 'Gee, Jack, that was a great win in the U.S. Open.' 'Yeah, sure it was. And boy, we should have more black players here or more women playing.' I mean, come on.

"[But] to answer the question, probably yes. Could I probably have done more? Could Arnold probably have done more? But nobody thought about it."

By 2003 the acceptance of a handful of black members at Augusta National and the dominance of Woods had muted the issue of race at the Masters and cleared room for the gender-bending brawl.

Nicklaus had female members at Muirfield Village and his Bear's Club in Jupiter, Florida, but, like Palmer, refused to take a public swipe at the tournament that helped define his career. It was only long after Martha Burk's protest outside Augusta National fell hopelessly flat in a dirt pit half a mile from the club gates, and after the coast-to-coast debate on the issue died a slow and painful death, that Nicklaus was willing to stray from the club rule forbidding its own from commenting on membership matters.

"If there's an outstanding woman who should be there," Nicklaus said of Augusta National, "why shouldn't she be there? I mean, that's my feeling.

"But I'm a member, and so when you're a member and you've accepted the membership, you accept the policies of that membership. So you publicly shouldn't say [anything] against the policies of that membership. That's the point. But do I believe we should have women at Augusta? I don't necessarily think we should have women, but I don't think we should exclude them."

Asked directly if he would have any problem with Augusta National bringing in a woman as a member, Nicklaus said, "Zero . . . If there's a woman that should be a member, there's no reason why we shouldn't [accept her]."

Palmer declined an invitation to follow Nicklaus's lead and address Augusta's Stone Age custom. "He never takes a position," Jack said of Arnie. "In many ways that's the beauty of Arnold . . . Arnold's loved because there aren't any negatives about him."

His silence actually counted for one. Palmer and Nicklaus both missed a wide-open fairway in their playing primes, when golf needed its two giants to speak loudly while carrying their big sticks.

CHAPTER 24

• Last Rounds

ARNOLD PALMER had just talked Joe Torre out of retirement. They were on a fishing boat off Maui, watching for whales, when Palmer invited the manager of the New York Yankees and fellow prostate cancer survivor to share a round of golf at Bay Hill.

Torre told Palmer he'd be free the following winter, after the 2004 season, since his contract was up and he was planning to call it a career.

"How old are you?" the seventy-four-year-old Palmer asked.

"Sixty-three," Torre answered.

"What the hell do you want to retire for?"

The manager was taken aback.

"Joe, you know, if I retired," Palmer said, "I wouldn't know what to do. I'd go crazy. I'm going to golf and do my thing and continue to work as long as I live."

Torre hung on every syllable. When Arnold Palmer spoke, even four-time World Series champions listened.

"You talk about charisma, man," the manager said. "Fuckin' sits there and the place lights up."

Three months later Palmer was retiring from the Masters, retiring from major championship golf. His charisma lit up Augusta National for fifty consecutive years, but his bones were too brittle and sore anymore to walk a lengthened course that had grown into a snarling beast for men half Palmer's age.

He had to settle for the smallest of victories. The year before, after shooting 83 in the first round at Augusta, Palmer stumbled into Barbara Nicklaus and glumly told her his score.

"Well, Jack had 85," she responded.

"Whaaaaat?" Arnold shrieked as his face widened into a smile.

"Oh, Arnold," Barbara said, "you guys are so bad."

The following April, Arnold suffered from shin splints for most of his final Augusta round. He'd grown accustomed to walking flat Florida courses in his old age and to using those carts he once campaigned against.

But with the hills of the Masters breaking him down muscle by muscle, stroke by stroke, the fans, as always, kept him on the march. Suddenly, at the fifteenth hole, the shin splints retreated and the pain disappeared. By the time he hit the eighteenth hole with his sixteen-year-old grandson, Sam Saunders, carrying his bag, Palmer was walking on air.

He lashed at his tee shot with his trademark fury, his last big April cut as wild as a March hare. As Palmer walked up the fairway, he thought about the four Masters victories and the couple he let get away. He thought about the legacy he established and the friends he made.

At the eighteenth green, with Palmer about to shoot a second consecutive 84 for a twenty-four-over total, Masters officials decided against posting Arnold's score with the plus fours registered by his playing partners, Bob Estes and Nathan Smith. Palmer finished off his bogey and waved to the adoring gallery as an active Masters competitor for the last time.

"I've had it," Palmer would say in the interview room. "I'm done. Cooked. Washed up. Finished."

Arnold had said he was done, cooked, washed up, finished two years earlier, but this time it was clear he meant it. No letter or age requirement was forcing him out. He knew if he kept playing, his scores in the 80s would become his scores in the 90s.

But two days earlier Nicklaus had mocked Palmer's intent, drawing belly laughs from the assembled press. "I think it's kind of nice that he's able to play fifty Masters," Nicklaus said. "Now, will this be his last one? I wouldn't bet on it. I mean, I think you all know Arnold well enough that even though he says it, how many times has he said it's his last one? Right?"

"Next year it will be, 'I always wanted to play over fifty Masters.'"

If some in the Palmer camp weren't thrilled with those remarks, all was forgiven on Friday afternoon, in the middle of the second round, when Arnold hit his tee shot at the par-three sixth and then looked down below and to his right toward the sixteenth green, where a certain someone was giving him his due.

Nicklaus was doffing his cap for Palmer, who in return doffed his for Nicklaus as the crowd cheered. They were all done beating each other up at Augusta, all done sliding those green jackets over each other's shoulders.

Palmer needed to hit a driver from the eighteenth fairway just to come up ten yards short of the green. Yes, it was time for him to go.

"Augusta and this golf tournament [have] been about as much a part of my life as anything other than my family," Palmer said. "I don't think that I could ever separate myself from this club and this golf tournament."

Breaking up was hard to do. Over the years Palmer would watch tapes of his Masters victories with Sam, an accomplished schoolboy player, and turn envious over the virile image of his younger self. "Why can't I swing that way anymore?" Arnold would ask his grandson.

Times change. Men grow old. Friends and associates fade away. In May of 2003 Palmer's manager, Mark McCormack, died four months after he suffered cardiac arrest and descended into a coma.

The agent went to his grave as the most powerful man in sports. McCormack built IMG into a dynasty with twenty-five hundred employees and offices in thirty countries; the company represented everyone from Tiger Woods to Derek Jeter to Itzhak Perlman.

Before he died, McCormack was told by Alastair Johnston that he was about to add a new high-profile client: Jack Nicklaus.

"You're kidding," McCormack said.

"I know how much that meant to Mark," Johnston said, "because it was the one asterisk in his career, that Jack Nicklaus had left him."

Nicklaus kept his own companies intact and hired IMG to move Golden Bear products, in Jack's words, "to countries where we would not have gone if not for IMG."

Through IMG Nicklaus landed a highly visible deal with the Royal Bank of Scotland. But forty years after the IMG pecking order was clearly established, Arnie was still Arnie.

Thanks to McCormack and IMG, Palmer was still banking $20 million in endorsements in 2004, or some $16.4 million more than the career sum of his regular tour and senior tour winnings on the golf course. He was still cashing in on licensing deals around the world, especially in Japan, "where Arnold Palmer is the hottest-selling brand of apparel for teenage girls," Johnston said.

"They're selling nose rings and tattoos and all sorts of stuff in Japan because they think Arnold Palmer is almost like a designer name. And we don't necessarily want to advertise that, because I don't want them thinking we took advantage of them or we've duped them. But Arnold said to me, 'Do you want me to come help you? Do you want me to visit Japan?' And I go, 'No, you can stay home.'"

The old man wasn't nearly as recognizable as Woods among the younger crowd and wasn't nearly as profitable a brand name either. But if Palmer wasn't playing in Tiger's league, he remained a most durable figure on Madison Avenue. After all, Arnie was the player most responsible for the $236.7 million in prize money for which PGA Tour professionals had competed in 2003.

"If it wasn't for Arnold," Woods said, "golf wouldn't be as popular as it is now. He's the one who basically brought it to the forefront on TV. If it wasn't for him and his excitement, his flair, the way he played, golf probably would not have had that type of excitement. He was at the forefront and that's why he's the King."

Outside the Augusta National clubhouse, half an hour after his grandfather took the last official stroke of his Masters life, Sam Saunders had a message for the young and naive who figured the sport had always revolved around Woods.

Sam had seen the films. He had admired a figure who, in the grandson's words, "was pretty jacked in those short-sleeve shirts.

"I guarantee you [Palmer] was just as good [as Woods]. He would've given Tiger a run for his money."

The grandfather wasn't about to call out the indomitable Woods. He had no more opponents to fluster, no more flagsticks to attack, no more charges to make.

Arnold Palmer could only choke back the tears as he left the tournament that made him Arnold Palmer.

"It's not fun sometimes," he said, "to know that it is over."

. . .

One year later Jack Nicklaus made it clear he was not going out at the Masters the way Arnold Palmer had. He had no use for a victory lap or a preplanned farewell tour. He had no designs on being propped up for the masses, a golfer with no legitimate chance of making the cut.

Nicklaus had said that loudly and clearly over the years, and it often sounded like a swipe at Palmer, the ultimate legend on parade.

"This is not a celebrity walk-around," Nicklaus would say of the Masters. "This is a golf tournament. It's a major golf championship, and if you're going to play in this championship, you should be competitive and you should be able to compete with who is out there."

Nicklaus wasn't planning on entering the 2005 Masters, not with his golf game a grim shell of its former self. He had played the tournament forty-four times, and he figured that was enough.

But a personal tragedy on March 1 compelled Nicklaus to tee it up at Augusta one more time. His seventeen-month-old grandson, Jake, had fallen into a hot tub and drowned, and the toddler's father, Steve Nicklaus, told his own father, Jack, that he wanted to play golf with him as a way of dealing with the pain.

Jack canceled all of his business meetings and trips to spend time on the course with his son. One day Steve turned to his father and asked, "Can we go to Augusta?" Steve loved the place. He'd caddied for his father in the 1998 Masters, the last time Nicklaus was really Nicklaus.

Father and son made the pre-Masters pilgrimage. They discussed the possibility of Jack competing in the tournament.

"Go play," Steve said. "You want to play anyway."

"I want to play," his father responded, "but I don't have much of a golf game."

"You'll have a golf game," Steve shot back.

And that was that.

Two days before the first round, Nicklaus's voice cracked in his news conference when he spoke of the loss of his grandson. His son and daughter-in-law had been crying themselves to sleep every night. Jake was just starting to develop his personality, just starting to talk. Of the seventeen Nicklaus grandchildren, Jake was the one who spent the most time in his grandfather's arms.

When the conversation moved to golf, Nicklaus didn't guarantee that this would be his final appearance at Augusta. But he did commit to the notion that his last go-around — if this was indeed his last go-around — would not be wrapped in Palmer-esque pomp and circumstance.

"I don't think I need to make a big deal out of whether I'm going to play or not going to play," he said. "My time has passed. I've had my time at Augusta. I don't need a lot of fanfare for that. When I decide to quit, I can't think that that's any big deal, at least certainly not to me. I don't know why it should be to anybody else.

"I think you all know me well enough. I'm not going to come back and clutter up the field if I don't have to."

He'd won the tournament six times, and he knew he couldn't possibly roll a lucky seven. But Nicklaus wanted another taste of 1998, a chance to sneak into the top ten. In his mind that was a realistic vision.

Nicklaus assigned his bag to his son Jackie, the one who caddied for him during the 1986 Masters, the greatest victory of the greatest golfing career. Only there was no magic this time around, just rust. Just a sixty-five-year-old man who would shoot 77 the first round and 76 the second and decide along the way that he couldn't play golf anymore at the Masters.

Not without cluttering up the field. Not without assuming Arnold Palmer's role.

Bad weather had plagued the early rounds and pushed Nicklaus to Saturday, a symbolic concession from the golf gods. The Bear didn't make the cut, but he did make it to the weekend.

The golf gods would demand compensation for this gift. They would force the Masters to send off groups from split tees, leaving Nicklaus to finish on the front side and make his farewell walk up the ninth fairway.

It didn't look right, and it didn't sound right either. The fans weren't sure how to act. They weren't certain this was Nicklaus's last Augusta round, and so the cheers were a few decibels short of resounding.

No, this wasn't Palmer's kind of goodbye, and that's exactly how Jack wanted it. His goal was to bid a dignified farewell and then to fade to black. "Just do it without making a fool out of yourself," Nicklaus said.

But as he approached the ninth green, Nicklaus couldn't prevent his throat from tightening and his eyes from welling up. He stopped, looked into the crowd, and lowered his head while wiping away the tears.

Jackie had been urging his father to score one last birdie for the ages, to go out the Nicklaus way. Jack had a four-footer for his three, but he couldn't get it home.

Nicklaus hugged his playing partner, Jay Haas, who had tears in his own eyes. Jack gave his ball and glove to Jackie and told him, "I don't want to see it on eBay tomorrow."

In the interview room the final formal question Nicklaus fielded as a competitor at the Masters wasn't a question at all. Jack answered it anyway, as definitively as usual. The exchange went like this:

"Arnold said he would like to be an honorary starter somewhere down the line."

"I have no interest in that whatsoever."

Of course he didn't. Nicklaus had as much interest in hitting the ceremonial first tee ball as he did in returning to the brink of bankruptcy.

Not that he didn't love the place with every inch of his champion's heart. Before he hit his second shot on his last hole at his last Masters, Nicklaus wanted to make sure his son knew exactly how he felt.

So he repeated his own father's words right before Charlie Nicklaus was wheeled into surgery in the final weeks of his life. Forty years after the Augusta galleries finally started cheering for Charlie's boy, making the father weep, Jack turned to Jackie and said, "Don't think it ain't been charming."

In July of 2005 Arnold Palmer played the U.S. Senior Open in Kettering, Ohio, if only to attend a dinner at the NCR Country Club honoring Jack Nicklaus's career. It was Arnold's final major championship of any kind, and two rounds in the 80s left him playfully bitching about Jack's decision to skip the event for a fishing trip in Iceland.

"He went fishing and I came out here and sweated my ass off," Palmer said. "That means he's just a little smarter than I am."

Two weeks earlier Nicklaus had made his own final appearance in a major of any kind, and this was one farewell set up to deliver him a Palmer-esque sendoff. Nicklaus was playing the British Open at St. Andrews, where he'd won in 1970 and again in 1978, when the overwhelming reception that greeted him on the seventy-second hole ranked among his most glorious.

There was no confusing Nicklaus's intent this time: the Royal and Ancient had its age limit of sixty-five in place, and it had moved St. Andrews's spot in the Open rotation up a year (it was originally scheduled to host in 2006) in order to get the sixty-five-year-old Nicklaus into the field one more time.

To mark the occasion, the Royal Bank of Scotland unveiled a five-pound note with his likeness, making Nicklaus the only person other than the Queen and the Queen Mother to appear on a Scottish note within his or her lifetime.

A three-time winner of the British Open on Scottish soil, and a seven-time runner-up in the tournament, Nicklaus was revered by the Scots, who were never moved to call him Fat Jack. In the entire United Kingdom, Nicklaus was never the antihero he was in the States, never the villain who shot the good guy right off his white horse.

The Scots had the greatest appreciation for him. Their homeland was the cradle of golf, a place where competitors weren't measured by their personalities or waistlines. The stoic Scots took to the stoic Nicklaus because they'd never seen anyone play their game quite the way he did.

The people of Scotland, Nicklaus said, "took me as one of theirs from the first time I went over there." So on exit they embraced him all over again.

Nicklaus played his last round without a hat because he wanted to take it all in. His goal was to make the cut, make it to Sunday, but by the final hole of his Friday round it was obvious he would come up a couple of shots short. He'd been afraid he'd shoot two rounds in the 80s, and yet he was about to follow up a 75 with an even-par 72.

"I was a golfer again today," Nicklaus would say.

He needed that feeling as much as he needed air to breathe.

Walking up eighteen with Tom Watson and Luke Donald, Nicklaus stopped on the famed Swilcan Bridge, propped up his left foot on the low stone wall, and waved and blew kisses to thousands of saluting fans. He called up his playing partners, their caddies, and his own caddie and son, Steve, to pose with him. They resumed their march to the green, and Watson, the one who had haunted him at Turnberry, was practically sobbing.

Nicklaus ordered him to knock it off. When he was done wiping away his own tears, the Golden Bear settled over the final birdie putt of his Grand Slam life. He had a left-to-right fourteen-footer, and his aim and stroke were entirely moot.

"I knew the hole would move wherever I hit it," Nicklaus said.

At 6:00 p.m. his ball banked in off the right side of the cup. Nicklaus raised his putter skyward. He embraced his wife and children, and then he was gone.

Jack, king of Scots. To those who witnessed both, Nicklaus's farewell at St. Andrews was wrapped in more affection and admiration than Palmer's farewell at the Old Course ten years earlier. The Golden Bear had traveled a long way to outscore the King on this card.

"The British Open," said Bev Norwood, who worked with Palmer at IMG, "was the one place where Jack ended up in the end getting more love than Arnold."

At the end of 2006 Jack Nicklaus would find himself matched against Arnold Palmer one more time. They had gathered at the ChampionsGate course in Orlando to play in the Del Webb Father/Son Challenge, Nicklaus teaming with his son Jackie and Palmer teaming with his grandson Sam.

The organizers of the event had the Normans, Trevinos, Caspers, Floyds, and Singhs among the contestants in the field, but they were no dummies.

Arnie and Jack would be paired together in the 9:30 a.m. slot.

Palmer and Nicklaus high-fived each other on the first tee. Palmer was wearing a tan baseball cap with the same umbrella logo that graced his left collar. Nicklaus was wearing a blue baseball cap carrying the image of the Golden Bear.

"Play well, young fella," the sixty-six-year-old Nicklaus had said.

"You too, old fella," the seventy-seven-year-old Palmer had responded.

"You want me to tee it up for you, Arnie?" Nicklaus asked as Palmer creaked over to prop up his ball.

"That's all right, Jack. You'll get as old as I am someday."

"I hope so."

The fans were already soaking in this vaudeville act, and the routine figured to get better as the day wore on. Three years earlier, at the same tournament, Nicklaus left a putt short and then advised Palmer that the greens were painfully slow. Palmer proceeded to run his attempt four feet past the hole before wheeling on Nicklaus and hissing through a thin smile, "You son of a bitch."

In their sunset years Palmer and Nicklaus had become better friends than they'd ever been. They had come to the same sort of unwritten arrangement that defined the relationship between Ted Williams and Joe DiMaggio.

Just as Williams would call the Yankee Clipper the greatest ballplayer he ever saw, and DiMaggio would call the Splendid Splinter the greatest hitter he ever saw, Palmer would call the Bear the greatest player of all time, and Nicklaus would call the King the greatest ambassador of all time.

"We never agreed on that," Palmer said. But it didn't require a contract or one of those Mark McCormack handshakes.

"At this point in our history," Arnold said, "Jack is the greatest player. And Tiger has a chance to maybe beat that, but he hasn't yet."

Nicklaus usually had his own concession at the ready. "Maybe I was a better player than Arnold," he said, "but Arnold was certainly a more popular player than I was."

Both truths fueled the competitive fires between the two men who combined for 135 tour victories, with Nicklaus accounting for 73 of them.

"He wanted what I had," Nicklaus said, "and I wanted what he had. And we both wanted to be both. Absolutely."

They still wanted to get the best of each other in the worst way. But by December 2006 Palmer and Nicklaus were each making so much money that it was hard for them to be envious of anyone or anything. *Golf Digest* estimated that they were raking in a combined $45 million in annual off-course income.

Nicklaus was still in the lead on the course design front. "Our fees run from $2.5 million [per course] with a percentage of what's going on," Jack said, "down to probably $400,000 to $500,000 when I'm not involved."

The King wasn't touching that $2.5 million figure, yet he was all over the Golden Bear on the endorsement front. Nicklaus did have a series of TV ads Palmer surely envied — the Royal Bank of Scotland commercials that kept running during major championships, the ones reminding Tiger that Nicklaus remains the one to beat.

"But Arnold does a lot more than I do," Jack said. "By choice I've limited mine to a very few."

Arnie and Jack could afford to be selective. They both had their own speeding jets, their own clothing and equipment lines, their own magazines, their own everything. Nicklaus had an Ohio State museum built in his name; Palmer had a USGA museum built in his name.

Nicklaus had his four sons—Jackie, Steve, Gary, and Michael—working in his course design company with his daughter's husband, Bill O'Leary. His children lived near his modified ranch-style house at Lost Tree Village, the same home where they were raised. Off Lake Worth, on three acres of property, Nicklaus kept a boat, grass tennis courts, a putting green, and a nursery for testing different grasses.

Palmer had his daughters help him with his Bay Hill tournament, newly christened the Arnold Palmer Invitational. Arnie lived in his modest condo at Bay Hill during the cold months and in his home at the Latrobe Country Club during the warm ones. He was presiding over the establishment of the Winnie Palmer Hospital for Women and Babies and the Winnie Palmer Nature Reserve, and he was a happily remarried man. He had wed Kathleen "Kit" Gawthrop in a Hawaiian sunset ceremony in January 2005—she could've passed for Winnie's twin sister—and he built her a house on the hill above the white colonial ranch where he and Winnie raised their two girls.

Once a small barn that housed sheep and then a pony for Peg and Amy, Palmer's office sat between his two homes. Measured against the three forbidding towers that made up Golden Bear Plaza off of U.S. Highway 1 in Palm Beach Gardens, the King's office in Latrobe wasn't much bigger than a snack stand.

Arnie didn't travel the world on business nearly as much as Jack; Palmer preferred a simpler existence at home, drinking his Ketel One on the rocks and playing afternoon money games with his Bay Hill friends, a daily contest he called the Shootout. Palmer's problems were locked up and stored away like the frayed brown box marked "Isleworth Lawsuit" that he kept five shelves up in the back of a Latrobe warehouse stuffed with trophies, memorabilia, course design documents, and about ten thousand golf clubs.

Palmer remained a study in humility. During an outing at Latrobe, when Pittsburgh Steelers quarterback Ben Roethlisberger brushed past a group of kids clamoring for his autograph, Palmer said to him, "Hey, Ben, looks like you have a fan club over there. Why don't you go over and say hello?"

"Do I have to?" Roethlisberger responded.

Palmer's look answered that question. No American athlete ever had more time for the fans than Arnold Palmer.

He only wished he could still treat them to a dazzling round of golf. Palmer hated growing old, but he was doing a damn good job of it. On the eve of his pairing with Nicklaus at the Father/Son, Palmer learned that he was about to become a great-grandfather for the first time.

"There is nothing I would love better," Arnold said, "than to hang around and play with that great-grandchild — girl or boy."

He would first play with his grandson Sam against Jack and Jackie Nicklaus at ChampionsGate, right across from the golf courses Arnie and Jack built separately at the Reunion resort. Sam was a promising young player at Clemson; he chose to stay clear of his grandfather's Wake Forest to better make his own way. Jackie was a forty-four-year-old amateur once good enough to have won the prestigious North and South tournament, just as his old man once did.

Team Palmer jumped out to the early lead in the two-man scramble format, as Saunders — a long driver who had his grandfather's habit of hitting out of hazardous places — dropped a birdie putt on the par-five eighth to push his team's score to three under, one shot better than Team Nicklaus. Arnie and Sam stretched their intramural advantage to three shots before Palmer nailed a thirty-five-footer at number eleven, putting Jack and Jackie in a major bind.

Only Jack followed with his own thirty-footer, burning Arnie one more time, and suddenly Team Nicklaus went on a tear. Jack drained a twenty-footer at number fourteen, a five-footer at number fifteen, and a fifteen-footer at number seventeen, with Jackie helping out here and there. Team Nicklaus ripped off seven consecutive birdies to move to nine under entering the final hole, two strokes ahead of Team Palmer.

Under a gray sky pierced by a razor-thin ray of faded, midafternoon sunlight, Jack Nicklaus stood over a thirteen-foot putt on the eighteenth green. Team Palmer was already in for birdie to finish at eight-under 64, and Jackie had already missed an attempt that gave his father the line.

Arnie stood off to the side of the green, exhausted and unable to recall the last time he'd walked eighteen holes. Palmer was standing on a downslope, one foot planted higher than the other, holding his scorecard and staring at his forever rival, Nicklaus. The two of them were sun-beaten, gray, and paunchy; both had lost two or three inches in height to the cruel forces of age. But with fifteen hundred fans surrounding this scene, they still looked every bit like the titans they were.

Nicklaus lowered himself over his ball as silence swept over the green like a warm breeze. He frightened the hole with that familiar glare of his, and then he sent his putt on its way. As the ball broke right and dropped into the hole, Nicklaus lifted that putter toward the clouds in his signature celebration. Team Nicklaus had finished its round with eight consecutive birdies for a score of ten-under 62.

Jack walked straight for Arnie, who was waiting for him in the rough.

"Well," Palmer said, "you putted pretty good coming in. Some things never change."

Arnie and Jack laughed out loud. Nicklaus wrapped his left arm around Palmer's back, and they headed off to the scorer's tent hip to hip as the fans applauded.

Outside the tent Palmer would be found shaking his head. "Jack was really grinding coming in," he said. "He was grinding as much as I've ever seen him grind."

"I've never played any other way," Nicklaus responded. "I played that way all my life. I still love the competition, but I just don't have the golf game to go with it anymore."

Neither did Palmer. He was finally ready to lay down his Wild West game, finally ready to stop barreling into saloons in pursuit of Jack Nicklaus, his most wanted man.

"At some point you need to turn in your guns and holsters," Palmer said. "Even the old cowboys did that."

Nearly half a century after they first met at Dow Finsterwald's day in Athens, Ohio, in 1958, Arnold Palmer and Jack Nicklaus gathered again to honor Finsterwald ninety miles to the northwest.

On May 29, 2007, Dow was the man of the hour at the Memorial Tournament in Dublin. His presenter, Palmer, didn't fly in this time to find an eighteen-year-old wonder boy with a wayward elbow itching to challenge him in a driving contest.

At sixty-seven, Nicklaus wasn't looking for a fight anymore.

"Is there a part of me that loves Arnold Palmer?" he said. "I absolutely love him. I love him for what he's done for me, the things he's stood for in the game, what he's given to the game, the friendship he's shown me, the favors he did.

"We've cried together and we've laughed together, both on the same day. Absolutely I love him, in a man's sort of way."

The two men took a walk together at the Memorial and talked about old times and how things had changed. Nicklaus had become quite the fisherman, for one. Forty-nine years earlier, when Palmer, Nicklaus, and Finsterwald grabbed some rods before the big exhibition at the Athens Country Club and settled over a pond full of catfish, the teenage Nicklaus wouldn't even slide down a hill to untangle his line from the rocks.

He was a suburban boy out of sorts in the country, afraid of the imaginary snakes lurking below.

By May 2007 Nicklaus was—in the estimate of some friends—a better fly fisherman than golfer.

So in a quiet moment at the Memorial, away from the fans who had cheered them and admired them and pitted them against each other, away from the heat and volume shaping the greatest rivalry the game has ever known, Nicklaus asked his friend to join him on a fishing trip.

Just drop everything, Jack told him. Just cancel your appointments and come out and join me on the river.

Five weeks later Arnold Palmer was sitting in a Latrobe office filled with programs to autograph and requests to honor, still pondering the offer of an escape. The Golden Bear wanted him to go fishing?

"Maybe I will," the King said. "Maybe I will."

Acknowledgments

NEITHER JACK NICKLAUS nor Arnold Palmer owed me a thing when I approached them about this book, yet each ultimately granted his time, attention, and trust without condition. Given the likely reaction Tiger Woods and Phil Mickelson would have had if asked to engage in a similar project offering no financial reward or editorial control, I will be eternally grateful to Jack and Arnold for their cooperation and professionalism.

In the course of researching and reporting this book, I had the distinct pleasure of interviewing members of two great American families. On the Nicklaus side, Jack's wife Barbara proved to be the saintly figure she was advertised to be. Jack's sister, Marilyn, was a big help, as was Jack's first-born, Jackie, and Jack's daughter, Nan.

On the Palmer side, Arnold's sister Cheech and brother, Jerry, couldn't have been more neighborly when I visited with them. Arnold's sister Sandy, daughter, Amy, son-in-law Roy Saunders, grandson Sam, and brother-in-law Marty Walzer were all kind enough to grant interviews. Arnold's first-born, Peg, proved to be as candid and thoughtful a person as I've encountered in twenty years of sports journalism; this work wouldn't have been half as interesting without her.

Nicklaus aides Scott Tolley and Andy O'Brien and Palmer aides Doc Giffin and Cori Britt were most gracious and responsive. Alastair Johnston and Bev Norwood were far more accessible and accommodating than their forbidding IMG badges would've suggested.

Palmer friends and associates Darrell Brown, Colonel Joe Curtis, Rita Douglas, Susan Eiseman, Howdy Giles, Bert Harbin, Ed Matko, Nancy McCormack, Mary Moran, and Joe Tito filled in the blanks, as did Nicklaus friends and associates Steve Auch, Kaye Kessler, Robin Obetz, Put Pierman, Harold Riley, Pandel Savic, Bill and Mary Lou Smith, and Ivor Young.

Scores of pro and amateur golfers were willing to share their thoughts on Nicklaus and Palmer. Those who made significant contributions include Tommy Aaron, Paul Azinger, Al Besselink, Paul Bondeson, Billy Casper, John Cook, Lee Elder, Dow Finsterwald, Jack Fleck, Raymond Floyd, Doug Ford, Bob Goalby, Jay Haas, Paul Harney, Hale Irwin, Peter Jacobsen, John Konsek, Billy Maxwell, Gary McCord, Johnny Miller, Bob Murphy, Bobby Nichols, Gary Player, Phil Rodgers, Chi Chi Rodriguez, Bob Rosburg, Mason Rudolph, Doug Sanders, John Schroeder, Charlie Sifford, Mike Souchak, Dave Stockton, Bob Toski, Lee Trevino, Ken Venturi, Lanny Wadkins, Tom Watson, and Ward Wettlaufer.

A number of golfing figures who added to this book passed away after granting interviews. My sincerest condolences to the families of Kermit Blosser, Gay Brewer, John Montgomery, Byron Nelson, and Ed Seay.

I received invaluable aid from numerous officials of golf's tours and governing bodies. Shannon Doody of the USGA and Dave Senko of the Champions Tour assisted me more than they even know. Jeff Adams, Walt Baker, Deane Beman, Michelle Berish, Tracy Dent, Ari Edelman, John Fitzgerald, Tim Finchem, Glen Greenspan, Kevin Hurst, Julius Mason, Brian Robin, Nelson Silverio, Banks Smith, and Tom Sprouse were among the tour, tournament, and club representatives who made my life easier during this process.

Robin Brendle and Leslie Anne Wade of CBS, Paul Melvin of ESPN, and Brian Walker of NBC provided me with tapes and films of golf events out of the goodness of their hearts. Other television officials and broadcasters who enhanced this book include Peter Alliss, Frank Chirkinian, John Derr, Peter Kessler, Verne Lundquist, Jim Nantz, Neal Pilson, Chris Svendsen, and Jack Whitaker.

Among the writers who chipped in, Larry Bohannan, Todd Jones, and Tom Metters did some legwork simply because they're nice guys. Larry Guest and Sid Matthew were terrific resources. The esteemed

Dave Anderson, Dan Foster, Ron Green, Jerry Izenberg, Dan Jenkins, and Edwin Pope graced me with their experience and wisdom. Bucky Albers, Bob Baptist, Jaime Diaz, Steve Elling, John Feinstein, Doug Ferguson, Johnette Howard, Dave Kindred, Marino Parascenzo, Bill Plaschke, Art Spander, George Strode, Bob Verdi, and Sam Weinman helped point me in the right directions.

The distinguished autobiographies of Arnold Palmer (*A Golfer's Life*, with James Dodson) and Jack Nicklaus (*My Story*, with Ken Bowden) were among the many books that provided a vivid roadmap through the two legends' lives, as were the impressive works of Guest (*Arnie*), Izenberg (*The Rivals*), Curt Sampson (*The Masters, The Eternal Summer*), and Howard Sounes (*The Wicked Game*).

I owe a debt of gratitude to the staff of the public library in Augusta, Georgia, and to the good people at the *Record* of New Jersey, including Stephen Borg, Frank Scandale, John Balkun, Dave Rivera, John Rowe, Thomas E. Franklin, Rich Gigli, Chris Bomeisl, Maria Bentivegna, and Nancy Pascarella.

Colleagues and friends who offered much-needed counsel include Harvey Araton, Wayne Coffey, Jack Curry, Tom Daly, Bob Klapisch, Joe Posnanski, Joel Sherman, Mike Vaccaro, Dan Wetzel, Adrian Wojnarowski, and Jay Young

My agent, David Black, only made this project possible by believing in it as much as I did, and I can't thank him enough for that. His trusted aide, David Larabell, lent a reliable hand.

At Houghton Mifflin, Will Vincent, Gretchen Needham, and Megan Wilson handled this project with extreme care, and Barbara Wood showed a true scout's eye in copyediting the manuscript.

Finally, like a ballplayer longing for the perfect coach, a writer can go a lifetime before finding the ideal editor. Susan Canavan was too tough and too damned good at what she does to allow me to settle. I'll be forever indebted to her for that.

Arnold Palmer's Record

NATIONAL TEAMS

    Canada Cup/World Cup: 1960, 1962, 1963, 1964, 1966, 1967
    Ryder Cup: 1961, 1963, 1965, 1967, 1971, 1973
    Ryder Cup Captain: 1963, 1975
    Captain and member of Chrysler Cup Team: 1986, 1987, 1988, 1989, 1990
    The Presidents Cup Captain: 1996
    UBS Warburg Cup Captain and Player: 2001, 2002, 2003

PGA TOUR VICTORIES: 62

1955	Canadian Open
1956	Insurance City Open
	Eastern Open
1957	Houston Open
	Azalea Open Invitational
	Rubber City Open Invitational
	San Diego Open Invitational
1958	St. Petersburg Open Invitational
	Masters Tournament
	Pepsi Championship
1959	Thunderbird Invitational
	Oklahoma City Open Invitational
	West Palm Beach Open Invitational
1960	Palm Springs Desert Golf Classic
	Texas Open Invitational
	Baton Rouge Open Invitational
	Pensacola Open Invitational
	Masters Tournament

	U.S. Open Championship
	Insurance City Open Invitational
	Mobile Sertoma Open Invitational
1961	San Diego Open Invitational
	Phoenix Open Invitational
	Baton Rouge Open Invitational
	Texas Open Invitational
	Western Open
	British Open Championship
1962	Palm Springs Golf Classic
	Phoenix Open Invitational
	Masters Tournament
	Texas Open Invitational
	Tournament of Champions
	Colonial National Invitation
	British Open Championship
	American Golf Classic
1963	Los Angeles Open
	Phoenix Open Invitational
	Pensacola Open Invitational
	Thunderbird Classic Invitational
	Cleveland Open Invitational
	Western Open
	Whitemarsh Open Invitational
1964	Masters Tournament
	Oklahoma City Open Invitational
1965	Tournament of Champions
1966	Los Angeles Open
	Tournament of Champions
	Houston Champions International
1967	Los Angeles Open
	Tucson Open Invitational
	American Golf Classic
	Thunderbird Classic
1968	Bob Hope Desert Classic
	Kemper Open
1969	Heritage Golf Classic
	Danny Thomas–Diplomat Classic
1970	National Four-Ball Championship
1971	Bob Hope Desert Classic
	Florida Citrus Invitational
	Westchester Classic
	National Team Championship
1973	Bob Hope Desert Classic

CHAMPIONS TOUR VICTORIES: 10

1980	PGA Seniors' Championship
1981	U.S. Senior Open
1982	Marlboro Classic
	Denver Post Champions of Golf
1983	Boca Grove Classic
1984	General Foods PGA Seniors' Championship
	Senior Tournament Players Championship
	Quadel Senior Classic
1985	Senior Tournament Players Championship
1988	Crestar Classic

OTHER VICTORIES: 19

1954	U.S. Amateur
1955	Panama Open
	Colombia Open
1960	Canada Cup (with Sam Snead)
1962	Canada Cup (with Sam Snead)
1963	Australian Wills Masters Tournament
	Canada Cup (with Jack Nicklaus)
1964	Piccadilly World Match Play Championship
	Canada Cup (with Jack Nicklaus)
1966	Australian Open
	Canada Cup (with Jack Nicklaus)
	PGA Team Championship (with Jack Nicklaus)
1967	Piccadilly World Match Play Championship
	World Cup (with Jack Nicklaus)
	World Cup (individual)
1971	Lancome Trophy
1975	Spanish Open
	British PGA Championship
1980	Canadian PGA Championship

OTHER SENIOR VICTORIES

1984	Doug Sanders Celebrity Pro-Am
1986	Union Mutual Classic
1990	Senior Skins Game
1992	Senior Skins Game
1993	Senior Skins Game

Information credited to PGA Tour and Champions Tour

Jack Nicklaus's Record

NATIONAL TEAMS

Walker Cup: 1959, 1961
World Amateur Team Championship: 1960
Canada Cup/World Cup: 1963, 1964, 1966, 1967, 1971, 1973
Ryder Cup: 1969, 1971, 1973, 1975, 1977, 1981
Ryder Cup Captain: 1983, 1987
The Presidents Cup Captain: 1998, 2003, 2005, 2007

PGA TOUR VICTORIES: 73

1962	U.S. Open Championship
	Seattle World's Fair Open Invitational
	Portland Open Invitational
1963	Palm Springs Golf Classic
	Masters Tournament
	Tournament of Champions
	PGA Championship
	Sahara Invitational
1964	Phoenix Open Invitational
	Tournament of Champions
	Whitemarsh Open Invitational
	Portland Open Invitational
1965	Masters Tournament
	Memphis Open Invitational
	Thunderbird Classic
	Philadelphia Golf Classic
	Portland Open Invitational

1966	Masters Tournament
	British Open Championship
	Sahara Invitational
1967	Bing Crosby National Pro-Am
	U.S. Open Championship
	Western Open
	Westchester Classic
	Sahara Invitational
1968	Western Open
	American Golf Classic
1969	Andy Williams–San Diego Open Invitational
	Sahara Invitational
	Kaiser International Open Invitational
1970	Byron Nelson Golf Classic
	British Open Championship
	National Four-Ball Championship
1971	PGA Championship
	Tournament of Champions
	Byron Nelson Golf Classic
	National Team Championship
	Walt Disney World Open Invitational
1972	Bing Crosby National Pro-Am
	Doral-Eastern Open
	Masters Tournament
	U.S. Open Championship
	Westchester Classic
	U.S. Professional Match Play Championship
	Walt Disney World Open Invitational
1973	Bing Crosby National Pro-Am
	Greater New Orleans Open
	Tournament of Champions
	Atlanta Classic
	PGA Championship
	Ohio Kings Island Open
	Walt Disney World Golf Classic
1974	Hawaiian Open
	Tournament Players Championship
1975	Doral-Eastern Open
	Sea Pines Heritage Classic
	Masters Tournament
	PGA Championship
	World Open Golf Championship
1976	Tournament Players Championship
	World Series of Golf

1977	Jackie Gleason Inverrary Classic
	MONY Tournament of Champions
	Memorial Tournament
1978	Jackie Gleason Inverrary Classic
	Tournament Players Championship
	British Open Championship
	IVB-Philadelphia Golf Classic
1980	U.S. Open Championship
	PGA Championship
1982	Colonial National Invitation
1984	Memorial Tournament
1986	Masters Tournament

CHAMPIONS TOUR VICTORIES: 10

1990	The Tradition at Desert Mountain
	Mazda Senior Tournament Players Championship
1991	The Tradition at Desert Mountain
	PGA Seniors' Championship
	U.S. Senior Open
1993	U.S. Senior Open
1994	Mercedes Championship
1995	The Tradition
1996	GTE Suncoast Classic
	The Tradition

OTHER VICTORIES: 25

1959	U.S. Amateur
1961	U.S. Amateur
	NCAA Championship (individual)
1962	World Series of Golf
1963	World Series of Golf
	Canada Cup (with Arnold Palmer)
	Canada Cup (individual)
1964	Australian Open
	Canada Cup (with Arnold Palmer)
	Canada Cup (individual)
1966	PGA Team Championship (with Arnold Palmer)
	Canada Cup (with Arnold Palmer)
1967	World Series of Golf
	World Cup (with Arnold Palmer)
1968	Australian Open
1970	World Series of Golf
	Piccadilly World Match Play Championship

1971	Australian Open
	World Cup (with Lee Trevino)
	World Cup (individual)
1973	Canada Cup/World Cup (with Johnny Miller)
1975	Australian Open
1976	Australian Open
1978	Australian Open
1983	Chrysler Team Championship (with Johnny Miller)

Information credited to PGA Tour and Champions Tour

Notes

INTRODUCTION

Author's Interviews

Frank Chirkinian, Johnny Miller, Jack Nicklaus, Arnold Palmer, Jerry Palmer, Gary Player, Peg Palmer Wears, Tiger Woods.

Other Sources

http://www.ArnoldPalmer.com, "Miller Says Beating Palmer Tougher Than Tiger," June 13, 2007.

PROLOGUE

Author's Interviews

Kermit Blosser, Dow Finsterwald, Tad Grover, Kevin Hurst, Babe Lichardus, Tom Metters, Jack Nicklaus, Arnold Palmer, Roger Pedigo, Dow Reichley, Bill Santor, Alice Saunders, Larry Snyder, Jean Sprague, George Strode, Fred Swearingen.

Other Sources

George Strode, "Palmer Shatters Country Club Course Record with 62," *Athens Messenger*, September 26, 1958.

1. POOR BOY

Author's Interviews

Don January, Ed Matko, Mary Moran, Arnold Palmer, Jerry Palmer, Steve Pipoly, Sandy Palmer Sarni, Lois Jean Palmer Tilley, Joe Tito, Bob Toski, Peg Palmer Wears.

Other Sources

Death Notices, *Washington Post*, October 26, 1983.

Gerry Dulac, "Winning the U.S. Amateur Championship Can Change a Golfer's Life Forever, As It Did for Arnold Palmer 49 Years Ago," *Pittsburgh Post-Gazette*, August 17, 2003.

ESPN, *ESPN SportsCentury,* profile of Arnold Palmer, July 18, 2000.

"For Love & Money," *Time,* May 2, 1960.

"Go Arnie Go! The History of Arnie's Army," http://www.ArnoldPalmer.com.

Thomas Hauser, *Arnold Palmer: A Personal Journey* (San Francisco: Collins Publishers, 1994).

Richard Johnson, "Meet the New King: 50 Years Ago Arnold Palmer Began His March to Glory," *Golf Magazine,* September 2004.

Mark McCormack, *Arnie: The Evolution of a Legend* (New York: Simon & Schuster, 1967).

Arnold Palmer: Golf's Heart and Soul, Golf Channel, 1998.

Arnold Palmer, *A Golfer's Life,* with James Dodson (New York: Ballantine Books, 1999).

Arnold Palmer, *Arnold Palmer Memories, Stories, and Memorabilia* (New York: Stewart, Tabori & Chang, 2004).

Arnold Palmer, *Go for Broke,* with William Barry Furlong (New York: Simon & Schuster, 1973).

Arnold Palmer, Orlando ChampionsGate press conference, December 1, 2006.

Arnold Palmer, SEI Pennsylvania Classic press conference, September 14, 2000.

"Tough & Tiring," *Time,* September 6, 1954.

USGA, *Heroes of the Game* (Warner Home Video, 1995).

USGA, U.S. Amateur Championship newsreel, 1954.

Lincoln A. Werden, "Test Goes 36 Holes," *New York Times,* August 29, 1954.

2. STARDOM

Author's Interviews

John Derr, Susan Eiseman, Doug Ford, Ron Green Sr., Dan Jenkins, Sid Matthew, Arnold Palmer, Gary Player, Ken Venturi.

Other Sources

Mercer Bailey, Associated Press, "'I'm Truly Sorry It Had to Be This Way,' Palmer Tells Venturi," *Augusta Chronicle,* April 12, 1960.

CBS telecast, 1958 Masters.

CBS telecast, 1960 Masters.

Johnny Hendrix, "The Long Wait," *Augusta Chronicle,* April 7, 1958.

Johnny Hendrix, "Venturi Wanted Masters More than Any Tournament," *Augusta Chronicle,* April 11, 1960.

Curt Sampson, *The Masters: Golf, Money, and Power in Augusta, Georgia* (New York: Villard, 1998).

Howard Sounes, *The Wicked Game: Arnold Palmer, Jack Nicklaus, Tiger Woods, and the Business of Modern Golf* (New York: Perennial Currents, HarperCollins, 2005).

David Sowell, *The Masters: A Hole-by-Hole History of America's Golf Classic* (Washington, DC: Brassey's, 2003).

Television Bureau of Advertising, television households, http://www.tvb.org, Nielsen Media Research-NTI.

Lincoln A. Werden, "Palmer's 284 Beats Ford and Hawkins by a Stroke in Masters Golf," *New York Times,* April 7, 1958.

Herbert Warren Wind, "Gasps for a Fabulous Finish," *Sports Illustrated,* April 18, 1960.

3. RICH KID

Author's Interviews

Paul Bondeson, Marilyn Nicklaus Hutchinson, Bob Jones IV, Kaye Kessler, Dom Lepore, Barbara Nicklaus, Jack Nicklaus, Robin Obetz, Harold Riley, Bill Santor, Pandel Savic, Jay Weitzel, Ward Wettlaufer, Stan Ziobrowski.

Other Sources

Steve Auch, Nicklaus Museum at Ohio State University, Nicklaus hospital birth certificate.

Tom Callahan, "Nine Holes before Dinner — Our Gaze Will Follow Nicklaus This Summer, and We Will Feel More than Just a Passage of Time," *Golf Digest,* February 1, 2000.

Craig Dolch, "From Cub to Golden Bear," *Palm Beach Post,* May 24, 2000.

ESPN, *ESPN SportsCentury,* profile of Jack Nicklaus, July 22, 2000.

John Meyer, "Nicklaus Meets Up with Old Friend," *Rocky Mountain News,* August 16, 1995.

Jack Nicklaus, *The Greatest Game of All: My Life in Golf,* with Herbert Warren Wind (London: Hodder & Stoughton, 1969).

Jack Nicklaus, Memorial Tournament press conference, May 30, 2006.

Jack Nicklaus, *My Story,* with Ken Bowden (New York: Fireside, Simon & Schuster, 1997).

Jack Nicklaus, Orlando ChampionsGate press conference, December 1, 2006.

Jack Nicklaus, Presidents Cup press conference, April 13, 2005.

"The Prodigious Prodigy," *Time,* June 29, 1962.

Leonard Shapiro, "Jack Nicklaus; Still Golden After All These Years," *Washington Post,* June 11, 1997.

Mark Shaw, *Nicklaus* (Dallas, TX: Taylor Publishing, 1997).

Sounes, *The Wicked Game.*

USGA, *Heroes of the Game.*

4. CHERRY HILLS

Author's Interviews

Deane Beman, Colonel Joe Curtis, Jack Fleck, Paul Harney, Dan Jenkins, John Konsek, Nancy McCormack, Jack Nicklaus, Robin Obetz, Arnold Palmer, Bob Rosburg, Mike Souchak, Marty Walzer, Ward Wettlaufer.

Other Sources

Colorado Historical Society, U.S. Open videotape, 1960.

George S. May International Company, profile of founder, http://www.georgesmay.com.

Palmer, *A Golfer's Life.*

"The Prodigious Prodigy," *Time.*

Curt Sampson, *The Eternal Summer* (Dallas, TX: Taylor Publishing, 1992).

Television Bureau of Advertising/Nielsen Media Research-NTI.

USGA, *Heroes of the Game.*

USGA, U.S. Open newsreel, 1960.

5. OAKMONT

Author's Interviews

Gay Brewer, Fred Bugna, John Derr, Dow Finsterwald, John Fitzgerald, John Garbo, Jerry Izenberg, Kaye Kessler, Billy Maxwell, Bobby Nichols, Barbara Nicklaus, Jack Nicklaus, Arnold Palmer, Gary Player, Bob Rosburg, Sandy Palmer Sarni, Alice Saunders, Banks Smith, Lois Jean Palmer Tilley, Joe Torre, Jay Weitzel, John Zimmers.

Other Sources

Steve Auch, Jack Nicklaus Museum at Ohio State University, Nicklaus letter to Joe Dey, Nicklaus first pro paycheck.

Charles Bartlett, "Nicklaus Ties Palmer in Open at 283," *Chicago Tribune,* June 17, 1962.

Charles Curtis, "Nicklaus Tabbed by Palmer in Open," *Los Angeles Times,* June 14, 1962.

Bob Drum, "Champ Littler Lets His Educated Clubs Do All the Talking," *Pittsburgh Press,* June 15, 1962.

Bob Drum, "Jack the Giant Kills Off Arnie," *Pittsburgh Press,* June 18, 1962.

Bob Drum, "Three-Putt Greens Called No. 1 Factor in Palmer Defeat," *Pittsburgh Press,* June 18, 1962.

ESPN, *ESPN SportsCentury* profile of Jack Nicklaus, Tom Weiskopf interview, 2000.

Maury Fitzgerald, "Palmer Favored As Open Starts," *Washington Post,* June 14, 1962.

Bob Harig, "Success Drives, Frustrates Nicklaus," *St. Petersburg Times,* June 15, 1992.

Jerry Izenberg, *The Rivals* (New York: Holt, Rinehart and Winston, 1968).

Arnold Palmer, Masters press conference, April 11, 2002.

Marino Parascenzo, "Shot That Haunts Arnie Still Tough," *Pittsburgh Post-Gazette,* June 13, 1994.

"The Prodigious Prodigy," *Time.*

USGA, U.S. Open highlight film, 1962.

United Press International, "Arnold Fears 'That Dude,'" *Washington Post,* June 17, 1962.

Lincoln A. Werden, "Nicklaus Shoots a 69, Palmer a 71 to Go into Golf Tie," *New York Times,* June 17, 1962.

6. AUGUSTA

Author's Interviews

Frank Chirkinian, Dow Finsterwald, Bob Goalby, Bert Harbin, Nancy McCormack, Jack Nicklaus, Arnold Palmer, Chi Chi Rodriguez, Mike Souchak, Ken Venturi, Peg Palmer Wears.

Other Sources

Associated Press, "Arnie's Hats Get Poohs from Winnie," *Chicago Tribune*, April 11, 1964.

CBS telecasts, 1963, 1964 Masters.

Will Grimsley, Associated Press, "Big Three Co-Favored," *Augusta Chronicle*, April 3, 1963.

Will Grimsley, Associated Press, "I Want to Win Them All," *Augusta Chronicle*, April 9, 1963.

Johnny Hendrix, "Nicklaus Splashes into Masters Lead," *Augusta Chronicle*, April 7, 1963.

Alastair J. Johnston, *Vardon to Woods: A Pictorial History of Golfers in Advertising* (Cleveland: Alastair J. Johnston, 1999).

"Loser Still No. 1, Says the Winner," *New York Times*, June 18, 1962.

Lloyd Shearer, "Mark McCormack: He Makes Golfers Rich," *Parade*, June 16, 1963.

United Press International, "Hogan's Tribute: Palmer Is Great," *New York Times*, April 13, 1964.

United Press International, "Talk of Decline Dogged Palmer," *New York Times*, April 13, 1964.

Lincoln A. Werden, "Palmer Gets New Supply of Inc.," *New York Times*, February 13, 1964.

Herbert Warren Wind, "Young Jack the Mighty Master," *Sports Illustrated*, April 15, 1963.

7. BACK TO BACK

Author's Interviews

Tommy Aaron, Ernie Accorsi, Miller Barber, Deane Beman, Frank Chirkinian, Ray DeBarge, John Derr, Raymond Floyd, Tommy Jacobs, Nancy McCormack, Bobby Nichols, Barbara Nicklaus, Jack Nicklaus, Arnold Palmer, Gary Player, Mason Rudolph, Pandel Savic, Lois Jean Palmer Tilley, Ivor Young.

Other Sources

Associated Press, "Masters Tourney Is Mecca of Golf," *New York Times*, April 3, 1966.

Associated Press, "Nicklaus, on 276, Takes Cup Golf," *New York Times*, December 7, 1964.

CBS, "RBS Presents Jack and Arnie: Talkin' Golf," *CBS Sports Spectacular*, 2006.

CBS telecasts, 1965, 1966 Masters.

Al Ludwick, "Ben Joins 'Army' Just for a Day," *Augusta Herald*, April 10, 1966.

McCormack, *Arnie: The Evolution of a Legend*.

Dudley Martin, "'Beat Jack,' and Gary Goes at It," *Augusta Herald,* April 3, 1966.

Nicklaus, *My Story.*

United Press International, "Palmer, Nicklaus Renew Golf Money Feud Today," *Washington Post,* November 18, 1964.

United Press International, "Title Settled by $81.13," *Washington Post,* November 24, 1964.

8. MASTER OF DISASTER

Author's Interviews

Billy Casper, Rita Douglas, Bob Goalby, Nancy McCormack, Jack Nicklaus, Arnold Palmer, Chi Chi Rodriguez, Art Spander, Lois Jean Palmer Tilley, Bob Toski.

Other Sources

ABC telecast, 1966 U.S. Open.

Associated Press, "Jack Nicklaus Fuming about USGA Speed-Up," *Chicago Tribune,* June 19, 1966.

Rick Reilly, "Seven Ahead, Nine to Go, and Then," *Sports Illustrated,* June 15, 1987.

USGA, U.S. Open highlight film, 1966.

9. BALTUSROL

Author's Interviews

Ernie Accorsi, Deane Beman, Bob Charles, Marty Fleckman, Nancy McCormack, Barbara Nicklaus, Jack Nicklaus, Put Pierman, Ken Venturi.

Other Sources

ABC telecast, 1967 U.S. Open.

Walter Bingham, "Hold On, Jack; A Guy Named Arnie Made Jack Nicklaus's Rise to the Top Unlike Anything Tiger Woods Will Ever Encounter," *Sports Illustrated,* June 9, 1997.

"Father's Day Win Old Stuff for Nicklaus," *Los Angeles Times,* June 19, 1967.

Hauser, *Arnold Palmer: A Personal Journey.*

Nicklaus, Memorial Tournament press conference, May 30, 2006.

Nicklaus, *My Story.*

Palmer, *Go for Broke.*

Bill Shirley, "Nicklaus (275) Wins Open by 4 Strokes," *Los Angeles Times,* June 19, 1967.

USGA, U.S. Open highlight film, 1967.

Lincoln A. Werden, "Nicklaus Shoots 8-Under-Par 62 in Tune-Up for U.S. Open Starting Today," *New York Times,* June 15, 1967.

Lincoln A. Werden, "Palmer Cards 68 for 137 and Takes One-Stroke Lead in Open at Baltusrol," *New York Times,* June 17, 1967.

10. TRANSFORMATION

Author's Interviews

Frank Chirkinian, Marilyn Nicklaus Hutchinson, Jerry Izenberg, Byron Nelson, Barbara Nicklaus, Jack Nicklaus, Mort Olman, Put Pierman, Phil Rodgers, Doug Sanders, John Schroeder, Charlie Sifford, Peg Palmer Wears, Ivor Young.

Other Sources

Associated Press, "Nicklaus Winner, but Veep Calls Arnie," *Los Angeles Times,* May 4, 1970.

Associated Press, "Palmer, Swamped by Remedies from His Army, Has Own Plan to Cure Slump," *New York Times,* June 8, 1969.

CBS, "RBS Presents Jack and Arnie: Talkin' Golf."

Izenberg, *The Rivals.*

Nicklaus, Memorial Tournament press conference, May 30, 2006.

11. PEBBLE BEACH

Author's Interviews

John Derr, Dow Finsterwald, Nancy McCormack, Barbara Nicklaus, Jack Nicklaus, Sandy Palmer Sarni, Bill Stathakaros, Dave Stockton, Lois Jean Palmer Tilley, Joe Tito, Lee Trevino.

Other Sources

ABC telecast, 1972 U.S. Open.

New York Times, "Nicklaus Rebuts Palmer's Charge," June 20, 1971.

United Press International, "Trevino Practices in Hospital, Plans Open Title Defense," *New York Times,* June 12, 1972.

USGA, U.S. Open highlight film, 1972.

Lincoln A. Werden, "Palmer Critical of Slow Play by Nicklaus," *New York Times,* June 19, 1971.

Lincoln A. Werden, "Palmer to Buy the Course Where He Learned to Play," *New York Times,* August 8, 1971.

12. LAST DANCE

Author's Interviews

Don January, Nancy McCormack, Todd McCormack, Jack Nicklaus, Arnold Palmer, Put Pierman, Edwin Pope, Lee Trevino, Lanny Wadkins, Peg Palmer Wears.

Other Sources

Associated Press, "Glasses Give Palmer 'Frightening' Vision," *Washington Post,* February 21, 1973.

Associated Press, "Yep, Arnie Finally Wins One," *Chicago Tribune,* February 12, 1973.

Braven Dyer, "Palmer Grabs 5th Crown in the Rain," *Desert Sun,* February 12, 1973.

Shav Glick, "Arnie Marches Troops Through Mud, Wins Day," *Los Angeles Times,* February 12, 1973.

Shirley Povich, "Greatest Golfer Grows Nice and Rich," *Washington Post,* December 3, 1972.

Bill Shirley, "Golf's Top 5? Nicklaus Can Name Only 3," *Los Angeles Times,* January 13, 1973.

13. OAKMONT REVISITED

Author's Interviews

Dave Anderson, Miller Barber, Billy Casper, John Fitzgerald, Johnny Miller, Jack Nicklaus, Bev Norwood, Arnold Palmer.

Other Sources

ABC telecast, 1973 U.S. Open.

Bill Christine, "Schlee Schleppes Around with 3 Drives on No. 1," *Pittsburgh Post-Gazette,* June 18, 1973.

Bill Christine, " 'They're 10 Shots Better' — Billy Casper: Nicklaus, Weiskopf . . . So Why Show Up?" *Pittsburgh Post-Gazette,* June 12, 1973.

Johnny Miller, U.S. Open press conference, June 12, 2007.

Marino Parascenzo, "Johnny Replaces Gary; A New Player on Board," *Pittsburgh Post-Gazette,* June 18, 1973.

Tom Tomashek, "Jack Declines Spot in Ranks of Arnie's Army," *Chicago Tribune,* February 18, 1973.

USGA, U.S. Open highlight film, 1973.

Lincoln A. Werden, "To Palmer, There's Only One Oakmont," *New York Times,* May 31, 1973.

14. GAMESMANSHIP

Author's Interviews

Doc Giffin, Hale Irwin, Johnny Miller, Bob Murphy, Jack Nicklaus, Sandy Palmer Sarni.

Other Sources

Bob Addie, "Jack Nicklaus' Empire Is at $200 Million, and Bearish," *Washington Post,* December 16, 1975.

Dave Anderson, "The P. T. Barnum Pairing," *New York Times,* April 13, 1975.

Dave Anderson, " 'The Record Book' Looks to the Slam," *New York Times,* April 15, 1975.

Tom Callahan, *The Bases Were Loaded (and So Was I)* (New York: Crown Publishers, 2004).

CBS telecast, 1975 Masters.

Al Corn, " 'Army, Pack' Create Problem for Heroes," *Augusta Chronicle-Herald,* April 13, 1975.

Jack Nicklaus, Senior PGA Championship press conference, June 5, 2002.

Edwin Pope, "Jack Beats Arnie, but Gives up Lead to Tom and Johnny," *Augusta Chronicle-Herald,* April 13, 1975.

Gerald Strine, "Murphy Fires 68 to Snare Gleason Golf," *Washington Post,* March 3, 1975.

United Press International, "Nicklaus Captures Lead in Gleason Golf with 66," *Chicago Tribune,* March 2, 1975.

15. REUNION

Author's Interviews

Colonel Joe Curtis, Bob Jones IV, Johnny Miller, Jack Nicklaus, Jack Nicklaus Jr., Arnold Palmer, Tom Watson.

Other Sources

ABC telecast, 1980 U.S. Open.

Dave Anderson, "'Jack Is Back, Jack Is Back,'" *New York Times,* June 16, 1980.

Thomas Boswell, "Pairing of Masters Elicits Devotion," *Washington Post,* April 14, 1980.

Larry Guest, *Arnie: Inside the Legend* (Nashville, TN: Cumberland House Publishers, 1993).

Al Ludwick, "It Was Nostalgic Time for Nicklaus, Palmer," *Augusta Chronicle,* April 14, 1980.

Jack Nicklaus, U.S. Open press conference, June 16, 1996.

John S. Radosta, "Nicklaus, in Full Swing at 40, Cards a 69 in Crosby Golf," *New York Times,* February 1, 1980.

USGA, *1980 U.S. Open,* highlight film.

16. SEPARATION

Author's Interviews

Doc Giffin, Howdy Giles, Jay Haas, Alastair Johnston, Gary Koch, Barbara Nicklaus, Jack Nicklaus, Nan Nicklaus O'Leary, Arnold Palmer, Neal Pilson, Tom Watson, Jack Whitaker.

Other Sources

ABC telecast, 1982 U.S. Open.

Jaime Diaz, "In Bear Market, Nicklaus Is Bullish on His Business," *New York Times,* February 2, 1992.

Florida International University, "Birth of the University," http://www.FIU.edu.

John S. Radosta, "Bogeys Derail Palmer," *New York Times,* January 17, 1983.

Sounes, *The Wicked Game.*

USGA, *1982 U.S. Open,* highlight film.

Barnet D. Wolf and Ron Carter, "From the Brink of Bankruptcy," *Columbus Dispatch,* May 24, 1998.

17. KING FOR A DAY

Author's Interviews

Dave Anderson, Marilyn Nicklaus Hutchinson, Sandy Lyle, Verne Lundquist, Gary McCord, John Montgomery, Jack Nicklaus, Jack Nicklaus Jr., Nan Nicklaus

O'Leary, Neal Pilson, Edwin Pope, Pandel Savic, Mary Lou Smith, the Rev. Dr. William E. Smith, Art Spander, Ken Venturi.

Other Sources

CBS telecast, 1986 Masters.

Ernie Els, Bay Hill Invitational press conference, March 15, 2006.

Jack Nicklaus, Masters anniversary conference call, March 14, 2006.

Alan Tays, "Nicklaus' Finest Hour Was a Great Way to Go Out," *Palm Beach Post,* April 6, 2006.

Wright Thompson, "A Golden Moment; Nicklaus Enthralled the Nation by Winning the Masters 20 Years Ago, but There's Even More to the Story," *Kansas City Star,* April 9, 2006.

Roger Whiddon, "Jack's Back, Roars out of Pack with 65 for Sixth Masters Title," *Augusta Chronicle,* April 14, 1986.

18. COLD WAR

Author's Interviews

Paul Azinger, Larry Guest, Alastair Johnston, Nancy McCormack, Johnny Miller, Jack Nicklaus, Bev Norwood, Arnold Palmer, Put Pierman, Chi Chi Rodriguez, Amy Palmer Saunders, Ed Seay, Lois Jean Palmer Tilley, Joe Tito.

Other Sources

Guest, *Arnie: Inside the Legend.*

"Roll, Jordan, Roll," *Forbes,* November 23, 1992.

19. HONOREE

Author's Interviews

Darrell Brown, Larry Guest, Peter Jacobsen, Lee Janzen, Alastair Johnston, John Montgomery, Barbara Nicklaus, Jack Nicklaus, Arnold Palmer, Put Pierman, Lois Jean Palmer Tilley.

Other Sources

ESPN telecast, 1994 U.S. Open.

Bob Green, Associated Press, "A Day for Walking with the Gods of Golf," *Los Angeles Times,* June 6, 1993.

Guest, *Arnie: Inside the Legend.*

Arnold Palmer, U.S. Open press conference, June 17, 1994.

Arnold Palmer, Jack Nicklaus, Bay Hill press conference, March 17, 1993.

George Strode, "Praise Flows for Palmer," *Columbus Dispatch,* June 3, 1993.

Len Ziehm, "Palmer Has His Day; So Might Norman," *Chicago Sun-Times,* June 3, 1993.

20. WINNIE AND BARBARA

Author's Interviews

Al Besselink, David Chapman, Mary Moran, Barbara Nicklaus, Jack Nicklaus, Arnold Palmer, Jerry Palmer, Amy Palmer Saunders, Pandel Savic, Lois Jean

Palmer Tilley, Bob Toski, Marty Walzer, Tom Watson, Peg Palmer Wears, Ivor Young.

Other Sources

Steve Auch, Jack Nicklaus Museum at Ohio State University, Barbara Bash homecoming queen ballot.

Ron Green Jr., "Tiger Leaves Nicklaus Spewing Superlatives," *Charlotte Observer,* April 11, 1996.

Randall Lane, "The Golden Bull and the Golden Bear," *Forbes,* December 19, 1994.

Jack Nicklaus, Senior PGA Championship press conference, May 23, 2001.

Sounes, *The Wicked Game.*

Bob Verdi, " 'I Had My Century'— His Most Personal Interview: Jack Nicklaus on Life, Love, Beer, Business — and Winning the Big Ones," *Golf Digest,* July 1, 2000.

21. THE KING AND THE BEAR

Author's Interviews

Louie Bartoletti, Ed Bignon, Kurt Bowman, Tim Finchem, Gina Hull, Jason Kubel, Steve Lafrance, Bob Murphy, Jack Nicklaus, Arnold Palmer, Ed Seay, Wayne Sloan.

Other Sources

ESPN, "2001 Palmer vs. Nicklaus Exhibition," *Shell's Wonderful World of Golf,* March 26, 2001.

Michael Patrick Shiels, "Palmer Shoots His Age, Finishes Ahead of Nicklaus," http://www.PGATour.com, March 27, 2001.

Summary Notice, Golden Bear Inc. lawsuit, United States District Court, Southern District of Florida.

Hunki Yun, "Nicklaus, Palmer an Odd Couple," *Orlando Sentinel,* December 12, 1999.

22. CEREMONIAL

Author's Interviews

Jack Nicklaus, Jack Nicklaus Jr., Gary Player, Tiger Woods.

Other Sources

Jerry Potter, "Nicklaus to Play On after Death of Mother," *USA Today,* August 17, 2000.

23. OPPORTUNITY LOST

Author's Interviews

Lee Elder, Tim Finchem, John Montgomery, Jack Nicklaus, Gary Player, Charlie Sifford, Peg Palmer Wears.

Other Sources

Don Harrison, interview with Jack Nicklaus, the (Vancouver) *Province,* July 1994.

Hootie Johnson, Jack Nicklaus, Arnold Palmer, Tiger Woods, Masters press conferences, April 9, 2003.

Joan Mazzolini, interview with Hall Thompson, *Birmingham Post-Herald,* June 20, 1990.

Jack Nicklaus, Northville Long Island Classic press conference, July 27, 1994.

Palmer, Masters press conference, April 11, 2002.

Guy Yocum, "50 Greatest Golfers of All Time: And What They Taught Us," *Golf Digest,* July 1, 2000.

24. LAST ROUNDS

Author's Interviews

Alastair Johnston, Jack Nicklaus, Bev Norwood, Arnold Palmer, Joe Torre, Peg Palmer Wears.

Other Sources

Kurt Badenhausen, "King of the Court," *Forbes,* July 5, 2004.

Doug Ferguson, Associated Press, "A Moving Day at the Masters," http://www.Golf.com, April 9, 2004.

Brian Murphy, "King Says Goodbye; Palmer Finishes His 50th; Rose Still in Lead," *San Francisco Chronicle,* April 10, 2004.

Jack Nicklaus, British Open conference call, June 31, 2005.

Jack Nicklaus, Masters press conference, April 5, 2005.

Jack Nicklaus, Masters press conference, April 7, 2004.

Jack Nicklaus, Masters press conference, April 9, 2005.

Arnold Palmer, Masters press conference, April 9, 2004.

Palmer, Orlando ChampionsGate press conference, December 1, 2006.

Arnold Palmer, U.S. Senior Open press conference, July 29, 2005.

Ron Sirak, "Profit Sharing: The Golf Digest 50 Are Not Only Making Millions, They're Spreading the Riches," February 1, 2007.

Tiger Woods, Masters press conference, April 6, 2004.

Bibliography

BOOKS

Buckley, James Jr., and David Fischer. *Greatest Sports Rivalries.* New York: Barnes & Noble Books, 2005.

Callahan, Tom. *The Bases Were Loaded (and So Was I).* New York: Crown Publishers, 2004.

Gleason, Dan. *The Great, the Grand and the Also-Ran: Rabbits and Champions on the Pro Golf Tour.* New York: Random House, 1976.

Graubart, Julian I. *Golf's Greatest Championship: The 1960 U.S. Open.* New York: Donald I. Fine Books, 1997.

Guest, Larry. *Arnie: Inside the Legend.* Nashville, TN: Cumberland House Publishers, 1993.

Hauser, Thomas. *Arnold Palmer: A Personal Journey.* San Francisco: Collins Publishers, 1994.

Izenberg, Jerry. *The Rivals.* New York: Holt, Rinehart and Winston, 1968.

McCormack, Mark. *Arnie: The Evolution of a Legend.* New York: Simon & Schuster, 1967.

Nicklaus, Jack. *The Greatest Game of All: My Life in Golf.* With Herbert Warren Wind. London: Hodder & Stoughton, 1969.

———. *My Story.* With Ken Bowden. New York: Fireside, Simon & Schuster, 1997.

Palmer, Arnold. *Arnold Palmer Memories, Stories, and Memorabilia.* New York: Stewart, Tabori & Chang, 2004.

———. *Go for Broke.* With William Barry Furlong. New York: Simon & Schuster, 1973.

———. *A Golfer's Life.* With James Dodson. New York: Ballantine Books, 1999.

———. *My Game and Yours.* New York: Simon & Schuster, 1963.

Parascenzo, Marino. *Oakmont: 100 Years.* Oakmont, PA: Fownes Foundation, 2003.

Sampson, Curt. *The Eternal Summer.* Dallas, TX: Taylor Publishing, 1992.

——. *The Masters: Golf, Money, and Power in Augusta, Georgia.* New York: Villard, 1998.

Shaw, Mark. *Nicklaus.* Dallas, TX: Taylor Publishing, 1997.

Shedloski, David S. *Golden Twilight: Jack Nicklaus in His Final Championship Season.* Chelsea, MI: Sleeping Bear Press, 2001.

Sommers, Robert. *The U.S. Open: Golf's Ultimate Challenge.* New York: Atheneum, 1987.

Sounes, Howard. *The Wicked Game: Arnold Palmer, Jack Nicklaus, Tiger Woods, and the Business of Modern Golf.* New York: Perennial Currents, HarperCollins, 2005.

Sowell, David. *The Masters: A Hole-by-Hole History of America's Golf Classic.* Washington, DC: Brassey's, 2003.

BROADCASTS/VIDEOS

ABC. U.S. Open broadcasts, 1966, 1967, 1972, 1973, 1980, 1982.

CBS. Masters broadcasts, 1958, 1960, 1963, 1964, 1965, 1966, 1986.

CBS. "RBS Presents Jack and Arnie: Talkin' Golf." *CBS Sports Spectacular,* 2006.

Colorado Historical Society. U.S. Open videotape, 1960.

ESPN. *ESPN SportsCentury* profile, Arnold Palmer. July 18, 2000.

ESPN. *ESPN SportsCentury* profile, Jack Nicklaus, July 22, 2000.

ESPN. *Shell's Wonderful World of Golf.* 2001 Palmer versus Nicklaus exhibition.

ESPN. U.S. Open broadcast, 1994.

Golf Channel film. *Arnold Palmer: Golf's Heart and Soul.* 1998.

NBC. U.S. Open highlights, 1960, 1962.

USGA. *Heroes of the Game.* Warner Home Video, 1995.

USGA. U.S. Amateur newsreel, 1954.

USGA. U.S. Open highlight films, 1962, 1967, 1972, 1973, 1980, 1982.

USGA. U.S. Open newsreel, 1960.

INTERVIEWS

The author conducted interviews with the following people between December 14, 2005, and September 7, 2007.

Tommy Aaron	Al Besselink	Bob Charles
Ernie Accorsi	Ed Bignon	Frank Chirkinian
Peter Alliss	Kermit Blosser	Charles Coody
Dave Anderson	Paul Bondeson	John Cook
Billy Andrade	Kurt Bowman	Bob Cousy
Paul Azinger	Gay Brewer	Colonel Joe Curtis
Bob Baptist	Darrell Brown	Ray DeBarge
Miller Barber	Fred Bugna	Jim Dent
Louie Bartoletti	Billy Casper	John Derr
Deane Beman	David Chapman	Jaime Diaz

Rita Douglas
Pete Dye
Susan Eiseman
Lee Elder
Brad Faxon
John Feinstein
Tim Finchem
Dow Finsterwald
John Fitzgerald
Jack Fleck
Marty Fleckman
Raymond Floyd
Doug Ford
Dan Foster
Fred Funk
John Garbo
Doc Giffin
Howdy Giles
Bob Goalby
Ron Green Sr.
Tad Grover
Larry Guest
Jay Haas
Bert Harbin
Paul Harney
Bill Hook
Gina Hull
Kevin Hurst
Marilyn Nicklaus
 Hutchinson
Hale Irwin
Sadao Iwata
Jerry Izenberg
Tommy Jacobs
Peter Jacobsen
Mark James
Don January
Lee Janzen
Dan Jenkins
Alastair Johnston
Bob Jones IV
Kaye Kessler
Dave Kindred
Gary Koch
John Konsek

Jason Kubel
Steve Lafrance
Dom Lepore
Babe Lichardus
Verne Lundquist
Sandy Lyle
Roger Maltbie
Ed Matko
Sid Matthew
Billy Maxwell
Bob Mazero
Gary McCord
Nancy McCormack
Todd McCormack
Tom Metters
Johnny Miller
John Montgomery
Mary Moran
Bob Murphy
Byron Nelson
Bobby Nichols
Barbara Nicklaus
Jack Nicklaus
Jack Nicklaus Jr.
Bev Norwood
Robin Obetz
Nan Nicklaus O'Leary
Mort Olman
Arnold Palmer
Jerry Palmer
Marino Parascenzo
Roger Pedigo
Put Pierman
Put Pierman Jr.
Neal Pilson
Steve Pipoly
Gary Player
Edwin Pope
Dow Reichley
Harold Riley
Phil Rodgers
Chi Chi Rodriguez
Bob Rosburg
Mason Rudolph
Doug Sanders

Bill Santor
Sandy Palmer Sarni
Alice Saunders
Amy Palmer Saunders
Roy Saunders
Sam Saunders
Pandel Savic
John Schroeder
Ed Seay
Charlie Sifford
Wayne Sloan
Jeff Sluman
Banks Smith
Mary Lou Smith
Reverend Dr. William
 E. Smith
Larry Snyder
Mike Souchak
Art Spander
Jean Sprague
Bill Stathakaros
Jerry Steelsmith
Dave Stockton
George Strode
Fred Swearingen
Lois Jean Palmer Tilley
Joe Tito
David Toms
Joe Torre
Bob Toski
Lee Trevino
Ken Venturi
Lanny Wadkins
Marty Walzer
Tom Watson
Peg Palmer Wears
Jay Weitzel
Ward Wettlaufer
Jack Whitaker
Tiger Woods
Ivor Young
John Zimmers
Stan Ziobrowski
Fuzzy Zoeller

MAGAZINES

Forbes   *Golf Magazine*   *Sports Illustrated*
Golf Digest   *Parade*   *Time*

MEDIA GUIDES

Bay Hill/Arnold Palmer   The Masters   PGA Tour
  Invitational   Memorial Tournament   USGA/U.S. Open
Champions Tour   PGA of America

NEWSPAPERS

Athens (Ohio) *Messenger*   *Columbus Dispatch*   *Pittsburgh Post-Gazette*
Atlanta Journal   *Desert Sun*   *Pittsburgh Press*
Augusta Chronicle   *Kansas City Star*   *Province* (Vancouver)
Augusta Chronicle-Herald   *Los Angeles Times*   *Rocky Mountain News*
Birmingham Post-Herald   *New York Daily News*   *San Francisco Chronicle*
Charlotte Observer   *New York Times*   *St. Petersburg Times*
Chicago Sun-Times   *Orlando Sentinel*   *USA Today*
Chicago Tribune   *Palm Beach Post*   *Washington Post*

WEBSITES

http://www.ArnoldPalmer.com   http://www.Nicklaus.com
http://www.ASAPsports.com   http://www.PGATour.com
http://www.FIU.edu   http://www.Sabr.org
http://www.Golf.com   http://www.USGA.org

WIRE SERVICES

Associated Press
United Press International

Index